the Peoples' Companion to the BIBLE

the Peoples' Companion to the BIBLE

EDITED BY

CURTISS PAUL DeYOUNG · WILDA C. GAFNEY
LETICIA A. GUARDIOLA-SÁENZ · GEORGE "TINK" TINKER
FRANK M. YAMADA

Fortress Press
Minneapolis

THE PEOPLES' COMPANION TO THE BIBLE

Further materials for this volume can be found online at www.fortresspress.com/
peoplescompanion.

Fortress Press Publishing Team for *The Peoples' Companion to the Bible:*
Neil Elliott, project director; Julie O'Brien, project editor; Josh Messner, development
editor; John Goodman, cover design; Hillspring Books, interior design, typesetting;
Donn McLellan, copyediting

Library of Congress Cataloging-in-Publication Data

The peoples' companion to the Bible / edited by Curtiss Paul DeYoung ... [et al.].
    p. cm.
  Includes bibliographical references.
  ISBN 978-0-8006-9702-0 (alk. paper)
  1. Bible--Criticism, interpretation, etc. I. DeYoung, Curtiss Paul.
  BS511.3.P46 2010
  220.07--dc22
                        2010003060

Printed in the U.S.A.

14 13 12 11 10   1 2 3 4 5 6 7 8 9 10

Contents

EDITORS AND CONTRIBUTORS xi

IMAGES AND MAPS xv

PREFACE xvii

INTRODUCTION TO A NEW WAY OF READING   *Neil Elliott* xxi
The Reading Difference Makes xxi
Reading through Others' Eyes xxii
Reading Again through Our Own Eyes xxiii
The Peoples' Companion to the Bible and the Biblical Studies Classroom xxiv
A Guide for Students xxvi
A Self-Inventory for Bible Readers xxix

PART I

THE BIBLE AT THE CROSSROAD OF CULTURES

1. CULTURE AND IDENTITY   *Leticia A. Guardiola-Sáenz and Frank M. Yamada* 3

2. THE BIBLE AS A TEXT OF CULTURES   *Randall C. Bailey* 10

3. THE BIBLE AS A TEXT IN CULTURES 17
   An Introduction   *Fernando F. Segovia* 17
   African Americans   *Vincent L. Wimbush* 23
   Latinas/os   *Francisco Lozada Jr.* 26

Native Americans *George "Tink" Tinker* 30

Asian Americans *Frank M. Yamada* 34

Euro-Americans *Nicole Wilkinson Duran* 39

4. JESUS AND CULTURES *Leticia A. Guardiola-Sáenz and Curtiss Paul DeYoung* 43

5. THE BIBLE AS AN INSTRUMENT OF RECONCILIATION *Curtiss Paul DeYoung* 51

6. THE BIBLE AND EMPIRE *Neil Elliott* 57

7. THE GOD OF THE BIBLE AND THE PEOPLES OF THE EARTH *Kosuke Koyama* 67

8. WOMEN, CULTURE, AND THE BIBLE *Choi Hee An* 73

9. RESPONSIBLE CHRISTIAN EXEGESIS OF HEBREW SCRIPTURE
Johanna W. H. van Wijk-Bos 78

10. THE "PEOPLE OF GOD" AND THE PEOPLES OF THE EARTH
Ann Holmes Redding (with Neil Elliott) 83

PART II

THE HEBREW BIBLE

11. THE HEBREW BIBLE AS A TEXT OF CULTURES
Frank M. Yamada (with Neil Elliott) 93

❖ Timeline for the Hebrew Bible 103

12. THE TORAH (OR PENTATEUCH) 107

Introduction to the Pentateuch *Frank M. Yamada* 107

Genesis *Randall C. Bailey* 111

Exodus *Jorge Pixley* 112

Leviticus *Madeline McClenney-Sadler* 114

Numbers   *Wilda C. Gafney* 115

Deuteronomy   *Frank M. Yamada.* 116

13. THE HISTORICAL BOOKS 119

Introduction to the Historical Books   *Uriah Y. Kim* 119

Joshua   *Dora R. Mbuwayesango* 124

Judges   *Wilda C. Gafney* 125

Ruth   *Wilda C. Gafney.* 127

1 Samuel   *Uriah Y. Kim* 128

2 Samuel   *Uriah Y. Kim* 129

1 Kings   *Francisco García-Treto* 130

2 Kings   *Francisco García-Treto* 131

1 Chronicles   *Gregory Lee Cuéllar* 132

2 Chronicles   *Gregory Lee Cuéllar* 133

Ezra   *Alejandro F. Botta* 134

Nehemiah   *Alejandro F. Botta* 135

Esther   *Willa E. M. Johnson* 136

14. WISDOM AND POETRY 139

Introduction to Wisdom and Poetry   *Francisco García-Treto* 139

Job   *Cheryl A. Kirk-Duggan* 143

Psalms   *Stephen Breck Reid* 145

Proverbs   *Joseph F. Scrivner.* 147

Ecclesiastes   *Madeline McClenney-Sadler* 148

The Song of Solomon   *Alice Hunt* 149

15. THE PROPHETS 151

Introduction to the Prophets   *Lai Ling Elizabeth Ngan* 151

Isaiah   *Hyun Chul Paul Kim* 154

Jeremiah   *Angela Bauer-Levesque* 156

Lamentations   *Cheryl A. Kirk-Duggan* 158

Ezekiel   *Gale A. Yee* 159

Daniel   *Barbara M. Leung Lai.* 161

Hosea   *Lai Ling Elizabeth Ngan* 162

Joel   *Claude F. Mariottini* 164

Amos   *Valerie Bridgeman* 165

Obadiah   *John J. Ahn.* 167

Jonah   *Claude F. Mariottini* 168

Micah   *Daniel L. Smith-Christopher* 169

Nahum   *Daniel L. Smith-Christopher* 171

Habakkuk   *Valerie Bridgeman* 173

Zephaniah   *John J. Ahn* 174

Haggai   *Steed Vernyl Davidson* 176

Zechariah   *Steed Vernyl Davidson* 177

Malachi   *Osvaldo D. Vena* 179

PART III

THE APOCRYPHAL/DEUTEROCANONICAL BOOKS

16. **THE APOCRYPHAL/DEUTEROCANONICAL BOOKS** 183

   Introduction to the Apocryphal/Deuterocanonical Books   *Wilda C. Gafney* 183

   Tobit   *Anathea E. Portier-Young* 187

   Judith   *Wilda C. Gafney* 188

   Esther (Greek)   *Nicole Wilkinson Duran* 190

   The Wisdom of Solomon   *Scott Tunseth* 191

   Sirach   *Scott Tunseth* 192

   Baruch   *Frederick Houk Borsch* 193

   The Letter of Jeremiah   *Frederick Houk Borsch* 195

   The Prayer of Azariah   *Wilda C. Gafney* 196

   Susanna   *Wilda C. Gafney* 197

   Bel and the Dragon   *Wilda C. Gafney* 197

   1 Maccabees   *Anathea E. Portier-Young* 198

   2 Maccabees   *Anathea E. Portier-Young* 199

   1 Esdras   *Stacy Davis* 200

   The Prayer of Manasseh   *Stacy Davis* 201

   Psalm 151   *Frederick Houk Borsch* 202

   3 Maccabees   *Stacy Davis* 203

   2 Esdras   *Stacy Davis* 204

   4 Maccabees   *Stacy Davis* 205

PART IV

THE NEW TESTAMENT

17. THE NEW TESTAMENT AS A TEXT OF CULTURES
   Neil Elliott (with Ann Holmes Redding) 209

   ❖ Timeline for the New Testament 233

18. THE GOSPELS AND THE ACTS OF THE APOSTLES 237
   Introduction to the Gospels   *Cain Hope Felder* 237
   Matthew   *Leticia A. Guardiola-Sáenz* 240
   Mark   *Emerson Byron Powery* 241
   Luke   *Stephanie Buckhanon Crowder* 243
   John   *Fernando F. Segovia* 244
   The Acts of the Apostles   *Rubén R. Dupertuis* 245

19. THE LETTERS OF PAUL 247
   Introduction to the Pauline Letters   *Elsa Tamez* 247
   Romans   *Elsa Tamez* 251
   1 Corinthians   *Demetrius K. Williams* 253
   2 Corinthians   *Demetrius K. Williams* 254
   Galatians   *Ediberto López-Rodríguez* 256
   Ephesians   *Raj Nadella* 257
   Philippians   *Aquiles Ernesto Martínez* 259
   Colossians   *Gordon Zerbe* 260
   1 Thessalonians   *Abraham Smith* 262
   2 Thessalonians   *Abraham Smith* 263
   1 Timothy   *Aída Besançon Spencer* 264
   2 Timothy   *Aída Besançon Spencer* 266
   Titus   *Aída Besançon Spencer* 267
   Philemon   *Cain Hope Felder* 269

20. THE GENERAL LETTERS AND REVELATION 271
   Introduction to the General Letters and Revelation   *Henry W. Morisada Rietz* 271
   Hebrews   *James Earl Massey* 276

James   *Margaret Aymer Oget* 278
1 Peter   *David Cortés-Fuentes* 279
2 Peter   *David Cortés-Fuentes* 280
1 John   *Craig S. Keener* 282
2 John   *Craig S. Keener* 283
3 John   *Craig S. Keener* 283
Jude   *David Cortés-Fuentes* 284
Revelation   *Greg Carey* 285

NOTES 287
SELECT BIBLIOGRAPHY 288
ACKNOWLEDGMENTS 290

EDITORS

Curtiss Paul DeYoung
Bethel University
*Editorial Team (Originating editor;
responsibility for Articles; Art; Maps)*
*The Bible as an Instrument of
Reconciliation; Jesus and Cultures
(with Leticia A. Guardiola-Sáenz)*

Wilda C. Gafney
Lutheran Theological Seminary
at Philadelphia
*Editorial Team (responsibility for Hebrew
Bible; Apocrypha)*
*Introduction to the Apocryphal/Deutero-
canonical Books*
*Numbers, Judges, Ruth, Judith, Azariah
and the Three Jews, Susanna, Bel and
the Dragon*

Leticia A. Guardiola-Sáenz
Seattle University
*Editorial Team (responsibility for New
Testament)*
*Culture and Identity (with Frank M.
Yamada); Jesus and Cultures
(with Curtiss Paul DeYoung)*
Matthew

George "Tink" Tinker
Iliff School of Theology
*Editorial Team (responsibility for Articles;
Art)*
*The Bible as a Text in Cultures: Native
Americans*

Frank M. Yamada
McCormick Theological Seminary
*Editorial Team (responsibility for Hebrew
Bible)*
*The Bible as a Text in Cultures: Asian
Americans*
*Culture and Identity (with Leticia
Guardiola-Sáenz)*
The Hebrew Bible as a Text of Cultures
Introduction to the Pentateuch
Deuteronomy

CONTRIBUTORS

John J. Ahn
Austin Seminary
Obadiah, Zephaniah

Randall C. Bailey
Interdenominational Theological Center
The Bible as a Text of Cultures
Genesis

Angela Bauer-Levesque
Episcopal Divinity School
Jeremiah

Frederick Houk Borsch
The Lutheran Theological Seminary at
Philadelphia
Baruch, The Letter of Jeremiah, Psalm 151

Alejandro F. Botta
Boston University School
of Theology
Ezra, Nehemiah

Valerie Bridgeman
Memphis Theological Seminary
Amos, Habakkuk

Greg Carey
Lancaster Theological Seminary
Revelation

Choi Hee An
Boston University School of Theology
Women, Culture, and The Bible

David Cortés-Fuentes
San Francisco Theological Seminary of
    Southern California
1 Peter, 2 Peter, Jude

Stephanie Buckhanon Crowder
Belmont University
Luke

Gregory Lee Cuéllar
Texas A & M University
1 Chronicles, 2 Chronicles

Steed Vernyl Davidson
Pacific Lutheran Theological Seminary
Haggai, Zechariah

Stacy Davis
Saint Mary's College
*1 Esdras, 2 Esdras, 3 Maccabees,
    4 Maccabees, The Prayer of Manasseh*

Rubén R. Dupertuis
Trinity University
Introduction to Acts

Nicole Wilkinson Duran
Trinity Presbyterian Church,
    Bryn Mawr, Penn.
*The Bible as a Text in Cultures:
    Euro-Americans
Esther (Greek)*

Neil Elliott
Fortress Press
*Introduction to a New Way of Reading
The Bible and Empire
The New Testament as a Text of Cultures*

Cain Hope Felder
Howard University School of Divinity
*Introduction to the Gospels
Philemon*

Francisco García-Treto
Trinity University
*Introduction to Wisdom and Poetry
1 Kings, 2 Kings*

Alice Hunt
Chicago Theological Seminary
Song of Solomon

Willa E. M. Johnson
University of Mississippi
Esther

Craig S. Keener
Palmer Theological Seminary
1 John, 2 John, 3 John

Hyun Chul Paul Kim
Methodist Theological School in Ohio
Isaiah

Uriah Y. Kim
Hartford Seminary
*Introduction to the Historical Books
1 Samuel, 2 Samuel*

Cheryl A. Kirk-Duggan
Shaw University Divinity School
Job, Lamentations

Kosuke Koyama
Union Theological Seminary, emeritus
*God of the Bible and the Peoples of the
    Earth*

Barbara M. Leung Lai
Tyndale Seminary
Daniel

Ediberto López-Rodríguez
Seminario Evangélico de Puerto Rico
Galatians

Francisco Lozada Jr.
Brite Divinity School, Texas Christian
    University
The Bible as a Text in Cultures: Latinas/os

Claude F. Mariottini
Northern Baptist Theological Seminary
Jonah, Joel

Aquiles Ernesto Martínez
Reinhardt College
Philippians

James Earl Massey
Anderson University, School of Theology,
    emeritus
Hebrews

Dora R. Mbuwayesango
Hood Theological Seminary
Joshua

Madeline McClenney-Sadler
ExodusFoundation.org
Leviticus, Ecclesiastes

Raj Nadella
Seabury-Western Theological Seminary
Ephesians

Lai Ling Elizabeth Ngan
Truett Theological Seminary, Baylor
    University
*Introduction to the Prophets
Hosea*

Margaret Aymer Oget
Interdenominational Theological Center
James

Jorge Pixley
Seminario Teológico Bautista, Managua,
    emeritus
Exodus

Anathea E. Portier-Young
Duke Divinity School
Tobit, 1 Maccabees, 2 Maccabees

Emerson Byron Powery
Lee University
Mark

Ann Holmes Redding
Abrahamic Reunion West
*The "People of God" and the Peoples of the
    Earth*

Stephen Breck Reid
Bethany Theological Seminary
Psalms

Henry W. Morisada Rietz
Grinnell College
*Introduction to the General Letters and
    Revelation*

Joseph F. Scrivner
Samford University
Proverbs

Fernando F. Segovia
Divinity School, Vanderbilt University
*The Bible as a Text in Cultures:
    An Introduction*
John

Abraham Smith
Southern Methodist University
1 Thessalonians, 2 Thessalonians

Daniel L. Smith-Christopher
Loyola Marymount University
Micah, Nahum

Aída Besançon Spencer
Gordon-Conwell Theological Seminary
1 Timothy, 2 Timothy, Titus

Elsa Tamez
United Bible Societies & Universidad
    Bíblica Latinoamericana
Introduction to the Pauline Letters
Romans

Scott Tunseth
Fortress Press
Wisdom of Solomon, Sirach

Johanna W. H. van Wijk-Bos
Louisville Presbyterian Theological
    Seminary
*Responsible Christian Exegesis of Hebrew
    Scripture*

Osvaldo D. Vena
Garrett Evangelical Theological Seminary
Malachi

Demetrius K. Williams
Marquette University
1 Corinthians, 2 Corinthians

Vincent L. Wimbush
Claremont Graduate University
*The Bible as a Text in Cultures: African
    Americans*

Gale A. Yee
Episcopal Divinity School
Ezekiel

Gordon Zerbe
Canadian Mennonite University
Colossians

IMAGES AND MAPS

GALLERY

The Bible at the Crossroad of Cultures

The gallery follows page 160. Acknowledgments can be found on page 291.

Maps

Map 1: World of the Bible

Map 2: The Ancient Near East and Key Locations in Genesis

Map 3: Exodus and Sinai Wilderness Wanderings

Map 4: Palestine and Key Locations in Joshua and Judges

Map 5: The Twelve Tribes of Israel, 1200-1030 BCE

Map 6: Ancient Jerusalem

Map 7: United Kingdom of Israel, 1000-924 BCE

Map 8: The Kingdoms of Israel and Judah, 924-722 BCE

Map 9: The Assyrian Empire

Map 10: The Babylonian Empire

Map 11: The Persian Empire

Map 12: The Greek Empire

Map 13: Palestine in the Time of the Maccabees, 175-63 BCE

Map 14: Palestine in Jesus' Time, 6-30 CE

Map 15: The Roman Empire

Map 16: Paul's Missionary Journeys

Map 17: The City of Jerusalem in Jesus' Time

PREFACE

We present *The Peoples' Companion to the Bible* mindful of a cultural transformation going on around us. The United States is rapidly becoming a nation of widely different cultures with a multiplicity of worldviews. Similar diversification is evident around the globe, particularly in the major cities of the world. Before the midpoint of the twenty-first century, white people of European descent are expected to constitute less than 50 percent of the total U.S. population, in a nation with an ever increasing plurality of races, ethnicities, and cultures. This textbook embraces multiple cultural approaches that reflect the current and future cultural mosaic in our society. It relies on established historical-critical, literary-critical, and social-scientific approaches to the Bible, but also on the perspectives of postcolonial, feminist, and Afrocentric criticism, to name a few. Thus *The Peoples' Companion to the Bible* highlights interpretations that emerge from diverse and particular perspectives.

Our purpose in *The Peoples' Companion to the Bible* is to shatter the misperception that the Bible is somehow "color-" and "culture-blind." We intend to open our readers' eyes to the complex interactions of peoples, at cultural crossroads through centuries of history, that gave rise to our Bible. We mean to draw the reader into a new encounter with the Bible as the product of many ancient cultures, at home in many contemporary cultures, and to show that the Bible really is a peoples' Bible. We seek here to draw people who have often felt left out and voiceless in their encounter with the Bible. In order to give voice to those readers and communities who have been silenced by dominant narratives in Western culture, *The Peoples' Companion to the Bible* offers some of the best insights of scholars from a wide array of different cultures and ethnicities. The editorial team and writers comprise scholars from communities traditionally underrepresented in mainstream biblical scholarship in the United States: African Americans, Asian Americans, Latinas/os, and Native Americans. Some white interpreters who have a track record of offering rarely heard perspectives have also contributed to this textbook, and the editors have sought a balance of men and women writers as well.

The Peoples' Companion to the Bible invites a peoples' interpretation of these ancient writings through each reader's own unique social lens. How we read the Bible, like our understanding of life itself, is affected by many dimensions, including our age, gender, race, culture, socio-economic class, religion, ability, sexual orientation, and nation of origin. *The Peoples' Companion to the Bible* taps into this reservoir of feeling and insight to inform the reader's understanding of these ancient texts. Studying the Bible with only one's own set of lived experiences or educational viewpoints limits the possibilities for gaining meaning from biblical texts. This textbook brings together the interpretive lenses of scholars from many peoples, whose many perspectives produce a mosaic of wisdom and affirmation. We hope that the reader's own view is enriched by the vast cultural diversity of scholarly knowledge offered here, even as readers resonate with voices speaking from life settings similar to their own.

Not only does *The Peoples' Companion to the Bible* offer the reader the space to explore the Bible from multiple social locations, it also invites a fresh discussion of the critical issues facing citizens of the twenty-first century. Many people have dismissed the Bible as irrelevant and of little or no value for addressing contemporary racism and injustice. The writers in this textbook, to the contrary, engage with passion the Bible's potential for social justice and liberation, originally meant for times and peoples long past, yet still proclaiming a timely word today. They also describe how the biblical authors struggled with the limitations of their own settings as they tried to interpret what they understood to be their god's will and work. Scholars in *The Peoples' Companion to the Bible* speak with a refreshing candor about how, throughout history, the Bible has been manipulated and misused to support colonization, slavery, genocide, ethnic cleansing, sexism, and a host of other forms of oppression. The residue of oppression still marks much current biblical interpretation and theological musing, and that, too, is part of the context in which we write.

The contributors to *The Peoples' Companion to the Bible* envision the Bible as a crossroads: a place of both collision and convergence. On the journey of biblical interpretation there are collisions between one or another culture and the biblical writings, between cultures themselves, between dominant and marginal perspectives, and across imbalances of power in society. These realities are reflected here as scholars often present multiple perspectives on a biblical text. Yet the Bible is also a place of convergence, where people meet at the crossroads to find points of common ground and shared interest. We invite you to join us at the crossroads as you read *The Peoples' Companion to the Bible*.

THE EDITORS

Because where we stand determines what we can see and hear, we have asked the authors of the following chapters to identify their own standpoints as they write about different books of the Bible and different aspects of its interpretation. Here are our own brief self-introductions.

Curtiss Paul DeYoung — I am a white male of Dutch and English ancestry who is a citizen of the United States. I am ordained in the Church of God (Anderson, Ind.) and Professor of Reconciliation Studies at Bethel University. My biblical interpretation has been transformed from what was a de facto Eurocentric bias to a more multicultural perspective through theological training at the historically black Howard University School of Divinity and through years of reading biblical scholars and theologians from Native American, Asian, Latin American, African, Arab, and African American perspectives. My racial self-understanding was interrupted at age fifty with the genealogical discovery of a black ancestor. My cultural self-understanding has been affected by socialization in African American communities and by having my consciousness raised by multiple visits to South Africa and Palestine and Israel. As a person with race, class, and gender privileges in the United States, I have committed my life to social justice and reconciliation. This collision of birthright privilege and experiential transformation informs my interpretation of the Bible.

Wilda C. Gafney — I teach the "Scriptures of Israel"—by which I mean a wealth of literature including the Hebrew Bible (the Scriptures of contemporary Judaism); the ancient Jewish writings treasured by many Christians as the Apocrypha or Deutero-canonical biblical writings; the Septuagint, the Greek translation of Jewish Scriptures made in North Africa; the Samaritan Pentateuch; and the writings represented in the Dead Sea Scrolls. As a black feminist with postcolonial commitments to and beyond the African Diaspora, my interest in these overlapping bodies of literature and their languages leads me to explore how translations, theories, and practices either open up or cover up biblical texts. I am an Episcopal priest who is a member of two congregations, the African Episcopal Church of St. Thomas and the Dorshei Derekh Reconstructionist (Jewish) Minyan, both in Philadelphia.

Leticia A. Guardiola-Sáenz — Just as the Bible has shaped the way I read and understand my life, my life has shaped the way I read and understand the Bible. Through my experiences as a Latina woman of Mexican heritage, born and bred in the bicultural borderlands between Mexico and the United States, I have come to appreciate and read the Bible as a hybrid text where many borders, voices, and meanings converge. So, as a reader, believer, and lecturer of the Christian Scripture, I find myself constantly negotiating and contesting the meanings and stories of the Bible as I seek responsibly to interpret and appropriate its message in a culture and time that is thousands of years and miles away from its original context. Ultimately, my goals as an informed reader of the Bible are to empower minority readers as agents of historical change in the ongoing process of decolonization and liberation; to dismantle interpretations of the Bible that are oppressive; and to offer inclusive and transformative readings that can bring about justice and liberation for all of the earth's people and all that the Bible describes as God's creation.

George "Tink" Tinker —I am an enrolled member of the Osage (*Wazhazhe*) Nation and Professor of American Indian Cultures and Religious Traditions at Iliff School of Theology. I have taught at Iliff for nearly twenty years, bringing an Indian perspective to a predominantly Euro-American school. As an American Indian academic originally trained in biblical studies (Ph.D., Graduate Theological Union), I am committed to a scholarly endeavor that takes seriously both the liberation of Indian peoples from their historic oppression as colonized communities and the liberation of white Americans, the historic colonizers and oppressors of Indian peoples.

Frank M. Yamada —I am Sansei, third-generation Japanese American, who grew up on the west coast of California, which locates me one generation after the internment of over 200,000 Japanese and Japanese Americans during World War II. I grew up in a nominally Buddhist home, before converting to Christianity when I was in college. I received my training as a scholar at a Protestant seminary, where historical criticism was the dominant form of investigation. Ironically, this is also where I began to develop interest in the destabilizing practice of postmodern biblical interpretation. All of these forces of cultural conflict and fusion are reflected in my identity—a hybrid construction that seeks to refuse oversimplified characterizations of Asia or America in my Asian American body. Because of my identity, I am often drawn to conflicts and contradictions in the biblical text, seeing them not as a problem to be fixed, but as difficult and sometimes painful openings into another people's understanding of the world and God.

Introduction to a New Way of Reading

Neil Elliott

There are many ways to study the Bible, and any number of textbooks that, in different ways, introduce the academic study of the Bible. You are about to embark on a different kind of Bible study in the pages that follow.

Some textbooks—and some courses on the Bible, for that matter—approach the Bible as if one or another part of it meant or means just one thing. Often, however, different textbooks, like different instructors or different students, can't agree on what that one meaning is! The result can be frustrating. A student who enters a course with a pretty clear idea of "what the Bible means" may be surprised, disappointed, or even angry when the text or the instructor suggests that it means, or meant, something else. Both this student and the instructor may feel pulled into an argument: Who is right? Who gets to decide what the Bible means? Meanwhile, another student who enters the same course without any background with the Bible may feel like an outsider who has wandered into someone else's family gathering (or family feud).

The Reading Difference Makes

We all know, of course, that different people read the Bible in different ways. That's not just a matter of individual preference: historical processes and cultural factors, differences in ethnic experiences and perspectives, and diversity in privilege and socioeconomic position all influence the ways we hear and read the Bible. Teachers often work to bring that diversity into class discussion. Despite those efforts, however, we often continue to perceive the very real diversity among people as something *external* to the Bible, which we (wrongly) assume remains just *one* thing with just *one* meaning.

It is always easy for the members of a dominant majority group to imagine themselves at the center of things, and others as peripheral. But I can speak more personally. I grew up in almost all-white churches, listening to white missionaries plead for our support to "take the Bible" to benighted dark-skinned people in distant lands. Such moments were possible because of a long history in which European conquest and colonialism were intertwined with Christian missionary efforts among other lands and peoples, including North America, and the particular history of slavery, conquest, and wave after wave of immigration that has produced the present diversity in the United States. It never occurred to me, as a white, Euro-American Christian, to imagine that the Bible was anything but "ours" in a way it could never belong to others. We could read ourselves into the biblical story, spontaneously identifying ourselves with the people of God. Meanwhile, as some of the contributors to this textbook point out, it has been harder for people from other groups to read the Bible as connected with *their* story. Someone who has grown up in a church where all the pictures of Jesus and his contemporaries are white—but the congregation isn't—might find it more difficult to connect with the Bible, its world, and its people. How much more difficult is it when one's ancestors were told by European missionaries that they would have to give up their culture and traditions to become part of the "people of God," while those same Europeans could simply identify their culture with Christianity?

I read it differently now, but that doesn't make me unusual. It is now less and less a possibility for any single group to imagine that the Bible is "theirs" any more than it belongs to others. The rich variety of peoples—including the diversity of communities of faith—has now made impossible the assumption that any one people or group "owns" the Bible.

That insight has long been at home in the university classroom. Even colleges that were originally founded by Christian denominations now offer classes in religious studies where asking students to subscribe to one or another religious doctrine would be out of the question. Nevertheless, many resources available for biblical study in the classroom—textbooks, commentaries, and study Bibles alike—have perpetuated the impression that the questions raised in multicultural and culture-critical scholarship are somehow extraneous ones, imposed by marginalized "others" onto a Bible that itself remains transcendent, universally authoritative, and ethnically "neutral."

READING THROUGH OTHERS' EYES

The Peoples' Companion to the Bible puts cultural diversity at the very center of reading the Bible. This textbook brings together the voices of many different biblical scholars from many places, all of whom speak candidly about what the Bible means to them and for their people. As the editors observe in the Preface, the *Companion* has been conceived as a crossroads where we may *all* find ourselves invited to other folks' family gatherings.

The editors and contributors believe that more is at stake in biblical interpretation than promoting a healthy campus climate of multicultural understanding or making visible the true diversity of biblical scholarship today, though those are worthy goals. The men and women who write here have for decades been taking part in conversations at the cultural "crossroads" in biblical scholarship. Their presence and their insights have dislocated some long-dominant habits of interpretation and broken open the rich diversity evident in the Bible itself. We now understand that the biblical writings were produced out of the complex interplay of peoples and cultures, whether those encounters involved conquest or cooperation, conflict or convergence, warfare or the discovery of new neighbors. *The Peoples' Companion to the Bible* highlights both the way the Bible continues to be read as a text *in* different cultures and the way we now understand the Bible as the multilayered product *of* ancient cultures.

READING AGAIN THROUGH OUR OWN EYES

The unique perspective at the heart of this textbook offers the student of the Bible the opportunity to encounter the Bible "again for the first time." If the Bible is familiar to you, you have the opportunity to encounter it new through the experience of others and thus rediscover new meanings for yourself. If the Bible has been foreign territory, it no longer needs to remain a matter that seems to belong only to others. You can explore it in the company of women and men who have taken very different paths across its landscapes and, in so doing, you may find worthy guides and companions for your own journey. Whatever your previous experience with the biblical writings, here is an opportunity to engage its stories and characters, its myths and heroes—and the communities that shaped them all—and find your own voice as a reader and an interpreter alongside others.

THE PEOPLES' COMPANION TO THE BIBLE AND THE BIBLICAL STUDIES CLASSROOM

Professors of biblical or religious studies who wish to bring multicultural perspectives and the diversity of interpretive options into the classroom will find *The Peoples' Companion to the Bible* a welcome resource. The following remarks will highlight the distinctive approach taken here.

First, *The Peoples' Companion to the Bible* is designed to be used alongside another classroom Bible of the professor's choice, for example, one of the accepted academic study Bibles (such as the *New Oxford Annotated Bible,* 4th edition, or the *Harper Study Bible*), or in courses where no specific version of the Bible is required. Instructors who wish to adopt a single study Bible incorporating the perspective of this *Companion* may wish to consider *The Peoples' Bible* (Fortress Press, 2008), which includes the entire Old and New Testaments and the Apocrypha in the New Revised Standard Version as well as many of the chapters and all of the book introductions that follow.

Chapters in this book are organized in the order in which the biblical books appear in the Protestant canon; Deuterocanonical/Apocryphal books are discussed after the Hebrew Bible and before the New Testament. Students should understand that the books of the Bible are not arranged in the chronological order of their composition. In fact, a thoroughly historical approach to the Bible would discuss the biblical books in a very different order, and would likely first discuss sources and "layers" of tradition that lay *behind* the biblical writings. Students and instructors interested in this history should give particular attention to chapters 11, "The Hebrew Bible as a Text of Cultures," and 17, "The New Testament as a Text of Cultures," and to the Timelines that accompany each of those chapters. These have been included in *The Peoples' Companion to the Bible* precisely to address many of the historical-critical insights into the development of the biblical writings, while keeping the role of cultures clearly in view. On the other hand, professors who know they will use a more extensive historical-critical textbook in class may wish to adopt *The Peoples' Companion* as an important second textbook that will supplement the historical introduction with its own distinctive approach.

While the historical-critical approach to the origins and development of the biblical writings has been the dominant approach in biblical studies for more than a century, it has not escaped questions and challenges from those who ask, what it is *for*? Are "historical-critical" scholars out to wrest control of the Bible's interpretation away from faith communities that have traditionally read these writings as Holy Scripture? Once scholars have identified and elaborated the historical origins of one or another writing—what then? Does the value of an ancient text become "fixed" in the past, or can it still speak to people today? Who gets to decide? The historical-critical scholar? And to whom are scholars accountable?

These are lively questions in contemporary biblical studies, not least among scholars who themselves work with and are committed to the historical-critical method. Readers of *The Peoples' Companion to the Bible* will benefit not only from the historical-critical perspective adopted especially in the key introductory chapters on the Hebrew Bible and the New Testament but also from watching carefully to see how and to what purposes individual writers use historical-critical insights in their own appreciation and appropriation of the Bible.

Students and instructors who wish to explore the *literary character of the biblical writings* will want to read each chapter attentive to those particular aspects of the biblical text that have caught the ear, and eye, of one or another community today. Those interested in different *methods of biblical interpretation* will note that no single method is adopted by all the contributors to this textbook and that none of them claims to present "the" authoritative reading. By design and intention, each contributor presents a deliberately personal angle of vision and invites the reader to see the text from that angle. Think of each writer not as making authoritative pronouncements on the meaning of a biblical text, but as offering to accompany the reader with an informed, but nevertheless personally inflected perspective. Of course, especially where that angle of vision is different from the reader's own, the difference is an opportunity for the reader to become aware of his or her *own* standpoint—an intentional goal of this textbook (see the Guide for Students and the Self-Inventory for Bible Readers, below).

We realize there are almost as many ways to organize a course in biblical studies or an introduction to the Bible as there are instructors! Some will want students to begin by encountering a biblical text directly and reflecting on it, then turning to the textbook for a broader view. Others may want to lead students through a more directed narrative, whether a historical account of the emergence of the Bible or a survey of themes in the Bible. Still others will want to highlight the plurality of voices in contemporary Bible interpretation. *The Peoples' Companion to the Bible* is suited to all these purposes. Sample syllabi for each of these approaches are available at the Web site, www.fortresspress.com/peoplescompanion.

For any of these approaches we recommend spending time with the Reader's Self-Inventory early in a course. Instructors may wish to devote at least one class session to discussing responses to it. The heart of *The Peoples' Companion to the Bible* is the concentration of varied perspectives of scholars writing from very different social locations—but the *Companion* is not really about those scholars; it is about the role of culture and angle of vision in *anyone's* interpretation of the Bible. For that reason we also recommend returning to the Reader's Self-Inventory at the end of the course. That may be a time for students to identify their own social locations as interpreters and describe how that location influences the way they read and experience the Bible.

A final recommendation concerns the online forum at www.fortresspress.com/peoplescompanion. This forum gives students a range of opportunities to interact with the biblical text and with scholar and student readers from a variety of perspectives. Visit the forum and explore how it might add to your class.

A GUIDE FOR STUDENTS

The point of a "companion" to the Bible is to *accompany* you as *you* read the Bible. Nothing can substitute for your own encounter with the biblical writings. The chapters in this textbook provide you with a wealth of information, much of it from perspectives not your own—probably not so different from the mix of viewpoints and experiences in your classroom! But the Bible isn't the only subject of this textbook. Neither is one or another of the viewpoints expressed by the scholars writing here. This textbook is also about *you* and your own awareness of how you encounter the Bible.

Your instructor may assign reading whole books of the Bible, or select passages from the biblical books. Either way, we recommend the following approach as a way to get the most from *The Peoples' Companion to the Bible.*

1. Read the introduction to the assigned biblical book in this textbook.

2. Ask yourself: *What is the author's perspective? How does it compare with my own? What does the author find significant in his or her encounter with this book in the Bible? What value does the author find in the writing? What challenges?*

3. Read the biblical book (or the selection) for yourself, making notes as you go.

4. Ask yourself: *What strikes me as a reader? What surprises me? What value do I find in the writing; what challenges?*

5. Reflect: *How do your own responses to the biblical writing compare to the author in this textbook? In what ways does the textbook present a different way of encountering the Bible? How do you account for the difference? What does the difference tell you about your own social location, about the influences that have shaped your own perspective?*

6. Synthesize: *In the wake of your own encounter with the text, how would you introduce this biblical writing (or selection) to another person? What do you consider the most important things you would want someone else to know about it?*

7. *An online option:* Visit the online forum at www.fortresspress.com/peoples companion. Is the biblical passage to which you have responded already the topic of a discussion? If so, you can add your synthesis (above) or respond to the posts of other students using *The Peoples' Companion to the Bible.* If there is no posting on your passage, you can start one!

The point of the online forum is to assemble a body of biblical interpretation similar, in some respects, to ancient Jewish interpretation. It is instructive to compare a page of a contemporary biblical commentary—for example, a commentary from the respected Hermeneia series from Fortress Press—to a page from the "rabbinic Bible," the Bible as used in rabbinic Judaism from the sixth century onward. Note that on one page, the Hermeneia commentary provides a scholar's translation of the biblical text, with notes to the right on the history of the text and on the translation; below that, a running commentary representing the scholar's best judgments about the meaning of the text; and at the bottom, a selection of other references in notes where the scholar interacts with previous interpreters.

Jeremiah 23:1–4

Yahweh Will Punish the Evil Shepherds and Replace Them with Good Ones

Bibliography

On 23:1–8:
Klein, Ralph W.
"Jeremiah 23:1–8," *Int* 34 (1980) 167–72.

On 23:1–4:
Holladay
"Recovery," 420–24.

23

1 Woe to the shepherds who destroy and who scatter the sheep of "my pasture!"— [oracle of Yahweh.]ᵇ 2/ Therefore thus Yahweh God of Israel has said concerning the shepherds who shepherd my people: You for your part have scattered my sheep and chased them and have not tended them: I am going to attend to you for the evil of your doings, [oracle of Yahweh.]ᵇ 3/ And I for my part shall gather the remnant of my sheep [from all the lands where I have chased them,] and I shall bring them back to their fold, and they shall be fruitful and multiply. 4/ And I shall appoint over them shepherds who shall shepherd them, and they shall not fear any longer nor be panicked, ᵃnor be missing, ᵃoracle of Yahweh.

Text

1a—a G reads "their pasture" (מרעיתם); given 10:21 this is an equally plausible reading.

1, 2b These occurrences of נאם־יהוה are lacking in G and are probably expansionist glosses here.

3a This is a gloss (compare v 8) which specifies the reality of exile to a greater degree: note that in the bracketed words the exile is Yahweh's work rather than that of the shepherds (see further Interpretation, and compare the emendation of Volz).

4a—a The expression is lacking in G; it nevertheless probably belongs here, given the fact that it is a further play on פקד (compare v 2, and see Structure and Form).

Structure and Form

Some commentators deal with vv 1–8 as a unit (Rudolph, Bright, Thompson), but there are surely three units here. Verses 7–8 are a passage duplicated in 16:14–15. Verses 1–4 deal in general with irresponsible shepherds, while vv 5–6 deal with a specific future king who name is a play on that of Zedekiah; except for the word "I appoint" (והקמתי, vv 4 and 5), there is no duplication of vocabulary between the two sequences. There is no way to be sure whether vv 1–4 and 5–6 were added to chapter 22 as a unit or whether they were added separately. If they were added separately, vv 1–4 are appropriately added to the general array in chapter 22 regarding the kings of Judah; in particular the double use of "shepherd" in vv 2 and 4 ("shepherds who shep-

herd") can be linked to the similar double use of the root in 22:22.

The passage is a carefully crafted sequence of structured prose (*Kunstprosa*).[1]

It is a "woe" oracle like 22:13–19: an accusation in the third person introduced by "woe" (הוי, v 1, compare 22:13–17), followed by "therefore Yahweh has said concerning" (v 2, compare 22:18). But 21:13–19 is a judgment speech to an individual, while this passage is to a whole group. Westermann points out that "woe" oracles directed to a group resemble more closely the judgment speech to individuals than the judgment speech to the nation.[2] One expects the messenger formula at the beginning of v 2 to be followed directly by the judgment speech (compare 22:18–19), but in this

---

1 Against my proposal that it is poetry: Holladay, "Recovery," 420–24.
2 Westermann, *Basic Forms*, 191–92; compare also

Zimmerli, *Ezekiel* I, 291, and Wolff, *Joel and Amos*, 243 n. 108, g.

A page from William Holladay's commentary on *Jeremiah*, vol. 1, in the Hermeneia series.

The rabbinic Bible, *Mikraot Gedolot*.

In contrast, two pages in the "rabbinic Bible" (*Mikraot Gedolot*) provide, first, in the upper right-hand corner, the Massoretic text of the Hebrew Bible (here, of Exodus); beside it, the Aramaic paraphrase of the Targum Onkelos, and at the top of the facing page, that of pseudo-Yonatan. Beneath these columns are commentaries from revered Jewish scholars from the twelfth to the eighteenth centuries, including Shabbethai Bass (*Siftei Chakhamim*), Rabbi Shlomo Yitzakhi ("Rashi"), Rabbi Shmuel ben Meir ("Rashbam"), Abraham Ibn Ezra, Rabbi Moses ben Nachman Girondi ("Ramban"), and Obadiah ben Jacob Sforno.

That is, while the Hermeneia commentary page is designed to focus attention on the most accurate determination of "the meaning" of the text that a single scholar can provide, the Rabbinic Bible is designed to draw on a *variety* of voices interpreting a single text.

The Peoples' Companion to the Bible is something in between these examples. The writers of the following chapters do not strive to provide a single authoritative interpretation; on the other hand, space permits only one voice to respond to each book of the Bible. *That's where you come in.* By going to the online forum (at www.fortresspress.com/peoplescompanion) you can take part in an ongoing interpretive conversation that in some ways resembles the process and format of the rabbinic Bible.

A Self-Inventory for Bible Readers

Throughout history and today, men and women have differed among themselves in their interpretations of the Bible.[1] Given the many different perspectives evident in the essays and introductions in this *Companion* alone—and probably represented in your classroom as well—it is inevitable that you will encounter voices different from your own. One goal of the *Peoples' Companion to the Bible* is to help you understand the different perspectives from which others hear and read the Bible—and thus to think seriously about where *you* are coming from as well.

Some readers might consider their religious background a sufficient explanation for how they read the Bible: "That's just what I believe." The following exercise asks you to go deeper. Even within a religious community, a variety of experiences have shaped different people to perceive their faith—and to find their place in the Bible—in very different ways. Ask yourself: do most of the people whom I expect to think like I do share other characteristics with me as well?

Different readings of the Bible are only partly due to the nature of the Bible itself. They are also due to differences between our experiences and identities as people who read the Bible, whether we are approaching it for the first time or have read it often. The point of the following self-inventory is that none of us comes to the Bible as a "blank slate." Its goal is to assist you in identifying and reflecting on some of the factors at work in the way *you* read or hear the Bible and to gain a stronger sense of your own voice as an interpreter of the Bible.

This inventory will be most helpful if you spend some serious time with it on your own and then have an opportunity to discuss it with others. For example, in a college class, the inventory could be the basis for at least one hour-long discussion period early in the course. It would also be valuable to take the inventory again at the end of the course to see what has changed as a result of engagement with the writers in *The Peoples' Companion to the Bible*—and what hasn't!

You don't have to know much about the Bible to answer the following questions. There are no right or wrong, or better or worse answers. The point is to be as honest as you can, both in answering these questions and in discussing them with others. Pay attention to which questions are more difficult for you, and to the questions for which you don't have an answer. (Leaving a question blank is preferable to making up an answer.)

Other students have used similar inventories before you. They attest that this is serious work. Readers who enjoy certain privileges in society—because of wealth, education, ethnicity, gender, sexual orientation, or other factors—may find themselves thinking that these factors "don't matter" for them as much as they might for others. If a question seems unimportant or irrelevant, one might well ask *why*?

Questions 1–4 address your own sense of your religious background and identity. Questions 5–8 concern the standards in whatever religious community may have influenced the way you look at the Bible now. (If your views have not been shaped by a particular religion, are there particular individuals or groups that *have* influenced your thinking?) Questions 9–17 have to do with other aspects of your background and identity that may or may not be related to your religious self-understanding.

1. *Your personal religious background.* How do you describe your religious background? Have you grown up in a religious community? How do you describe yourself now in terms of religious affiliation? Have you grown closer to or farther from a religious community?

2. *Your family religious history.* What was the characteristic view of the Bible in your childhood home? Have you stayed in touch with that point of view, or do you now see the Bible differently? If there have been major changes in the way you see the Bible, how did these happen? How do you feel now about any differences within your family regarding the Bible?

3. *Your life experience.* Have you experienced a crisis in your life in which the Bible played a role? Did you come to a deeper or a different understanding of the Bible through that crisis? How do you describe the lasting effect on your understanding of the Bible?

4. *Your spirituality.* What has been your experience of the role of the Bible in your own spiritual awareness, your sense of a spiritual path, or your spiritual practice? Have particular themes or images in the Bible been important for your spiritual awareness?

5. *Your religious community.* If you identify yourself now with a particular religious community, how would you describe the way the Bible is understood and read (if it is) in that community? What is the cultural or racial makeup of your religious community? Is a diversity of people an important value in your religious community? Does this affect the way the Bible is understood?

6. *Authoritative standards.* In that religious community, what are the "norms" or standards outside the Bible that are recognized as bearing authority on the way the Bible is read or heard? Is there a "founder," an authoritative organization or group, a creed or set of beliefs, a set of authoritative customs, a type of personal experience, a particular social commitment, or some other principle?

7. *Customary exposure to the Bible.* Describe the ways you have been or now are ordinarily exposed to the Bible. Such exposures might include worship services, group Bible studies or discussions, classes, friends and roommates, family members, radio, TV, Internet, or your own private reading. How do these exposures influence the way you read or hear the Bible?

8. *Your own "philosophy" regarding the Bible.* What is your own "working" approach to the Bible—how do you honestly think about it? Is that different from the way your religious community or the authoritative standards of your community regard it?

9. *Your ethnicity and/or race.* How do you identify yourself ethnically or racially? How does your own ethnic history, racial group, culture, and identity influence the way you read or hear the Bible?

10. *Your gender.* How do your gender and the way your culture perceives your gender influence the way you read or hear the Bible?

11. *Your class.* How do you describe yourself in relation to class? How does your class location or background influence the way you read or hear the Bible? (This is a tough question, especially in the United States, since the dominant attitude is that economic classes don't exist or are unimportant in U.S. society. It may help in answering this question to think in terms of your work experience; your inherited wealth; your income; your education to date, and your expectations for further education; your social and career expectations; and so on. You can ask these questions about yourself, about your parents, your grandparents, the people you hang with, your neighborhood, or your religious community.)

12. *Your education and professional aspirations.* How do your education so far and your educational and professional aspirations influence the way you read or hear the Bible? If you have some specific education or training in other fields (for example, your major in college), how does that influence your perception of the Bible?

13. *Your community's priorities.* How do the values, the welfare, and the survival needs of your community influence the way you read or hear the Bible? (This also may be a difficult question in the United States, since much of the dominant culture focuses strongly on the individual rather than on membership in a community. If you have trouble identifying "your community," that, too, is valuable information for reflection!)

14. *Your* explicit *political position.* How does your avowed political position influence the way you read or hear the Bible? (This can mean a lot more than which political party you identify with, if any. It can mean how much you feel the impact from the larger society or the government on your own life, or how much responsibility you take for society and government, and may also involve any political position you think is characteristic of your religious community.)

15. *Your* implicit *political stance.* Even if you do not think of yourself as very political, how does your being *not* political influence the way you read or hear the Bible? How about the religious community with which you identify (if any): Does that community claim to be "not political"? How does that influence the way the Bible is read or heard in that community?

16. *The media to which you are exposed.* Specifically, which books have you used when you have read the Bible (if you have)? Which books have influenced the way you think about the Bible? What movies, music, plays, or other cultural media come to mind when you think about the Bible?

17. *Preachers, teachers, leaders, and scholars in your life.* Are there particular individuals who are professionally trained and professionally involved in interpreting the Bible—clergy or professors of biblical studies or religion, for example—who have had an important influence on your thinking? How do they regard the Bible; how does their perception influence the way you read or hear the Bible? Do you perceive a difference between important leaders in your life and scholars of the Bible? How do you relate to that difference?

18. *How would you rank the factors you've just described?* Which are more important, which are less important? Are some foundational or pivotal or even nonnegotiable for you? Are there other factors that are important to the way you read the Bible that you haven't discussed here?

19. *What have you learned about yourself?* Are you surprised by any of the factors you've described; have you identified influences on the way you read or hear the Bible that you hadn't much thought about before now?

20. *What next?* Do you have any different sense of yourself as a Bible reader now that you've taken this inventory? Are there some aspects of the way you perceive the Bible about which you want to learn more? Are there some aspects that you'd like to change? If so, in what ways, and why?

Part I

THE BIBLE AT THE CROSSROAD OF CULTURES

1. CULTURE AND IDENTITY
   Leticia A. Guardiola-Sáenz and Frank M. Yamada

2. THE BIBLE AS A TEXT OF CULTURES
   Randall C. Bailey

3. THE BIBLE AS A TEXT IN CULTURES
   An Introduction *Fernando F. Segovia*
   African Americans
       Vincent L. Wimbush
   Latinas/os *Francisco Lozada Jr.*
   Native Americans *George "Tink" Tinker*
   Asian Americans *Frank M. Yamada*
   Euro-Americans *Nicole Wilkinson Duran*

4. JESUS AND CULTURES
   *Leticia A. Guardiola-Sáenz
   and Curtiss Paul DeYoung*

5. THE BIBLE AS AN INSTRUMENT OF
   RECONCILIATION *Curtiss Paul DeYoung*

6. THE BIBLE AND EMPIRE *Neil Elliott*

7. THE GOD OF THE BIBLE
   AND THE PEOPLES OF THE EARTH
   Kosuke Koyama

8. WOMEN, CULTURE, AND THE BIBLE
   Choi Hee An

9. RESPONSIBLE CHRISTIAN EXEGESIS
   OF HEBREW SCRIPTURE
   Johanna W. H. van Wijk-Bos

10. THE "PEOPLE OF GOD"
    AND THE PEOPLES OF THE EARTH
    Ann Holmes Redding (with Neil Elliott)

Culture and Identity

Leticia A. Guardiola-Sáenz
and
Frank M. Yamada

If there is one clear commonality between twenty-first-century readers of the Bible and the peoples of the biblical world, it is that each of us, like each of them, belongs to a culture and has an identity. Of course, our contemporary cultures and identities also set us apart, in various ways, from the peoples of the Bible. How, then, can understanding culture and identity help us understand the biblical text, considering our sameness but without losing sight of our differences?

Our initial encounter with culture and the process of identity formation is subtle and imperceptible; it begins with our first breath. Our first interactions with those who care for us and with the environment we share with them give us our first appreciation of sameness and difference; we learn to

reject or to accept certain differences in other people. Later, as we grow and pass through the stages of life, participating in new cultural spaces such as school, church, workplace, and community, we encounter other ways to value diversity, which can either affirm or challenge our earlier perceptions. Sadly, more often than not, we are socially trained to assimilate that which is similar to us and reject that which is different from us. What is similar and familiar appeals to our trust, but what is different and strange tends to trigger fear and suspicion in us. But as nations are becoming more and more culturally diverse because of immigration and political, social, and economic factors, the face of the world is changing and new identities and cultural spaces are emerging. With these changes we are offered an opportunity to gain a new appreciation for the richness of diversity.

Within this new social reality, understanding culture and the process of identity formation not only can give us new light to appreciate the social complexities of the biblical text; it can also help us realize how our own cultural diversity as readers affects the ways we read the Bible and live in a multicultural world.

DEFINING CULTURE

Culture is a word we commonly use but rarely define. Culture can be explained as the sum total of our everyday practices and "texts"—the ways we live everyday life; our behavior, beliefs, social interactions; and all human production, such as food, clothing, art, ideology, institutions, and, most importantly, language. Culture is the collective space where the meanings we produce are assimilated or resisted; it is the battleground where the ideologies of those in power are established or dissolved; it is the public and private terrain where we create our personal and social identities. Culture—with its values, points of view, and traditions—shapes the way we see life, understand the world, define ourselves, think, act, create community, relate to others, and express our sense of belonging to family, groups, and nations.

All the creation, expression, and transmission of culture and identity is only possible through the fundamental vehicle of *language*. Through language we create meaning to express ourselves, and because meaning can only be understood in context, language is intrinsically connected to culture. Through the acquisition of language we enter into a cultural dialogue already in progress as we go through a process of socialization.

Language is fundamental for cultural identity: it shapes our perception of reality, past and present.

Our native languages express our identity and culture in ways that no foreign language can. Language is a maker of identity; when languages disappear, cultures die. Losing a native language means losing aspects of a culture and an identity. On the other hand, speaking other languages creates the opportunity for different or multiple identities as we immerse ourselves into other cultures. As a strategy of colonization, native languages were suppressed in order to undermine a native people's sense of nation, community, culture, and therefore identity. In some other instances, immigrants who arrive in a new country, or later generations of their offspring, have refused to speak their native language to avoid being identified with a certain group. This is a way of erasing an identity that is not equally valued in a new context.

With the help of technology, we have managed to increase our mobility in the world more than ever before. Now we find ourselves negotiating our identities in a new world where multiple cultures converge in neighboring spaces in most big cities. With an abundance of new cultural traits around us, we find ourselves constantly modifying our identities, looking for new ways to communicate with others in a changing world.

IDENTITY FORMATION

Identity, or how we speak about ourselves, can be defined in different ways. The spectrum of definitions ranges from those that assign autonomy and power to the self—as a being not only in control of the process of self-definition but also capable of changing social structures—to those that barely recognize the existence of the individual. The latter definitions assert that the multiple external forces at play in the formation of our identities hardly give us any control over the ways we define ourselves, let alone any power to create change apart from what current social structures allow.

Identity formation is complex and not easily defined, but three main ideas are crucial in this process. First, identities are shaped by power relations; they are created in relation to outsiders (thus Western representations of the non-Western "other" in terms of ethnic identities are often seen as subordinated to the West). Second, identities are not unified; they are fragmented, ruptured, discontinuous, and contradictory. We are split among political allegiances; we have multiple identities that sometimes struggle within us. Third, identities are constantly in flux; they are always changing, not fixed products; they are productions in process.

By and large, although we could say that there are some genetic predispositions involved, the formation of identity is mostly a social process. Even identity markers such as ethnicity, skin color, gender, sexual orientation, or physical disabilities cannot really be said to affect our identity because of biological predispositions; rather, they are identity markers because of the cultural value we have assigned to such characteristics. Identity is formed within culture and in relation to those around us. We learn to become ourselves by observing others, mirroring behaviors, trying out new patterns of action, following in the steps of those we admire, or by those we feel pressured to imitate. Our identity is formed in community, and therefore understanding others helps us understand ourselves.

Even before we can speak, the formation of our identity has already started. We come into a world that has a culture and a language with ready-made labels, names, and expectations that begin to shape our identity even without our knowledge. At first, our existence is automatically explained through those labels. Later on, once we have acquired language and a sense of the culture that surrounds us, we can escape some of those labels and choose others on our own. Our power to define who we are is limited, however, by language, a system already established by society before we participate in it.

Despite the sense of being trapped by language, identity is fluid and dynamic. It changes as we move in life and adopt new cultures, new ideologies, new beliefs, new languages. Identity is in constant motion, just as culture and language are, which in turn helps us create new and complex identities shaped by our cultural heritage, family, geography, religion, and social identity. Identity is a *process*. At any moment, identity is only a snapshot of a person who continues to grow, develop, and identify herself or himself in diverse ways. We are not born with an essence of identity within ourselves that we need to discover; identity is rather a social and public process linked to the personal and emotional ways we define ourselves at different conscious and unconscious levels.

The construction of our identity is not an abstract process in a vacuum; it is historically grounded in culture and involves a lot of emotions and feelings. For many it can be traumatic as we move from childhood to adulthood if we do not find the support to be ourselves in the face of stressful or even harmful social and cultural expectations.

Our identities are also grounded in larger histories. Just as our nations are characterized geographically by specific terrains shaped by natural forces over time—mountains, rivers, deserts, and plains—so our identities are affected by government, religious, educational, and other cultural institutions that have been shaped by the sweep of history.

CULTURE, IDENTITY, AND THE BIBLE

As complex as it may sound, we all experience culture and identity in our daily lives, and it is through these social realities that we learn to understand the world that surrounds us. As we read the Bible, we should keep in mind that although we may find some stories very familiar because of our experiences in life, it is still important to ponder the stories in their own cultural context before translating their message into our own. Just because we find a point of correlation between a biblical story and our own lives does not mean that we can ignore the temporal and cultural gap between us and the Bible. Some of the most oppressive readings of the Bible arise, for example, when we lose track of the liberating message of a text and seek instead to reproduce the cultural settings of the text—trying, say, to reproduce the social mores of the first-century church in a twenty-first-century context.

As we explore aspects of culture and identity in the Bible, we should also keep in mind that just as we are constantly negotiating our identity in complex cultural settings, the people of the Bible were also negotiating their own identities in the midst of different cultures. In the First Testament we see the Hebrews forming a new identity as the people of God in the midst of a hostile environment, surrounded by cities and nations with different and often opposing cultures and customs. Later we see a similar struggle in the Second Testament when those who believed in Jesus were called to adopt a new identity in the midst of political, cultural, and religious opposition. In both cases, the process of identity formation as people of God became a constant struggle as men and women seemed at times to adopt the identity of those around them as a strategy of survival, and at other times to strive to establish a clearly different identity that distinguished them from their neighbors—even when that might have implied oppression, violence, and death.

CULTURE AND IDENTITY IN THE BIBLE

Most discussions among biblical scholars about cultural identity focus on the issue of ethnicity. For example, scholars tend to understand Israelite identity in relationship to Israel's emergence and history as a nation—from a confederation of tribes to a monarchy, from a divided monarchy to Assyrian and Babylonian deportations, from exile to repatriating peoples in the province of Yehud (Judah). In contemporary North America, especially in the United States, while ethnicity also plays an important role for cultural groups, the issue of race is one of the key identifying marks of cultural identity, especially for people of color. "Race" usually refers to particular physical traits (for example, skin color) around which groups understand a common culture. However, the division of peoples into racial categories is arbitrary, varying from one Western society to another and having no basis in human genetics. The practice developed among the pioneers of the social sciences in the West and had racist underpinnings and assumptions. In spite of this history, African Americans, Latina/o Americans, and Asian Americans have continued to use these racial designations strategically to build community and to obtain a collective political and social voice.

Contemporary understandings of racial identity are not used as prominently in the Bible to mark identity as are ethnicity or religion. Historically, "ethnicity" tends to refer to issues of identity that are related to the identity of a people or a nation. In biblical terminology, the Greek word *ethnos*, from which we derive the word *ethnicity*, refers to a people or a nation (although in the New Testament the NRSV consistently translates the plural *ethnē* as "Gentiles"). In early Judaism, and in the New Testament (where early Christians of whatever ancestry often considered themselves to be in continuity with Judaism), other "peoples" or "nations" fell under the generic collective term *ethnē*.

The writers of the Hebrew Bible assumed that their place in and perspective of the world was normative for all humankind. The contemporary reader of the biblical text must recognize, however, that the Hebrew Bible is told from the perspective of a small, colonized group of peoples who lived in successive generations in the land first called

Canaan. Most of these writings were compiled in the sixth and fifth centuries BCE, though some books, sources, and texts were written earlier in Israel's history. Moreover, most of the biblical authors wrote from the perspective of the southern kingdom of Judah (928–586 BCE), which had its capital in Jerusalem. Northern traditions are still present in a significant way, but the point of view is heavily skewed toward that of the Southern Kingdom. All these factors influence the way that a people understood its identity as Israel and how Israel came to be represented in relation to other peoples in the biblical text.

National identity, or ethnicity, certainly plays a large role in Israel's self-understanding. Israelite traditions show an awareness of different national identities within Canaan and beyond, represented in the various nation lists that appear in biblical narrative and law (Gen 10; Deut 7:1) and in oracles against the nations within prophetic materials (Amos 1–2; Jer 46–51). As far as the biblical text indicates, Israelite cultural identity tends to understand itself as fundamentally different from these foreign "others." Hence, in Deuteronomy 7, part of what makes Israel a chosen nation before its God is its religious and cultural distinctiveness from the surrounding peoples. Israelites are not to worship as those other peoples do, nor are they to make covenants with them or intermarry with them (see Deut 7:1–6). Thus, the people are called to be holy, that is, separate or set apart to their God. This language of religious and cultural distinctiveness must be understood in light of Israel's status as a small nation in the shadow of great empires. Archaeologists and biblical scholars now recognize that the cultural artifacts and religious traditions of earliest Israel were actually very consistent with the traditions from surrounding Canaanite society. In fact, on the basis of its similarity in material culture, many scholars now hold that early Israel was ethnically indistinguishable from the Canaanites.

They further contend that the sharp differentiation that later biblical writers, living under the aegis of the Persian Empire, sought to maintain between Israelite and "Canaanite" is not as much related to an actual ethnic difference between their ancestors and the people of Canaan as it is a cultural, social, or religious construction serving particular purposes in the sixth and fifth centuries BCE. We can certainly understand the perceived need for constructing such a difference. When small groups or peoples feel the impact of larger empires (such as the Egyptian, Assyrian, Babylonian, or Persian empires), the need for cultural identity and particularity increases. Thus, in the Hebrew Bible we see ancient Israel constructing its self-understanding as religiously and culturally unique: they are a chosen people who are in a special relationship to their God.

Within the New Testament, the language of cultural specificity and religious uniqueness takes on a similar tone. Even though some early Christians saw their missionary activity as being inclusive of the whole world (Matt 28:19; Acts 1:8), cultural identity in early Christian groups was often maintained by dividing the world into two parts—God's chosen people (the elect, understood as the church) and outsiders, who are often described as the "other" nations (the "Gentiles"). While the early apostolic communities sought to join Jews and non-Jews together in the circle of those who were considered chosen (a process that plays out in different ways through the letters of Paul and the book of Acts), that very distinction shows that the cultural assumptions of Roman-era Judaism remained strong among these communities. We see in Paul's letters the concern to establish a new identity for non-Jewish believers that is neither Jewish nor "Gentile" (see, for example, 1 Cor 5:1, where the NRSV translates *ethnesin* as "pagans"). When later New Testament writings begin to speak of Jews (or "Judeans"; in Greek, *Ioudaioi*) as the "other," scholars see evidence that the composition of the early Christian movement shifted decisively from a

Jewish to a non-Jewish majority, probably soon after the fall of Jerusalem in 70 CE. The reader of biblical material must remember that, similar to what we find in the Hebrew Bible, the New Testament writings represent the perspectives of small groups of people living under an imperial authority (so the traditions of Jesus' birth are set within an environment of Roman occupation: Matt 2; Luke 2:1-2). Even though the Christian church was later accepted by the Roman Emperor Constantine, the New Testament writings show a more conflicted relationship between early Christian identity and empire. But the drive to establish group identity by distinguishing insiders from outsiders, whether those outsiders are "Gentiles" or Jews, may be understood as different responses to the pressures of an imperial culture.

Culture and Identity of Readers

It is well beyond the scope of this essay to address the multiplicity of contemporary readers and the cultural contexts in which they seek to find meaning in the Bible. However, one of the important features of *The Peoples' Companion to the Bible* is that it represents a shift in the way scholars approach the biblical writings. Indeed, in recent decades, scholars of both the Hebrew Bible and New Testament have increasingly recognized the importance of identifying the cultural and social location of readers in a more disciplined and concrete way. For most of the nineteenth and twentieth centuries, a method of investigation known as historical criticism had been the dominant mode of scholarly exploration of the biblical text. In its basic form, historical criticism, which emerged in Europe among other intellectual developments in the Enlightenment, believed that contemporary readers must set aside their own self-understanding in order to examine the historical contexts of the biblical authors and readers. In this way, historical critics understood

that contemporary readers' biases could substantially influence the ways they read the text. Hence, historical critics recognized the importance—and in their minds the potential danger—of people reading their own self-interest into the Bible.

What historical critics often failed to recognize, however, was that their own ways of reading were not universal principles through which the biblical text became evidently clear to all peoples of the world. Historical criticism itself is a culturally contextualized approach to the biblical text—one that is heavily shaped within the context of post-Enlightenment Europe, especially Germany. It served the purpose of helping biblical scholars to be objective in their approach to the biblical text. This objectivity had at least two functions. First, similar to broader trends within theology, biblical criticism was seeking to define itself as a legitimate form of "scientific" inquiry (in German, *Wissenschaft*). Within this methodology, objectivity became an important value in presenting biblical criticism as a legitimate form of knowledge within European intellectual life. Second, biblical scholarship during this time sought to distance itself from the traditional and confessional interpretations that emerged from faith traditions. Hence, objective, disinterested inquiry was championed as a way to create a safeguard against interpretations of the Bible that sought to reinforce the positions of the church in an age of increased secularization.

During the last third of the twentieth century, which saw the emergence of racial and cultural identities following the Civil Rights era, biblical scholars and theologians began to understand the vitality and importance of new perspectives from African Americans, Latinas/os, Asian Americans, Native Americans, and many other historically marginalized groups. In his important essay "Toward a Hermeneutics of the Diaspora: A Hermeneutics of Otherness and Engagement" (1995), Fernando Segovia argued that biblical scholarship must take seriously the "real reader" of the Bible. Segovia's argument represents a larger trend in biblical scholarship that moves beyond historical criticism's objective reader and fully engages the social and cultural location of real readers with the same disciplined rigor that has been a hallmark of biblical scholarship from its inception. This shift highlights the important role that a reader's cultural context plays in generating meaning in relation to the biblical material. Hence, within culturally contextual biblical interpretation, scholars and readers find importance not only in the cultures of ancient Israel, Judaism, and early Christianity, but they also highlight the significant contributions of people of color to the interpretation of the biblical text. All interpreters, regardless of their social location, benefit from the powerful interpretative insights of African Americans and Latin American liberation theologians in their expositions of the exodus and liberation narratives of the Hebrew Bible. Native American and Palestinian perspectives on the conquest narratives, in which readers often find themselves sympathizing with invaded Canaanites, help all of us to understand the problematic side of the language of chosenness that is so prevalent in both the First and Second Testaments. Asian American interpretations of the Ruth and Esther stories help all of us to see the various cultural nuances and conflicting responses that happen when a group seeks to establish their identity in a dominant culture that sees them only as foreign others.

CULTURE AND IDENTITY IN OUR READING OF THE BIBLE

Culture, whether it is understood through identity markers such as race, ethnicity, class, gender, or sexual orientation, affects the way we understand the biblical text. But this does not lead us toward a negative understanding of Babel—the confusion of too many tongues all speaking different languages. Rather, this great polyphony of different cultural voices challenges the assumption that one can learn only through the limited experience of voices similar to one's own. Within all of the great religions of the world that assume some form of god or gods, we find a common theme: human beings do not learn from what is similar to them but from what is different. Within the Bible, people of faith also maintain that humans have a great capacity to be transformed when they come in contact with the holy Other, whose desire it is to dwell among human beings. What goes for human interactions with the divine holds true as well for human-to-human interactions. We learn from difference. We can be mutually transformed as we listen attentively to our very different understandings of the God that we may encounter in and through the biblical text.

As we read the Bible, let us keep in mind that culture shapes our faith and how we read. Since meaning is bound to context, there is no single general understanding of the Bible that will be valid for everyone; understanding is always particularized, modified by our context.

Cultural diversity is an integral part of who we are. Learning to appreciate its richness can help us overcome our biases, our racism and our discrimination, so that we can see our interdependency with others. We are formed in light of others who have preceded us. Devaluing or seeking to destroy cultural diversity hinders and limits our understanding of the world and of the Word. Valuing diversity and the richness that it brings makes us stronger as a people and allows us to discover and respect the otherness in ourselves as well. ❖

Chapter 2

THE BIBLE AS A TEXT OF CULTURES

Randall C. Bailey

One of the difficulties in approaching the Bible is that we have been conditioned to look at it as "the Word of God," which gives it a sense of universalism and timelessness, and elevates it as a reality above culture. This way of viewing the Bible has helped in transporting it from one culture to another; it has also made it easier for people to read the Bible as though their own cultural biases were embodied in the text itself. The sense that there is but one way to view the text and only one way to interpret it has been reinforced by a view that "our way of doing it is the right way." Too often we have failed to look at the biblical text as a cultural production within its own time and geographical location, and we have not recognized that our interpretations of the biblical text have been prodded and shaped by our own

cultural understandings and time. This has robbed us, as readers, of the rich textures of the text and, ironically, has inflated the importance of our own readings to equal the high status we have attributed to the Bible itself.

One exception to this way of reading comes when we see something in the text that is embarrassing or upsetting. For example, in Genesis 16, Sarai tells Abram to have sex with her Egyptian slave, Hagar, so that Sarai can take Hagar's baby as a way of fulfilling God's promise to Abram—that he will be the father of a great nation (Gen 16:1-6). We readily recognize that this is about raping a slave, as we would see it in our own time. Yet we seek to explain it away, saying, for example, "That is just how it was in those times. This wasn't sexual abuse—it was just the custom of people back then." At a wedding in Cana, in John's Gospel, Jesus responds to his mother, "Woman, what concern is that to you and to me?" (John 2:4). Most of us know that were we to address our own mothers that way, we probably wouldn't be able to finish the sentence! But since Jesus is the speaker, we imagine, "That must have been a term of endearment in those days." In other words, we have been trained to read the Bible as though there isn't much difference between the culture of our time and place and that of the text— *except* when it becomes so obviously problematic that we assert, rightly or wrongly, that the culture behind the biblical text must have been dramatically different from our own!

Scripture and Culture

In approaching the biblical text, we should understand that the books that finally won places in the canon were not originally written by people who thought they were contributing to such a limited and authoritative collection. There was no collection, no Bible, and no plan for a Bible when people first composed the books that ended up in the Hebrew Bible, or First Testament. There was no doctrine of inspiration of the writings in either the First or Second Testament at the time those writings were being composed. (True, 2 Tim 3:16 states, "All scripture is inspired by God and is useful for teaching, for reproof, for correction, and for training in righteousness." But at the time that verse was written, only the Hebrew Bible and the Septuagint—that is, the Greek translation of the Hebrew Bible—had been compiled as Scripture. Even those two collections did not agree as to which books should be included or excluded, nor regarding order or wording of those books. The statement in 2 Timothy cannot refer to the New Testament, which wasn't assembled into its current order until some two hundred years later.)

The doctrine of the Bible's inspiration as an article of faith is a modern concept, developed in response to the critical study of the Bible in the eighteenth and nineteenth centuries.

The authors of the books we find in our Bibles today were writing to people of their time, exploring ideas of what life was about and how God wanted them to live. They were talking to people of their era, in languages, and using metaphors and symbols that made sense to their contemporaries. It isn't surprising that the biblical authors primarily used symbols and ideas that would make sense to *men* from the upper classes—their readers—because in the ancient world only upper-class men were taught to read and write. Some examples help make the point clear.

In the world of ancient Judah and Israel, polygamy—the marriage of a man to several women at the same time—was the norm. Thus, we see that Jacob was married to Leah and Rachel (Gen 29:21-30); David was married to Michal (1 Sam 18:27), Abigail (1 Sam 25:42), Bathsheba (2 Sam 11:27), and other women as well (2 Sam 15:16); and Solomon is reported to have married 700 princesses and 300 concubines (1 Kgs 11:3)! In the New Testament, we read that a bishop can only have been married once (1 Tim 3:2)—but we are not told that this was a requirement for other "Followers of the Way," much later called Christians. Today, however, we practice monogamy as though it were a clear biblical mandate.

An interesting aspect of this reading of the biblical text is that when African and other men who practice polygamy convert to Christianity, they often are required to divorce all but one of their wives. Given the clear acceptance of this marriage style in much of the Bible, it is a matter of curiosity—and of concern—to see that the church has often disrupted families because of false claims about "what the Bible says." While Paul in 1 Corinthians 7 speaks positively regarding marriage, he describes it as a distant second choice to asceticism and celibacy, and as an alternative appropriate only for those who cannot live his own lifestyle.

The ancient world also knew the practice of levirate marriage. In essence, when a man died without a male heir, his brother was to impregnate the widow, so that the first son born to her would carry the name of the deceased man. This practice is the basis of the story of Tamar in Genesis 38, of Ruth and Boaz in Ruth 3–4, and of the question the Sadducees pose to Jesus about a woman who had multiple husbands (Matt 22:23-30). It may surprise us to note that Jesus says nothing to question the practice of levirate marriage. Here again, understanding a culture different from our own helps us better understand what is going on in the Bible.

Scholars have noted that the royal administrations of David and Solomon's courts use the Egyptian form of government in the incorporation of the offices of recorder and secretary (2 Sam 8:15-18; 20:23-26; 1 Kgs 4:1-6). Even in this example we see a wider pattern in the Bible: the political life of ancient Israel and Judah was influenced by the ways of the peoples and nations with whom they lived and interacted. Similarly, Jesus likely spoke Aramaic and, as many scholars have observed, would probably have been perceived by many of his contemporaries in Galilee and Judah as a prophet with a politically incendiary message. That his speeches come to us in Greek means that early on they were subjected to a certain Greco-Roman spin—as incongruous, I imagine, as presenting Billy Graham's sermons in hip-hop.

There is evidence that biblical writers borrowed directly from other cultures. For instance, Ps 110:1-3a says:

> The LORD says to my lord,
> "Sit at my right hand
> until I make your enemies your footstool."
> The LORD sends out from Zion

> your mighty scepter.
> Rule in the midst of your foes.
> Your people will offer themselves willingly
> on the day you lead your forces
> on the holy mountains.

Here "the LORD" is a reference to God. On the other hand, "my lord" is a reference to the king—note the "scepter" in verse 2 and "your people" being led in verse 3. In verse 1, the statement that the king's enemies will be his footstool appears to be a direct reference to Egyptian court custom: the Pharaoh was seated on a throne, with his feet on a stool that bore the carved names of his enemies.

In the New Testament we have lists that scholars call the Household Codes (Eph 5:22—6:9; Col 3:18—4:1; 1 Pet 2:18—3:7). These passages talk about relationships of wives and husbands, children and parents, and slaves and masters. To varying degrees they talk not only about the responsibility of the subordinate members of each pair to the dominant ones; they also to some extent instruct the dominant ones to be nice to their subordinates. Although we know of no Greco-Roman document that bears such instructions, the ordering of God, husband, wife, child, and slave is a New Testament adaptation of the social organization of families in the Greco-Roman world. In other words, these instructions tell the members of the early Followers of the Way groups that they should be organized in line with Roman customs.

DIFFERENT CULTURAL VIEWS WITHIN SCRIPTURE

Within the biblical writings as well we find examples of writers debating with other writers over issues of culture and cultural theologies. For example, 2 Sam 24:1 states, "Again the anger of the LORD was kindled against Israel, and he incited

David against them, saying, 'Go, count the people of Israel and Judah.'" As the story has it, once David does what God incited him to do, he is punished and given three choices: three years of famine, being pursued by his enemies for three months, or three days of pestilence. He chooses pestilence (vv. 13-15). We may be surprised to hear of a biblical character being punished for doing what God urged him to do, until we recognize that there are other places in the books of Samuel—for example, 1 Sam 16:14, which tells us that God sent an evil spirit on Saul—where God is described as doing good and bad things to people. The writers of Chronicles— probably written in the fifth century BCE—didn't like this theology. So when the same story is retold, 1 Chr 21:1 states that "Satan"—not God!—"stood up against Israel, and incited David to count the people of Israel." Chronicles was written during the Persian period, when Yehud (Judah) was a colony of Persia. The writers of Chronicles were influenced by Persian thought and theology, including a dualism that positioned one power, responsible for good, against another power responsible for evil. The writers of Chronicles could blame Satan for inciting David to do something that would get him and the nation into trouble—a conception that wasn't available to the earlier writers of Samuel, because they lived in a different time and a different culture. The contrast allows us to recognize that those who today chant "God is good—all the time!" agree more closely with the theology of 1 Chronicles than that of 2 Samuel.

Similarly, in the New Testament, when Paul is asked whether it is all right to eat meat purchased in the marketplace (that is, meat that had been sacrificed to other gods), he responds that, yes, it is: since our God is God of all the earth, sacrificing to other gods was nothing more than wasted activity on the part of the Corinthian butchers and those making the sacrifice (1 Cor 10:25-29). His only disclaimer is that eating such meat is not allowed if someone else is offended by the practice. Paul takes the stand that when there is a conflict between the practices of the broader culture and tenets of the faith, unless the issue is one of crucial import, believers should "go along with the flow" culturally.

But the writer of Revelation totally disagrees on this and other issues. Addressing meat sacrificed to idols, he compares it to fornication and presents the risen Christ as threatening harm to those who do it (Rev 2:14-16). So this writer says one should not accommodate to culture but, rather, stand fast.

Here again we have two different biblical writers addressing the same episode or situation and taking different positions. Paul may have regarded the prospect of making it to Rome as a high point in his career; Luke certainly presents his preaching in Agrippa's court as a climax of Paul's story in Acts. The writer of Revelation, on the other hand, was living through a time of great persecution by the Romans, so he viewed any accommodation to them or their culture as evil. Two different biblical writers, at different times and under different social circumstances, disagree—and both of their contrary positions end up in the biblical text. Perhaps we should take this as a signal that those who put the Bible together recognized that culture and times influence theology, and that there is more than one way to look at things.

Readers from different cultures and different times have looked at the same text and come up with radically different ways of interpreting the text. The Pilgrims who migrated to North America in the seventeenth century read Exod 3:7-8:

Then the LORD said, "I have observed the misery of my people who are in Egypt; I have heard their cry on account of their taskmasters. Indeed, I know their sufferings, and I have come down to deliver them from the Egyptians, and to bring them up out of that land to a good and broad land, a land flowing with milk and honey, to the country of the Canaanites, the Hittites, the Amorites, the Perizzites, the Hivites, and the Jebusites."

The Pilgrims saw this passage as inspiration to leave their homes in England, where they were being persecuted for their religious beliefs, move to Holland, and then to travel to the "New World," which they called the "Promised Land." They saw both their leaving a place of oppression and their taking the lands of the native peoples in the Americas as following divine warrant. The Afrikaner Dutch Reformed Church in South Africa read that text in much the same way.

Enslaved Africans in the Americas heard those same verses as saying that God would free them from enslavement. They sang "Go Down, Moses" and interpreted their experience as paralleling Israel's. They even called Harriett Tubman the "Black Moses." Their hopes for manumission were inspired by such biblical passages. As a biblical scholar I find it interesting that enslavers and enslaved alike looked on the same passage as a way of justifying their actions, and as a Black man in the United States, I consider it of utmost importance that we all reflect deeply on that fact.

Latin American liberation theologians also looked to the Exodus story as a way of arguing that God had a special "preferential option" for the poor. They saw this narrative as encouragement to struggle against oppressors in their context. South African theologians opposed to apartheid appropriated this text in similar ways, and for similar reasons.

But some Native American theologians challenged black and liberation theologians on their use of the Exodus paradigm. They noted that the liberation of the people of Israel, spoken of in verse 7, is followed by a foreshadowing of the conquest of the Canaanites in verse 8. The God of liberation, they declared, was also a God of dispossession.

Given their experience with the conquest of their lands in the Americas, these Native American theologians found themselves identifying more with the Canaanites than with the Israelites. They asked black and liberation theologians why they didn't also identify with the Canaanites, given their oppression at the hands of those who had come from Europe and had brought many of them to the Americas as slaves.

READING OUT, READING IN

We read what Scripture says differently—and sometimes we may be reading what we believe as much as what Scripture itself says! Some have read Genesis 19, the story of the destruction of Sodom and Gomorrah, as a condemnation of homosexuals. That argument is based on one way of reading verse 5, which says the men of these cities "called to Lot, 'Where are the men who came to you tonight? Bring them out to us, so that we may know them.'" If we assume that the word *know* here means—as we often put it—"to know *in the biblical sense*," that is, sexually, then we might further assume that the men of Sodom are making a sexually threatening request. This view finds some reinforcement in Lot's response in verses 7-8:

> I beg you, my brothers, do not act so wickedly. Look, I have two daughters who have not known a man; let me bring them out to you, and do to them as you please; only do nothing to these men, for they have come under the shelter of my roof.

Lot responds as if he thinks this is a sexual request and feels that letting his neighbors rape his daughters is better than letting them rape his male guests. Part of our problem is that many contemporary readers would agree with Lot on both counts!

However, several observations call that interpretation into question. When the LORD tells Abraham that these cities are to be destroyed (18:20-21), there is no description of the behaviors to which the LORD objects. Further, we regularly recognize the difference between gang rape (which may be carried out against vulnerable persons—for example, in prison or military settings—by men who understand themselves as heterosexual) and same-gender sexuality. The men of Sodom and Gomorrah might well have expected to assault Lot's guests and then go home to their wives. Finally, Ezek 16:48-49 clearly suggests that the sin of Sodom was its lack of hospitality; nothing indicates it had to do with homosexuality.

Others have argued that this story is really about the sexual abuse of daughters. The verb *know* appears twice later, in Gen 19:33 and 35, when Lot's daughters committed incest with their drunken father. We read that Lot "did not know" when his daughter "lay down or when she rose." Clearly, in these verses the verb refers to awareness, not to knowing in the sense of sexual activity. Could it be that the men of Sodom just wanted knowledge of who was in the city? Note that it is *Lot* who thinks their request has sexual intention, and responds by offering his daughters for abuse. Lot is not the most morally reliable of characters. Later he seeks to exonerate himself with regard to incest with his daughters by saying that he was so drunk, he didn't know what was happening. Those who regard the "sin of Sodom" as simply a lack of hospitality might bear in mind that Lot's understanding of hospitality is to sacrifice his daughters. My point is that often our readings are shaped by what in a passage seems either to help or to hurt us; often we ignore what else is going on, either in the passage or in our own interpretations.

Another example is presented in the Magnificat, Mary's song in Luke 1:46-55, which reads in part:

My soul magnifies the Lord,
  and my spirit rejoices in God my Savior,
for he has looked with favor on the lowliness of
    his servant.
  Surely, from now on all generations will call
    me blessed;
for the Mighty One has done great things for me,
  and holy is his name.

This song often is held up as an example of how the women in the Gospel according to Luke hold a special role. So, for example, the birth story in Matthew 1 concentrates on Joseph and his feelings, but Luke's account of the birth concentrates on Mary and even allows her to speak. The song ends with verses 52-55:

He has brought down the powerful from their
    thrones,
  and lifted up the lowly;
he has filled the hungry with good things,
  and sent the rich away empty.
He has helped his servant Israel,
  in remembrance of his mercy,
according to the promise he made to our
    ancestors,
  to Abraham and to his descendants forever.

Churches that celebrate and lift up Mary for veneration and prayer look to this song as validating their claims of her special role in the life of Jesus. After all, there is no Song of Joseph. This song has also had great appeal to some liberation theologians, because it speaks of a God of reversal who helps the oppressed. These verses strengthen the claim of a special option for the poor in the Gospels.

Yet there are feminists and womanists who ask, How long will women have to put themselves in harm's way to save others and to be part of the struggle? How long will women, even when involved in shared community struggles, be expected to do "women's work" rather than taking true leadership roles? These critics see Mary's song as a way of encouraging women to go along, even in times of struggle, and to put themselves in jeopardy. Again we see that wherever one enters the story—whether in line with one's own experience, that of one's people, or of one's race, gender, social class, or sexual orientation—may dictate how one reads and interprets a text.

Sometimes we feel compelled to take other people's readings and make them our own. At other times we may feel compelled to struggle with these texts, to discern how they fit—or whether they fit—with our lives. For these texts not only grow out of certain historical and cultural contexts, they are also read and interpreted by people who live in very different contexts. Perhaps our goal could be to hear one another's readings and to see what is guiding them. Perhaps in this we can learn to see the richness in the texts, in the interpretations—and in the interpreters. ❖

Chapter 3

The Bible as a Text in Cultures

An Introduction

Fernando F. Segovia

Biblical interpretation involves widely differing ways of reading the text. For instance, a dogmatic-theological reading is used as official church doctrines are formulated. An ecclesial-liturgical reading is concerned with the conduct and worship of the church. A popular-devotional reading is at work in the daily practices and common piety of church members. Cultural readings of the text show up in literature, music, art, film, and the like. Social readings pertain to politics or the economy. And the academic-scholarly tradition puts the text into the world of higher education and knowledge production. Each of these reading traditions can be varied and complex, using any number of approaches or perspectives.

Ideally, biblical criticism—a term reserved for the academic-scholarly strand—should have within its angle of vision and study *all* of these reading traditions. Historically, however, that has not been the case. The discipline has mostly confined itself to analysis of its own trajectories and discourses. As a result, biblical criticism has pursued the study of the Bible as a text "in culture" but not "in cultures." *Culture* should be understood broadly, as meaning not only cultural production of symbols but also the material matrix of a culture. Consequently, it would be better to say that biblical criticism has pursued the study of the Bible as a text "in society and culture," but not "in societies and cultures." Thus, until recently, biblical criticism has pursued such study as focused solely on ancient society and culture.

Within this narrow academic way of seeing, any mention of contemporary Euro-American readings or of African American, Asian American, Latina/o American, or Native American readings of the Bible was unthinkable. For me to specify that my own reading had something to do with my particular social location—as someone born and raised in Cuba, who had lived first in the world of the colonized as a citizen of a dependent country, and then in the world of the colonizer, as a member of what was in the United States a minority ethnic group—would have been regarded as intrusive and ruled out of order. The appearance of *The Peoples' Bible* is one indication that this situation no longer pertains. To understand this transformation it is necessary to retrace the history of the discipline.

THE RISE OF BIBLICAL CRITICISM

Biblical criticism emerged as a tradition of reading in the early part of the nineteenth century, following upon the ferment of the French Revolution and paralleling the rise of several other areas of studies now formally pursued as disciplines in higher education. Its aim was to understand the texts of the Bible within their respective contexts, cultural as well as material, and, in so doing, to liberate the Bible from the doctrinal constraints placed upon it by the church. For this task of contextualization, biblical criticism was inspired by another new academic discipline of the time—historical studies. Biblical criticism latched onto the new historical methodology in its own investigation of texts from the past, yielding what could be described as an "umbrella" model or paradigm—a model of models—of interpretation that became known as historical criticism. The historical-critical method, which over time came to encompass a succession of varying but related models or angles of inquiry, proved dominant for about 150 years, right up to the final quarter of the twentieth century.

For historical criticism, the core challenge of contextualization was to bridge the historical gap that was perceived to exist between ancient writings and modern readers. This was done in a way that would avoid both reading the present back into the past (anachronism) *and* reading the critic's individual concerns and interests (or those of the critic's group) into the texts. This required, first, amassing as much historical knowledge as possible about the material and cultural realities of the particular time and place of the text being read, particularly focusing on religious knowledge and practices. Second, because scholars wanted to avoid reading the critic's personal concerns and interests into the text, they technically called the task of interpretation *exegesis*, meaning "reading out of" the text, or letting the texts speak for themselves. Its opposite, *eisegesis*, "reading into" the text, or imposing on it the personal agenda of the modern reader, was considered to be a fundamental misreading of the text.

Historical criticism, then, represented itself as a scientific method, objective and impartial in character, trying to understand the original meaning of the ancient texts in their own contexts, within the limits of the evidence available to us. For proper learning and deployment of the method, it was necessary for critics to put aside all markers and preoccupations of identity, removing themselves from their own material and cultural contexts and become instead universal and informed readers. In the eyes of historical criticism, therefore, all other reading traditions were deemed to be fundamentally defective, yielding inaccurate and compromised perceptions of the past. Biblical criticism had set itself up as the one proper key to unlock the biblical past—the Bible in (ancient) society and culture—and hence the norm for any and all interpretation of the Bible.

NEW APPROACHES

The ascendency of this mode of biblical criticism was unchallenged until the mid-1970s. The challenge to establish biblical criticism followed the social ferment of the 1960s and ran parallel to the way similar questions were being asked across the humanities and social sciences. Following the earlier example of historical criticism itself, new models posed themselves as a liberation from the constraints imposed upon biblical interpretation by the old historical criticism. The challenge came from two different sides.

On the one hand, the first stirrings of what would eventually become two new umbrella models signaled a parting of the ways with traditional historical criticism. Literary criticism, interested in texts as texts rather than as windows to the world, turned to literary studies (narratology, reader response, rhetoric, psychology) for direction. Sociocultural criticism, focused on social contexts as contexts rather than as mere backdrops for texts, looked to the social sciences (sociology, anthropology) for its grounding. From each direction, and in very different ways, the reigning view of a faithful retrieval of the past by neutral critics began to undergo destabilization. The literary turn showed

that texts were multidimensional, that readers were actively involved in producing the meaning of texts, and that this process produced multiple readings. The sociocultural turn accentuated the placement of texts and readers in society and culture, and hence emphasized the gap between antiquity and modernity. This first deviation from the standing paradigm arose from within the discipline itself: it was pursued by its traditional practitioners, dissatisfied as they were with the state of affairs in criticism.

On the other hand, the new undertaking of what would in time become another umbrella model, ideological criticism, was more intent on identifying and analyzing relations of power in society and culture. Ideological criticism marked another dramatic departure from traditional historical criticism. For instance, feminist criticism pressed the question of gender constructions and gender relations, while liberation criticism questioned the effects of political economy and social class on biblical texts. These developments seriously shattered what had been an entrenched view of the objective and impartial recovery of the text's meaning and its history. The established critical tradition was instead portrayed as thoroughly situated and interested—highly patriarchal as well as highly middle-class in nature—despite its claim to and its mask of objectivity.

NEW INTERPRETERS, NEW LOCATIONS

This second deviation from the ruling paradigm originated outside the traditional ranks of the discipline and involved a variety of newcomers, such as women scholars from the dominant culture in the West and male scholars from the non-Western world—especially Latin America at first—who had pursued graduate studies in the West. Ideological criticism continued to develop through the 1980s and 1990s as literary and sociocultural criticism as well as feminist and liberation criticism solidified and increased their hold. Minority criticism pursued racial-ethnic constructions and relations; queer criticism attended to sexual constructions and relations; and postcolonial criticism raised the issue of imperial-colonial relations. As a result, any claim to a single correct reading by informed and universal critics stood demolished. The older established critical tradition was again depicted as profoundly biased and not nearly as objective as it had claimed. It was now seen to be highly Euro-American, heterosexual, and empire-based. New models challenged the old model as having masked its social location and political agenda under the guise of objectivity. More importantly, this further shift from the standing paradigm was generated by people whose social location was even farther outside the traditional discipline: men and women scholars from non-Western minority groups in the West, especially African Americans at first; gay and lesbian scholars from within the West; and men and women scholars from the former colonies of the West.

By the end of the century, biblical criticism had come full circle since its inception, paralleling similar developments in other fields of study. The changes in question were momentous. Instead of a single defining model, several competing models were now in operation and in dialogue with one another. Instead of a privileged and normative model standing guard over interpretation, the presence of a variety of models alongside one another yielded acknowledgment of multiple points of entry and multiple results in interpretation. Instead of readings producing a faithful recovery of meaning and history from the past, readings were now regarded as contextualized and "perspectival," offering constructions or representations of meaning and history that were themselves subject to critical analysis. Instead of critics who sought to transcend

material and cultural contexts through scientific methodology, critics now emerged as embodying cultural contexts and engaged in those contexts, worthy of critical analysis in their own right.

Biblical criticism could now be envisioned in a different way altogether. Its objects of study were no longer only the texts and contexts of antiquity, as envisioned by traditional historical criticism, but also the modern and postmodern interpretations of ancient texts and contexts and the interpreters behind such interpretations. With the scientific ideals of objectivity and impartiality in retreat, biblical criticism now pursued more fully the study of the Bible as a text "in cultures and societies," meaning simultaneously in antiquity, modernity, and postmodernity. Texts, interpretations, and interpreters were now seen as not independent of one another but rather thoroughly enmeshed in and constitutive of one another.

The new lens provided by ideological criticism focused on the biblical text in terms of placement and ideology in society and culture, and hence on unequal relations of power. Suddenly, it was not only acceptable but imperative to critique the dominant tradition of interpretation, identified with Euro-American readings and the world of the North Atlantic, most evident in tradional historical criticism but present as well in the umbrella models of literary and sociocultural criticism. Now it was imperative as well to speak of feminist, liberationist, minority, queer, and postcolonial readings. Now it was possible and necessary to speak of African American, Asian American, Latina/o, and Native American readings, where the central axis of discussion was the problem of race and ethnicity, in association with such related concepts as migration, the "nation," borders, racialization, and ethnicization. In each case, and in minority criticism as a whole, the discussion became at once ever more subtle and ever more complex. This is the state of affairs at present in biblical criticism.

MOVING BEYOND
THE CIRCLE OF EXPERTS

But a further and crucial development in the discipline needs to be mentioned. As a result of this transformation, there has been a fundamental change in attitude toward the other major traditions of reading the Bible. Biblical critics no longer work alone, apart from a world of others who read the Bible. Given all this emphasis on location and agenda regarding texts, readings, and readers coming from sociocultural and especially ideological criticism, plus the intense focus on the multiple voices of texts, the agency of readers, and the diversity of readings coming from literary and ideological criticism, another principle of established criticism had to give way. Biblical analysis could no longer be restricted to the experts, to the world of learned readings and readers. The line of argument was clear and to the point. If the academic-scholarly tradition of reading was no longer viewed as guaranteeing proper and impartial interpretation, but constituted at all times a situated and positioned exercise in reading, why should criticism not extend its field of vision to the other reading traditions? If the goal of contextualization was no longer considered applicable only to the texts of antiquity (via a faithful recapturing of past meaning and history) but was now construed as applicable to *all* constructions of the past and their agents (given their character as localized and engaged), why should criticism not include similar representations and their agents from the other reading traditions? In sum, why should the use of the Bible in the theological-dogmatic, the ecclesial-liturgical, the popular-devotional, and the cultural-social reading traditions not be subject to the same degree of attention and analysis?

Countless possibilities for research opened up as a result. Why not examine the use of the Bible in works of popular theology or in official church pronouncements? Why not explore appeals to the Bible in missionary endeavors or in preaching traditions? Why not inquire into applications of the Bible in small church communities or in daily religious practices? Why not examine invocations of the Bible in works of poetry or in political discourse? Such a move signaled a much more expansive view of criticism, involving a broad conception of the Bible as text and of interpretation as task. The biblical writings no longer constituted just texts from the past bearing stable meanings. Now they represented living texts, drawn upon and reconfigured in ever so many ways, to ever so many ends, and with ever so many consequences. And biblical interpretation no longer represented simply an exercise in writing the history of ancient times, as if to retrieve one stable meaning from the past; now interpreters were fully aware of the problem of claiming to represent what history was "about" or what it "meant." Interpretation now became an exercise in cultural studies as well, attentive to all applications, their objectives, and their consequences.

PUTTING OUR INTERPRETATIONS
IN CONTEXT

With this extension of criticism into other reading traditions, a further principle of established criticism was revisited as well: the limitation of comparative analysis to the historical times and cultural areas of the ancient texts. For the goal of contextualized interpretation, comparative analysis of both symbolic and material aspects of culture was essential so that the biblical texts could be set as fully as possible—and thus explained as fully as possible—within their historical and cultural frameworks. As criticism moved to include analysis of modern and postmodern interpretations and interpreters, comparative analysis underwent an initial and corresponding expansion. It became imperative to situate such interpretations and interpreters, as constructive renditions of the biblical text, within their respective social-cultural contexts in modernity and postmodernity. Now, as criticism proceeded to include other major reading traditions as constructive renditions of the biblical texts, comparative analysis followed suit. It became similarly imperative, first, to situate such interpretations and interpreters within their respective social-cultural contexts; second, to place such interpretations and interpreters alongside one another, either within the same context or across a variety of contexts; and third, to place such interpretations and interpreters alongside the academic-scholarly tradition, either within the same context or across a variety of contexts.

By the end of the twentieth century, biblical criticism had indeed come full circle. These changes proved as momentous as those at its beginning. Instead of setting firm boundaries around the academic-scholarly tradition, other reading traditions were brought under its critical gaze. Instead of reserving comparative analysis to the academic-scholarly tradition, other reading traditions were now brought into critical juxtaposition with the academic-scholarly tradition and with one another. This was truly biblical criticism in a different key. Its object of study now comprehended all other major traditions of reading and their discourses. As a result, biblical criticism now pursued in full the study of the Bible "in societies and cultures"— in the world of learning as well as in all cultural appeals to it and renditions of it.

Within this comprehensive perspective, the issue of location and ideology in society and culture— that is, of power relations—was in the foreground in all areas of inquiry. Now it was not only imperative to speak of a dominant Euro-American tradition of interpretation in biblical criticism; it was proper to keep such a dimension in mind in *all* reading traditions. Now it was not only imperative to speak of feminist, liberationist, minority, queer, and postcolonial traditions of interpretation in criticism; it was proper to keep *all* such dimensions in mind across the other reading traditions. Now it was not only imperative to speak of African American, Asian American, Latina/o American, and Native American traditions of interpretation in criticism; it was proper to keep such dimensions in mind throughout the other reading traditions. In such minority approaches, the problematic of race and ethnicity and their related concepts functioned as the axis of discussion. The result in each case, as in minority criticism as a whole, was an even more subtle and more complex discussion.

The result of this recent transformation has been, for many, a far more demanding, far more engaging, and far more fulfilling conception and practice of the discipline. Today's biblical criticism continues to look back to the past, but it also looks around in the present and forward to the future. It is a biblical criticism in full dialogue with others, within the discipline, across disciplines, across societies and cultures, and across all realms of societies and cultures. In sum, it is a criticism for which the Bible has become truly a text *in societies and cultures*. ❖

The Bible as a Text in Cultures

African Americans

Vincent L. Wimbush

African American engagements with the Bible suggest much not only about who the people of the Bible are, how they sound and think, and what they mean and communicate but also about how Scripture functions in society and culture. African American use of the Bible as Scripture is varied and wide-ranging and has a storied history. These engagements should be understood as reflections of a people's long and continuing efforts to define and empower themselves. They are at once "readings" of the people and of the worlds with which they were forced to negotiate. These engagements reflect the people's consistent aspiration for power to signify upon, speak back to, and reshape the worlds and situations forced upon them.

One useful way to capture the complexity of African Americans' engagement with the Bible is through use of a framework of historical "readings." Such a schema will account for some of the recurring sentiments, practices, and orientations of a large segment of a people who have been called by many names, all reflecting marginal status, but in recent times most often "African Americans." The sketch presented here is organized historically, but the characteristics of each "reading" extend across the different types of readings, allowing us to observe different stages in orientation to the world.

First Reading: Awe and Fear— Initial Negotiation of the Bible and the New World

From the beginning of their captivity in different parts of the west coast of Africa and their traumatic translation to the Americas, where they experienced slavery and subjugation, peoples of African descent were confronted with the "civilizing" and missionizing agenda of the white-controlled system of black enslavement. One of the most important ideological tools used to advance this agenda was the Bible, held in common as an iconic text by all the European slave-trading nations.

Testimonies from European sailors, teachers, and missionaries, on the one hand, and from African, African American, and Afro-British autobiographies of the eighteenth and nineteenth centuries on the other, register the Africans' initial lack of understanding of European socio-religious orientations and their uneasy socialization into them. In arrogant presumption, European cultures violently imposed particular types of psychosocial scripts (ways of being), forms, and practices of literacy that at first frustrated the "conversion" of the Africans made to be slaves. Scripting and literacy per se were not the issue. But not only were the Africans on the whole incapable of meeting the culture-specific literacy requirements for conversion, they also were not emotionally disposed toward the book religion of the slavers. The notion of the divine communicating via a book was odd and scary, as should have been expected upon first contact. But at the same time, Africans perceived behind such a notion something awesome, mysterious, fascinating, and full of potential for future negotiation and empowerment. This was the period of the foundation and cultivation of the folk traditions among the Africans made slaves in the Americas. The complex engagement with the Bible was an important part of the cultivation of such traditions.

SECOND READING:
CRITIQUE AND ACCOMMODATION

Not until the late eighteenth century, with the phenomenal growth of dissenting, evangelical movements in England and in its colonies that were about to become the United States, did large numbers of the mostly enslaved Africans in the latter begin to engage the Bible explicitly and in ways that were more and more self-interested. Finding themselves directly appealed to by the new evangelicals and revivalists in vivid, emotional biblical language, and seeing that nearly the entire white world explained its power and authority by appeal to the Bible, the Africans could hardly fail to be drawn closer to it. With great ingenuity, reflecting their awareness of their situation and the times, they began to change the Bible from the sacred book of the white, aristocratic slavers and the mostly lower-class dissenting evangelical exhorters into a close-at-hand source of psychic-spiritual power and hope. It offered inspiration for learning and language that was readymade for a stinging, if veiled, critique of their situation. The Bible became for them a freighted site of social memory.

This reading extends well into the late twentieth century and may be considered the most popular, significant, and certainly the most enduring of the readings. It antedates but came to define and shape the independent African American churches and denominations that began in the late eighteenth century, as well as schools, colleges, and other organizations throughout the nineteenth century. It supplied the rhetoric and fueled many of the ideological-political positions of the civil rights movements and related campaigns of the mid-twentieth century. This reading of the Bible played an important role in the cultivation, in the late nineteenth to mid-twentieth century, of worldviews, initiatives, and political orientations that offered "racial uplift" to African Americans.

This reading—of both the Bible and of U.S. culture—expressed considerable ambivalence. It was at once critical and accommodationist. On the one hand, its respect for the primarily Protestant canon reflected its desire to be included within the nation's mainstream. On the other hand, its interpretations, including some burgeoning black "nationalist" sentiments, were on the whole from a social and ideological location "from below" and outside the mainstream—and these interpretations projected a blistering critique of Bible-believing, slave-holding, racist America.

THIRD READING:
CRITIQUE FROM THE MARGINS

Another reading was cultivated in the early decades of the twentieth century, primarily in urban centers of the United States. It reflected the sentiments of rural and small-town residents who migrated to the big cities in search of better job opportunities, greater social freedom, and a sense of power. These displaced individuals formed new religious communities that gave them a sense of solidarity.

The reading of the Bible and of the world among such communities also reflected a particular attitude about society and culture. It was a more critical, even radical, attitude about America. It held out little hope of full integration into the mainstream. The United States was seen as racist and arrogant, and was to be rejected as such. The use of the Bible and the creation and uses of other religious texts clearly reflect this attitude. Among the movements associated with such an attitude were the Garvey Movement, Father Divine and the Peace Mission Movement, the Black Jews, the Nation of Islam, the Spiritual churches, and the Pentecostal movement. These fairly marginal groups involving marginal peoples exerted considerable pressure upon mainstream groups to take note of the sentiments and practices to be found at the margins. But as a nonconfederated mix of communities, these folks remained marginal in numbers and power only for a few generations. They and the reading they fostered have in many respects come in the last few decades to define the center of African American religious life, including engagement with the Bible.

FOURTH READING: FUNDAMENTALISM— LEAVING RACE BEHIND

Another African American reading of the Bible and American culture emerged as a significant phenomenon in the late twentieth century. Sometimes called Fundamentalism, it was and continues to be in many respects a reaction to both the accommodationist and the separatist readings discussed above. This particular reading of the Bible is a sharp departure from the traditional African American use of the Bible. To be sure, African Americans have historically been evangelical in their religious sensibilities. For example, many African Americans continue to attach primary importance to the Bible as guide in all domains of life, including religious doctrine, morality, and ethics. Yet for a variety of reasons—including the politics of literacy and class divisions within and beyond religious denominations and also the richness of oral traditions and sensibilities among African peoples—most African Americans have historically been much more inclined toward playfulness and ingenuity than toward doctrinalism and moralism in their engagement with the Bible. In much the same way that the rise of Fundamentalism among whites in the early decades of the twentieth century represented a rejection of modernism, so within the world of African Americans a turn toward the universalism and color blindness offered in Fundamentalism can be seen as rejecting the significance of the particularities of African Americans' historical experiences.

The growth of such a reading, seen in the change in orientation of more traditional African American churches and in the founding of new churches and alliances with white Fundamentalist denominations and organizations, has resulted in the heightening of some tensions and the deepening of some fault lines within African America. These tensions are especially evident with regard to political initiatives and alliances.

DRAWING THE CIRCLE MORE WIDELY: WOMEN'S READING

In evidence throughout the history of African American readings of the Bible are the special readings of African American women. From Phyllis Wheatley to modern womanist interpreters, women have not only participated in each of the readings distinguished above; they have also constructed and transmitted those readings. Across all of these readings, differences in historical periods, locations, classes, and other factors notwithstanding, women collectively have for the most part added special emphases and intensities. Especially important has been their radical challenge to their male contemporaries, in every historical period and situation, to be consistent in striving for the prophetic ideals of justice and fairness.

Seen as a thread running through the story of a historically enslaved and subjugated people, we may see the Bible as a freighted cultural and political phenomenon, and a site for poignant social memories. Seen through this people's history, the Bible should not be viewed merely as holding different meanings for African Americans. The Bible must no longer be solely the object of historical criticism. We should see it as a focal point in critical histories of peoples and their journeys, orientations, practices, and politics. ❖

The Bible as a Text in Cultures

▪ LATINAS/OS ▪

Francisco Lozada Jr.

What distinguishes a Latina/o reading of the Bible from a European-Anglo reading or an African American, Asian American, or Native American reading of the Bible, to name only a few perspectives? One way to address this question is to examine the various ways Latinas/os have read the Bible through the lens of our experiences of *diaspora*—that is, of being unsettled, traveling, and resettling. These experiences are understood broadly; they involve not only an external diaspora, traveling from home country to host country, but also an internal diaspora, movement within a home or host country.

People and communities leave their home countries (into an external diaspora) for many reasons: political (for example, civil unrest or colonialism), economic (for example, globalization, scarcity of jobs), cultural (for example, social migration to reunite with family or escape religious intolerance), and those related to acts of nature (like earthquakes and hurricanes). Internal diasporas also have many causes: socioeconomic (searching for jobs), political (to escape anti-immigration laws), cultural (for example, in the United states, English-only laws), and, again, acts of nature (such as famines). Diaspora has traditionally been viewed in a temporally linear way, assuming that after the experience of resettlement, the diaspora experience ceases, both physically and mentally. But a more inclusive view sees diaspora as a temporally circular event that entails an ongoing experience. In other words, with every new wave of migration from Latin America, the process of diaspora starts over again for people from that particular country of origin, and for the Latina/o community in general. In addition, this circular understanding includes the view that diaspora involves social psychology and, in particular, the memory of many Latinas/os. This sense of diaspora is reflected in the titles of some biblical and theological books, including *Galilean Journey, Strangers in our Own Land,* and *A Dream Unfinished.*

Finally, the idea of diaspora is not fixed and stable but is fluid, extending beyond the first generations. Still, we should not assume that all Latinas/os have given a lot of reflection to either the concept or experience of diaspora.

A word about what I mean when I use the term *Latina/o.* It is Spanish nomenclature that is often mistranslated in English as "Latin." But Latina/o usually refers to communities whose cultural roots are traced to Latin America rather than to Spain. It is also a term that suggests permanency in the United States and that one has agency in claiming this identity for oneself. Finally, it is a term that is used loosely in the collective community, so as not to overshadow the unique cultural and historical particularities of the various Latina/o communities in the United States—Mexicans, Cubans, Puerto Ricans, Dominicans, Guatemalans, Salvadorans, Costa Ricans, Colombians, Venezuelans, Argentineans, and so on.

BEING UNSETTLED OR UPROOTED

Due to the violent encounter of indigenous American peoples with the Spanish empire in the sixteenth to the eighteenth centuries and to the colonial and imperial involvement of the United States throughout much of Latin America and the Caribbean from the nineteenth century to the present, the history of Latinas/os in the United States involves a great deal of dislocation and migration to and within the United States. Many Mexican Latinas/os in the U.S. Southwest found their political identity changed overnight, against their will, when the United States acquired the Southwest territory (known by Chicanos/as as *Aztlán*) after the Mexican–U.S. War and the Treaty of Guadalupe Hidalgo in 1848. Similarly, Puerto Ricans became subjects of the United States overnight with the colonization of their island in 1898. Such experiences of colonialism led many Latin Americans to unsettle themselves, within their home countries, as well as from their homelands to various host countries, including the United States. This experience of being uprooted is reflected in the way many Latinas/os read the Bible and is part of what we mean by a Latina/o perspective. It is especially visible in the reading strategies, principles, and assumptions of many Latina/o Christians.

Prior to the 1980s, the traditional way to read the Christian Scriptures was to borrow from the long-reigning and normative model of historical criticism. This model, focused primarily on identifying the written sources used by biblical authors, the oral traditions, histories, and settings behind the biblical texts, and the authors' special emphases and theologies, became a dominant way to read the Christian Scriptures. It was the way many Latinas/os learned to read the Bible, particularly if they were trained to read in the United States or Europe or by institutions in Latin America informed by historical criticism. As U.S. power and influence increased throughout the nineteenth and twentieth centuries, so did the dominance of the historical-critical approach. However, certain forces began to create a kind of uprootedness among Latin Ameri-

can scholars in the field of biblical studies. Leaving behind the traditional methods (but not altogether), many (including Latinas/os in the United States) began to depart from the historical-critical approach. These scholars began to challenge its principles of positivism and universality and to abandon its notions that meaning is apolitical and that the reader is invisible. This departure led many Latinas/os to borrow from the theology of liberation the interpretive push to decolonize and contextualize the experience of the interpreter. One of the earliest examples of this is Virgilio Elizondo's *Galilean Journey: A Mexican American Promise*. He draws from the historical, social, and theological experiences of Mexican Americans to read the Gospels through the experience of *mestizaje*, the cultural and racial intermixing of the Mexican people following the often violent cultural encounter between the Spanish (Roman Catholic) and indigenous communities of the Southwest. Elizondo argued that both Jesus and Mexican Americans were *mestizos*; that is, they were marginalized and outcasts within their societies. Another example is Justo González's strategy of reading "in Spanish," reflected in his book *Mañana: Christian Theology from a Hispanic Perspective*, in which he reads the Christian Scriptures from the experiences of exile (as a stranger in a new land) and oppression. Both readings are representative of this uprootedness. Dissatisfied with historical criticism's promises of prosperity, Latinos and Latinas stood up and began to travel to a new interpretive location. Drawing upon their experience of being unsettled, they began to explore where to go next. At the same time, filled as they were with a new consciousness and dismayed by dead-end historical-critical readings, they embarked on the risk of a new journey, back and forth sometimes, to "el norte," across the sea, and crossing the Southwest, always toward a new terrain, always in the hope of something new for them and their community.

TRAVEL:
CROSSING BORDERS AND WATERS

The experience of travel is not the same for all Latinas/os. These journeys are as diverse and unique as are the identities within the community. For many, it is extremely dangerous, while for others it is relatively safe. Some travel because of civil war (for example, Central Americans, Argentineans), political repression (Cubans, Dominicans), or economic disparity (Puerto Ricans, Mexicans). Others engage in social migration to rejoin family, as many women and children are doing today to join husbands and fathers who cannot travel back to their home country because of stricter immigration policies. Some travel because people of their sexual orientation are persecuted. Diasporic communities are just as diverse. Some are considered migrants (legal or "illegal"); others are viewed as political exiles and refugees. Some travel across state lines (for example, from Texas to Oklahoma) as internally displaced migrants, while others travel across national boundaries—which may involve crossing treacherous deserts or rivers. The diasporic experience of travel is distinctive for each of the Latina/o communities in the United States and diverse within each particular national or ethnic group as well. This experience of travel is usually a matter of crossing borders and waters. That is reflected in the biblical reading strategies of many Latinas/os, and it is another part of what is meant by a Latina/o perspective.

The experience of travel is the moment of searching—of trying to find space to stake one's own claim, to speak one's own voice, within the academic world of biblical studies as well as throughout various ecclesial communities and the larger society. Travel is also a moment of combating the closing of the borders of the mind, of opting for perforated borders and "crossing over" into different discourses. Much of this sense of combativeness

was due to the experience of cultural clash when Latinas/os arrived physically in the United States, or perhaps only later when they felt that their consciousness had arrived in the United States. Many Latinas/os began to experience systematic mistreatment in their host country, and as a result they inevitably turned their experience, language, and culture into tools of resistance. They sought to achieve full equality within their host country and within the Christian tradition. Many who were trained in the rich tradition of historical criticism "migrated" to other discourses—ranging from literary criticism to cultural studies, as well as to initial collaborations with other modes of interpretation, particularly that of liberation—that were reshaping the field of biblical studies. Traveling back and forth across borders was a common enough experience, allowing Latinos and Latinas to draw nourishment from their various homelands and, at the same time, to come under the influence of other discourses and ways of reading. Many of their readings now are infused with the cultural and ethnic pride that was awakened by the cultural clash of travel—but that also owes much to being *in* the United States but not really part of it.

This cultural clash also exists within both academy and church. As a result, Latina/o culture and language were employed in strategies of resistance and as tools to demand full equality within the host society. This spirit of resistance is part of what makes up the Latina/o perspective.

This experience of the diaspora is perhaps best represented by Harold J. Recinos's reading approach, which some have called *barrio* reading. Reading the Christian Bible through the lens of the experience of the inner city (the barrio), with its socioeconomic third-world conditions that make the people poor, Recinos correlates the marginalized experiences of the people in the world behind the biblical text with the marginalized people (Latinas/os) in front of the text. In effect, his strategy is crossing over, back and forth, between two different worlds. In the biblical scholarship from the early 1990s we find that many readings of the Bible begin with the social location of the reader and involve a similar crossing-over. This approach is sometimes called social-location hermeneutics, and it typically begins readings with the expression "I read from the perspective of…" or "My social location is…." Another scholar who represents this diasporic travel experience is Ada María Isasi-Díaz. Drawing upon her experience as a *mujerista* (womanist) theologian, she reads the Bible with a hermeneutic of suspicion and recovery. That is, she seeks to reclaim the voice of women that has been suppressed or obscured in the biblical text, in order to reclaim the Latina voice within the contemporary community.

A Latina/o perspective is conscious of the reader's social location and of the purpose of interpretation, which is to challenge any negative representation of Latinas/os in the United States, in the academy, and in ecclesial communities. Latina/o interpretation works with the principle that all readings of the Bible are socially and culturally located constructions. Thus all meaning is particular. And drawing from their experience of diaspora, Latinas/os seek to negotiate where interpretation itself is to be located. Latina/o interpreters continue to look back to their homelands at the same time they look forward to their new home.

RESETTLEMENT: TRANSFORMING SPACE AND VOICE

The experience of resettlement varies among Latina/o communities. Latinas/os have resettled in all regions of the United States. Many of these resettlements have led to the formation of new transnational identities, that is, the creation of new social identities that span borders, thus creating dual or multiple identifications. Sometimes this is reflected

in new modes of cultural production, such as new hybrid cultures (for example, the Nuevo Latina/o cuisine, or *Reguettón*, a blending of many Latin American musical styles). Recently, transnational identities have allowed Latinas/os—Mexicans or Cubans in the United States, for example—to influence the economics and politics of their homeland countries as well as their host countries through monetary remittances. Finally, transnational identities allow Latinos and Latinas to change or transform their particular locales to reflect their home cultures (think, for example, of Little Havana, Club San Lorenzo, Puerto Rico, or La Michoacán). I characterize this moment as one of "transforming space and voice." Respect shown to the culture of the host country is reciprocated by the host country respecting its various Latina/o communities. This transformation is also part of what is meant by a Latina/o perspective.

During this experience of resettlement, many Latinas/os are beginning to establish their homes in the host country. This is particularly reflected among those Latinas/os who have been in the United States since the 1960s or even earlier in the twentieth century, as well as by their children (second- and third-generation Latinas/os). These younger people are beginning not only to draw from their grandparents' cultures and homelands, but also to fuse them with other Latina/o and marginalized cultures found throughout the United States. What results is a cultural amalgamation, among Latinas/os themselves and others, through intermarriage, through shared knowledge regarding food, traditions, music, language, and religion, through uniting to combat anti-Latina/o ethnic racism, and through people of different cultural and ethnic identities being shunted into the same segregated neighborhoods, areas, and churches throughout the United States. During this period of resettlement, Latinas/os aim to preserve their language and their traditions, and gradually fuse them with other cultures in the United States. The result is a postcolonial hybridity or ambiguity as a way to survive within their new home. This "transforming space and voice" is also part of what makes up a Latina/o perspective.

This transformation is best represented in Fernando F. Segovia's reading strategy of intercultural hermeneutics and his push to make the discipline of biblical studies more interdisciplinary. Segovia seeks to bring biblical studies into dialogue with other discourses, whether it is with other theoretical discourses (around feminism, racism, sexuality) or with the cultural production of any contemporary period (such as globalization). A Cuban American, Segovia reads the Bible out of his own Latino context, using postcolonial studies as the optic or lens in which to read the Bible and providing interpretive strategies that other colonized people may use if they prove liberating, or refuse if they prove oppressive. Another representative example is the reading strategy of Efraín Agosto. Using postcolonial

studies, Agosto reads Philippians, for example, through the lens of the colonization of Puerto Rico by the United States. This reading provides readers a way to reinsert the voices of the colonized (Puerto Ricans) back into history with the colonized voices in the text. In effect, Agosto entertains a dialogue between the colonization evident in the text and the colonization of Puerto Rico.

It should be evident that reading the Bible through the perspective of the Latina/o experience includes diverse possibilities, as reflected in the diverse makeup of the community. Any attempt to flatten this collective diversity fails to capture the unique characteristics of the community. The framework of diasporic experience is one small way to understand not only the diversity of experiences and cultures among Latinos and Latinas, but also how they read the Bible through their cultures. All diasporas are different, and every diaspora is poignant—but every diaspora also holds the possibility of leading new, hybrid lives filled with much hope. ❖

The Bible as a Text in Cultures

▓ Native Americans ▓

George "Tink" Tinker

American Indians will read a biblical text differently than Amer-European readers because they live a distinctly different cultural reality. Sometimes American Indian cultures and our historical experiences of conquest mean that the biblical text collides with our idea of good in the world.

Take, for example, the Exodus story. American Indians will always see themselves as the aboriginal Canaanite owners of land that has been invaded.

The Pilgrims and Puritans arriving in America saw the situation in exactly those terms, calling themselves the "new Israel" as they justified their invasion and theft of Indian property. In the nineteenth century, in the age of imperialism, German scholars read the exodus as a pure act of colonial conquest. By the late twentieth century, on the other hand, some scholars were arguing for understanding the emergence of Israel in Canaan on the model of a peasant revolt. Those last two interpretations present a significant problem for Native American readers. The Indian reading of Exodus will always raise hackles, because Indians will always identify with the Canaanites as indigenous, colonized peoples.

This is problematic enough on the face of it, but there is another, more serious, dilemma inherent in the Euro-Christian/Indian intersection. While we will not deal here with the place of Scriptures in the faith of Indian Christians, we have to notice that Christian Scriptures cannot have the same place among Indian Christians as they do in Amer-European church communities. The missionary imposition of the Hebrew Bible on Native American Christians as an "Old Testament," a practice that denominations continue today, has two primary effects that prove destructive for Native American communities. First, it challenges the validity of Native American traditions, which were castigated as "demonic" by the missionaries. Second, it inherently prescribes replacing one's own history with someone else's as a prerequisite for conversion. Christian conversion typically mandates the learning and embracing of a completely foreign history—the history of Israel and Judaic Palestine—as one's own. Today many Indian Christians are increasingly insistent that their own historic covenants with the Creator, once labeled demonic by the missionaries, should receive continued respect and attention. Many Indians participate both in church liturgies and in their own tribe's ancient traditional ceremonies.

TIME, SPACE, AND THE KINGDOM OF GOD

We will mention here two significant cultural differences between American Indian and Euro-Western peoples that deeply affect interpretation of biblical text. First, American Indian peoples are characteristically spatial in their thinking, while Euro-Western folk tend strongly toward being temporal thinkers, emphasizing time as a priority. Second, the radical individualism of Euro-Western people continues to be distinctly foreign to American Indians because it is opposed to an Indian worldview.

If we take a single text, Mark 1:14-15, as an example, the foundational Indian cultural perception of spatiality changes the reading of the text from one focused on time and eschatology—the theology of the last days of the world—to one much more interested in a theology of creation. At stake here is the interpretation of the "kingdom" of God (*basileia tou theou* in Greek). As it stands in the Greek or in a literal English translation, this metaphor presents a particular challenge for any American Indian reader or listener. Beyond the inherent sexism of the usual "kingdom" translation, the concept is problematic simply because Indian peoples in North America never functioned with political systems that included ruling monarchs. For American Indian peoples, who come out of communities that are historically more egalitarian and genuinely democratic and participatory, the kingdom metaphor is culturally foreign and must be completely recast. The only possible point of comparison for the notion of *basileia* (bah-si-LAY-ah) in Indian experience might be the Bureau of Indian Affairs or the U.S. War Department!

Comparing an American Indian interpretation of *basileia* (kingdom) with those generally proposed by Western biblical scholars will show how the principles of creation and spatiality might function. Euro-Western scholarly discussion for the last century has assumed a universal validity across cultures, when otherness and difference may have been much closer to reality. Until recently, these scholars interpreted the meaning of *basileia* as related to time, based on contemporary notions of eschatology. That is, the only appropriate question to ask about the *basileia* has been, *When* will the kingdom come? It is not that scholars did not consider other possibilities. The question of *where* has been consistently dismissed! A wide variety of temporal answers have been argued, each generating a new technical term. We have been given notions of "realized eschatology," "actualized eschatology," "immanent eschatology," and "future eschatology." But each merely addresses a different perspective on the time-related "when-will-the-kingdom-come" question.

It seems obvious enough that spatial categories do not necessarily exclude the temporal, or vice versa, but the orientation assumed by the interpreter becomes crucial. In the Gospel of Mark especially—the verses cited above notwithstanding—there seems to be a distinct sense of the priority of the spatial in its language. Any Indian reader of Mark, or of the other two Synoptic Gospels, Matthew and Luke, is bound to think first of all about the question Where? with regard to *basileia*. An American Indian reading, then, must begin with a spatial understanding of the *basileia* as a place where God rules. That place, in the Indian mind, must be the place God created, namely, the world in which we exist. Thus, *basileia* is read spatially, as a creation metaphor.

My argument is that those two different ways of thinking have to do with time and space, the when and the where of the *basileia* in Mark. Space and time are not necessarily two dimensions of equal value in human thinking. For any given culture, one is usually primary, the other secondary. American Indian people tend to think out of a spatial cosmology. Their most fundamental and powerful images, metaphors, and myths have to do primarily with space and places. An American Indian spatial interpretation raises the likelihood that all of Western biblical scholarship has worked for a century with a transcultural blind spot. Why, after all, would the kingdom of God not be a realm or a place where God rules, or a community that God rules?

For the Western intellectual tradition, time is primary, and space is a subordinate category. From notions of progress to the casual revelation that "time is money," from the sacred hour on Sunday morning and the seven-day cycle of work, play, and spiritual obligation, to the assumption of progress in philosophical and scientific inquiry in the West, time always reigns supreme. In much of Western thought, all of space is rendered a mere function of time. It is no wonder that the *basileia tou theou* (kingdom of God) is also discussed consistently as a function of time.

An American Indian spatial reading of the Gospels combines spatiality and creation, resulting in a reading that naturally understands *basileia* as a creation metaphor that images ideal harmony and balance. It represents a symbolic value whose parameters might be outlined as follows. First, the Gospels seem to view divine rule as something that is in process. It is drawing near. It is emerging (Mark 1:15). Yet it is also "among" us, in our midst (Luke 17:21). It is something that can be experienced by the faithful here and now, even if only anticipated, while its full emergence is still in the future. Second, the symbolic value captured by this imagery in no small part includes a view of an ideal world. Finally, the structural definition of that ideal world is, above all else, relational and spatial.

The imagery of divine rule in the Hebrew Scriptures is essentially creation imagery. That is, the ideal world symbolically represented in the Hebrew Bible builds on the divine origin of the cosmos as an ideal past and points to an ideal future. American Indian readers would assume that the ideal world is the real world of creation in an ideal relationship of harmony and balance with the creator. It is relational, first, because it implies a relationship between the created order of things and its creator and, second, because it implies a relationship between all created things. As the creator, *theos* (God, in the Christian Scriptures) is the rightful ruler of all. Hence, the ideal world to which Jesus points in the Gospels is precisely the realization of that proper relationship between creator and created in the real, spatial world of creation.

For an American Indian reader of the Bible's creation stories, whether human beings were created first of all the mammals or last of all the "createds" is not nearly as important as affirming the harmony and balance of the created order. While the balance of that order is repeatedly shaken by the human creatures, it is still the ideal state of being that we attempt to restore. While the ideal state of balance and harmony can never be achieved for all time, all—meaning all of creation—are part of the ongoing process of restoring balance. In his letter to the Romans, Paul says that all of creation groans in travail, that is, in childbirth (Rom 8:22). A Christian Indian perspective would naturally assume that Paul sees the Christ-event as having the same purpose as Indian ceremonies: to restore a world in travail.

In this American Indian interpretation, the *basileia* must be understood as all-inclusive. That is, if it symbolizes the harmony and balance of all creation, then it must include all things created. In an American Indian anthropology, the *basileia* must include two-legged, four-legged, winged, and all the living and moving things, since all are created by the creator and leader of all existence. The *basileia* is inclusive of all human beings, whether or not all recognize the divine creator. Those who are considered to be standing outside the kingdom are there because they have somehow excluded themselves by failing to recognize the balance and harmony intended in creation. This state of unawareness is often the result of an individual's attempts to establish her or his own sense of control within or over the creation.

While Native Americans know little about either rulers or kingdoms, only a spatial response to the question Where? begins to make any sense of the metaphor. Whatever the *basileia* is, it must be a

place. The verb *ēngizein* ("the kingdom has drawn near," Mark 1:15) allows for and even predicates a primary meaning of spatial nearness. In Luke 17:21, Jesus instructs the Pharisees that the *basileia* is "in your midst" (*entos hymas*), that is, already spatially present. Removing the Amer-European emphasis of temporality of course lessens the emphasis on the future establishment of God's kingdom. In an American Indian reading, the *basileia* has little, if anything, to do with what happens in the future. Rather, it is concerned with how one images oneself in the present in relationship to the Creator and to the rest of creation.

THE KINGDOM, REPENTANCE, AND RESTORATION

In Mark 1:15 the *basileia* is linked with the imperative, *metanoiete* (repent). We need not discuss at length the nature of the word for time in this verse. It is enough to acknowledge the cyclical and seasonal nature of *kairos* (meaning the "right or opportune moment"), used here, over against the more linear concept of *chronos* (meaning "continuing time"). The mention of a time element should not distract us from a spatial, and now creational, understanding. More important for a Native American reading is a spatial understanding of *metanoiete*. Here the underlying meaning of the Aramaic-Hebrew *shuv* (return) is spatial, rather than the Greek notion of "change of mind." Repentance is key to the establishment of divine oversight, because it involves a return to God and a proper understanding of God's rule over all of creation.

Feeling sorry for one's sins is not part of repentance at all, although that may be the initial act of confession. In the Acts of the Apostles, repentance does not yet carry a penitential, emotive connotation but instead carries the Hebrew sense of *return*. In Acts 2:37-39, people feel penitential emotion (they are "cut to the heart") as a result of Peter's sermon and come to him and the others to ask what they must do. His response: "Repent, and be baptized." Since they already feel sorry for their sins, "repent" here cannot imply the Latin *penitentio*, penitence. The Hebrew notion of repentance really is calling on God's people to recognize the divine rule of God, to return to God, to return to the ideal relationship between Creator and created, to live in the spatiality of creation fully aware of God's rule, of human createdness, and of the interrelatedness of all the createds.

In the Native American world, we recognize that interrelatedness as a peer relationship between the two-leggeds and all the others— four-legged, winged, and other living, moving things. This is the real world within which we hope to actualize the ideal world of creational balance and harmony.

These examples only begin to articulate an American Indian reading of the Christian Bible. That this reading of the *basileia* may be quite unlike standard Amer-European interpretations should signal that in a multicultural, pluralistic world of diversity there will necessarily be many readings of the Bible. A single normative interpretation seems to be further from reality today than ever. ❖

The Bible as a Text in Cultures

░ ASIAN AMERICANS ░

Frank M. Yamada

Asian American biblical interpretation reflects the diverse perspectives and experiences of peoples from many different ethnic backgrounds, whose ancestry can be traced back to the various nations and rich cultures that make up Asia. The question "How does one read the Bible from an Asian American perspective?" is complicated. For many Asians in the United States, their experience of the Bible has been heavily shaped by missionaries from the West who sought to convert peoples of Asian descent to Christianity and to Western cultural ideals. The Bible, however, is just one influence among many religious texts and traditions for Asian groups within the United States. The very term "Asian American" complicates biblical interpretation from this U.S. cultural location. Asian Americans include peoples from China, Japan, Korea, Vietnam, the Philippines, India, Thailand,

Laos, and many other nations. Because of this, it is difficult to identify a single or unified Asian American way of being. Though each of these groups would maintain the importance of their ethnic heritage for understanding community identity, no one group can speak for the others. Moreover, the history of U.S. racism, both in law and in culture, has affected the ways these groups and individuals have experienced life in the United States. To understand Asian American biblical interpretation, one must first begin to understand the complex experiences, cultures, and histories that emerge from Asian peoples who live in the United States.

It is necessary to make an important qualification. The term *Asian American* has been a useful and politically strategic classification. During the civil rights movement, this identification helped unite peoples of different Asian ethnicities to gain a more unified and powerful political voice. Since that time, several Asian American organizations, activist groups, and student agencies have benefited from the collective energies that come from such diverse gatherings. In the latter part of the twentieth century, Asian American studies programs began to emerge at universities and colleges around the country, especially in or near big cities and on either coast. Asian Americans are now also more prominently visible throughout popular culture, even as many pernicious stereotypes persist.

The civil rights energy and the social activism surrounding the racial classification "Asian American" suggest that it has been a helpful designation for many Asian peoples within the United States. But it is also inherently limiting. The category does not take into account the many and varied ethnicities and cultures that are an important part of the lives of Asians living in America. Even within a single ethnic designation, such as Japanese American, for example, it is difficult for one to take into account generational, geographical, cultural, and social differences. A Japanese American who grew up during World War II on the West Coast will have a different perspective than one who grew up in Hawaii during those same years. Similarly, a Nisei (second generation) female will think very differently about gender roles than a Sansei (third generation) male like myself. One begins to see the difficulty in defining what it means to be Asian American when one expands these few examples to include all of the ethnic and cultural groups that make up the rich diversity of Asians in the United States.

Additionally, Christianity has had a long and complicated relationship to Asia, which affects the ways Asians receive the Bible. The Bible was introduced to many Asian countries within the context of Western European colonialism. Different forms of U.S. Christianity, including Evangelical, mainline, and Roman Catholic traditions, have all had a major impact on the practice of Asian American Christians. Because this racial designation is both useful and problematic, Asians in the United States are empowered through the building of Asian and Asian American communities, while they simultaneously seek to resist oversimplified stereotypes of Asians within Western culture.

It is difficult, therefore, to suggest that there can be a single, unified way to understand how Asian Americans read the Bible. Asian American biblical interpretation is as diverse as the many different ethnic groups that make up the peoples of Asian descent in the United States. One helpful way to understand Asian Americans and their relationship to the Bible is to examine the historical experiences of these peoples and the history of the development of Asian American theological thought.

THE EXPERIENCE OF ASIAN AMERICANS

Themes of exclusion and the persistence of community characterize the history of Asians in the United States. Asians began immigrating to the United States as early as the eighteenth century, with large groups from East Asia, especially the Chinese and Japanese, relocating to the United States in the 1800s. Many worked on the railroads during their westward expansion in the latter third of the nineteenth century. With this new wave of immigrants came fear from the existing populations. Legislation soon followed that sought to limit the population of Asians in the United States. Congress passed a series of laws that prohibited Asians from gaining citizenship or owning property, including the Chinese Exclusion Act of 1882. The Immigration Exclusion Act, also passed in 1882, halted further migration of the Chinese to the United States.

During World War II, after the Japanese bombed Pearl Harbor, President Franklin D. Roosevelt signed Executive Order 9066, which allowed for the imprisonment of more than 120,000 Japanese and Japanese Americans into internment camps, located mostly in remote areas of the western continental United States. Many families were only given forty-eight hours to pack up their belongings and relocate to the camps. The government enforced this legislation without due process of law, even though many in the camps were U.S. citizens by birth. Forty years later, the Commission on Wartime Relocation and Internment of Civilians determined that the government's actions were unjustified, based as they were primarily in racism and war hysteria. The government issued an official apology and provided a financial settlement to survivors of the camps, but the effects of the camps have been devastating and long-lasting in the Japanese American community.

More recently, groups primarily from South Asia have experienced violence and hostility in the aftermath of the terrorist attacks that occurred on September 11, 2001. In this case, racism has been manifested in religious and ethnic stereotypes. Asians in America, whether or not they were religiously observant Muslims, faced discrimination at the hands of a nation gripped with fear, suspicion, and prejudice. Islam, similar to other monotheistic religions, is multifaceted and complex. It is neither more nor less inherently violent than the other Abrahamic monotheistic religions, Christianity and Judaism. In a culture of fear, however, people's irrational actions and thought processes took hold. Thus, even other Asian American religious groups, which differ from Islam in their religious practices and beliefs, were often identified erroneously as "Middle-Eastern terrorists" by an uninformed American public after the attacks. For example, many Sikhs, who wear traditional head coverings as part of their religious observance, were publicly harassed or violently assaulted shortly after 9/11. This happened in spite of the clear religious differences between Sikhs and Muslims. Similar incidents were reported among Hindus of Asian descent.

In these cases, stereotypes of Middle-Eastern Islamic terrorists were projected upon peoples who were neither Middle Eastern nor Muslim and whose religious practice discourages violence against others.

Even though Asian Americans have contributed greatly to U.S. history and society, stereotypes of Asians exist within contemporary U.S. culture. Two such stereotypes are prominent: the "model minority" and the perpetual foreigner. Because certain Asian Americans have been relatively successful in American society, they are often viewed as a model minority. On the surface, this stereotype could be viewed as a positive description. However, the idea of the model minority is problematic for Asian Americans, both internally and externally. Internally, it limits identity. For many, the designation means that Asian Americans are good citizens who do not cause problems. Thus, this stereotype doesn't envision Asian Americans engaging in the sorts of civil disobedience or dissent that were typical in the 1960s and 1970s. Moreover, the model-minority label makes invisible those Asian Americans who do, in fact, suffer from poverty or social dislocation. Externally, this stereotype also creates tension between Asian Americans and other people of color, since it functions within the dominant society to pit one racial group against another.

The second dominant stereotype of Asians in American culture is the perpetual foreigner. Even though some Asian American groups have been in the United States for centuries, spanning many generations, the Asian population continues to be portrayed in American culture as foreign or alien. Asian American men and women are commonly depicted in the media as exotic, often speaking with a heavy accent. In some cases, Asian foreignness is characterized as disloyalty or untrustworthiness. Even as late as 1999, the U.S. government falsely accused Wen Ho Lee, a Taiwanese American scientist, of being a spy for the Chinese government in a highly publicized case that ultimately proved embarrassing for U.S. officials. The perpetual-foreigner stereotype is tied to the history of Asian immigration to the United States—a history in which legislation such as the Chinese Exclusion Act sought to keep Asians foreign to protect the status quo. The perpetual-foreigner label is another way the dominant U.S. culture tells people of Asian descent that they are not wanted or that their acceptance in this country has limits.

In spite of this history and culture of exclusion, Asian American communities have persisted and flourished. Peoples from Asia continue to immigrate to the United States, building communities that grow and thrive. During the 1960s, Asian American activist groups worked toward social change during the civil rights movement, resulting in empowerment and political voice. Religious centers, including Christian churches from a variety of traditions, are locations in which Asian American identity and culture is fostered. For example, immigrant churches continue to serve as both worship centers and places where future generations can practice the language and culture of their ancestry. Asian Americans as a group tend to be upwardly mobile socially and economically, integrating well into mainstream American society. Asian American studies programs are now well established at universities and colleges across the nation. Moreover, in the twenty-first century many Asians in the United States, including mixed-race Asian Americans, have become prominent public figures and celebrities in politics, sports, literature, the media, and other areas. The communities of Asian America continue to grow and expand in vital and diverse ways.

ISSUES IN ASIAN AMERICAN BIBLICAL INTERPRETATION

The experience and culture of Asian Americans informs how these communities read the Bible.

However, there are specific factors within the academic study of the Bible that have also contributed to what we know as Asian American biblical interpretation. For most of the nineteenth and twentieth centuries, biblical scholars employed a method of study called historical criticism. This useful methodology, developed primarily in Germany, had a lasting impact on modern biblical scholarship. Historical criticism emphasizes that the meaning of a text must be situated in its original context in history. But in the 1970s and 1980s, biblical scholars began to emphasize the importance of recognizing the role the *reader's culture* plays in developing the meaning of a text. For example, someone reading from an African American perspective would not necessarily see the same things in a text as someone coming from a white, Western-European understanding. It is from within this change of perspective in scholarship that Asian American biblical interpretation emerges.

Asian American academic study of the Bible has its roots in Asian American theology, which began to blossom in the last three decades of the previous century. These scholars, primarily from Protestant Christian traditions, began to write theologies that emphasized the experiences of Asians in the United States. Therefore, ideas such as marginality and *liminality* (the experience of being in an ambiguous in-between or "threshold" state) became prominent. As in all liberation theologies, when one understands God from the perspective of the margins, important themes begin to emerge. For example, Jesus' status as mediating between humanity and deity within the Christian Scriptures allows us to understand him as someone who responds to those who are marginalized in society. Much of Asian American experience, especially in early generations, is described as being located *between* two worlds—their land of origin and the United States. Because of this, Asian American theology identifies with a God who is on the margins or who works in those in-between places. Thus, Asian American theology is based in the experiences of Asians in the United States, stressing the rich cultural and religious heritages that come from the continent of Asia.

Asian American biblical scholarship has followed a similar trajectory. Biblical scholars have sought to read the Bible through characters and themes that emphasize margins or spaces in-between. In the Abraham-Sarah stories, for example, an Asian American reading might understand the marginalized status of a childless couple in the ancient world, who are wandering in a place between their land of origin and an unknown destination promised to them by God. One would also be attentive to characters such as Hagar and Ishmael, whom God blesses even when they are excluded from the center because of their ethnic (Egyptian) difference.

Asian American scholars also have used cultural and religious themes from Asia to help in their understanding of the Bible. Some have sought to see tensions within the biblical texts through the lens of yin-yang. Rather than thinking of diverse opinions as opposites, this East-Asian philosophical idea understands differences as mutually intertwined—not either/or, but both/and. Thus, the differentiations God/human, grace/law, or insider/outsider are held together in tension. Still other scholars have stressed the similarities between biblical understandings of human existence with religious ideas within Taoism, Buddhism, or Confucian thought.

The trajectories described above have greatly enhanced biblical interpretation from the context of Asian America. These themes, however, have tended to stress the Asian-ness of Asian American biblical interpretation. Ideas such as marginality or liminality make most sense among early generations, where the context of immigration is central. But later generations do not have the same longing for homeland that their parents or grandparents experienced. For Asian Americans who have been in the United States for three to five or more generations, their relationship to the U.S. context is complicated and conflicted in a different way. Themes such as hybridity or the fluidity of identity become more important. Interpretations in this vein might stress the ways that biblical identity is conflicted rather than stable. Within this interpretative mode one might ponder, for example, how the identity "Israelite" is developed largely to deflect another identity, "Canaanite." Israel's religious practice is fully dependent on Canaanite religion, even as it tries to be different from it. Later-generation Asian American biblical interpretation would complicate clear distinctions between Asian and American, between Israelite and Canaanite, or between Jew and Gentile, preferring instead to see the complexity that is inherent in any cultural identity.

Asian American biblical interpretation is as complex and diverse as the many different ethnicities, cultures, and experiences that make up the populations of Asians in the United States. While the inherent diversity within Asian America threatens the usefulness of this racial designation, Asian Americans continue to form alliances across these social boundaries to form meaningful communities. This movement in Asian American theology and biblical scholarship mirrors what is happening in churches across the nation as later generations form congregations through their shared experience of growing up as Asians in America. This meaningful connection suggests that generations of Asians in the United States will continue to generate biblical interpretations that will empower their understanding of God at work in their midst and give voice to their own rich cultural heritages. ❖

The Bible as a Text in Cultures

Euro-Americans

Nicole Wilkinson Duran

The Bible, which in the Christian use of the term includes Hebrew and Greek writings, has nowhere else exerted the kind of deep influence on culture that it has had in the West. Europe certainly had religious and cultural traditions before the Bible was introduced. But as long as it has been called "the West," the Bible has been profoundly involved in its history. Robert Alter has maintained that the linear quality of Hebrew narrative constituted a revolution in literary culture and that the Bible consequently stands as the most influential source for Western literature and historiography. Certainly one cannot read European literature without becoming familiar with biblical themes and stories. The Bible has exerted a major influence on most elements of Western culture, from art to astronomy.

Like most peoples of the world, the peoples of the West have always read the Bible in translation. The native speakers of biblical Hebrew and *koine*, or common, Greek were not Westerners, and Westerners, once there was a West, on the whole did not read or speak those languages. When Christianity became the official religion of the Roman Empire, it made sense to translate the Hebrew, Aramaic, and Greek of the original texts into Latin, at the time the most common spoken language in the Empire. This translation was quickly seen as sacred in itself. The holy words of Scripture, and of the Christian Mass in which it played an integral role, were Latin words, even among peoples who did not understand Latin. The Bible could exert its strong cultural influence only because of the mediation of the clergy, who, unlike the populace, were literate in Latin and interpreted the text to common Christians, both by translating it and by making it relevant.

In far too many cases, the ecclesiastical hierarchy interpreted and taught its clergy to interpret the Bible to serve its own interests. The poor were poor as part of God's plan, merely lower links on what came to be known as the Great Chain of Being. Earthly authorities, said these interpreters of the church's Bible, were ordained by God, as were slavery, war, chauvinism of all kinds, and even torture.

THE LEGACIES OF THE REFORMATION AND ENLIGHTENMENT

For centuries after the West became predominantly Christian, the Bible's worldview mingled with that of Western culture almost imperceptibly. Sometimes the Bible adapted and reshaped native European traditions, with the result that we (I speak as a person of white European descent) learned to portray biblical saints with the sun god's radiant halo, and to read three wise men into Matthew's story because three was for us a magical number. During the Reformation some of this interplay of older culture with biblical interpretation was noted and, in a word, protested. Various strains of the Protestant movement rejected certain elements of interaction between the Bible and native cultures: the array of local gods alongside Christian saints and the adoption of the winter solstice as the birth of Christ, for example. The Protestant ideal was to cleanse the Bible of cultural influences and to cleanse the church—and the culture—of every authority but the Bible. Of course this ideal was never achieved. Cultural influences can be reshaped, but they cannot be undone. The Bible, like any text, cannot be received except through human hands, mediated and interpreted by culture.

But if Protestant leaders wanted to free the Bible of certain "foreign" cultural entanglements, most concluded that it was neither possible nor desirable to have a Bible free of all cultures except those of biblical times. Not surprisingly, these European Protestants looked with some favor on their own culture. Eventually, they understood the Bible to give authority to the rise of European power and to European imperialism. The biblical mandate to conquer the promised land and destroy idolaters, as well as Christ's command in Matthew (the "great commission") to go out into all the world, lent support and offered satisfying rationalizations for those who sought adventure, trade, power, and wealth in the European imperial project, from the Crusades to the conquest of the Americas and beyond.

On the other hand, some of those same biblically supported ventures brought back news that seemed to threaten the Bible's authority. Europe's science for the first time came into conflict with what was understood to be the worldview of the Bible. If the Bible said that God created humanity as the pinnacle of creation, then surely the earth, humanity's home, was the point around which the heavens turned. To threaten that inference, as new astronomical discoveries did, was to diminish the Bible and, perhaps more importantly, detract from the authority of the Bible's appointed interpreters. For the first time, what were understood as advances in European culture were shunned by the church. The unity of religion and elite culture had been broken.

The rift between at least one stream of European culture and the biblical text became a central issue during the Enlightenment. The concept of natural law seemed to fly in the face of the Bible's miracle stories, and it was difficult to enlist the Bible on the side of equality and democracy when it had historically been one of the greatest defenders of hierarchy. Secularism became almost a belief system in itself, and the cultural space for those who had no use for any religion widened considerably. In response, those who stayed with some form of the church regrouped into two separate camps—camps that continue in the West, with little development, to this day and are particularly evident in U.S. Christianity.

On one side are those who see the rift between the Bible and the Enlightenment as a series of errors in the insights, premises, and conclusions of the Enlightenment. From this perspective, the Enlightenment's very establishment of a secular space from which to begin contemplating the world and humanity emerges as its central error. The concept of natural law must be flawed, since it fails to take into account God's complete freedom and excludes miracles from the start. Likewise, the Enlightenment value on equality, particularly when applied to gender, is seen as based on human vanity; it flies in the face of biblical teaching that long had been understood to be confirmed in biological realities. At the same time, writers and preachers from this perspective often insist that the Bible is supported by scientific facts (appealing, paradoxically, to an Enlightenment category), if the scientific facts are properly interpreted. But like the Bible's influence, the influence of the Enlightenment is difficult to escape, even among those who would like to.

On the other hand, some portions of the church attempt to make peace with the Enlightenment, while still holding on to the Bible. This school of thought reads the biblical story of creation, for example, as symbolic and theological, a narrative about God's relationship to all things, rather than as a historical or scientific account. The resurrection, rather than requiring a hole in the fabric of natural law, likewise becomes symbolic and a statement about God and Jesus, rather than a miracle verifiable by science. In this view, the Bible's value lies not in its usefulness as a compendium of all knowledge worthy of the name but as a story that centers and frames human history. The limitation of this position has been its relatively weak hold on the biblical text or on Christianity in general. Its aversion to dogma and its sympathy for secular thought has meant, at least until recently, that its supporters are reluctant to claim much of anything for the Bible—least of all to speak out loudly in defense of the Bible as Scripture or as definitive in some way for human life.

With the problematic exception of the United States, the West has effectively given the Bible away in its travels to other parts of the globe, often forcing Christian Scripture upon peoples who did not want it, while back home in Europe the Bible—or at least active public participation in the church—dwindled into a pale relic. In the United States, however, the Bible remains culturally prominent. Our courts hear lawsuits about monumental governmental displays of the Ten Commandments. Our politicians cite Scripture when they can. Our news magazines run cover stories on new interpretations of the biblical Jesus. Historically, arguments both for and against such major issues as slavery, abortion rights, and stem-cell research have been couched in biblical language.

Conservative politicians and citizens often reinvent the American Revolution as a biblically based event organized by faithful Christians, although it in fact emerged directly from Enlightenment secularism and included prominent atheists and deists as well as the occasional churchgoer. The religious revivals washing over the country almost since its founding have raised the Bible to new heights in American public life. It remains on those heights—though often unread—offering a sacred space for some and simply a distinguishing feature of the landscape for others. Perhaps it is because of our lack of a common cultural history—for the United States is a country made up of people descended from immigrants, slaves, and the battered remains of once prosperous indigenous peoples—that Euro-Americans have looked so often to the Bible as a foundation on which to build some kind of commonality, by force if necessary.

THE LEGACY OF APOCALYPSE

Much political rhetoric and cultural production across the U.S. spectrum continues to draw on the biblical imagery and drama of apocalypse. It is no accident that when Joseph Conrad's novel *Heart of Darkness* was Americanized in film, the subject became war and the title became *Apocalypse Now*. Visions of the end time fueled the nonviolent force of the civil rights movement but also produced the Branch Davidians and their arsenals in Waco, Texas. From the Civil War to the post-9/11 "War on Terror," every U.S. conflict has been effectively sold to the public, in song, slogan, and speech, as a biblical confrontation between good and evil. Likewise, the U.S. branch of the environmental movement almost relishes its prophecies of impending doom, rhetoric shaped and informed by biblical prophecy. We seem to be in love with the apocalypse—ready to read each cultural or historic change as a sign that it is coming, and prepared to break down history's doors and drag it in if it delays too long.

Many citizens of the United States love the Bible best at its end—the end of the book and the end of the world. The urgency of ultimate justice intoxicates us so that, as a historian of the Ku Klux Klan once wrote, "being an American is a heady experience." At the end of the world, after all—facing the ultimate enemy, whether that means God's own enemy or that of the planet—all bets are off; all forgiveness is at an end; and all violence and torment, as well as all sacrifice and effort, are justified. Then the biblical message of God's overarching justice is at its most powerful and most volatile, like the terrifying power of the atom, or that of the nation itself. Like a child with a gun, we are consumed equally by visions of justice, vengeance, and chaos, visions we aspire to make reality, even as we fear that they may mean our own destruction.

The challenge for us who read the Bible as inheritors of these distinctive European and Euro-American legacies is to read with discernment. How can we negotiate these mixed and often conflicting visions in order to contribute with others to a just and peaceable world? ❖

Chapter 4

JESUS AND CULTURES

Leticia A. Guardiola-Sáenz
and
Curtiss Paul DeYoung

Throughout the centuries and around the world, almost every culture has represented Jesus in characteristic ways that are relevant and appropriate to the faith, ideologies, and social contexts of a people. The resulting titles, names, images, and symbols used to speak of and to characterize Jesus are as diverse as the readers of the biblical text. Jesus can also be appreciated in a wide range of imagery that goes from the classic works of art found in museums around the globe to the contemporary renditions of pop art images and movies.

The representations of Jesus are so many that it would be impossible to cover all of them in this short article. What we offer here is a small sample, highlighting the cultural context from where they have emerged. First, we look at some of the images of Jesus as described in the New Testament, within his own culture and the culture of the early church. Then we briefly describe the quest for Jesus within the academic culture; and finally we present some of the ways Jesus has been depicted in contemporary cultures.

JESUS IN HIS CULTURE

Right from the start, the New Testament validates the plurality of images of Jesus by giving voice to the unique perspectives of four evangelists (the Gospel writers, from the Greek word *euangelion*, "gospel"). The Gospels, our main sources for the life of Jesus, give him many different names and titles that convey particular roles and symbolize distinct aspects of his identity. Despite their similarities, each Gospel renders a particular representation of Jesus. In Matthew, for example, Jesus is predominantly presented as the teacher, the rabbi; for Mark, Jesus is the suffering son of God; the Gospel of Luke highlights Jesus as the savior of the world; and in John, Jesus is the incarnate Word (from the Greek *logos*). Together with these titles, some of the most familiar names and images of Jesus in the New Testament are Messiah or Christ, Son of David, Son of Man, King of Kings, Lord of Lords, Almighty, Lamb of God, High Priest, Light of the World, and Good Shepherd. All of these are linked to particular aspects of Israel's experience.

The influence behind the formation of these images of Jesus comes mainly from three cultural arenas: the political, the religious and philosophical, and the economic.

The first influence involves political reality not only in ancient Judea but also in the neighboring nations. After the Babylonian destruction of Jerusalem, the Jews who returned from Babylon included in their sacred writings the expectation of a future king, anointed (in Hebrew, *moshiach*) as the great David had been, who would free them from foreign domination and oppression. It is important not to exaggerate the scope of this expectation, as if all Jews were "waiting for a messiah." Early Jewish literature, in the Hebrew Bible and outside it, shows a wide range of expectations for priestly, royal, military, or even heavenly figures who would bring salvation, alongside movements to reform worship in the temple or law observance among the common people. In the era of Roman rule in Judea, the language of kingship or messiahship was apparently most used in a number of brief popular movements that rallied around militant figures (termed "bandits" by the Romans) whose careers were inevitably short-lived. Typically, such movements did not devote their energy to leaving literary remains for posterity.

The idealized expectation of a messiah nevertheless was crucial to the circles that first acclaimed Jesus as Messiah (in Greek, *christos*) or Son of David. It was in these circles that the concept of a suffering Messiah, who would die to cleanse the people of their sins, first appeared, based on innovative readings of Psalms 22 and 69 and Isaiah 53 (notice, for example, how phrases from Psalm 22 are woven into the accounts of Jesus' crucifixion in the Gospels). This concept was never part of earlier Jewish expectations, however, and these passages of Scripture were never read as referring to a messiah before the Jesus movement.

The conception of a suffering and dying messiah helped the first believers in Jesus to understand his death, and in subsequent centuries Christian theologians developed it into the predominant understanding of salvation through the atoning death of Jesus. More recently, however, theologians have noted that an overemphasis on the divine necessity of the Messiah's suffering has the potential to make suffering as such seem a spiritual necessity. Historically, just such interpretations have brought much pain when they have been used—in contexts of slavery, conquest, imperialism, and the subjugation of classes of people—to tell the mistreated that their suffering is somehow justified.

New Testament images of Jesus were also influenced by the political context of Roman imperial rule. In the midst of an oppressive empire, ruled by emperors who were hailed as sons of God, saviors of the world, kings, and lords, it was a bold move—but a crucially important one—for emergent Christianity to acknowledge Jesus as the true Savior of the world, the only begotten Son of God, the King of kings, the Lord of lords, and the Almighty who would redeem his people from oppression. Early Christianity did not dismiss Jewish expectations of a powerful warrior-messiah, one capable of neutralizing the power of foreign adversaries like Rome. Instead, in the distinctive doctrine of the second coming of the messiah, believers assigned the traditional roles of Jewish messianic expectation—ruling over the earth in peace, subduing enemies, securing justice, restoring the oppressed—to Jesus at his future advent (see for example 1 Cor 15:24-28 or the prophecy of Rome's defeat in Revelation 18).

The second cultural arena that influenced images of Jesus is the world of religious and philosophical experience and practice. The images of Jesus as the *great high priest* and Lamb of God derive from Israel's worship. The first, predominant in Hebrews, announces Jesus as the supreme mediator who surpasses all human priests who had served in the temple; the second speaks of Jesus as embodying and surpassing the sacrificial rituals in which the blood of an unblemished lamb was offered in expiation for sins (Lev 4:32). The New Testament writings, and especially the Gospel of John, refer to Jesus as the sacrificial lamb, unblemished and innocent, offered to expiate the sins of the people. It is interesting that the lamb for the sin offering had to be a female. A similar application of feminine imagery to Jesus appears when he is represented as the personification of divine Wisdom (1 Cor 1:24, 30). Wisdom personified (the Hebrew, *Hokmah*, and Greek, *Sophia*, are both feminine nouns) appears and speaks in Proverbs 8 and became the subject of greater speculation among more philosophically minded Hellenistic Jews (Philo and the author of the Wisdom of Solomon). Such speculation apparently stands behind the masculine metaphor of the *Logos* in the Gospel of John. *Logos* and the imagery of Jesus as Light of the world both emerge from the cosmopolitan, hellenized society in which the church grew in the late first and early second centuries; they are related to the Greek philosophical view of the creating force that originates and sustains the order of the cosmos.

The third cultural arena of influence is Israel's agrarian society. In a land of shepherds, whose livelihoods depend on taking good care of their flocks, the image of a good shepherd is greatly valued. The New Testament—and many of the earliest visual representations of Jesus in Christian art—represent him as the *Good Shepherd* who takes great care and protects the flock (see John 10:1-5), just as YHWH did (Psalm 23).

The plurality of images of Jesus in the New Testament opened the door for new interpretations, some coming from theologians and teachers in the church, past and present, but many others coming from ordinary readers who have felt invited to appropriate Jesus in personal ways.

JESUS IN ACADEMIC CULTURE

In an effort to explain Jesus of Nazareth as a historical figure—apart from the interpretations of the church and the faithful appropriations of individual believers—scholars have used modern historical methods to analyze the Gospels in their cultural context. This historically oriented scholarship, begun at the end of the eighteenth century, is known as "The Quest for the Historical Jesus." As controversial as some of the reconstructions of the "historical Jesus" have been, it is important to learn about them, because they help us understand the cultural conceptions and expectations that Jesus' followers may have had of him, and they help present-day readers understand better what the New Testament says about him. The contemporary quest for the historical Jesus has its roots in the Enlightenment, when the Bible became an object of historical science and of the historical-critical method. The quest for the historical Jesus thus far can be explained succinctly as a three-phase endeavor: the first or original quest (late eighteenth to early twentieth century); the second or new quest (early 1950s to early 1970s); and a third quest (late 1970s to the present).

FIRST QUEST

Attempting to depart from what they considered the unreal and "inhuman" Christ of faith created by the institutionalized church of the fourth and fifth centuries, the first "questers" for the historical Jesus stripped away the cloths of dogma and faith, hoping to find the human Jesus they assumed was hidden in the Gospels. Some of these interpreters proposed that Jesus should be seen in political terms, having had messianic intentions, thinking of himself as future king of a new kingdom, and at last entering Jerusalem and trying to seize power as a worldly messiah. Others sought to re-create Jesus' mental and social outlook, depicting him as a supporter of a pure worship, a religion with no priests or external rites, based on feelings and emotions— an idealist who highlighted the infinite value of the human soul and had as his core message love and the fatherhood of God. The goal of this first quest was to recover the Jesus of history hidden behind the Christ of faith, and its main result was the realization that the Gospels were products of faith, not historical records. By the end of the nineteenth century a consensus had emerged that the Jesus of history had been lost behind the Christ of faith.

The original quest ended when, at the beginning of the twentieth century, William Wrede and Albert Schweitzer challenged these interpreters, revealing their biases and subjectivity in creating modern, liberal images of Jesus with whom they felt more comfortable. Schweitzer proposed a counter-image of Jesus, in light of his religious-historical context, as an eschatological enthusiast who, claiming to be the Messiah, sought to bring God's longed-for kingdom but instead died tragically on the cross.

SECOND QUEST

Following Schweitzer's work, many academic interpreters became convinced that the Gospels offered no reliable accounts as sources for the historical figure of Jesus. In the 1950s, however, in the wake of the Second World War and influenced by the existentialist philosophy of Søren Kierkegaard and Martin Heidegger, a "new quest" for Jesus began. Its proponents believed that the New Testament evangelists had said little about the person and life of Jesus because they were not interested in those details. What had mattered to them, rather, was the question of how to interpret our existence when confronted with Christ's teaching.

With such an existentialist message, these scholars took it as their task in this new quest to seek out the history embedded in the early church's *kerygma* (proclamation), understanding that the Gospels had no historical interest apart from faith. Their goal was to reconstruct the historical context where the message about Jesus, the *kerygma*, was preached, rather than to reconstruct the historical Jesus per se.

THIRD QUEST

By the late 1970s, after the decline of existentialism and a period in which the quest for the historical Jesus became dormant, something of a renaissance in Jesus scholarship started a third quest, which has been characterized by its widely contrasting representations of Jesus and by a lack of common methodology. There are, however, three points of consensus: the image of Jesus as an eschatological prophet has faded; a new image of Jesus as teacher has emerged; and the social world of Jesus has become central to the quest.

The goal of the third quest has been to free Jesus from the prison of Scriptures, where we have incarcerated him. Some of the portraits of Jesus that emerge from this third quest see him as a Jewish-Cynic peasant; a prophet of restoration eschatology; a Hellenistic-type Cynic sage; an egalitarian prophet of Wisdom; a social prophet; and a spirit person.

In the end, it may seem to some that the logic behind the battle between the Christ of Christian faith and the Jesus of history has destroyed both figures, leaving no winner. The result of the quest for the historical Jesus has been in some cases an ahistorical Jesus, dispossessed both from his Jewishness and from the community of faith that portrayed him in the Gospels. On the other hand, the Christ of faith has become "unbelievable" because he had been so extremely divinized and removed from the sociocultural context of what Christians affirm as the incarnation. In the same way that too much light or too little light prevents us from seeing clearly, polarizing the question of Jesus' identity in the stark terms of history versus Christian faith may prevent us from understanding him in new ways, including ways that accept the tension inherent in the Christian claim of his full humanity *and* his full divinity. Some of this new light has come through the images of Jesus current in contexts outside the West.

Jesus in Multicultural Contexts

In the same way that the cultural context of ancient Israel and the context of the Roman Empire influenced the titles and representations of Jesus, every cultural context in Christian history has contributed its own particular images of Jesus. For the Christianized Platonic philosophy of the third century, Jesus was essentially the Cosmic Christ, the *Logos* who ruled the universe and in whom all things had their being. In a sixth-century mosaic, dressed in Roman armor and driving the chariot of the sun (in the figure of Apollo), Jesus was transformed into the Christ Militant. For the medieval Benedictines, Jesus became a monastic figure who simultaneously ruled the world. In the Renaissance he was turned into the Universal Man (though distinctly European!). As themes of judgment came to the fore in popular European imagination, the reformers

found in Christ the Mirror of God's parental love that justified the sinner. For the philosophers of the Enlightenment, he became the Teacher of Common Sense. The multicultural quest for Jesus today emerges as a response to contemporary racism, the colonial captivity of much of the world, and the thwarting of indigenous images of Jesus.

Dominant White Eurocentric Images

When Jesus of Nazareth walked in Galilee, he looked visibly like his first-century Galilean Jewish contemporaries and shared their common culture. He came culturally from the region today called the Middle East, and he was ethnically like others descending from Afro-Asiatic Hebrews. Yet the image of Jesus that has been pervasive throughout much of the world is that of a white Northern European male with fair hair and blue eyes. How did that white Jesus become the prevailing image?

The earliest representations of Jesus were symbols such as a fish or a lamb. Early likenesses of Jesus show him as a beardless young man with a brown complexion. Only under the Byzantine Empire of the fifth and sixth centuries—which often depicted Jesus, with a beard and his hair parted down the middle, after the fashion of the Byzantine court, as a monarch, seated on a throne, his hand raised in command—did artists begin to create what has come to be the standard representation of Jesus. Like other regions, Europe developed culturally relevant representations of Christ for communicating the biblical story of Jesus.

But why did Europe's culturally appropriate Christ become the dominant image of the historical Jesus beyond Europe? The "European" Christ image was used to support European colonial expansion into Africa, Asia, and the Americas, as well as the genocide of indigenous peoples and the capture and enslavement of black Africans. In effect, a white likeness of Jesus served the purpose of being God's stamp of approval on the actions of white conquerors and demonstrated that the white "race" was superior to peoples of color by virtue of the whiteness of Jesus.

Missionaries from Europe could have discarded the Western images of Jesus upon arrival in Africa, the Americas, Asia, and the islands of the great oceans. With the help of indigenous people, new images of Jesus could have been shaped that spoke powerfully to the people encountered. But this did not happen. The propagation of white images of Jesus continues even to our own time through media portrayals in movies and television, as well as in the pictures of nearly every Bible produced for use around the world.

The effects of a Western image of a white Jesus have been far-reaching. In contexts outside of Europe, the whiteness of the image makes Jesus seem like a foreigner, a stranger, or even an enemy. If your oppressor is white and the oppressor's image of Jesus is white, it appears that Jesus has endorsed your domination—an impression the oppressors were often only too happy to promote. In this way, the Jesus who taught the love of enemies (Matt 5:44, Luke 6:27) has repeatedly been transformed into the enemy, a monarch who presides over brutal oppression carried out by those who look like he does.

When white Western images of Jesus appear in contexts outside of Europe, Jesus seems like a captive of the West. This makes it difficult for non-European people to understand Jesus as separate from those who brought him from Europe. When the Bible is interpreted from a Western bias, Christian faith and Western culture come to appear synonymous. White images of Jesus subtly give the impression that European and Euro-American ways of thinking and acting are normative. The effects of regarding Western Christianity as the normative and superior form of the Christian faith demeans

any other form of Christianity, including ancient rites like the Eastern Orthodox Church and the Egyptian Coptic Church.

White images of Jesus have been used to deny the biblical message of liberation. The Jesus who preached good news to the poor and freedom for the oppressed (Luke 4:16–19) was altered to sustain systems of exploitation. For example, the religion of the slaveholder in the United States required only a belief in the incarnation (God made flesh in Jesus Christ): there was limited concern for the historical Jesus. Christianity was a religion of right belief. As long as one subscribed to the right belief or doctrine, one could enslave people in good conscience. Slave masters forced enslaved Africans to bow down in worship to this white image who looked racially like the brutal overseer. But the effects on white people in the United States have been no less troubling. In order to bless slavery and condone the white man's divine right to own Africans, the Bible was stripped of its liberating power. The Jesus that preached, practiced, and prayed for freedom and liberation was replaced with a Christ who was a symbol of right belief. Christian faith was domesticated, stultified into a pale reflection of white power and privilege.

RESTORING CULTURALLY APPROPRIATE IMAGES OF JESUS

Today we know that the colonizer, the slaveholder, and the white supremacist lied about Jesus. Yet the image of a white Jesus remains deeply imbedded in our psyches. In order to change perceptions, people need to see that Jesus was not white. Jesus must be returned to his rightful place in a faith with roots in Africa and Asia. Even white people may need an Afro-Asiatic Jesus to be set free from racism. Whites who assent to an Afro-Asiatic Jesus will find it more difficult to accept society's racial hierarchy.

There is also a need for culturally relevant depictions. Some Native Americans describe Jesus as a respected spiritual leader. Latina/o scholars living in the United States have connected with a Galilean Jesus who knows the experience of feeling cut off from one's culture of origin and unaccepted by the dominant culture in a new land. African Americans have claimed a black Jesus who is friend, fellow sufferer, confidant, and liberator. Of course, the historical Jesus with African blood flowing through his veins (at least one drop!) could easily blend in among the wide range of skin colors and hues found in the African-American community today.

Jesus must also be internationalized. Asian scholars remind us that the Jesus of history lived and breathed on the Asian continent. We need to reclaim this cultural connection. Latin American images of Jesus are diverse and include traditional portrayals of the infant Jesus and the suffering Jesus, as well as modern images such as the Indian Jesus, the black Jesus, the revolutionary Jesus, and Jesus as friend and liberator of women. Africans are contributing images of Jesus like Greatest Ancestor, First Ancestor, Elder Brother, Healer, Liberator, and Mother (or Nurturer of Life).

It is interesting to note that there are also some representations of Jesus coming from Asian non-Christian contexts. Within Islam, Jesus has been known as *Isa Masih* (Jesus the Messiah). Isa is known as one of God's most prominent and beloved prophets, who was called to guide the people of Israel. A Hindu view of Jesus recognizes him as one of the *Avataras*, the incarnations of the divine. Within Buddhism he has been called *Bodhisattva* ("one whose existence is enlightenment"), a being whose wisdom lies in the commitment to redeem all of life.

In our contemporary multicultural context, Jesus is emerging with new faces that are relevant to those who live in a culture different from the West. Following are a few examples.

JESUS THE LIBERATOR

In the midst of the economic oppression of poverty, the social oppression of dehumanization, and the spiritual oppression of sin, Jesus has emerged in Latin America as liberator from all oppressions. Jesus' miracles in the Gospels are seen not so much as demonstrations of Jesus' divinity but as actions of liberation that freed the oppressed as a consequence of their participating in the creation of God's kingdom. Jesus' followers must do what Jesus did: generate partial liberations in anticipation of the future liberation of all that God will bring about. As liberator, Jesus is also seen as a prophet who questioned the religious-political authorities and demanded justice, challenging the oppressive systems of his time. This image gives hope and liberation to the powerless to demand justice. Jesus the liberator does not arise exclusively from Latin America: a similar Jesus has emerged from the realities of oppression and poverty in Asian and African nations and of racism in the United States.

JESUS THE GALILEAN–MESTIZO

This Jesus emerges from the Latina/o reality of marginality in the United States. Jesus' identity as a Galilean, on the boundaries of Judean culture, is a symbol of marginality, a mirror where the marginalized community today can find a clear cultural identity. This Galilean Jesus was a human being with no particular privilege (Phil 2:6-7); he even assumed the form of a slave, in the eyes of the slaveholder less than human. He came into the world of the voiceless, the sick, the hungry, and the oppressed, not to do things for them, but to become one of them. The challenge of this Jesus today is to understand what Galilee was and what it means to be a Galilean today, and to seek out those who live on the cultural margins in today's world. It is there, in the most unsuspected places, that God continues to work.

JESUS THE ANCESTOR

In some African cultures the concept of communion with the dead is an important part of their worldview. Those relatives who have died acquire a sacred status that implies supernatural powers and closeness to God. In that position they can act as mediators between God and humanity. For many, the deceased ancestors are liturgical companions of the living. Being an ancestor is more than simply having died; it means one lived an exemplary life, was married and transmitted life to another generation, then died a natural death. With the intention of translating the Christian faith into categories that are familiar to African people, the image of Jesus as Ancestor conveys the important role of Jesus as mediator between God and humans. A complementary understanding of Jesus as Elder Brother emphasizes his companionship in daily life.

JESUS AS CHIEF

The concept of chief among some African communities is that of the guardian. The chief is the leader over political and religious matters in the community and is seen as a hero who can conquer enemies in both the earthly and the spiritual realms. Located at the intersection of both realms, the chief receives strength and authority from the ancestors and is considered an ancestor himself. In such position the chief is mediator between members of the tribe, the ancestors, and even those who have not been born. The identity of the community is derived from the chief. Just as the chief mediates between the tribe and the ancestors and gives identity to the community, Jesus mediates

blessings to the church from God and gives identity to the church.

THE PEOPLES' JESUS

As history shows, each of us has a particular vision of Jesus that may be influenced by our faith, ideologies, traditions, experiences, and all the other cultural elements that play a role in shaping our vision of reality and our own identity. No matter how diverse all these individual images of Jesus are, it is always important to acknowledge his historical context in first-century Judea and the fact that Jesus was a Jew. When our images of Jesus are divested of his cultural and ethnic background, they risk becoming anti-Semitic.

With so many images of Jesus available already, it is impossible not to ask, is there a limit to the images and representations of Jesus that we can create? Our answer: not really. As long as diverse people come to Jesus, approaching him with particular images in mind, personalizing their own distinct encounters with him and perhaps coming to call upon him with distinct names, there will be no such limit. However, we could say that a limit is set by the spirit of love and liberation that the Gospels convey. Images that depict a Jesus contrary to the spirit of the Gospels go beyond that limit. It should be inconceivable, for example, to represent Jesus as someone who meant to inflict oppression and pain. Imperialist images of Jesus, or the Aryan, Nazi Jesus who sponsored racism, or a violent, armed, revolutionary Jesus—all are distortions of the gospel depiction of a Jesus who preached the love of God.

The first-century Jesus of Nazareth had a particular culture and a distinct ethnic look. Jesus as the Christ has come to reside in all cultures, embraces all cultures, and speaks forth from all cultures. The Jesus of history and the Jesus who emerges from the pages of the Bible has come to be and remains the peoples' Jesus. ❖

Chapter 5

The Bible as an Instrument of Reconciliation

Curtiss Paul DeYoung

The biblical story commences in an idyllic garden setting in Genesis, with God creating the world and breathing life into the first human couple. The Bible concludes in Revelation in an envisioned future utopian paradise where all of humanity is gathered around the throne of God in perfect unity. Between creation and eternity the biblical story juxtaposes human alienation and God's desire for reconciliation. For us who live in a post-biblical, pre-paradise world, the Bible still remains a powerful source for understanding separation and God's hope for reconciliation.

The Hebrew Scriptures illustrate the story of God's relationship with the entire human family by highlighting a particular relationship between God and the Hebrew people. The narrative emerging from the pages of the Hebrew Scriptures describes the cycle of separation and reunion in the Hebrew peoples' relationship with God. Yet God never gives up on humanity and constantly pursues a relationship with the peoples of the earth.

One of the most powerful stories illustrating God's love for the Hebrew people is found in the writings of the prophet Hosea. Hosea's relentless pursuit of his unfaithful wife serves as a prophetic parable of God's constant pursuit of a relationship with humanity. This theme of relational reconciliation with God, or atonement (at-one-ment), is found throughout the Hebrew Scriptures. There are also many examples of alienation and reconciliation within the human family itself, including Adam and Eve, Jacob and Esau, Joseph and his brothers,

Queen Esther (representing the Jews) and King Ahasuerus (the Persians). The Hebrew Scriptures offer insights into the dynamics that produce just relationships among people.

In the New Testament Gospels, Jesus of Nazareth is the model of reconciliation with God and others. The Gospel writers went to great lengths to present Jesus as a radically inclusive person and an exemplar of reconciliation. Their accounts of his birth and upbringing describe a relevant preparation for his reconciling task. Mary gave birth to Jesus in a livestock barn (Luke 2:7). Poor and despised shepherds in Palestine witnessed the event (2:8-20). Rich magi from Asia went to Bethlehem to see the infant Jesus, and the family escaped to the continent of Africa as refugees (Matt 2:1-15). Jesus the Jew was raised in Galilee of the nations (NRSV: "Gentiles," Matt 4:15). While Jesus maintained his own Jewish cultural and religious identity, he was enriched by various cultural elements from many nations.

The ministry of Jesus was also radically inclusive, beginning with his choice of disciples. He selected both a tax collector who collaborated with the Roman Empire and a zealot who called for the violent revolutionary overthrow of Rome (Matt 10:2-4; Luke 6:14-16). Jesus took the unheard-of step of including a number of women in the circle of his followers (Matt 27:55-56; Mark 15:40-41; Luke 8:2-3). His broad table fellowship reached to individuals outside of his socioeconomic class and ethnic/cultural world. Even at the death of Jesus, an African named Simon of Cyrene carried his cross (Matt 27:32; Mark 15:21; Luke 23:26) and a Roman centurion uttered words of faith (Matt 27:54; Mark 15:39).

In Acts and the apostolic writings Jesus the Christ, by virtue of his death and resurrection, is presented as the mediator between God and humanity, person and person, group and group. The apostle Paul and his circle of disciples were the theologians of reconciliation for the first-century church. The Greek words for "reconciliation" or "reconcile," *katallassō, katallagē, apokatallassō,* are used only a few times (Rom 5:10, 11; 11:15; 2 Cor 5:18, 19; Eph 2:16; and Col 1:20, 22), but are a powerful way of expressing the meaning of the life, death, resurrection, and abiding presence of Jesus Christ. Biblical reconciliation implies friendship with God and each other, radical change and the transformation of a relationship or of a society, and the restoration of harmony.

The biblical discussions are not limited to embracing a loving God in relationship or affirming a good theology of reconciliation. Those of us who read the Bible as Scripture understand biblical reconciliation as a message we must announce and a ministry we must pursue. We are called to become God's "ambassadors" of reconciliation (2 Corinthians 5), working as catalysts for inclusive community, peace among nations, social transformation in society, and unity amidst religious diversity. The following biblical resources can empower us in that ambassadorial work.

RECONCILIATION AND INCLUSIVE COMMUNITY

Congregations in the first century, as described in the Acts of the Apostles and in the Pauline letters, present an inviting possibility for developing a community that is inclusive. The mother church in Jerusalem (Acts 2–6) was a multilingual congregation of Jews from Jerusalem, Galilee, and the broader Roman Empire. The community was also diverse socioeconomically. The faith community in Antioch of Syria (Acts 11, 13; Galatians 2) was founded by Greek-speaking Jewish leaders originating from North Africa and Cyprus. From its beginning the Antioch congregation was multiethnic, including not only Jews raised in different cultural settings but Greeks and others. They had a multicultural and multiracial leadership team and survived a possible schism along ethnic lines through a courageous confrontation by the apostle Paul (Galatians 2). In Acts 13 and subsequent chapters, the author narrates the founding of many other congregations launched on the model of multiethnic inclusiveness found in Antioch. In many first-century congregations, women also emerged as leaders. (See Rom 16:1-15, where Paul mentions thirty-four church leaders, sixteen of whom are women.)

The congregations in the first-century church offer insights for reconciliation and creating inclusive communities through their empowering ministry with the poor, spiritual disciplines, courageous social action, and bilingual, multicultural, and gender-inclusive leadership teams. The New Testament details both the successes and failures of these faith communities in their efforts to be ministers of reconciliation.

RECONCILIATION AND PEACE AMONG NATIONS

The Bible not only portrays the possibility of unity in faith communities; it also offers a vision for peace among nations. The prophet Isaiah proclaimed, "They shall beat their swords into plowshares, and their spears into pruning hooks; nation shall not lift up a sword against a nation, neither shall they learn war any more" (Isa 2:4). The author of Revelation saw a time when "a great multitude that no one could count, from every nation, from all tribes and peoples and languages" would be gathered together (Rev 7:9).

One of the most dramatic biblical episodes of two nations reconciling is the reunion of Jacob and Esau (Genesis 32–33). At the surface this seems to be only the reconciliation of two estranged brothers. And it is that. But by the time they met, after

years of separation, they were no longer just individuals but growing communities—soon to be nations. The meeting of these leaders of two large tribal groups provides clues to the possibilities of peacemaking among nations in our own day.

Before the meeting, Jacob, the offender, sent gifts ahead to symbolically replace what he had taken from his brother Esau. He surmised, "I may appease him with the present that goes ahead of me, and afterwards I shall see his face; perhaps he will accept me" (Gen 32:20). Then Jacob spent the night prior to the meeting wrestling with God, purifying his motives, and preparing for the worst. The encounter with God left him wounded and ready to meet his brother with humility and repentance—"I have seen God face to face, and yet my life is preserved" (32:30). On the appointed day Jacob went ahead of the others and led his nation to meet Esau, "bowing himself to the ground seven times, until he came near his brother" (33:3).

It seems that Esau, the offended, had also met with God. When he saw his brother Jacob he "ran to meet him, and fell on his neck and kissed him, and they wept" (33:4). Jacob came to the meeting with humility and a demonstrated willingness to make reparation. Esau came to the meeting ready to forgive and seek a new future for the relationship. Esau at first refused Jacob's gifts, saying he already had enough. But Jacob insisted, "If I find favor with you, then accept my present from my hand; for truly to see your face is like seeing the face of God (for) God has dealt graciously with me" (33:10-11).

Peace in the world becomes a greater possibility when the leaders of nations embrace the spirit of Jacob and Esau. Too often kings, queens, prime ministers, presidents, and other leaders approach the table of international dialogue with an agenda that is informed by a sense of ethnic or racial superiority, a punitive desire for revenge, self-centered arrogance, and an apparent lack of interest in an inclusive view of humanity or of social justice.

These two biblical leaders of emerging nations had such a strong desire for reconciliation, they set aside real and rightful feelings of hurt, anger, shame, fear, vengeance, and the like. A biblical framework for peace among nations requires leaders and citizens who emulate the attitudes and actions of Esau and Jacob.

RECONCILIATION AND SOCIAL TRANSFORMATION

Another key component of reconciliation is a focus on social transformation for justice. As noted above, 2 Cor 5:1—6:2 calls us to be ambassadors of reconciliation. "As we work together with [God], we urge you also not to accept the grace of God in vain. For he says, 'At an acceptable time I have listened to you, and on a day of salvation I have helped you.' See, now is the acceptable time; see, now is the day of salvation!" (6:1-2). Paul's quote from Isaiah 49 echoes Jesus' quotation of Isaiah 61 in Luke 4:18-19. The language of the "day of salvation" and "the year of the Lord's favor" speak of the year of Jubilee (Leviticus 25)—that great ideal placed in the legal code of the Hebrew people to ensure that social justice defined their community and nationhood. (Unfortunately, there is no record of it ever having been practiced.) In Luke 4, Jesus appeals to this divine intention in his opening sermon. In 2 Corinthians, Paul links the ministry of reconciliation with the prophetic call to social justice. Our reconciliation with God leads to reconciliation with each other. This means on the macro level the creation of a society that practices social justice.

Paul makes the link between social justice and reconciliation even clearer in Galatians 3:28. "There is no longer Jew or Greek, there is no longer slave or free, there is no longer male and female; for all of you are one in Christ Jesus." These words were part of a baptismal formula from the earliest days of the first-century church. This creedal statement was used to initiate new members into a reconciling faith that removed socially constructed boundaries and hierarchies and replaced them with relationships and societal interactions based on social justice.

Too often people of faith choose to focus on reconciliation with God but not with others. Others reconcile relationally across human boundaries but do not address the societal issues that created the boundaries. A biblical perspective calls for an integrated approach to reconciliation that includes our relationship with God, our relationship with other people, the dismantling of oppressive social structures that cause division, and the creation of just societies and nations.

RECONCILIATION AND RELIGIOUS DIVERSITY

The biblical writers focus primarily on the story of the Hebrew people and then of Jesus and the first-century Christians. Therefore, there is little in the Bible that speaks directly to interfaith reconciliation. Given the extreme conflicts in the twentieth century and beyond that involve the three major Abrahamic religions—Judaism, Christianity, and Islam—there is one biblical story that might symbolize the needed reconciliation. Jews and Christians claim Abraham as their father through Isaac, and Muslims claim Abraham through Ishmael. The story in Genesis 25 of Ishmael and Isaac coming together to bury their father could serve as a catalyst for reconciliation among these monotheistic religions. The story is simple. Upon Abraham's death at 175 years of age, "His sons Isaac and Ishmael buried him in the cave of Machpelah, in the field of Ephron son of Zohar the Hittite, east of Mamre, the field that Abraham purchased from the Hittites. There Abraham was buried, with his wife Sarah" (vv. 9-10). Ishmael, the older son and spiritual ancestor of Islam, joined together with his brother, Isaac, spiritual ancestor of Judaism and Christianity, and they buried their father Abraham in Hebron.

The biblical stories of Ishmael and Isaac reveal a history of favoritism, prejudice, manipulation, rejection, victimization, and mixed blessing. Yet the death of Abraham provided a reason for setting aside problematic histories and convoluted relationships to focus on a shared love and responsibility. Judaism, Christianity, and Islam share much in their understanding of faith, the importance of peace and social justice, and God's love for humanity. They also share a problematic history and convoluted relationships. The story of Ishmael and Isaac together burying their father, Abraham, offers a message to Judaism, Christianity, and Islam in our day: set aside histories and present animosities in order to focus on a world that desperately needs the values of compassion, reconciliation, social justice, and peace at the core of your respective faiths.

RECONCILIATION AND COMMUNITY

Usually the work of reconciliation is complex and multifaceted. Reconciliation issues are often intertwined and not easily separated. The Bible also offers scriptural resources for this reality. Paul's admonition in Gal 3:28 implies that race, gender, and socioeconomic class are all intertwined justice issues and that reconciliation cannot succeed without a strategy to address each that is simultaneous and interlinked.

A good biblical example of the complicated and multifaceted nature of reconciliation is the story of Jesus in conversation with a woman from Samaria by Jacob's well (John 4:4-42). This interchange represented differences in culture, gender, socioeconomic class, status, religion, and more. As the story is read, it becomes evident that Jesus arrived

at the encounter unashamed of the differences and well prepared for the nuances of such a conversation. This allowed reconciliation to occur rather than for alienation to fester further. Jesus engages with this Samaritan woman in public. As a Jewish male and itinerant rabbi, Jesus rejected social norms when he spoke publicly to a woman, requested a drink from a Samaritan, and was seen with a person of questionable moral standards. This single act of welcoming the woman from Samaria to a relational encounter meant Jesus had to cross at least three social boundaries. He could not decide to focus only on ethnic reconciliation, or gender inclusion, or moral questions. Jesus had to embrace all of who this woman was and he did it publicly, without any embarrassment or hesitation.

Not only was Jesus bold in a public display of his reconciliation intentions, he was also well prepared for the encounter. Most likely Jesus did not know that he was going to meet a Samaritan woman on this day. What Jesus did know was that his call to be a reconciler would lead him to all kinds of encounters, so he had to prepare himself even before the event. Given the proximity of Samaria, it seems that Jesus was likely familiar with their culture and religion. This is apparent in how he presents himself and his messianic mission to the woman. The Samaritans were seeking a messiah who would reveal truth and restore belief. When Jesus told the woman things about her life that he would have no way of knowing, he was not saying something about her. Rather, Jesus was revealing something about himself. He was informing her that he was the Revealer (*Taheb*), the Messiah. The woman told her neighbors, "Come and see a man who told me everything I have ever done! He cannot be the Messiah, can he?" (John 4:29). Jesus' knowledge of Samaritan culture and religious beliefs hurried the process of reconciliation at Jacob's well that day.

The theme of reconciliation runs throughout the Bible. Reconciliation calls us to inclusive communities, peace among nations, social transformation, and relationships across religions. Jesus said to the woman in Samaria, "Woman, believe me, the hour is coming when you will worship the Father neither on this mountain nor in Jerusalem" (John 4:21). Reconciliation calls us to such a time: a future era when neither race, culture, gender, socioeconomic class, religion, nor any other designator will serve as our primary identity or the identity we ascribe to others. Biblical reconciliation propels us to embrace our ultimate identity as humans created in the image of God, that is, as children of God. ❖

Chapter 6

THE BIBLE AND EMPIRE

Neil Elliott

Introductions to the Bible ordinarily discuss the rise and fall of empires as the background of biblical history, and for good reason. For most of recorded history, the peoples living in the land once called Canaan, later Israel, and still later Palestine, have lived under the sway of outside powers. From Egypt and its Canaanite vassal kings to the Hittite empire, the Mesopotamian empires of Asshur and Babylon, later Persia, then the Greeks and the Hellenistic Seleucids, and still later the Roman Empire—throughout this long history, empires exerted control over the land and the labor of the people who lived on it.

That history continued, of course, after the biblical period, with the Byzantine Empire; the rise of Islam and the Arab Caliphates; European Crusader kingdoms; and the Mamluk and Ottoman Empires. Following World War I, the land was controlled under the British Mandate. After World War II, the United Nations partitioned the land and created the State of Israel. Following the war of 1967, Israel occupied the Palestinian territories, continuing to hold them today under the plea of self-defense and with the indispensable protection from international sanction provided by the United States. The oil resources of the Middle East are only one reason—but an undeniably important one—that powerful foreign nations continue to influence the fortunes of people living in the land.

But there are other, more pressing reasons to consider the Bible's relationship to empire. In the 1960s and 1970s, many formerly colonized peoples in Africa, Asia, and South America began to throw off the rule of European and North American powers, following the example of India in the 1940s (and Haiti in 1791). These same peoples throughout the world are nevertheless keenly aware of the powerful continuing legacy of colonialism. Deprived of much of the natural wealth of their lands, often stripped of their cultural heritage, their kinship and community structures ravaged, and their new governments too often independent only in name, people of the "global South," and the surviving native peoples of North America as well, know that their futures are inevitably shaped by the political, economic, and military power of the same industrialized nations that formerly ruled them directly.

Because the Bible was so often wielded as an instrument of European and North American imperialism, justifying policies of genocide, enslavement, and cultural extinction, formerly colonized peoples now look upon the Bible with tremendous ambivalence. The profoundly varied ways that different communities have experienced the Bible—and come to read it for themselves—are well represented throughout the essays in this volume. This essay will focus on the role of imperialism in constraining the imaginations of the people who wrote the Bible itself. The communities who produced the Bible thought of themselves, their world, their God, and the future in ways that bear the unmistakable imprint of empire. These themes are at the center of biblical scholarship today.

THE EMERGENCE OF "ISRAEL" IN CANAAN

How did a people called "Israel" emerge in the land of Canaan in the thirteenth through eleventh centuries BCE? The Bible itself offers a conflicted picture. The book of Joshua tells of a swift and decisive military conquest of Canaan, carried out by a single people, Israel, who had been led miraculously out of slavery in Egypt and across the Sinai wilderness (according to the epic related earlier in Exodus–Deuteronomy). These people, also called "Hebrews," shared the lineage of Abraham, who had left his home in Ur (in modern Iraq) in answer to the call of a god he had not known before (Genesis 11–12). But the Bible also declares that "a mixed crowd" left Egypt with the Israelites (Exod 12:37-38); and after Joshua's time, the book of Judges describes Israel's failure to drive out "the Canaanites" and their continued struggle against Canaanite influences. The traditional picture of a decisive Israelite "conquest" that dispossessed and destroyed the Canaanites is called into question within the Bible itself.

Critical assessment of all the biblical, archaeological, and extrabiblical literary evidence suggests a much more complicated history. The Hebrews (ʿibrim) may have begun not as a distinct ethnic group but as a social class in Canaan. Canaanite documents (like the Amarna letters) refer to hapiru either as outsiders or persons of low status, or as political opponents who set themselves against the kings of Canaan's city-states and their Egyptian overlords. At least some of the hapiru settled in the highlands, beyond Egypt's reach; others controlled cities in defiance of Egypt. If the origins of the Hebrews are to be found here, it would appear that Israel first emerged in the hills of Canaan as the result of a social and cultural phenomenon, achieved in part through the displacement of peoples as Egypt's power over the land subsided, and in part through the overthrow of Canaanite cities from within as well as without. The term Israel first described a network of cities, villages, and clans, made up (on this theory) not of one but of different ethnicities, joined in cooperative agriculture, the sharing of resources, and responsibilities for mutual defense.

According to the Bible, this new people gathered around ceremonies and symbols that represented the centrality of the God of liberation in their shared life. Joshua 24 may reflect typical occasions on which the dispossessed were drawn to this new people and incorporated into it. They recited a common history that looked back to an unnamed migrant ancestor, "a wandering Aramean" (Deut 26:5). Note that it is Abraham's departure from Ur, not his "Aramaean" ethnicity, that makes him paradigmatic: see Deut 26:5-9. They spoke of miraculous deliverance from slavery in Egypt at the hands of a God who listened to the cries of the oppressed. That story was likely brought into Canaan originally by escaped slaves, but the story would have spoken just as powerfully to the people of the land who had borne the brunt of oppression by Egypt's vassal kings. (If one of Israel's most ancient poems is Miriam's celebration of the defeat of Pharaoh's army at the Red Sea, or Sea of Reeds, Exod 15:20-21, another celebrates the deliverance, at Deborah's hand, of "the peasantry" of Canaan from "the mighty," Judg 5:1-31.) They called upon God under the name YHWH, an enigmatic name, later read (but not spoken) in Hebrew, and translated into Greek and English as "LORD" (and so printed in the NRSV; see note at Exodus 3). The name probably originally meant "creator," and it was linked from the beginning with the downfall of earthly lords.

A decided antagonism to empire marks the earliest symbols that united this people. The identification of YHWH as the God of liberation is the first commandment given to the new people (according to Exod 20:2; compare Deut 6:12; 26:7-9). They were to worship this God alone and never to carve any image of God (Exod 20:4-6; compare Deut 4:15-20). In the context of ancient Near-Eastern empires, in which the gods were regularly carved in the likeness of a human monarch, that prohibition conveyed a clear message: the glory of YHWH the deliverer was incompatible with the grasping claims of pharaohs and kings. To similar and startling effect, early Israel gathered for prayer, or went

into battle, around the most disconcerting of symbols: the ark of the covenant, which resembled the portable thrones of other ancient Near-Eastern deities—except that it was conspicuously empty! (See 1 Samuel 4–6.)

THE RISE OF THE KINGDOM ISRAEL

In the eleventh century BCE, the waning of Egyptian power allowed a new people to invade the coastland of Canaan. The Philistines brought superior iron-age weapons to their conflict with bronze-age Israel. In a scenario often repeated in history, the militarily weaker people were able eventually to thwart more powerful opponents through collective effort and stealth. They gathered around a fearless bandit leader whose courage, loyalty, and cunning gained him tremendous popular support. This was David; and just as Saul, his predecessor, was raised up as "king" after leading an Israelite victory in the field, so the tales of David's daring exploits—single-handedly defeating a more powerful Philistine warrior, tricking Philistine raiders who mistook him for an ally, and at last capturing the fortified city of Jerusalem with a small band of warriors, without bloodshed—amply explain his rise to power as Israel's most renowned king (see 1 Samuel).

David moved swiftly to unite the people behind his monarchy, establishing Jerusalem as his capital and bringing the ark of the covenant into his city (2 Sam 6:12-19). David's reign and that of his son, Solomon, was the first period of Israelite independence. It is not surprising that Israel's first national epic, fragments of which scholars find in Genesis, Exodus, and Numbers, was written in this period or that it expressed buoyant defiance of imperial values (see the introduction to the Pentateuch).

While Mesopotamian creation accounts began with a city and its king being lowered from heaven, this Israelite epic spoke of a man and a woman bearing the image of God (Gen 1:26-27) as they walked, naked and unashamed, in a paradisal garden. Kings, cities, and the makings of sacrifice and warfare were not yet in sight (Gen 2:4-25). The epic moved from promises made to the ancestor Abraham toward their fulfillment in the reign of Solomon (compare Genesis 15 with the map of David and Solomon's reign). The centerpiece of this narrative was the exodus from Egypt, now elaborated as a great contest in which YHWH manifested his power at Pharaoh's expense. Everything that imperial Egypt held sacred—from the cleansing waters of the Nile and the fertile fields along its banks, to the Pharaoh's firstborn son, whose succession would guarantee dynastic stability, to the power to control the bodies of slaves through the threat of violence, represented in Pharaoh's mighty chariots—all this was polluted, struck down, or emptied of force (Exodus 3–15). Strikingly, Egyptian records give not a hint that the empire of the pharaohs ever faced a catastrophe like that described in Exodus; to the contrary, Egypt continued to influence Israel's history for centuries. The power of the exodus story lay not in its objective reporting of ancient history but in its potency to shape a new people around the imagination of a world where imperial power was no longer decisive.

CONTESTED MEMORY

The preceding account necessarily reads beneath and behind the biblical narratives, which reflect later efforts to manage the memory of Israel's origins. Like an archaeological tell or a geologist's trench, the Bible provides a wealth of information but often in complex layers that require critical interpretation. The Bible presents not a single voice but a chorus of sometimes conflicting voices struggling to articulate what YHWH had done, was doing, and would do in the future.

We find tensions between different views of Israel's monarchy, for example. In some of the psalms a distinct theological narrative appears, resembling the kingship ideology of other ancient Near-Eastern empires. Probably developed in the court of David and Solomon, this "Zion theology" represents YHWH's chief work in the world as the establishment of the royal city, Zion (the sacred name for David's Jerusalem), and of the king himself, through whose benevolent rule alone YHWH would bring justice to the earth (see Psalms 48 and 72). On the other hand, the books of Samuel and Kings present episodes in which one or another individual or group protests the actions of a king as excessive. Solomon's son Rehoboam's harsh rule was (according to 1 Kings 12) the occasion for the kingdom's division into a northern ("Israel") and a southern kingdom ("Judah"), a fault line that neighboring nations were eager to exploit. When in the eighth century the Assyrian Empire threatened the Northern Kingdom, the prophets Amos and Hosea read the geopolitical power shift as a warning from YHWH against the nation's infidelity and injustice. Similarly, Isaiah of Jerusalem warned the Southern Kingdom that what seemed pragmatic alliances with neighboring kingdoms was a failure to trust YHWH.

While we cannot identify a single institutional location for the rise of prophecy in Israel, the prophetic writings testify to sites and practices of advice and criticism, addressed to the monarch or the ruling class, in the name of YHWH and on behalf of the poor and needy. The book of Amos gives glimpses of the tensions when both an opposition prophet and the officials of a royal sanctuary claimed to speak for the same God. A similar tension appears elsewhere as the contrast between "true" and "false" prophets (see, for example, 1 Kings 22). While it is impossible to speak of a single "prophetic perspective," the tendency of the prophets to speak of YHWH as the sovereign God who governed earthly affairs would prove fatefully decisive when hostile empires loomed on Israel's horizon.

YHWH AND THE IMAGINATION OF EMPIRES

Unable to imagine the YHWH who had formed Israel through the defeat of mighty Egypt as in any way inferior to the gods of other empires, the prophets made the daring move of imagining the empire of Assyria and, later, of Babylon as themselves the instruments through which YHWH threatened judgment on a disobedient Israel. Although the book of Jeremiah shows that this viewpoint was unpopular in a nation that understood YHWH as their protector, after Babylon's capture of Jerusalem and deportation of many of its people to exile (587–86 BCE), what had been unpopular became self-evident. That Israel's defeat at the hands of Babylon was the expression of YHWH's anger seemed, paradoxically, to prove that YHWH alone was truly God. The necessary corollary of belief in YHWH's supremacy was the acceptance of humiliation at the hands of imperial powers as the will of heaven—a belief that subsequent empires would find little enough reason to challenge.

THE DOCUMENTS OF COLONIAL JUDAH

It was in Babylonian exile that the priestly and scribal elite of defeated Judah assembled the great compositional units of the Hebrew Bible: the Torah; the scrolls of the Prophets; and the epic history that reaches from Joshua to 2 Kings, called the Former Prophets in Jewish tradition and the Deuteronomistic History in contemporary scholarship. When Babylon in turn fell to the Persian empire—an event that Second Isaiah (Isaiah 40–55) hailed

as a new exodus, YHWH's unprecedented deliverance of his people—members of the exile community were allowed to return to their homeland (see Ezra and Nehemiah). They "restored" Judah, not as a vassal kingdom but as a tributary temple-state ruled by priests on behalf of their Persian overlords. The documents the exiles had created became the constitution of reorganized Judah. We may read the Torah and Prophets, then, as the artifacts of a colonial situation.

The returning elite had to negotiate the competing claims of the Persian Empire and of the indigenous population who worked the land. In their final form, the writings they placed at the center of the people framed earlier traditions around themes that implicitly showed the people their place in the colonial order. The account of creation and the earth's primeval history revealed a priestly focus on order and on the necessity of sacrifice to recover from catastrophe (Genesis 1–9). The grumblings and apostasies of an unworthy and recalcitrant people punctuated the account of the exodus and the wandering in the wilderness (Exodus–Numbers). Only repeated priestly interventions saved the people from much-deserved wrath; indeed, the presence of YHWH among the people was possible only because of a system of sacrifice. When Israel entered the land of Canaan, worship and the ingathering of tithes and offerings were to be centralized under priestly supervision in Jerusalem.

The postexile Torah warned that kings—the hallmark of sovereign nations—would prove disastrous unless they submitted to priestly supervision (Deut 17:14-20). Prophecy, originally an urgent challenge to the present, was redefined as the authoritative voice of the past (Deut 18:15-22). These two themes would govern the whole of the Deuteronomistic History as well. The Torah now concluded with warnings to the people, issued on the far side of the Jordan river, that their own willful disobedience to their covenant with God would make them unworthy of the land they were about to inhabit—a lesson illustrated at length in the history. Israel's early life as a federation of tribes was now recast in Judges as life under the shadow of self-destructive lawlessness and anarchy; the epic of the great king David was retold as a warning against the dangers of monarchic power. The succession of kings in Israel and Judah was evaluated according to a simple criterion: those kings who had obeyed "true" prophets and supported centralized worship in Jerusalem were good kings; those who had tolerated alternative modes of popular religion were evil. The artificiality of this scheme is apparent when one compares the evaluation of the "evil" Manasseh, who reigned for fifty-five years, to the reformer Josiah, who was struck down in battle—in punishment, the history insists, for the sins of Manasseh! (2 Kgs 21:1—23:30).

For the Deuteronomistic historians, Manasseh's sin was not the tolerance of Israelite popular religion but promotion of the "abominable practices of the nations" that YHWH had driven out "before the people" (2 Kgs 21:2). A single theological agenda informs the book of Deuteronomy and the Deuteronomistic History alike, according to which the greatest danger to Israel's future is the contagion of a "Canaanite" past. The book of Joshua represents Israel's violent conquest of Canaan as obedience to YHWH's command to invade the land and to exterminate and replace its unworthy inhabitants (explicit, for example, in Deut 20:16-18).

Long read as an actual description of divinely ordained conquest, this narrative has borne terrible fruit in recent centuries as the empires of Christianized Europe expanded into new lands. Their reading of Joshua emboldened more recent conquerors to view the indigenous peoples of the lands they invaded as inferior and expendable. In North America, the equation of European settlers with a "new Israel" and the native peoples with the unworthy inhabitants of a "new Canaan" was explicit (see

"The Bible as a text in Cultures: Native American"). Later secularized as the "manifest destiny" of the Anglo-Saxon race, this theme fueled violent American imperialist expansion throughout the late nineteenth and early twentieth centuries. But read as the product of the colonial elite in Persian-controlled Judah, the biblical command to "drive out" the Canaanites appears rather as a spasm of spectacularly violent wishful thinking. The reformers' zeal to suppress what they regarded as corrupting influences among their own people led them to rewrite Israelite origins as a sacred campaign to exterminate the contagion of the Canaanite population.

The messages of the prophets were assembled into scrolls and edited to convey a dominant rhythm of disobedience, judgment, repentance, and restoration—the same rhythm rehearsed in the Deuteronomistic History. YHWH's covenantal faithfulness was constant and undeserved. The fulfillment of ancient hopes was projected into a distant future and made dependent on the precarious prospect of the people's renewed obedience.

There were dissenting voices. The books of Job and Ecclesiastes (in Hebrew, *Qoheleth*, "the Preacher") protested, in their own ways, the crude equation of misfortune and defeat with divine judgment. The intimate narrative of Ruth has been read as an oblique rebuttal to Ezra's "reforms"; and the strident tone in some postexilic prophecy (for example, Isaiah 56–66) reveals controversies regarding the welfare of groups excluded from temple worship.

THE DISCIPLINING OF HOPE

Torah and temple alike were sites of contention between the national and religious aspirations of the Judean population—who by the second century BCE seem to have accepted both as ordained by God—and the successive Hellenistic and Roman empires that tried, ultimately without success, to cultivate a compliant ruling class in the land. Nothing so stirred up hopes for a future free of foreign domination as the successful uprising of the Maccabees against a brutally repressive Hellenistic rule (167–64 BCE; see 1 and 2 Maccabees). Judean independence was short-lived, however. The Hasmonean dynasty that followed the Maccabean revolt secured its position through pragmatic compromises with Hellenistic rulers that alienated many of the priestly class. We can see a range of responses in the splintering of the Judean priestly and lay ruling class into factions or schools: the Pharisees and Sadducees who appear later in the Gospels, for example, and the dissenters who withdrew from what they considered a corrupt temple to wait near the Dead Sea for YHWH's purging of Jerusalem (according to the generally accepted reading of the Dead Sea Scrolls). We can also recognize the knife-edge of negotiating the colonial situation in the flourishing of short stories that depict devout Judeans living faithfully in a foreign court (Esther, Daniel 1–6, and the story of Joseph in Genesis 37–48). When the colonizing power became intolerably harsh, the genre of apocalyptic vision offered heavenly reassurance that God remained in control and would vindicate the righteous in a spectacular redemption, if they only endured (Daniel 7–12, soon followed by an explosion of other apocalyptic writings).

In 63 BCE the intervention of the Roman general Pompey effectively made the Hasmonean dynasty a client kingdom of Rome (lamented in the Psalms of Solomon). Priestly and scribal elites facilitated the payment of tribute to Rome from the temple treasuries; in so doing, they may also have protected the people from bearing more directly the brunt of Roman demands. Some of the leaders of resistance to Rome also came from priestly circles, as did, at last, some of the instigators of revolt in 66 CE.

These aspects of the colonial situation characterized the world in which Jesus of Nazareth lived and died. The fact that Jesus was crucified beneath the derisive Roman title "King of the Jews" (see Mark 15:25 and parallels) requires that we understand him against the context of Roman imperialism. The Romans crucified rebels and fugitive slaves, including thousands of Judeans in the course of the first century CE, to punish the insubordinate and to display their bodies as a warning to others.

Scholars debate which aspects of the Gospels point us reliably to Jesus' own practice. There are nevertheless ample reasons to explain why Jesus was among Rome's victims. For example, though they appear now as allegories of God's dealings with the world, Jesus' parables may originally have functioned to shine the harsh light of the prophetic tradition on the fundamental injustice of the Roman economy in Palestine—juxtaposing sharecroppers and day laborers with cruel landowners and indifferent landlords. He apparently preached a coming reversal of fortunes (compare Matt 5:1-12 and Luke 6:20-26); he urged a mutual reliance among the poor that would have cut against the grain of Roman patronage, land appropriation, and taxation. He and his disciples are depicted performing exorcisms, as did other itinerant Judean wonderworkers in his day; but Jesus presented these as an assault on the present reign of Satan (see Mark 3), at a time when Roman propaganda boasted of having inaugurated a golden age of peace and justice. At length, Jesus made a dramatic entrance into Jerusalem, during Passover—a time when nationalist feeling was most intense—at the head of an excited crowd who hailed him as the Messiah. He entered the outer court of the temple and staged a disturbance there. While the Gospels disagree on his motives, comparison with similar actions by other Jews suggests that he intended a protest against a temple regime that some saw as collaborating with Rome (see Mark 11:7-18 and parallels).

Scholars also debate the precise responsibility for Jesus' arrest and execution. But there is near universal recognition that the ultimate responsibility for crucifixion lay with the Roman governor, Pilate, whom we know from other sources to have been spectacularly brutal (in marked contrast to his portrayal in the Gospels). Any of the actions just described might have provoked a reaction from agents of the temple regime, eager to maintain a precarious balance and avoid the sort of spectacular collective punishment of which Rome had repeatedly shown itself all too capable. (The high priest expresses this logic in a statement that may, ironically, hold a kernel of historical truth: see John 11:49-50.) The Gospels give troubling hints of broader unrest: Mark makes oblique reference to an "insurrection" (15:7), and reports that Jesus was crucified between two "bandits" (Mark 15:27). We must go outside the Gospels for evidence that a number of first-century Judeans similarly gathered crowds, staged provocative actions against the Roman client regime in Jerusalem, and were cut down, their followers scattered.

THE SUBLIMATION OF HOPE

During the forty years between the death of Jesus and the earliest of the New Testament Gospels, an international movement sprang up, centered in Jerusalem and including Judeans and non-Judeans alike in small assemblies that honored Jesus as Israel's true Messiah, miraculously raised from the dead. Our primary source for this period, and consequently for what account we should give of the spread of this movement beyond Palestine, remains controversial. On one account, the apostle Paul sought to move beyond the chafing boundaries of Jewish practice to establish a universal religion that transcended ethnic limitations. On another account, any "universalism" purchased at the price of Jewish identity is a false universalism; the interpretation of Paul thus becomes a conflict in cultural

values. The controversy is compounded by writings in the New Testament that many scholars contend were falsely attributed to Paul (see the Introduction to the Pauline Letters).

All the New Testament Gospels were penned years after Paul's death—and more importantly, in the aftermath of the Roman war that put down a rebellious Judea and destroyed the temple (66–70 CE). Though all of the Gospels affirm that Jesus had been raised from death and would return to usher in a messianic future, the Gospel writers thus faced circumstances that seemed to disconfirm those hopes. Each responded, in his own way, by providing Jesus a messianic past. Matthew and Luke specified his Davidic lineage and recounted the sort of birth prodigies and miracles that Hellenistic readers would have expected of heaven's favorite. They and Mark reframed Jesus' parables as allegorical teachings about God's sublime nature; and with John they set Jesus in opposition primarily to corrupt, venal, and hypocritical Jewish religious leaders who mercilessly imposed the Torah's purity codes to defraud and oppress the poor. The Gospels all ascribed Jesus' failure to bring in the messianic age to his devout refusal to seize power inappropriately (see the "temptation" scene in Matthew 3 and Luke 4) and to his obedience to a divine "necessity" that he die on behalf of others. Most fatefully, they attributed primary responsibility for his death not to Roman colonial policy but to the malice and dishonesty of the Jewish leadership in Jerusalem, the weak and ineffectual character of the Roman governor, and the fickleness of the Jewish mob. The crowd's paradigmatic choice of Barabbas, a murderous rebel, over Jesus, whom even Pilate identifies as an innocent man, seals not only Jesus' fate but that of the city itself; for as Jesus' own words make clear, the city's rejection of him will bring down the judgment of God (see especially Matthew 21–24).

In the decades after the horrors of Nazism, churches around the world repudiated the notion, prevalent in some Christian communities, that the Jewish people were culpable for the death of Jesus. In general, however, churches have not as readily embraced the insights of critical scholarship into the pivotal—but historically improbable—role that notion plays in the plot of the various Gospels. By portraying Jesus' fate as a miscarriage of justice for which hostile Jews were responsible, rather than as the predictable consequence of his own actions and words, the Gospels implicitly disavowed the cause of defeated Judea and presented belief in Jesus as politically innocuous. In this way the Gospels, too, reveal themselves as no less the products of a colonial situation than the Torah and Prophets of the Hebrew Bible.

TO THE PRESENT

In the decades following the apostolic age, Christian theology focused increasingly on Jesus' divine nature and on the necessity of his atoning death. The ancient priestly logic of sacrifice, which Judaism reinterpreted metaphorically after the temple was destroyed, became central to Christian atonement theology (as seen already in the Letter to the Hebrews). The political significance of the actions that led to Jesus' death was minimized, however. The thoroughly Judean character of his hope had become a liability, and the dejudaization of Jesus, evident already in early Christianity, continues even to the present.

In the fourth century, with the advent of a Christian emperor of the Roman Empire, the heavenly Jesus himself came to be represented in the likeness of a monarch: bearded, clothed in purple, and seated on a throne, his hand raised in command. That imperial depiction of Jesus as all-ruler ("Pantocrator") is one of the most widely recognized images in our world.

Closer to our own time, imperial powers have wielded the Bible as an instrument of colonization.

Yet from time to time, the colonized have also found in the Bible sparks to ignite resistance and the struggle for liberation. In our own day, leaders of the world's most powerful nation have candidly spoken of the possibility, even the necessity, of a benevolent imperialism and have appealed to the imperative of "national security" in laying claim to the resources of peoples from Venezuela to Iraq and beyond. In the two-thirds world, however, theologians describe devastating war, the proliferation of national security states, the forced displacement of millions of human beings, and the hijacking of national economies for the benefit of transnational corporations as the true nature of a new global imperialism, the savage face of capitalism.

Those who turn to the Bible as a compass as they try faithfully to navigate a course through these realities face great challenges, for the Bible presents a complex and bewildering legacy. Contemporary scholarship shows us that the sweep of biblical story was marked by the rise and fall of empires. We should hardly be surprised that the Bible's contents have been shaped by their sway.

The challenges facing contemporary readers of the Bible are, first, to recognize how powerfully the Bible itself was shaped by political realities. Second, and just as important, we may recognize the ways in which religious perceptions and practices in our own day—including the very definition of what counts as religion—have been shaped by the complex and subtle pressures of imperial culture. In the United States in particular, the rise of a powerful civil religion, the popularity of escapist fiction about the "rapture," and, paradoxically, the simultaneous marginalization of alternative religious voices from the public sphere are but a few important consequences of those pressures.

My own awareness of these pressures is admittedly limited: I live fairly comfortably as a well-educated, middle class, white professional male. My efforts at raising the issues just named from an Episcopal pulpit are generally tolerated by my congregation, either because of their liberal inclinations or their forgiving spirit! But perhaps these are symptoms of the problem I have been describing: many of us are quite comfortable with the religion in which we find ourselves, and many of those who have been most moved by the Gospel's demands have either moved on or have been made to feel unwelcome in the church. For all of us, the responsibilities to reassess the biblical heritage critically and to reevaluate the ways the Bible has shaped our perceptions of our global neighbors and what we owe them remain nothing less than moral imperatives. ❖

Chapter 7

The God of the Bible and the Peoples of the Earth

Kosuke Koyama

Speaking of "God"

The English word "god" is used in different ways. In general, when we speak of a "god" we mean a being who is beyond us, larger, wiser, and more powerful than we are. Routinely we speak of "God" (with a capital "G") as the *one* such being who actually exists, and we think of God in personal terms. On further reflection, we may realize we do not mean to refer to one more being alongside others but to a mysterious, invisible, and transcendent reality that is beyond all other beings—in traditional Christian terms, a Creator who is unlike all that is created—and that eludes being captured by human thought: in the words God speaks in Isaiah, "For my thoughts are not your thoughts, nor are your ways

my ways. . . . For as the heavens are higher than the earth, so are my ways higher than your ways and my thoughts than your thoughts" (55:8-9).

Some people have insisted that the reality we call God transcends even our understanding of what it means to be a person. The prominent scholar of religions Rudolf Otto described the human experience of a mystery that is at once fearsome and fascinating as the source of all religious expression. Though the character and intensity of this experience surely varies, this phrase describes what we can find in many diverse cultures. Some scholars who study cultures say that every language and dialect of the several thousand spoken in the world has a word that can be translated "deity(ies)" or "god(s)": *kami* in Japanese, *nkulunkulu* in Zulu, *mwari* in Shona, *khuda* in Tamil, *siong-te* in Chinese, *allah* in Javanese, *theos* in Greek, and so on. This is a remarkable fact, suggesting that every culture has some conception of a transcendent being or beings. Whether or not they speak of God in personal terms, in many cultures people perceive that they not only can speak *about* this transcendent reality but can be personally connected with it.

To be religious means being aware of such a connection. Dag Hammarskjöld, general secretary of the United Nations, wrote,

> I don't know Who—or what—put the question, I don't know when it was put. I don't even remember answering. But at some moment I did answer Yes to Someone—or Something—and from that hour I was certain that existence is meaningful and that, therefore, my life, in self-surrender, had a goal.[2]

A similar experience, from another culture, comes to us from the great Indian writer, Rabindranath Tagore:

> Almost every morning in the early hour of the dusk, I would run out from my bed in a great hurry to greet the first pink flush of the dawn through the shivering branches of the palm trees.... The sky seemed to bring to me the call of a personal companionship, and all my heart—my whole body in fact—used to drink in at a draught the overflowing light and peace of those silent hours.... I am certain that I felt a larger meaning of my own self when the barrier vanished between me and what was beyond myself.[3]

The Bible, too, offers scenes of encounters with God that are filled with awe and wonder: Moses's encounter with the Lord in a bush that "was blazing, yet it was not consumed" (Exod 3:1-6), for example, or Isaiah's vision of the LORD in the Jerusalem temple (6:1-13).

ISRAEL'S "ONE GOD"

In the great story of human awareness of the transcendent that reaches back to the dawn of civilization, the ancient people of Israel in the Near East made a remarkable contribution. The Hebrew Bible (what Christians call the Old Testament) gives evidence that from its beginnings as a people, Israel was keenly aware of the wealth of religious ideas and practices around and among them. Though other gods were worshiped in Israel, the Bible always presents that phenomenon as faithlessness and false worship, and depicts Israel's very life as founded on a relationship with one unique God. That God—whose name, spelled YHWH in Hebrew, is represented in the New Revised Standard Version by the form "the LORD"—was originally perceived as supreme among a host of gods: "For the LORD your God is God of gods and Lord of lords" (Deut 10:17; see Deut 13:2, Pss 77:13, 86:8, and Isa 44:6). Sometimes another god is specifically distinguished as a "strange god" or a "foreign god" (Ps 81:9).

Israel understood the LORD as the Creator of all things, who rules the world with sovereign freedom, justice, and love. Eventually, Israel came to hold a genuinely monotheistic faith, believing that the LORD was the only truly existing God:

> Thus says the LORD, the King of Israel, and his Redeemer, the LORD of hosts: I am the first and I am the last; besides me there is no god. (Isa 44:6)

This belief did not come immediately, or easily. The story of Israel's faith involves tortuous spiritual struggles both within Israel and against the polytheistic god-talk of the surrounding nations. The Hebrew Bible is fearlessly honest about the intensity of that struggle, though looking back on Israel's history the biblical authors also sought to portray their own monotheistic faith as a clear and obvious truth from the beginning. This required portraying alternative beliefs within Israel as the "stiff-necked" duplicity and faithlessness of some—at times, of the majority—in Israel (Exod 32:9, Jer 7:24). Through the prophet Hosea, the LORD complains against the worship of Baal within Israel: "She did not know that it was I who gave her the grain, the wine, and the oil, and who lavished upon her silver and gold that they used for Baal" (Hos 2:8). Again, we read of the spectacular contest between the prophet Elijah and 450 prophets of Baal in 1 Kgs 18:1-40.

The LORD insists that "You must not worship any other god, because the Lord, whose name is Impassioned, is an impassioned God" (Exod 34:14, the JPS Tanakh translation). This is not just a matter of "jealousy," as the NRSV translates the verse; in the Bible's perspective, "any other god" also refers to any god who allows injustice, cruelty, and the use of power to control people. Such gods must not be worshiped. Though the biblical God is sometimes depicted as responding in anger and wrath against an unfaithful nation, this is only one aspect of a larger and more comprehensive portrayal of the LORD yearning passionately for a relationship of mutual faithfulness with Israel and, indeed, the whole human race.

GOD SHOWS NO PARTIALITY

Israel's ancient faith in one God has decisively influenced the fundamental character of Judaism, Christianity, and Islam alike. Because Israel recognized one God over all people, the love, freedom, and justice of this one God apply to all people equally. This meant in particular that God showed no partiality or favoritism for the rich and powerful against the needy. So God speaks in Jeremiah:

> For if you truly amend your ways and your doings, if you truly act justly one with another, if you do not oppress the alien, the orphan, and the widow, or shed innocent blood in this place and if you do not go after other gods to your own hurt, then I will dwell with you in this place, in the land that I gave of old to your ancestors forever and ever. (Jer 7:5-7)

The message is clear: the worship of God must be expressed by doing justice, loving kindness, and walking humbly with God" (Mic 6:8). It will be seen in acts of loving the neighbor as one loves oneself (Lev 19:18). The same theme is voiced in the New Testament, as "the king" (here meaning the Messiah, the risen Jesus) says at the last judgment:

> I was hungry and you gave me food, I was thirsty and you gave me something to drink, I was a stranger and you welcomed me. I was naked and you gave me clothing, I was sick and you took care of me, I was in prison and you visited me. (Matt 25:35-36)

God's impartiality also means that the biblical God's purposes extended to all nations, not just to Israel (Isa 42:6-7; 49:6)—a theme picked up by Jews speaking in the New Testament as well (Luke 1:29-32; Rom 3:29-30). Israel's God was never a tribal god but the universal God, the God of all nations and all peoples who "judges the world with righteousness… [and] the peoples with equity" (Ps 9:8). The ancient promise given to Abraham was repeatedly reaffirmed: "in you all the families of the earth shall be blessed" (Gen 12:3). This is, so to speak, an "ecumenical God," from the Greek word for the peoples of the inhabited world (*oikoumenē*).

The ecumenical God is "the Creator of the ends of the earth" (Isa 40:28). The apostle Paul reaffirms the ecumenicity of the God of Israel: "Is God the God of Jews only? Is he not the God of Gentiles also? Yes, of Gentiles also, since God is one"(Rom 3:29). The words first spoken in Israel are now spoken to all the peoples of the earth: the whole cosmos is within the concern of this God. In the story of Pentecost (Acts 2), we read that the gospel is not limited to one specific language or culture but is spoken in many languages. Thus the horizon of the message of healing is widened: it becomes multicultural, inter-religious, inter-ethnic, international, and even cosmic. "All things came into being" through the Word, declares the Gospel of John, "and without him not one thing came into being. What has come into being in him was life, and the life was the light of all people" (John 1:3-4).

The ancient psalmist sings that God "who keeps Israel will neither slumber nor sleep" (Ps 121:4). The profound ecumenicity of the biblical God suggests that the same promise extends to all people, of any nation and any faith. "The one who keeps Nigerians will neither slumber nor sleep"; "the one who keeps Buddhists will neither slumber nor sleep."

THE WORD OF THE BIBLICAL GOD AND THE RELIGIONS OF THE WORLD

The inhabited world is the world of many religions. One scholar of religions, Mircea Eliade, has listed forty-four different religions. These religions, like human languages, are constantly encountering and influencing one another. The meeting of religions affects human spirituality with its languages and cultures, bringing about change and growth. Some religious symbols may cease to be meaningful, and new symbols may take their places. Some religions have transcended initial ethnic boundaries

to become universal religions (for example, Islam and Buddhism). Judaism, Christianity, and Islam all revere the biblical patriarch Abraham, and are called the Abrahamic religions: the growth and diversity of each religion expresses the biblical promise to Abraham, that he should be "the ancestor of a multitude of nations" (Gen 17:4-5).

The Bible insists that truth is one. That implies that truth found in Judaism and Christianity does not diminish the authenticity of truth found in other religions. Mahatma Gandhi expressed his understanding of a "public religion" when he said, "instead of saying God is Truth, I have been saying Truth is God." Similarly, the Jewish thinker Martin Buber wrote, "If one dares to turn towards the unknown God, to go to meet Him, to call to Him, Reality is present."[4]

The Buddha declares that our principal problem is greed; in the Hindu tradition, what you do to others will visit you without fail. We can read the Bible in order to separate ourselves from others; but as the American writer James Baldwin puts it, "one cannot demonize others without demonizing oneself." The very diversity of forms in which the Bible expresses the word of God—prose, poems, songs, visions, dreams, narratives, law, history, prophecy, accusation, vindication, maxims—and the wealth of picture-language for God's word, which can be like "drippings of the honeycomb" (Ps 19:10) or like "a hammer that breaks a rock in pieces" (Jer 23:29)—suggests that the breadth and depth of God's word cannot be contained by human religious knowledge.

Abraham Heschel wrote that the prophets tell "God's experiences of history." The Psalmist declares, "If I ascend to heaven, you are there; if I make my bed in Sheol, you are there" (Ps 139:8). Do not such texts in the Bible itself affirm that truths found in diverse human communities, such as the various expressions of the so-called Golden Rule (Matt 7:12), point to a single truth of history?

Empathy is a universal value, as the African proverb suggests: "One who would take a pointed stick to poke a baby bird should first try it on oneself to feel how it hurts." If we wish to learn the depth of "God's experiences of history," we are wise to listen to the experiences of those who are strangers to us.

THE HOLY GOD WHO CARES

God is always "God in relationship." To say, "God is" is to say, "God cares." "Can a woman forget her nursing child, or show no compassion for the child of her womb? Even these may forget, yet I will not forget you" (Isa 49:15; see Luke 13:34). Israel's God is a holy God (Isa 6:3), and holiness means separation: there is an unbridgeable distance between the holy God and humanity in what the Bible can call our uncleanness (Isa 6:5). Yet the Bible also likens this holy God to a woman with her nursing child! Here God is described as reaching out to overcome this distance. The prophet Hosea expresses the deeply felt desire of God for connection: "How can I give you up, Ephraim?" (11:8). The Gospel of John depicts the Word of God reaching across the separation between God and humanity: "And the Word became flesh and lived among us" (1:14). The Gospel of Mark portrays Jesus reaching across social boundaries for connection with others, prompting questions from observers: "Why does he eat with tax collectors and sinners?" (Mark 2:16). Jesus responds: "I have come to call not the righteous but sinners" (Mark 2:17).

The holy God cannot be boxed in. "Even heaven and the highest heaven cannot contain you," King Solomon prays at the dedication of the Jerusalem temple (1 Kgs 8:27). Christians affirm this transcendence, declaring (for example, in the words of the Westminster Shorter Catechism) that "God is a Spirit, infinite, eternal, and unchangeable in his being, wisdom, power, holiness, justice, goodness, and truth." Even this impressive chain of words

"cannot contain" God, any more than statements like the Apostles' Creed could "contain" God. "Death no longer has dominion over him [Jesus]," wrote the apostle Paul to the Romans (6:9). If even death cannot contain the power of God, why should we imagine we could "box in" God with our cultural, religious, ethical, moral, and theological words? As New Testament scholar Eduard Schweizer writes, our teaching and our theology cannot ultimately convey the reality of "the living God":

> It may even hinder his coming, though it may be totally correct. It is exactly the most correct and orthodox teaching that would suggest that we had got hold of God. Then he can no longer come in his surprising ways.[5]

A "boxed in" God is a convenient God, a portable God—but not the God of the Bible. "Their idols are like scarecrows in a cucumber field, and they cannot speak; they have to be carried for they cannot walk," declares Jeremiah (10:5). But God is not like a scarecrow in a cucumber field!

The holy God described in the Bible is invisible, which is one way to describe God's holiness. Yet the Bible also includes Job's hope for vindication: "in my flesh I shall see God" (19:26), and Jesus' saying, "Blessed are the pure in heart, for they will see God" (Matt 5:8). The pure in heart practice what Jeremiah said: "...do not oppress the alien, the orphan, and the widow" (7:6). And 1 John suggests that when we love other people, who are visible, we are showing love for the invisible (1 John 4:20). Love particularly strangers, orphans, and widows! Pay special attention to the welfare of children throughout the world. "Whoever welcomes this child in my name welcomes me, and whoever welcomes me welcomes the one who sent me," Jesus says (Luke 9:48). In welcoming children, we are welcoming God. In others, we "see" God.

It is our relationship with what we can see that determines our relationship with the invisible

God. If we may "see" God in our neighbors (Matt 25:40, John 13:35), then it is possible to "see" God anywhere, at any time! The reality that Jesus called the kingdom of God comes when we learn to see the "image of God" (Gen 1:27) in our neighbors and in ourselves. The apostle Paul spoke of the kingdom of God as "righteousness and peace and joy in the Holy Spirit" (Rom 14:17-19). Similarly, in loving the planet earth, our ecological concern (our care for our own home, from the Greek *oikos*, "house"), we "see" the Creator and Sustainer of the universe (see Ps 104:19). On the other hand, when we abuse our neighbors, we are also giving offense to God. Oppressing our neighbors is making "wrongful use of the name of the LORD your God" (Exod 20:7).

THE GOD OF THE BIBLE AND THE GOD OF JESUS

For Christians, God is best understood by looking to Jesus as Lord. The New Testament proclaims one God as "the Father, from whom are all things and for whom we exist, and one Lord, Jesus Christ" (1 Cor 8:6). While belief in Jesus' unique relationship to God is the most distinguishing hallmark of Christianity, the New Testament presents that relationship less as a doctrine to be believed than as an invitation. Jesus called God "Father," *abba* (using an Aramaic word indicating a close intimacy: Mark 14:36; compare Rom 8:15), and taught his disciples to address God as "Our Father in heaven" (Matt 6:9).

As feminist theologians have correctly insisted, New Testament language about God as "father" does not mean that God is a male person. Though biblical representations of God often use masculine pronouns and metaphors, the Bible also affirms that God transcends gender definition. Human beings, male and female, are alike created in God's image (Gen 1:27); and virtually alone in the religious cultures of the ancient world, the God of Israel—and the God of

the early church—did not have a "consort." Though we must take account of the patriarchal cultures in which the biblical writings were produced, we may also understand biblical language of God as "father" as a way of speaking metaphorically of "One who devotedly loves and cares."

Of course, the New Testament references to God as "father" often mean to affirm more: that God is to be understood as the "father" of Jesus Christ. "Whoever has seen me has seen the Father," Jesus declares in the Fourth Gospel (John 14:9; compare 10:38). Even in that Gospel, however, the relationship between Jesus and the Father is not a mere object of belief: it is a matter of participating in the "works" of God (see John 14:12, 15, 21). Elsewhere in the New Testament we find expressed the idea that following Jesus is a way to respond to God, or in the words of the prophet Micah, "to do justice, and to love kindness, and to walk humbly with your God" (Mic 6:8). The apostle Paul affirms that even people "who do not possess the law" may "do instinctively what the law requires" and that these may be justified before God (Rom 2:13-16). In Matthew's Gospel, Jesus declares that God's standard of judgment is simply whether we have met the most basic needs of others: providing food to the hungry, drink to the thirsty, welcoming the stranger, clothing the naked, caring for the sick, and visiting those in prison (Matt 25:31-46).

Though differences in religious belief often divide people, we find in many religions—and in important passages in the Bible as well—a vision that transcends difference: the affirmation that the God of the Bible, and the God of Jesus, is best honored when we live in peace, honoring one another in justice and mercy. As the apostle Paul exhorts the Philippians, "Finally beloved, whatever is true, whatever is honorable, whatever is just, whatever is pure, whatever is pleasing, whatever is commendable, if there is any excellence and if there is anything worthy of praise, think about these things" (Phil 4:8). ❖

Chapter 8

WOMEN, CULTURE, AND THE BIBLE

Choi Hee An

How we see ourselves shapes how we see the peoples of the Bible. But because of the importance of the Bible in Western culture, and especially in the history of the imposition of Western culture on other cultures through colonialism and imperialism, the reverse is also true: how the peoples of the Bible are represented to us influences the way we see ourselves and others.

Because of its predominance as a symbol in Western colonial cultures, the Bible and its values have been identified with the dominant values of those cultures. When this has meant that privileged classes in colonial cultures—whites, males, the powerful, and so on—have been identified with the peoples at the center of biblical narrative, the result has been the subordination, marginalization, and exclusion of nonprivileged others as the "others" of the Bible.

It has been easier in Western culture for privileged classes to identify themselves with the "we" of the Bible. At the same time, others—immigrants and foreign women, for example—have found just that identification difficult. The Bible has been regularly employed to define a "we" that marginalizes and excludes others in various ways—for example, through racism, classism, sexism and heterosexism, prejudices regarding different ages and different body abilities, and the prejudices of colonial powers toward the colonized.

The prominent forms of biblical interpretation in colonial cultures have regularly made these hierarchical ideologies appear natural. Consciously or unconsciously, Western interpreters have identified white Western males as the normative "we" of the Bible; but they have also identified, and thus devalued and negated, any other possible "we"—we women, we the marginalized, we the oppressed, we ethnic minorities, we immigrants—as the biblical "other." This dominant way of reading the Bible in colonial situations has consecrated white domination at the same time it has denied sacredness to other religious practices and cultures as "uncivilized," without moral or historical value. The way conventional biblical scholarship has discussed historical "backgrounds" to the Bible mirrors the way colonial culture has taught the colonized to habitually think of themselves, with their many religions and cultures, as "objects of investigation," in the phrase of postcolonial theorist Gayatri Chakravorty Spivak. Further, using the Bible to legitimate the supremacy of Western white males has led to the fusion of the biblical value of fearing the one God with obedience to Western colonial power.

READING THE BIBLE AS A "FOREIGN WOMAN"

Especially in the case of women who are immigrants, foreigners, or members of ethnic minorities in Western societies, approaching the Bible intentionally requires renegotiating what "we" means and who "we" are. Immigrant women like myself (I come from Korea), who find themselves an ethnic minority in a new land, have experienced the Bible as a symbol of Western colonial control—but also as a resource that offers them their own voice and legitimacy, an instrument through which their own voices can come to be heard.

In the transition from their own countries to life in a new land, immigrant women become "foreign." They are impelled to adapt from thinking of themselves as "we," as they could do in their own countries, to seeing themselves as "the other." They acquire a marginalized identity, exacerbated in the European and North American contexts by severe racism and unbounded individualism. When such women have read the Bible and tried to find a place for themselves in its story, they have often been compelled to erase their own unique ethnic memories, to forget their own histories, traditions, and cultures, in order to try to adopt the perspective of white culture and its religion, Christianity. Too often the place that Western culture assigns them in the biblical story is that of "the other."

But such forgetting of themselves remains incomplete. These women struggle to sustain their existence by remembering who they once were, reintroducing memories that become dangerous to the assumptions of white Western domination. Only by struggling to retrieve their own histories can these women discern what it means to be faithful and to live out their own lives authentically before the divine. Interpreting the Bible can be an important resource in this process.

THE PLACE OF THE FOREIGN WOMAN IN THE BIBLE

The Bible is not a single book but has always been the object of multiple and diverse readings. However, the predominant biblical interpretation in the West has presumed that the Bible speaks with a single voice and this singular voice is best understood and interpreted from within Western culture in general and the Western Christian tradition in particular. But this presumed unity is false. It could only be maintained through a sort of interpretive violence that privileged Western culture and denied any significance to the wide variety of other communities, not least the diversity of ethnic immigrant women. Ironically, this presumption of Western superiority has often been considered the "universal" perspective. Claims to read the Bible from any of the many alternative perspectives found in the majority of the world's peoples has too often been considered tendentious.

Within the presuppositions of this colonial pattern of interpretation, the only space relegated in the Bible to immigrant, foreign, and ethnic-minority women are a handful of images of non-Israelite women in the biblical narratives. But Euro-American scholarship has repeatedly read these images—for example, Rahab, Canaanite women in general, Tamar, Ruth, the wife of Uriah, or the unnamed Samaritan woman in John 4—through the lens of the contemporary valuation of immigrant or foreign women. Thus these biblical women are valued only as they could be assimilated as members of ethnic minorities within the normative people, "Israel" or "the church." These "outsider" women are often further characterized as unclean, impure, manipulative, illicitly sexual, and/or disloyal to their own countries and to the colonizers' countries as well.

Nowhere is this interpretive strategy more evident than in discussions of Matthew's genealogy of Jesus, which famously includes non-Israelite women. It is not unusual to find Matthew's inclusion of these women interpreted as affirming the necessity that outsiders, especially non-Israelites, be transformed in Christ. On this view, these foreign women obtained salvation and inclusion in the genealogy of the Messiah because they joined Israel, relinquishing their previous histories and identities. Without such transforming inclusion, the immigrant or foreign women of the Bible signify only dangerous seductiveness, or weakness—as when they are represented as the victims of the patriarchal oppression of their own native ethnic cultures, from which they must be rescued (by Christ or the Christians). In such interpretation, the saving incorporation into the normative people mirrors the solicitude of sympathetic white feminist or liberal theologians for immigrant and foreign women in their own contemporary culture.

When elite Western interpreters characterize non-Israelite women in the Bible in culturally marginalized terms, they implicitly disparage contemporary immigrant and foreign women as well. This tendency can perhaps best be read in interpretations of the story of Rahab. Some white feminists have described Rahab as a heroine, a faithful woman, and as Phyllis Bird put it, as the "pagan confessor," one who could discern what her neighbors failed to see and thus "committed her life to the people of Yahweh." However positively this characterization is meant, to immigrant and ethnic-minority women it evokes the culturally loaded image of the converted prostitute, the native woman who placed her sympathies with the conquerors (or fell in love with them or had sex with them), saving them and offering them assistance against her own people by embracing the colonizing religion and culture wholeheartedly. As Kwok Pui-Lan points out, Rahab becomes in effect a Canaanite Pocahontas, the "good native" who acquiesces voluntarily to the conquerors, offering them her body as well as her protection and assistance and, in so doing, enabling the subjugation of her own people. In biblical accounts Rahab's previous religion was condemned and her culture was portrayed as sexually lascivious and impure (see Lev 17–18; Deut 7:1-5). Thus, to welcome the Israelites, she was forced to despise her own people's religion and culture, erasing the knowledge of all that she had known in her past life. In subsequent readings of the text, she was held up (in Timothy Tseng's phrase) as "a model minority" who successfully adopted the colonizer's culture, being changed from a sexually illicit and heretic non-Israelite to a faithfully civilized woman. She could be cited in colonial efforts to proselytize colonized peoples. She nevertheless remained, so far as the book of Joshua was concerned, a foreigner, an alien, and an outsider.

In a constant effort to distinguish the biblical "we" from the biblical "other," this colonial-preferred interpretation discriminates not only against Rahab the Canaanite, but also against the ethnic identities, cultures, traditions, languages, and spiritual practices of all immigrant and foreign women. It both presumes and implicitly represents the legitimacy of colonial domination, thus putting in suspense the legitimacy of these women's memories and traditions and precluding any notion that they might participate in divine creativity as do the normative "people of God."

FINDING ONE'S OWN PLACE IN THE BIBLE

Paradoxically, immigrant and ethnic-minority women have also read the Bible in ways that offer them an alternative to the place assigned them by colonial cultures and a way to understand who they are before God in their situation as immigrants, "foreigners," and "others." These alternative reading strategies start from remembering the historical injuries of colonialism. By remembering the experiences of colonial intervention and immigration, women start to integrate their previous selves with their current situation in new and imaginative ways.

They are compelled to adapt to a new situation—not just to survive but to try to live in hope. Their memories, ethnic identities, and consciousness of their own history and culture may appear as dangerously different in a new and often oppressive world. When immigrants were in their own land, their orientation was to the community, to "us." When they move into a new land, the land of the (former or present) colonial power, they are forced to think more individually—not just as "I" but "I as *the other*," an identity shaped by the racism and individualism of the new culture. When

they experience a clash between their former "we" identity and the new "I as other" identity, they may try to engage both identities in a transformative way and to create a new self: "*I and We among others.*" I call this the struggle to establish *a postcolonial self.* This self is characterized by *connection* rather than separation, and it can become the core of a new identity. In this evolution, colonial struggles are not experienced as historic baggage to leave behind but as part of a history that immigrant women deliberately carry with them as they move, not just *into* a new culture but *beyond* it, to participate in global-majority communities.

In this process, the Bible can provide a space for women that is not just the marginalized space assigned by the legacy of colonial interpretation. By reinterpreting non-Israelite women's lives in light of their own, immigrant and "foreign" women revalue those biblical figures and themselves, no longer as the colonial "other" but as participants in a greater "we" in which we are aware of our own power for transformation.

For example, immigrant and "foreign" women can find in the story of Naomi and Ruth a biblical image in which solidarity is nurtured not only among one's own ethnic group but also among the many immigrant, ethnic minority, and "foreign" communities that surround us. Ruth chose to stay in the society to which she had immigrated not only out of necessity for her own survival as a widow but also out of solidarity with Naomi—that is, out of the solidarity of "I and we among others." This was not an easy choice. It involved inevitable danger. She risked enduring bitter experiences of marginalization in her new culture, but she accepted the risk in order to cherish her relationship with her mother-in-law. This was an expression not of patriarchal virtue but of an embraced connectedness with Naomi, also an "other," as "we."

Reading the story of Ruth in this way challenges the individualistic orientation of Western culture, which emphasizes the difference between "we" and "other." It opens a space for a new "we" to be realized, a "we" that welcomes our different ethnicities and honors our histories without accepting the marginalized status of "other." The solidarity Ruth shows in choosing to live with Naomi is an instance of resistance against the social forces that would marginalize them both. Reading the story this way allows the Bible to become a space for immigrant women—and other "others"—to exercise, communally and individually, a different way of being "we" together.

Such a reading does not come easily, especially in a society where the Bible enjoys tremendous importance, but, as we have seen, is usually read as a unitary voice that legitimizes the distinction between a normative "we" and marginalized "others." But such a reading *frees* the Bible from the role of legitimizing the privileged and powerful in Western society. The presence of the "foreign" woman belies and resists the normative representation of "the other" in the biblical text and in contemporary global society alike, and opens up the possibility that the Bible will be a space of solidarity and welcome. ❖

Chapter 9

RESPONSIBLE CHRISTIAN EXEGESIS OF HEBREW SCRIPTURE

Johanna W. H. van Wijk-Bos

How we read Holy Scripture has been important as long as there has been a text to read.

One of the earliest examples of what might be called "Christian exegesis" is found in the Gospel of Luke, written at least two generations after Jesus' death. The scene depicts a conversation between Jesus and an expert in the Torah (Luke 10.25-29; compare Matt 22.34-40, Mark 12.28-34). Here is my translation:

> And, look, a certain expert in the Torah stood up to test him and said: "Teacher, what must I do to obtain eternal life?" And he said to him: "What is written in the Torah? How do you read?" He answered: "You shall love the Holy One your God with your entire heart and with all your soul and all your strength and your whole mind, and your neighbor as yourself." He said to him: "You answered correctly. Do this and live." He, wanting to justify himself, said to Jesus: "And who is my neighbor?"

Luke presents Jesus as confronted by a member of his community who knows the most important part of Scripture for his day, the Torah. He is an expert in reading and interpreting what he reads in the Torah. Luke paints the incident as a confrontation. This person stood up to test Jesus, as if laying a trap. Contrary to what we might expect, he asks Jesus a question not about interpretation, but rather about action. He asks: "What must I *do*?"

Jesus excelled at clever interaction with members of his own faith community and turns the question right back into his questioner's field of expertise. He asks, "What is written in the Torah? How do you read?" In other words, if you want to know what to do, pay attention not only to *what* you read, but to *how* you read.

EXEGESIS AND RESPONSIBILITY

Exegesis, a Greek word meaning "interpretation" or "explanation," is the study of the biblical text. Exegetes intend to provide a solid foundation for reading the Bible. Exegesis is a technical word, and many exegetes are specialists who concentrate on this technical work. Yet all of us who are interested in the Bible—who read it, who study it, who listen to it being taught and preached—are in an informal way exegetes of the text. Exegesis, reading the text, is of crucial importance because it is directly connected to our actions. When we ask how to read we are also and always asking what to do.

Those of us who are Christians do Christian exegesis, meaning that we read the Bible from the perspective that in Jesus the God of Israel became incarnate so that Gentiles might become a beloved community, taken into covenant by the God who is revealed in Israel's Scripture. That part of the Bible, which in Christianity has traditionally been called the Old Testament, we also call *Hebrew Scripture* out of respect for the faith that recognizes this book as its Bible. (Jews also call it *Miqra'*.) Christian exegetes are aware that in reading this part of the Bible we are in sacred literature that was not in the first place created for our benefit and that is still the entire Bible for Judaism, a faith with adherents around the world. Although the term *Hebrew Scripture* has its own shortcomings, it does not imply that these writings are in any way surpassed or superseded, as the term *Old Testament* might.

Christian exegetes must read Hebrew Scripture responsibly. We may begin by assuming that, like the Torah expert in Luke 10, Christian exegetes are responsible to both God and our neighbor. We are responsible to God as we read, insofar as we consider the Bible to be the sacred literature that speaks to us of God's dealings with us and with all creation. We are responsible to God insofar as we believe that God addresses contemporary believers somehow through the words of these texts. Before reading from the Bible on Sunday morning, many Christian preachers may invite their congregations to listen to these words as a, or *the*, word of God.

Exegetes are also responsible to our neighbors in our work. First, we are responsible to the neighbors of the past, those who in faith spoke and eventually wrote these texts, the community that went before, the "great . . . cloud of witnesses" of Heb 12:1. Exegetes are responsible to all who have devoted themselves to reading these texts so that it might benefit them, strengthen their faith, and guide their actions. Next, exegetes are responsible to our neighbors today. They include those who are potentially hurt and alienated by a certain way of reading the Bible; neighbors who belong to another community of faith; and neighbors within our own community who read, study, and listen so they may hear as fully as possible from these texts about God and God's will for their lives.

RESPONSIBILITY AFTER THE HOLOCAUST

What, then, constitutes responsible Christian exegesis of Hebrew Scripture? First and foremost, responsibility to the neighbor requires that Christian exegesis of the Hebrew Scripture proceeds from an awareness that we read the Bible today in a post-Holocaust world. We are aware that previous Christian ways of reading at the very least contributed to a political climate that made the Holocaust (or Shoah) possible. The Holocaust has forever changed the way in which the Hebrew Bible is read theologically by Jews and Christians alike.

Second, responsible Christian exegesis acknowledges that Judaism has its own legitimate claim on these sacred texts, comprising a community of direct descendants of the people who produced the Hebrew Scriptures, who have their own centuries-long tradition of interpretation. Third, responsible Christian exegesis recognizes that there is a connection between the idea that the Hebrew Bible is somehow incomplete or unfulfilled without the "New" Testament and active Christian persecution of the Jews and defamation of Judaism throughout the centuries. Christian exegesis must repent of past actions of discrimination and persecution against Jews, and insist on reading both Testaments from a perspective of honor and respect for Jewish sisters and brothers and their faith convictions. Finally, responsible Christian exegesis understands the Christian faith community to be in great need of direction for its way of life—for its relation to God and neighbor. It looks to directives in the Hebrew Scriptures to complete and deepen the instructions given to the early followers of Jesus, and at times even to correct these later directives, especially as found in the epistles of the New Testament. This responsibility means attempting at every turn to dissolve the tension between gospel and Torah found in much traditional Christian exegesis, insofar as gospel is identified with Christianity and Torah with Judaism. In all these ways, Christian interpreters exercise responsibility to the neighbor.

What about responsibility to God? Responsible Christian exegesis of the Hebrew Bible takes seriously the conviction that Christians believe in one God who is revealed in two parts of the Bible, in Christian terminology the Old and the New Testa-ment. It affirms that the good news, the gospel, of God's presence with the world permeates the entire Bible, and did not begin with the arrival of Jesus Christ. Moreover, responsible Christian exegesis of the Hebrew Scriptures recognizes that the witness of the Hebrew Bible to the God of Israel does not need the witness of the New Testament to speak fully of God and God's presence in the world. Conversely, however, this kind of exegesis understands that the witness of the New Testament is incomplete and can easily be misunderstood without the foundational testimony of the Hebrew Scripture.

Responsible Christian exegesis takes note of the entire Hebrew Bible, not just the parts that fit with certain New Testament texts, and engages in a continuous reading of the biblical text. This is a particular challenge when a church lectionary takes fragments of a book of the Hebrew Bible out of context and juxtaposes them with fragments from a New Testament writing. In light of the responsibilities discussed here, it is desirable to provide for the continuous reading of a book—or of a complete unit within a book—of the Hebrew Bible and to do the same with Second Testament writings (though not in isolation from the Hebrew text). Such procedures allow us to engage First and Second Testament texts in conversation with each other and thus to arrive at a Christian interpretation that takes a full account of the diverse voices of Scripture.

In many ways, irresponsible Christian exegesis represents the opposite of what has just been described. Irresponsible Christian exegesis of the Hebrew Scriptures ignores the events of the Holocaust/Shoah and how Christian anti-Judaism contributed to make those events possible. It ignores, as far as possible, the existence of contemporary Judaism and the contributions that Jewish tradition has made to interpretation of the biblical text. Irresponsible Christian exegesis continues to view Christianity as superior to Judaism and as the sole true inheritor of the promises made to ancient Israel. It judges the Hebrew Scriptures to be unfulfilled and incomplete without the witness of the "New" Testament and considers the community that produced these sacred texts ultimately to be a failure.

This type of exegesis understands the New Testament to be the final arbiter of the value of biblical texts in revealing God and speaking of the Christian life to the believer. It understands texts of Hebrew Scripture to have revelatory value only insofar as they speak to the revelation of God in Christ. Thus, an irresponsible Christian exegesis never reads texts from the Hebrew Scriptures unless they are followed by, and in practice subordinated to, New Testament texts in Sunday morning preaching. New Testament texts, on the other hand, may be read and preached on their own during large parts of the so-called Christian year. Such practices imply that New Testament texts are self-sufficient to describe what is worthwhile and to speak of God to the community.

Finally and more subtly, irresponsible Christian exegesis ignores the historical context of the Hebrew Scriptures and the significance and meaning of the election of ancient Israel as God's covenant community. It ignores the distance in time and space between the Christian reader or listener and texts from the Hebrew Scriptures and reads them only as they have application to the church and the contemporary Christian reader.

The problems with this type of Christian exegesis are multiple. It sustains barriers between two faiths and their adherents who by common sense ought to consider each other sister faiths. It blocks avenues to the richness of the biblical text as God's self-revelation. It has created the impression among many Christians that the Bible speaks of two deities, one threatening and violent, of which the Hebrew Scripture speaks, and one loving and kind, to which the New Testament testifies. Such

exegesis in effect not only ignores the existence and contributions of contemporary Judaism, but erases the historical roots of the Jews. In this way, it belongs on a continuum of indifference and hostility toward Jews, a continuum with a long history of persecution of Jews that culminated in Christian complicity in the Holocaust/Shoah.

Irresponsible Christian exegesis of Hebrew Scripture not only belies the self-understanding and identity of believing Jews but also prevents Christians from a full sense of their own identity as believers in the God of the Bible. In the end, this kind of exegesis is irresponsible to God, to neighbors both past and present, and to the self as well.

EXAMPLES OF READING

The roots of the sort of irresponsible Christian interpretation of Hebrew Scripture discussed here are very deep. The fifth-century bishop Augustine of Hippo, for example, was one of the first theologians to put anti-Jewish interpretation of the Bible on the Christian map with his reference to Jews as a "cursed people" (*Faust.*, 12.11). But it is not difficult to find examples of irresponsible Christian exegesis of Hebrew Scriptures today, not only in many Christian churches in the United States, but also in scholarship. Introductory textbooks on the Old Testament rarely make consideration of the Holocaust/Shoah a primary point of departure, or even consider it at all. Recognition of the Holocaust's importance is thus often confined to "specialized" literature. While today one rarely encounters such crass hostility toward the Jewish neighbor as found in Augustine, it is not so unusual to hear a sermon on an Old or New Testament text in which the existence of the Jews and their faith is completely ignored, making the Jews as invisible as if Hitler had been successful with his program of extermination. In Christian scholarship, too, one not infrequently meets generalizations about Israel and Jews in the past tense, as if they no longer existed, and to their covenant with God as obsolete and superseded. This is often especially egregious in Christian theological and historical discussions of Jesus that set him in opposition to the benighted attitudes and practices of his contemporaries, as in some modern liberationist theologies. Christian theologians may then read the "Old Testament" as pointing to the *church* as the "New Israel," or to the Exodus as a paradigm for the liberation of the oppressed, without acknowledging the particularity of the original covenant people. They may ignore the continuing covenant relationship that another community has with God or imply that the other community's relationship has ended in failure so that Christians may lay claim to all the promises made to that original covenant people.

WHO IS OUR NEIGHBOR?

Taking our cue from the Gospel story with which we began, with the Torah expert we may well ask: "Who is our neighbor?" When Jesus responds with the story of the Samaritan who rescued the victim of a robbery, he points to both neighborly action and the recipient of this action. The one to whom we should show the love of neighbor may not be like us, may not be of our "family." In this regard, Luke places Jesus in a direct line with Torah's teaching concerning love for God and neighbor, which ultimately means love for the *stranger* (see Lev. 19:34). The stranger need not be distant or an outsider; the stranger may be one close by—but different. Responsible Christian exegesis will read the Hebrew Scriptures especially with an eye toward the Jewish neighbor. If Christians do not read in ways that directly connect them in compassionate action to this particular neighbor, how can they aspire to read in ways that lead to the love of any neighbor? ❖

Chapter 10

THE "PEOPLE OF GOD" AND THE PEOPLES OF THE EARTH

Ann Holmes Redding

with Neil Elliott

In the voice of the priest presiding at the Episcopal church I attend, I hear a Caribbean lilt; and on the faces of the assembly I see features and hues that reflect ancestral origins from several continents. The racks in the pews hold *Lift Every Voice and Sing II,* a hymnal that draws on the African American tradition, alongside the standard-issue *Hymnal 1982.* I stand among folks like me, descendants of enslaved Africans, as well as descendants of those who enslaved Africans, a heritage I also share. In our midst are young children whose parents left the United States to find and bring them from other countries home to America to become a family. Also in the mix are adults who were conceived or reared in the U.S. internment camps to which their parents were transported after they lost their property

and liberty during World War II. This Sunday and every Sunday, we bring with us a complex array of cultural and ethnic legacies; "we are surrounded by so great a cloud of witnesses" (Heb 12:1a). But on this particular day, the Sunday after the Fourth of July, there is an additional layer to the texture of our social fabric, because we, like many Episcopal congregations, celebrate Independence Day as a feast day in our denominational calendar. As I watch the American flag follow the cross in the procession, I wonder, "What happens as we listen together to the readings from the Scriptures on such a day? How do the host of social identities and narratives we bring affect and inform both our listening and our relating to one another as the people of God?" A metaphor that comes to mind is that the liturgy is a kind of loom threaded with the warp of the scriptural witness and ritual action, and the members of the assembly are interwoven into the tapestry with their own stories and selves as the colorful strands of the woof.

THE PEOPLE OF GOD ON A JOURNEY

In recent decades, another metaphor for the encounter between congregation and Scriptures has been that of the people of God on a *journey*. In the latter half of the twentieth century, perspectives from the liturgical renewal movement, biblical theology, and "postliberal" theology combined in creating a focus on Scripture as an enveloping and unified narrative recounting the movement of God's people toward God's future. In their encounters with the text, present-day believers retrace the steps of their forebears, even as they continue together on the path. The liturgical renewal movement, especially in the 1960s and '70s, emphasized the participation of the assembly and the recovery of biblical language and imagery. Both biblical and postliberal theology brought a shift in emphasis *from* the Bible as either a body of laws or a set of doctrines providing a basis for constructing architecturally complex theological systems and *to* Scripture as an engaging narrative, replete with recitations of "saving history." This approach invites the identification of the congregation with "the people of God" in the biblical story and tradition.

The appeal of this approach has grounding in the biblical text itself. The canonical ordering of the texts, beginning with the creation of the world and the launching of human community in Adam and Eve, embeds all the smaller genres of the Bible in a narrative sweep centering on the establishment of a people accountable to God. The family tree repeatedly laid out and reworked in the First Testament and reconfigured in the Christian writings makes the connections explicit between the main characters so that readers have sense of reading a continuing saga. As the scriptural journey continues, this people of God is constantly in formation and transformation. In the family scrapbook of Scripture, certain figures and their offspring appear and reappear, while other branches of the family drop out of sight. For example, Abraham, the father of many nations, and his wife, Sarah, are the primary family connection linking the Jewish and Christian testaments. In Paul's writings in the Christian testament, faith in Jesus admits his followers into the family of Abraham (Gal 3:29), who is the symbolic progenitor of all people of faith and the actual forebear of Jesus (Matt 1:1-2; Luke 3:34). In the process of reconfiguring these family lines, Paul explicitly reads Hagar, the mother of Abraham's older son, out of the family, ignoring her privileged position as the first person in the Hebrew Bible to receive an angelic announcement of promise and the only human in both volumes to name God (Gal 4:22-31; Gen 16:10, 13).

Among the prophets, Isaiah is perhaps the clearest in proclaiming that membership in the family of God will eventually extend far beyond the bounds of the blood lines established earlier in the narrative (see Isa 49:6; 56:6-7). In the New Testament, Jesus radically redefines familial ties by saying that "whoever does the will of my Father in heaven is my brother and sister and mother" (Matt 12:50). The social reality of the "new creation" in Christ that Paul announces means that "there is no longer Jew or Greek, there is no longer slave or free, there is no longer male and female; for you are all one in Christ Jesus" (Gal 3:28).

The dynamism of the development of the people of God is not only temporal, but also spatial; they are people on the move. Adam and Eve and the expulsion from Eden; Noah and company on the ark; Abram, the wandering Aramean; Hagar and her flight; Joseph's abduction to Egypt; Moses and the exodus from Egypt; another Joseph's escape *to* Egypt with his endangered family; Jesus' sending forth his disciples to all nations—the constantly shifting venues in the text give a sense of the extensive reach of a Deity who invites, inveigles, prods, pulls, and marches those called down the path.

As communities of faith read the biblical text together as witnesses of "the people of God on a journey," this reading strategy allows them to see the coherence of the Bible as the divinely guided formation and movement through history of a people. Furthermore, as they trace the steps of the textual "pilgrimage," this model invites readers to identify with the characters in the biblical stories and to connect powerfully with their own stories as individuals and communities. The biblical stories become their stories, and this sense of ownership in turn reinforces their identity as "the people of God."

However, as appealing as this perspective on the encounter with Scripture may be, it also presents us with significant challenges, again arising both from the text itself and from its readers. Over the three centuries before anything like a centrally authorized version of the Bible appeared, a multitude of manuscripts were in use among Christians, not only in the Greek language most scholars believe was the original language of the New Testament texts, but also in Coptic, Latin, and Syriac. To the extent that language is a constitutive element of cultural identity, it is fair to suppose that cultural and ethnic tensions arose during the process of translation and compilation that resulted in the earliest Bibles.

Within the text as it exists, we can see that from early on in the narrative, there is ambiguity, discontinuity, displacement, and hierarchical ranking in the development of the mythic social configuration of "the people of God." The solidarity of the common origin of humanity is ruptured in the second generation, when Cain slays Abel and asks the archetypal question, "Am I my brother's keeper?"

The listing of the nations of the earth in Genesis 10, following upon Noah's curse on Canaan and blessing of Shem, gives the offspring of the latter pride of place in the continuing story. Genesis 11 begins with the famous story of the Tower of Babel, in which diversity of language arises, not seemingly as a gracious gift, but rather as the consequence of human arrogance.

In other places, lines of affiliation and loyalty shift and blur. In Exodus, for example, to lead the Hebrew people to freedom, Moses must turn against the Egyptian pharaoh whose daughter had saved Moses's life as an infant. Tribal prejudice and ethnic strife are met at some times with divine rebuke; on other occasions, cultural chauvinism is sanctioned, if not encouraged. The description of the removal of the Canaanites from their land at God's behest in the first half of the book of Joshua reads like divinely ordained ethnic cleansing. When Jesus encounters a woman labeled a "Canaanite" in Matt 15:22, his initial refusal to heal her child on ethnic grounds betrays an ethnocentrism that calls the story of the conquest to mind. His tone, though not his position, stands in stark contrast to Paul's anguish in the collision of loyalties he feels as tensions between Jewish and Gentile Christian escalate in Rome. "For I could wish that I myself were accursed and cut off from Christ," he writes, "for the sake of my own people" (Rom 9:3).

When Christians like me with no cultural or ethnic ties to Judaism, approach the whole Bible and identify ourselves as legitimate heirs to "the people of God" in the text, we can scarcely relate either to Jesus' or Paul's deep attachment to their Jewish heritage. Indeed, the question becomes, *if Christians are the "people of God," then what about the Jews?* In the wake of the Holocaust, a number of Christian New Testament scholars began to address with greater clarity the dangers of a biblical theology implicitly based on the assumption of supercessionism, that is, the claim that in Christianity God has removed the validity of and need for Judaism. A renewed emphasis on the Jewishness of Jesus, of the movement he started, of his earliest followers, and of Paul has been a priority in the scholarship ever since. However, the understandable appeal to gentile Christians of being biblical heirs of Jews has led some into dangerous territory. Christian scholars have been known sometimes to characterize Jesus and the earliest followers of his movement as progressive and enlightened, in contrast to the rest of the Jews of their time. Jewish feminists, among others, have rightly challenged the stereotype of Jesus as an exceptional champion of women's liberation, bravely opposing the intransigent patriarchy of his Jewish culture. The attitudes of gentile Christians who assume that Jesus handed over to Christianity (hence to Gentiles) the best of Judaism give license for the cooptation of Jewish practices (for example, Passover seders) without understanding the implicit condescension and disrespect for Jewish people such behavior can indicate and convey.

Because of widespread unfamiliarity with Islam, the other Abrahamic sibling of Christianity, many Christians have not grappled with the reality that its holy book, the Qur'an, recapitulates, augments, and reinterprets significant portions of the Christian Scriptures. In so doing the Qur'an declares itself to be one part of the "mother of the Book," a heavenly source that also includes prior revelations to Jews and Christians (Qur'an 13:38-39) and, therefore, a significant segment of the revealed story of the people of God. I was profoundly surprised and humbled when I first heard about and then read the accounts of Moses, Abraham, Noah, Jesus, his disciples, Mary, and other familiar figures, in the Qur'an. Mary, in fact, has an entire chapter devoted to her, more material than in the entire Christian testament. As a Christian who has been embraced by and has extended her religious affiliation to include Islam, I find that Jesus

is at least as at home in Islam as he is in the Judaism of his birth and practice and that reading the Bible alongside the Qur'an illuminates both texts.

The metaphor of journey or pilgrimage so powerful in the Bible—especially when construed in sequences like exodus to conquest and settlement of the land, the "on the road" structure in the Gospels, and the expansionist narrative in Acts—can easily be manipulated into a tool of oppression when it is read through the lens of the Eurocentric fantasy of cultural progress. By contrasting and ranking societies along a spectrum of "progress," this perspective functions to legitimate the claims of superiority of white-skinned Christians, who identify themselves as "the people of God" (and who, not surprisingly, came up with that idea of progress in the first place). This viewpoint blessed the unholy union of European mission strategy and colonialism by readily equating Christianity with European civilization and "enlightenment," which in turn spawned such destructive offspring as the construct of racism and the devastation of the African continent. The history of the indigenous peoples of the Americas bears witness to the destruction wrought by the white Europeans who came as "the people of God" to dispossess them of their land by whatever means necessary, including genocide. Then the missionaries asked the survivors to read the Bible "against" themselves—to identify with "the people of God" and deny their own origins and heritage.

A similar vantage point plays out in contemporary imperialism and myths of exceptionalism—the fusion of civil religion and Christianity in U.S. churches—which claim the United States specifically as a Christian nation with the unique vocation from God to bring freedom, democracy, and prosperity to others, even through war. Choi Hee An has written about the difficulty of Southeast Asian immigrant women who feel they are "outsiders" when they read a Bible that seems to be wholly owned by white Americans. (See chapter 8, "Women, Culture, and the Bible.") Especially since September 11, 2001, these ideas underlie the political rhetoric of "crusade" and opposition to the "Axis of Evil" and function to mask the complex cultural, economic, and social dynamics of the situation. Christians, of course, are not alone in interpreting Scripture as a warrant of superiority. In his book *How to Win a Cosmic War*, Muslim scholar Reza Aslan points out the dangers of reading the holy books of Judaism, Islam, and Christianity to sanctify an unending cycle of violence and vengeance. The recognition in recent years by a few political leaders in the United States of the importance of expanding national identity to include those who do not see themselves as part of the Christian story could mark a turning point in the history of American religious consciousness.

Another manifestation of the process of ethnic and cultural usurpation of the biblical narrative is in the artistic representations of biblical characters and geography. Like many Christian children of African descent, I grew up never seeing anyone with skin color close to mine in the children's bibles and church school curricula I read. Despite the maps of "the Holy Land," many of us, no matter our ethnicity, grew up thinking of Jesus' homeland as being a southeastern extension of Europe, rather than as southwest Asia or northeast Africa. I have my friend and former colleague Randall Bailey to thank for the realization that the very term "the Middle East" functions to sever from its context the cultural and social ties of the territories where most of the action in the biblical narrative takes place. (See the Gallery in this volume for a rich collection of biblical images from across a spectrum of cultures and times.)

The notion of a "chosen people" is rooted in Scripture and often stands behind the metaphor of "the people of God." If we understand "the people of God" in the text to be those chosen and privileged by God, then we can interpret their successes as divinely ordained and sanctioned. When we bring to the reading of the text our own strong sense of "peoplehood"—whether our identification is with a nation, an ethnicity, a race, a culture, a denomination, or simply the people in the room at any given time—that identification often informs the choices we make about the particular passages and episodes to which we give priority. Depending upon the position of our own group as, for example, conquerors, victims, or survivors, we home in on those portions of the narrative that may lend credence to our social or political agendas. In the process, after identifying our own group with the "in group" in the story, we wield the polemical labels in the biblical narrative against our own designated antagonists. How often have we heard—or used—the term "Pharisee," for example, in and of itself a neutral or even honorable title, as a blanket condemnation of a person or a group deemed hypocritical or untrustworthy, simply because the Pharisees in the New Testament are depicted as Jesus' opposition?

In my own experience, while my mother never made explicit our claim as members of the chosen people, the African American spirituals she sang to my sisters and me at bedtime painted the picture of a world with dark-skinned biblical characters, including Jesus, to whom we knew we were closely related. His experience of unmerited persecution at the hands of the ignorant but powerful combined with his ultimate victory as God's chosen provided strength, comfort, and hope. A testimony to the complexity and power of the scriptural text is that it has never been completely subject to those who have wielded it as proof of their exclusive pedigree as the people of God and therefore as a sanction for conquest and exploitation of others. Throughout history, examples abound of peoples who first heard the words of the Scriptures from would-be colonizers or enslavers—but discerned the strains of common humanity and liberation underneath the messages to submit and obey. Anglican archbishop and Nobel laureate Desmond Tutu frequently has observed that the Europeans sowed the seeds of their eventual downfall when they made the strategic error of bringing Scripture to the African peoples of the land they had intended to conquer.

SPREADING A TABLE AT THE CROSSROADS

In proposing one more metaphor for the encounter with Scripture, I return to the scene at my parish church described at the beginning of this chapter. On that Sunday morning, I was mindful of our gathering as a point of convergence for a complex web of pathways—social, ethnic, and cultural; personal and communal. We stood together at the crossroads of our shared faith, powerfully represented and enacted in the words of Scripture and the gathering at the table of communion. We met at a table spread at the crossroads. In this image the text is a meeting ground, a territory where people come together for refreshment, nurture, and edification. No matter where they come from, Scripture provides a common ground for those who gather. The spread table sets the tone of the occasion. All are welcome to lay down their armor, sit down at the table, and eat. The boundaries traced by the text form an enclosure that is—like the heart of the Islamic holy city of Mecca—*haram,* a sacred precinct where no aggression or hostility is permitted. Reading the text together becomes an act of worship, or "liturgy," according to its root meaning as "the people's work."

This strategy for reading Scripture both preserves the idea of people of God on the journey and expands it in several ways. It does justice to complexities of the journeys that occur inside the narratives of the biblical texts, in the history of revelation and composition of the sacred Scripture, and in the lives of the readers. Exodus and exile,

the conquest of Canaan and the Maccabean revolt, Jesus' triumphal entry into Jerusalem and the *via dolorosa*—all the comings and goings, the advances, withdrawals, and detours, are encompassed in this image. Rather than reflecting a linear, singular march through time whose participants are enrolled by conscription, the metaphor of the crossroads focuses on encounter and interaction, with all the accompanying possibilities of choice, conflict, collision, convergence, conversion, and communion. In this model, there are no eternal good guys and bad guys; instead, the body identified as "the people of God" includes everyone who shows up at the crossroads. Those who come as readers and interpreters are encouraged to bring their own stories—personal and communal—into the interpretive occasion.

For the image of the presence of a table at the crossroads in our encounter with Scripture, I am indebted to J. Louis Martyn, wise and beloved first adviser in my doctoral studies. To help students put academic biblical study into perspective, Martyn would speak about the two tables. One was rectangular and stood in a brightly lit, sterile operating room in a hospital. Around it was an array of well-trained medical practitioners, peering down at an anesthetized patient. Cut open, exposed, inert, and susceptible to the probing activities of the professionals around the table, the patient represented the biblical text. "With any luck at all," Lou would say, "when the time comes for sewing the patient up again, the medical team will have used their expertise to clear up any problems and will leave the patient in better shape than when they began." At the second table in Lou's story, no one stood. Unlike the operating table, it was round, spacious, and made for conversation. Seated around it, side-by-side, were the students in the class and others whom they and Lou chose to invite. Jesus always had a place at Lou's table, along with biblical authors, editors, and compilers—known and unknown—who together embodied the text. "Think about those to whom you are accountable whenever you read and interpret Scripture," Lou would say; "they also belong at your table, as part of your conversation."

To set this kind of table at the crossroads further defines the nature of the encounter. It honors the age-old traditions of hospitality that often characterized the cultures through which the text came—and of many of the peoples who claim the text today. Reminiscent of the meal offered by Abram and Sarai to their angelic visitors (Gen 18), the feast of "fat things" foretold for the fullness of time (Isa 25:6), and the cup of water Jesus requests from the Samaritan woman at the well (John 4), this image suggests the possibility of nurture and renewal. It also implies that no given social, religious, or cultural group has proprietary rights in the occasion; rather all bring to the table their own contributions to supplement the bounty already provided.

When we come together at the crossroads of the text, our meeting can become an unanticipated family reunion. Whoever is there—those in the text as characters; those behind the text as authors, collectors of traditions, editors, and prophets; and those present at the table both in the flesh and in the legacies we represent—whoever is there is a child of God, part of the people of God. Whoever shows up is kin. When familial relationship is assumed, uniformity of religious creed is not required. The conversation partners at the crossroads can share their differences of vantage point in light of their own stories and experiences.

For those of us who are Christians, Jesus always shows up at the table at the crossroads. Our relationship to him inspires believers to embrace the full humanity of all whom we encounter there. Paul urges a similar kind of awareness when he warns the Corinthian congregation that without "discerning the body" when they come together for the Lord's Supper, they will not treat one another with due honor and respect (see 1 Cor 11:18-29). Can the presence of Jesus at our table indeed stretch us to recognize the deep interconnectedness of all the peoples of the earth as the people of God? The answer to this question is not as obvious as it may seem, given that Jesus apparently is in the habit of showing up incognito from time to time in the likeness of those whose human dignity and value have been compromised. In the story he tells in Matt 25:31-46, Jesus must explain to those who are baffled by his praise for coming to his aid when he was hungry, naked, sick, and in prison that when they acted on behalf of "the least of" his brothers and sisters, they were unknowingly doing it for him.

As the one whom Christians confess as the Word of God *incarnate*, the Word who "was made flesh and camped out among us" (John 1:14a, my translation), Jesus embodies the sacred reality of God's will to communicate not only through the words on the pages of our holy book, but also through the living words of our shared flesh and blood in our common trek toward God. In our coming together at the table, we can only hope that we do not miss or dismiss a word—or thereby, the Word—in the conversation. ❖

Part II

THE HEBREW BIBLE

11. THE HEBREW BIBLE
    AS A TEXT OF CULTURES
    Frank M. Yamada (with Neil Elliott)

❖ TIMELINE FOR THE HEBREW BIBLE

12. THE TORAH (or Pentateuch)

    Introduction to the Pentateuch
    Frank M. Yamada
    Genesis   *Randall C. Bailey*
    Exodus   *Jorge Pixley*
    Leviticus   *Madeline McClenney-Sadler*
    Numbers   *Wilda C. Gafney*
    Deuteronomy   *Frank M. Yamada*

13. THE HISTORICAL BOOKS

    Introduction to the Historical Books
    Uriah Y. Kim
    Joshua   *Dora R. Mbuwayesango*
    Judges   *Wilda C. Gafney*
    Ruth   *Wilda C. Gafney*
    1 Samuel   *Uriah Y. Kim*
    2 Samuel   *Uriah Y. Kim*
    1 Kings   *Francisco García-Treto*
    2 Kings   *Francisco García-Treto*
    1 Chronicles   *Gregory Lee Cuéllar*
    2 Chronicles   *Gregory Lee Cuéllar*
    Ezra   *Alejandro F. Botta*
    Nehemiah   *Alejandro F. Botta*
    Esther   *Willa E. M. Johnson*

14. WISDOM AND POETRY

    Introduction to Wisdom and Poetry
    Francisco García-Treto
    Job   *Cheryl A. Kirk-Duggan*
    Psalms   *Stephen Breck Reid*
    Proverbs   *Joseph F. Scrivner*
    Ecclesiastes   *Madeline McClenney-Sadler*
    The Song of Solomon   *Alice Hunt*

15. THE PROPHETS

    Introduction to the Prophets
    Lai Ling Elizabeth Ngan
    Isaiah   *Hyun Chul Paul Kim*
    Jeremiah   *Angela Bauer-Levesque*
    Lamentations   *Cheryl A. Kirk-Duggan*
    Ezekiel   *Gale A. Yee*
    Daniel   *Barbara M. Leung Lai*
    Hosea   *Lai Ling Elizabeth Ngan*
    Joel   *Claude F. Mariottini*
    Amos   *Valerie Bridgeman*
    Obadiah   *John J. Ahn*
    Jonah   *Claude F. Mariottini*
    Micah   *Daniel L. Smith-Christopher*
    Nahum   *Daniel L. Smith-Christopher*
    Habakkuk   *Valerie Bridgeman*
    Zephaniah   *John J. Ahn*
    Haggai   *Steed Vernyl Davidson*
    Zechariah   *Steed Vernyl Davidson*
    Malachi   *Osvaldo D. Vena*

THE HEBREW BIBLE AS A TEXT OF CULTURES

Frank M. Yamada

with Neil Elliott

In my writing, I am trying to make central what is marginal,
to re-create and reveal what others say should not be spoken of.
Imagination is intervention, an act of defiance. It alters belief.

—David Mura[9]

David Mura is a Sansei—third-generation Japanese American—and a poet, author, and performance artist. In his memoir, *Where the Body Meets Memory: An Odyssey of Race, Sexuality and Identity,* he attempts to wrestle with the legacy of his parents' silent response to the internment of Japanese Americans during World War II and the effects of these events on his own physical body. He appeals to memory as a source for identity and as an imaginative act of resistance against the silences in American history that would repress the stories and experiences of Japanese Americans. This form of defiance to a dominant national script is subtle and profound. Mura speaks truth to power through the rearticulation of his own narrative, which is also simultaneously his family's story. In this way, he claims his identity as he seeks to write against the wrongs of American history.

Drawing an analogy from Mura's reflection, with its way of configuring identity, writing, and culture, is a fitting entry point for readers of the

Hebrew Bible. The diverse collection of writings that make up the First Testament represents the efforts of communities in Israel's history to preserve their collective memory in all its complexity, contradiction, pain, and power. The Hebrew Bible, however, represents not a single cultural perspective but many. In this way, it is a text of cultures. Moreover, it is not simply a text in the singular but is a compilation of hymns, myths, legal materials, laments, prophetic oracles, and wisdom texts that represent multiple perspectives spanning hundreds of years.

The Hebrew Bible is a culturally complex montage of historical memories. These texts represent the cumulative perspectives of different communities who, over time, made their own claims to be in a significant relationship with their God. If we read those memories and texts synthetically as a single narrative, we perceive the history of a single people that we may call biblical Israel. As we shall see, however, there are other ways to read these texts.

"HEBREW BIBLE," "TANAK," AND "OLD TESTAMENT"

People who adhere to the religious traditions of Judaism, Christianity, and Islam claim the texts of the Hebrew Bible as a significant component of their communal and historical identities, designating them as scriptures. The name for this collection varies among different religions. Modern Jewish communities often use the acronym *TNK,* or *Tanak,* to refer to the threefold structure of the Hebrew Bible. The three divisions are:

- *Torah*, or the Law (though *torah* is better translated "teaching"), which consists of the Five Books of Moses (Genesis through Deuteronomy), also known as the Pentateuch

- *Nebi'im*, or the Prophets, which are organized in the Jewish scriptures to include the "Former Prophets," the books of Joshua, Judges, Samuel, and Kings, as well as the "Latter Prophets," Isaiah, Jeremiah, Ezekiel, and the Twelve (Hosea through Malachi)

- *Kethubim*, or the Writings, a variety of literary genres including liturgical and poetical texts (the Psalms and Song of Songs), Wisdom literature (Proverbs, Ecclesiastes or Qoheleth, and Job), and historical narratives such as Ezra-Nehemiah, Daniel, Esther, Ruth, and Chronicles.

These three divisions are best understood in Judaism as concentric circles with the Torah at the center. The Prophets are the great interpreters of this core tradition. The Writings represent—in song, wisdom, and story—faithful expressions of a life lived under the Torah.

Christians call this collection the Old Testament. The term *testament* is synonymous with "covenant." Jeremiah 31:31-34 refers to a "new covenant" that will be made with the house of Israel and the house of Judah. It is important to note that the twofold designation, New Testament/Old Testament, bears specifically Christian connotations. The Christian understanding of the Bible sees a continuous story that begins with God's covenant with the people of Israel and culminates in the establishment of a new covenant in the person of Jesus of Nazareth. Paul and early Christian traditions used the language of "new" and "old covenants" to articulate their understanding of what God was doing in the person of Jesus Christ (2 Cor 3:5-6). The early Gospel traditions characterize this "new" covenant through Jesus' well-known words at the last supper, "this is my blood of the covenant, which is poured out for many" (Mark 14:24, compare Matt 26:28 and Luke 22:20).

Biblical scholars who are interested in interreligious dialogue have advocated using the term *Hebrew Bible* because it is more descriptive of these writings (although Ezra and Daniel contain sections written in Aramaic, which was the official language

The Hebrew Bible	The Christian Bible
Torah	Law
Prophets	Historical Books
Former Prophets	= Former Prophets +
Latter Prophets	Ruth, 1–2 Chron., Ezra, Neh., Esther)
Writings	Poetry
Psalms, Proverbs, Job	Job, Psalms, Proverbs, Eccles.,
Megillot: Song of Sol., Ruth, Lam.,	Song of Sol.
Eccles., Esther	
Daniel, Ezra-Neh., Chron.	Prophets (= Latter Prophets + Lam., Daniel)

of the Persian Empire during the fifth century BCE) and because it is less a specifically Christian designation. Other Christian scholars choose to use the language of "First" and "Second Testaments" in an attempt to avoid the theological implication that the "new" supersedes the "old": many Christian traditions recognize the Old Testament as their Scripture no less than the New. Still others use religious distinctions such as "Jewish Scriptures" or "Christian Scriptures" (meaning First and Second Testaments together) to highlight the distinctive character of the collections within these two religions. In these ways, people seek to recognize that the Hebrew Bible, which is itself a diverse set of texts with multiple cultural perspectives, also serves as sacred writings for multiple religious traditions, informing and reshaping the cultural identities of different religious communities.

NARRATIVE HISTORY, FORMS, AND SOURCES

The Hebrew Bible tells a story. Though there are multiple authors, sources, and traditions contained within it, the collection as it now stands recounts the journey of a diverse set of peoples and groups, who locate their identity within the narrative history of Israel with its God.

The "Grand Narrative" of the Hebrew Bible

This narrative begins with myths about the beginning of the world in Genesis 1–11 and continues by tracing the story of a particular ancestral line whose descendents will be the Hebrew people: Abraham and Sarah, Isaac and Rebekah, Jacob and his wives Leah and Rachel (Genesis 12–50). When the children of Israel become enslaved in the land of Egypt, the LORD miraculously delivers them at the Sea of Reeds by making a way through the waters (Exodus 1–18). The Hebrew Bible often refers to Israel's God by a proper name represented by the Hebrew consonants y-h-w-h, translated in several English versions as "the LORD." According to Exod 3:13-15, the revelation of this name is tied closely to the memory of the deliverance from Egypt. The LORD makes a covenant with this people at Mount Sinai (Exodus 19–20; in Deuteronomy the mountain is named Horeb), giving them ten words or commandments around which the community is to structure its life together (Exod 20:1-17; see Deut

5:6-21). After sojourning in the wilderness, a place of testing in which the LORD provides for the people's needs (Numbers), the Hebrews invade the land of Canaan and settle there among the peoples of the land (Joshua–Judges).

Eventually, Israel becomes like the surrounding nations in their desire to have a king. The LORD appoints a series of kings (1 and 2 Samuel and 1 and 2 Kings), beginning with Saul, David, and Solomon, and later establishes a central place of worship and political governance at Jerusalem. After Solomon, a struggle for succession ensues, which results in the division of Israel into the Northern Kingdom, which takes the name Israel, and the Southern Kingdom, or Judah, with their respective capitals at Samaria and Jerusalem.

The two kingdoms are eventually conquered by two major empires. Israel falls to the Assyrian Empire in 722 BCE and Judah to Babylon in 587 BCE. The Babylonians destroy the temple and send many of Judah's religious and social elite into exile. After decades in Babylon, a remnant of this elite returns to the province of Judah (in Hebrew, Yehud) following the edict of Cyrus, king of Persia, who conquered the Babylonians in 539 BCE. After much struggle, the people rebuild the temple and establish a new colony in their former homeland.

The Sociocultural and Historical Frame of the Hebrew Bible

Several features of this history reveal the points of view of the biblical authors. These in turn suggest social and cultural contexts that modern interpreters seek to keep in mind as they read the Hebrew Bible.

First, although multiple perspectives are contained within this collection, in their final form they show a marked focus on the history and destiny of the southern kingdom of Judah. Although northern traditions are present in the Pentateuch (Deuteronomy) and within the prophets (Jeremiah

and Hosea), a strong "southern" or Judahite bias can be seen especially in the traditions surrounding King David and in prophets such as Isaiah of Jerusalem (Isaiah 1–39). Second, the geopolitical location of ancient Israel determines both the theological outlook of this grand narrative and its perspectives on the broader history of the ancient Near East. Israel was a very small vassal state within much larger world empires. The periods in which the biblical texts were generated span at least three or four major empires—those of Assyria, Babylon, Persia, and Greece. Egyptian and Hittite empires also played significant roles during this time, given their proximity to ancient Canaan and Israel. Israel was a minority presence, caught in the middle of much larger social and political forces.

Because of this, Israelite theological perspectives can truly be regarded as voices from the margin. Israel's self-identity and understanding of God must be understood within this context of imperialism and colonialism. For example, the Zion traditions, which emphasize God's twofold choice of a place (temple/city) and of a Davidic king, must be interpreted through the lens of a people that were struggling to forge their own identity in the midst of much larger empires. Such biblical themes reflect both Israel's internalized colonial desire to be a kingdom in its own right and a theologically imaginative act of self-definition and defiance of outside powers.

Lastly, the cultures and theologies that make up the Hebrew Bible reflect their engagement with the broader social context of the ancient Near East. Thus, the biblical authors borrowed literary forms and religious themes from Mesopotamian, Canaanite, and Egyptian cultures. Archaeologists have discovered wisdom, prophetic, liturgical, legal, and narrative texts in other ancient cultures that are very similar to what we find in the Bible. These important discoveries help the modern interpreter to understand that ancient Israel was deeply enmeshed with and engaged in its cultural context even as it sought to forge its own sense of identity apart from its neighbors. Moreover, many scholars recognize that most if not all of the earliest Israelites were indigenous Canaanites (see above). Therefore, when the biblical texts make sharp differentiations between Israel and the other peoples in the land of Canaan (as, for example, in Deuteronomy 7), one must understand that such sharp distinctions are the social constructions of later authors. Thus, the people of Israel—through their understandings of God, their religious practices, and their sense of cultural identity—sought to make sense of their particular place in the world by differentiating themselves as unique from other peoples with whom they shared obvious similarities.

THE LITERARY FRAME

The history of composition that I have just described leads scholars to conclude that the Hebrew Bible disrupts its own impression of unity. The Pentateuch, for example, reads on the surface as a continuous story. The careful contemporary reader, however, will recognize that there are many seams in the story, places where the story overlaps itself.

The opening chapters of Genesis provide a good example. Genesis 1:1—2:4a is a creation story, which culminates with God creating humanity on the sixth day and resting on the seventh. The following account, beginning in Gen 2:4b, also contains a creation narrative with a beginning and an end, concluding with humanity's expulsion from the Garden of Eden. Thus, Genesis contains two complete creation stories. However, there are significant differences between these two accounts. In Genesis 2–3, the name of the deity changes from the more generic "God" used in Genesis 1 (*'elohim* in Hebrew) to the proper name of Israel's God, represented in the four Hebrew consonants

YHWH. (Most translations substitute the name of God with the word "Lord," following the Jewish custom of saying *'adonai* rather than pronouncing the name of God.)

The two creation stories also differ in style and form. The first account is liturgical and repetitive; it involves the categorization of the animals; and it contains a particular emphasis on the Sabbath rest (which even God observes). The second, by contrast, has the characteristics of a folk tale; it focuses on the issue of human knowledge and explains why human beings are not immortal. Moreover, the order of creation differs between the two accounts. In the first story, animals are created before the human beings, and humanity is created in the image of God (Gen 1:27) on the sixth day. In the second creation narrative, the Lord creates animals in response to the dilemma of the first human's loneliness: "It is not good that the man should be alone" (Gen 2:18). That is, the Lord creates animals *after* the *'adam*, the first human. Finally, the images of the deity differ in the two accounts. In Gen 1:1—2:4a, *'elohim* is a transcendent god who commands the created order. In Gen 2:4-25, the Lord has humanlike characteristics, forming humanity out of the ground and walking in the garden.

The Diversity of Sources

The textual seams discussed above and many more like them have helped scholars to recognize that the Hebrew Bible is made up of multiple sources that were later edited together to make a more continuous story. In the Pentateuch, for example, biblical scholars have identified four sources:

- The J or Jahwist/Yahwist source, which receives its name because it uses the name of God (*y-h-w-h*) for its designation of the deity, is written from the perspective of the southern kingdom of Judah during the period of the

$$J \text{ (c. 950)} + E \text{ (c. 850)} + D \text{ (c. 622)} + P \text{ (after 587)} = \text{Torah}$$

United Monarchy (c. 950 BCE.). It emphasizes the theme of the promises to the ancestors, which include blessing, land, and progeny.

- The E or Elohist source focuses on the point of view of the northern kingdom of Israel during the Divided Monarchy (c. 850 BCE.). It uses *'elohim* as its name for God. The Elohist stresses themes of prophecy, in which the deity often communicates through intermediary figures such as angels (the Hebrew word for "angel" means messenger). The J and E sources were combined at a later point, after the Northern Kingdom fell to Assyria in 722 BCE, to create a national epic.

- The D or Deuteronomist source, which makes up the majority of the book of Deuteronomy, was written during the reign of King Josiah of Judah (c. 622 BCE) and is distinctive for its emphasis on the theme of the LORD's choice of a centralized location for worship in Jerusalem.

- The P or Priestly source was written in the Babylonian exile (after 587 BCE) and stresses purity laws, the Sabbath, and cultic or worship regulations. There is also a strong covenantal theme within the Priestly source. Some scholars have argued that the Priestly writers were also editors who collected the earlier traditions and combined them into a collection that eventually led to what we now have as the final form of the Pentateuch.

Other well-known stories in the Hebrew Bible such as the flood narrative (Genesis 6–8) and the exodus story (Exodus 14–15) are also composite texts, containing multiple source traditions within the final version of the story.

Unity Out of Diversity

These sources were combined in such a way that a fairly coherent story emerges in the Pentateuch, even as this larger narrative contains evidence of multiple sources through overlapping events, repetitions, and even contradictions. More importantly, the presence of multiple sources suggests to the modern reader that ancient Israel had multiple perspectives and traditions. In the wisdom of the ancient editors, these traditions were incorporated in a way that preserves both their specific messages and theologies, even as each source contributes to the telling of Israel's larger story.

In other sections of the Hebrew Bible we can also see this unity and diversity among the texts. In the prophetic literature, for example, a prophet like Isaiah of Jerusalem (Isaiah 1–39), who promoted a theology of the LORD's double election of a Davidic king and of a temple located in Jerusalem, is placed side by side with Jeremiah, who remained critical of temple theology throughout his prophetic ministry. The result is a tension between the ideal of the LORD's purpose for and protection of the chosen city and the temple authorities' failure of nerve just prior to the Babylonian captivity.

Similarly, in the Wisdom Literature, books like Proverbs maintain a theology of just retribution, where the righteous and wise are blessed and the wicked and foolish are cursed. Books like Job and Ecclesiastes, however, bring into question an oversimplified understanding of this wisdom ideal, observing that sometimes the righteous suffer and the wicked prosper. Even with these differences, however, the Wisdom traditions all maintain the primary place of human experience in their understanding of God's ways, emphasizing the centrality of wisdom in their ponderings of the human condition in God's creation.

A Diversity of Social and Cultural Experiences

Because the formation of the Hebrew Bible spans several hundred years, there are also different types of cultural identity formations evident within the Hebrew Bible. As mentioned earlier, the period of the United Monarchy represented a time when Israel was forging its national identity as a vassal state in the middle of much larger empires. Texts like Deuteronomy and books like Joshua–Kings include older stories and traditions from this period that reflect tensions and struggles among king and court, land-owning elites, prophetic circles, and common people to define the identity and destiny of the nation.

After the Babylonian exile, Israelite identity took up themes of diaspora (or "dispersion") as a displaced people sought to understand itself in the wake of national disaster. Prophetic books like Jeremiah and Ezekiel and the Priestly source in the Pentateuch (see above) address this situation in Israel's history, asking how the people are to relate to the LORD away from their own land and without their own state.

Still later, when a segment of these exiles were permitted by the Persian government to return to their homeland, another set of issues involving cultural identity emerged. How were these returning exiles supposed to relate to those who had remained in the land of Judah all this time? Who were the true Israelites? Books like Ezra, Nehemiah, Chronicles, Ruth, and Esther are best understood within this social-cultural context.

In its multiple sources, traditions, and theological perspectives, then, the Hebrew Bible witnesses to both ancient Israel's unity and diversity. While a larger story emerges from this richly diverse collection of texts, the different perspectives that are represented resist any attempts to see only one Israel, only one story—or only one understanding of God. Israel is, by its very self-definition, a people moving through many different times and situations and thus inevitably taking multiple cultural forms and identities.

Nor should we think of the Hebrew Bible as only a single collection of texts, fixed in time. These texts were taken up, reread, reinterpreted, reorganized, and reappropriated by different communities that laid claim to them practically from the beginning. Among the many traditions active in the first century CE, for example, were communities that treasured different ancient versions: the Samaritan Pentateuch, Aramaic traditions that would be written down in the Targums, and the Septuagint, a Greek translation of Hebrew texts. All these represent early efforts to translate the Hebrew texts, but also to reinterpret them as a way of making them meaningful to a new community, in part by introducing some new materials not present in the Hebrew writings. The ancient texts from Qumran, also known as the Dead Sea Scrolls, included versions of some books (like Jeremiah) that are different from those that appear in our Bibles today. The Scrolls include other, nonbiblical texts as well that were obviously important to the community. It appears the process of collecting and interpreting texts was unique for each ancient community.

Christianity emerged in the first century CE as a particular form of messianic Judaism, around the same period as the rise of the Pharisees, who came, after the destruction of the Second Temple in 70 CE, to emphasize a form of Judaism centered on the teaching and interpretation of Scripture. Within subsequent Christianity, different communions receive the Hebrew Bible in different ways. The Old Testament collections of Roman Catholics and Protestants differ, and neither is identical to the organization of the Jewish *Tanak*.

Hearing Biblical Themes from Different Standpoints

Speaking out of their own historical and cultural experiences, the authors of the chapters that follow provide their own responses to different parts and individual books of the Hebrew Bible. All of these scholars are well versed in the contemporary discipline of biblical studies, which has been decisively shaped by specific developments in European history: the Enlightenment, the Reformation, and the rise of modern science, for example. These developments had particular consequences for the way European and Euro-American Christians came to read the Bible. As the chapters in Part I suggested, these developments led to an emphasis in Western biblical interpretation on the Bible's intelligibility and integrity, a rather individualistic understanding of salvation, and a widespread presumption, manifest especially in the age of European imperialism, colonization, and "missions," that Eurocentric interpretations of the Bible were self-evident and universally valid.

Despite their familiarity with this received scholarly tradition, the authors of the chapters that follow beg to differ with its emphases. They—and the peoples whose experiences have shaped them—have read and heard the Bible differently and often connect with biblical themes in ways very different from the Euro-American tradition. The following observations are meant to highlight some of the distinctive angles of vision you will encounter in Part Two.

Creation and Ancestry

Western interpretation has long been preoccupied with the cosmological aspects of creation in Genesis 1–2, especially as these figure in the exploration of the physical universe and the evolution of life on earth. Christian theology has found in Genesis 3 the basis for doctrines of evil and human sinfulness. Compared to these emphases, the ancestral traditions in Genesis and elsewhere in the Hebrew Bible have received much less attention (except as one or another ancestor has been taken up as an exemplary model of individual faith).

In contrast, many of the earth's peoples, from African, Asian, and Native American cultures, have very explicit religious traditions that connect them to their ancestors. Furthermore, in many of these cultures, the way one finds one's place in the world is directly connected both to accounts of the origins of the world and to accounts of one's ancestors. That is, "creation" and "ancestry" traditions are parts of a seamless whole. To recite the story of one's family origins is simultaneously to rehearse the beginning of the world and to find one's place in it in powerful, life-giving, and healing ways. For persons formed in such cultures, the connections Israel made between the God of creation and the ancestors seems natural. God is not an abstract entity about whom we theorize but is "the God of Abraham, Isaac, and Jacob"—the God of our ancestors.

Exodus and Liberation

The story of the exodus has at its heart a very particular historical memory, yet this is a memory embraced today whenever people gather for the Passover Seder and declare that "with a strong hand the Almighty led *us* out from Egypt, from the house of bondage." The story of the exodus has proven a powerful force beyond Judaism as well, as poor and oppressed peoples and communities of color have identified themselves with the people awaiting deliverance, struggling for it, or rehearsing the precious memory of its attainment. Theologies of liberation—first given voice as authentic expressions of African American and Latin American protest, hope, and exhortation, then taken up in Minjung, Palestinian, Hispanic, Dalit, and many other forms—are oriented around the story of the exodus. Just so, scholars insist, the exodus memory so galvanized the imaginations of generations in Israel that it is rightly regarded as the historical fountainhead of the Hebrew Bible.

Settlement and Invasion

If the exodus story has proven powerfully attractive across cultures, its aftermath is far more troublesome.

The biblical accounts of Israel's "conquest" of the land of Canaan and their violent eradication of the indigenous peoples, carried out at the explicit command of a deity who has "given" the land to Israel, have been played out again and again in colonial history. English colonizers of North America, Boer colonizers of southern Africa, and Jewish settlers in the Palestinian West Bank have all made explicit appeal to the biblical accounts in Joshua and Judges as they have dispossessed peoples and—in the case of North America—destroyed nations. The thematic movement from deliverance to settlement in a "promised land" has proven an almost irresistible paradigm for the notion that military force can determine the course of history and achieve ultimate peace. Needless to say, those who have suffered the transfer of these ideas to their own lands hear the biblical language of promises for Israel with great ambivalence.

Monarchy

Israel's story of the rise of its greatest king, David, from humble beginnings, through tests of courage, integrity, and wits, to political and military triumph proved intoxicating to European fantasies of the ideal king. The point of the biblical sequel—David's corruption through power and the resulting destruction of his family and his dynasty—have proven less influential in the West, although the themes seem just as applicable. Historians and archaeologists have shown that the real kingdom of David was far more modest than the biblical accounts suggest. From the experience of colonization, advocates of postcolonial theory suggest that we understand biblical accounts of David's glory as manifestations of internalized colonization. That is—to quote the Bible itself—Israel's desire for a powerful king sprang from their longing to be "like other nations" (1 Sam 8:5). That desire led the small nation into entangling relationships as the vassal of

powerful surrounding empires—a phenomenon all too well known in our own world today.

Prophecy

Though the theological tradition of Western Christianity has tended to mine the writings of the prophets for predictions of Jesus Christ, the prophetic books are clearly less interested in predicting the distant future than in warning and exhorting the people about the more imminent consequences of their collective actions. The political dimension of Hebrew prophecy has not been lost on marginalized and disfranchised communities. As the Bible presents it, the prophetic call to justice is always a call for *social* justice—in the streets, in the markets, in the courts. And it is always contested by the powerful and those who represent their interests (whom the Bible calls "false prophets"). These themes are hardly mysterious to peoples today who have suffered injustice and cry out for vindication against powerful oppressors.

But just such experiences of shared injustice and oppression can be internalized, as if exploitation and violence are all the poor and oppressed deserve. When the prophets speak of the judgment of God or identify the overwhelming power of neighboring empires as the will of God, are they giving voice to the same experience of internalized oppression?

Exile and Restoration

The biblical theme of exile resonates powerfully with many of the world's peoples who have been colonized in their own lands, dispossessed from their homes, resettled in refugee camps or interned as politically suspicious, expelled from their own countries or kidnapped and sold into slavery in distant lands. The powerful and immediate connection such persons feel with biblical passages that describe exile may be beyond the imagination of others who have only heard of such experiences second hand. But people who have lived under colonial rule or in client states serving powerful foreign interests are often not romantic about the biblical themes of exile and restoration. Biblical scholars point out that the Hebrew Bible was given its final shape in the period when Judah was under Persian colonial rule—by scribes who played a vital role in maintaining the equilibrium of colonial power. It is easier for communities who have known dispossession to identify with cries of lament than to welcome the message that a new regime rules by the will of God.

Some of the most poignant tensions evident between writings in the Hebrew Bible—for example, between Ezra and Nehemiah on one hand and Jonah and Ruth on the other—reflect social tensions within Israel under Persian rule. Issues of community purity, group boundaries, and the people's right to live on the land were implicated in the delicate negotiations with the colonial power. Contemporary immigrant communities—where nostalgia for "the old country" and belonging to "our people" struggle against the requirements of survival in an often hostile environment—provide unique vantage points for understanding these biblical texts.

Wisdom and History

Israel's wisdom tradition has often been an afterthought in Western biblical theology. In many marginalized communities, however, the wisdom of the community's elders is prized. The experiences of those who have gone before us and the wisdom and knowledge they have attained are the foundation upon which we and our descendants thrive and renew ourselves. Wisdom has often appeared too static to Western thinkers absorbed with loftier ideals of the powerful and purposeful movement of history, but for peoples who have suffered great harm as the wheels of history have ground forward, the wisdom of the past appears far more life-giving.

Worship

The Western tradition, especially Protestant Christianity, has put a premium in worship on preaching and the prophetic word. This has sometimes meant appealing to the rational and industrious individual, moving him—it has usually been *him*!—to carry out God's will on earth. For other communities, however—communities of color, immigrant communities, communities of the poor—the invitation to realize the realm of God in our midst has had little to do with enjoying the power to shape the course of history. It has had more to do with the ecstatic sharing of joy, pain, sorrow, and hope with our neighbors. Worship is the context in which we knit together our daily experiences in the presence of God. We rehearse and receive again our identities as members of a community and as a people among nations. Worship is the means by which we experience healing and renewal—a genuine coming back from the dead and living into the glory that is already breaking into our present suffering.

The point of these observations is not to draw hard and fast lines of distinction and separation. Rather it is to invite readers both to explore the experiences of others and to examine their own perspectives. How we read has much to do with how our cultural and historical experiences have formed us.

This doesn't mean that we interpret the Bible, or reflect on how we interpret the Bible, for its own sake. Rather, in many of our communities we read the Bible against a broader horizon: our common efforts to bring about greater equality, more harmonious relationships, and deeper respect for human dignity. How we shape the world in which our children will follow us may have much to do with how we read; and when we read, we always read from our own particular place in the world. ❖

❖ TIMELINE FOR THE HEBREW BIBLE ❖

9000–8000 BCE   NATUFIAN CULTURE (STONE AGE)
The earliest culture whose artifacts have been recovered in modern Israel.

6000–4000   NEOLITHIC (NEW STONE AGE)
Pottery emerges c. 5000.

4000–3200   CHALCOLITHIC (COPPER) AGE

3200–3000   ESDRAELON AGE

3000–2100   EARLY BRONZE AGE (EB)
The Egyptian Old Kingdom lasted c. 2700–2200; the Akkadian Empire, 2400–2200. Sumerian city-states, including Ur, flourished 2800–2400. The cultural practices found in the stories of **Abraham, Isaac, and Jacob** lead some scholars to date the ancestral period as early as the end of this period (EB IV, 2300–2100). Others place them in the Middle or Late Bronze Age.

2100–1550   MIDDLE BRONZE AGE (MB)

1550–1200   LATE BRONZE AGE (LB)
Moses and the exodus are most often dated to the rule of Ramses II (1290–1224, in the Egyptian New Kingdom).

1200–900   EARLY IRON AGE (IRON I)

     1200–1150   (Iron Age Ia). Settlements in the hill country point to the beginnings of ancient Israel.

     1150–1025   (Iron Age Ib). Period of the **Judges**.

1025–950	(Iron Age Ic). Rise of the Israelite monarchy (**Saul, David, Solomon**). 1 Sam 13:19-22 indicates that in the early days of Saul, the Philistine cities along the coast held a monopoly on iron; Israel was effectively still in the Bronze Age.
c. 1000	David captures the Jebusite city of Jerusalem and takes it for his capital; he ceremonially appropriates the Ark of the Covenant. David's reign deteriorates into civil war against his son Absalom. Traditions favoring David (1 Samuel 16—2 Samuel 5 and in 2 Samuel 9—1 Kings 2) are developed.
c. 950	After Absalom's death, Solomon succeeds David. The earliest saga of Israel's history, the **Yahwist** epic, may have been written in Solomon's court.
950–900	(Iron Age Id). Division of the monarchy into north (Israel) and south (Judah). Alternative northern traditions of Israel's history (such as the **Elohist** source) are developed.
900-600	**MIDDLE IRON AGE (IRON II)**
800–700	(Iron IIb). Expansion of the Assyrian empire (1100–612) to the west prompts anxieties in Israel and Judah, addressed by the eighth-century prophets **Amos, Hosea, Micah,** and **Isaiah of Jerusalem.**
734–702	Syro-Ephraimite War, in which kings Rezin of Syria and Pekah of the northern kingdom of Israel invade Judah. King Ahaz, the southern king, appeals to Tiglath-Pileser III and later pays tribute to Assyria. This conflict is the context for Isaiah 7–8. The story is recounted, with a strong Judahite bias, in 2 Kgs 16:5-18.
722	Northern Kingdom falls to the Assyrian Empire; northern traditions such as those found in **Deuteronomy** begin to migrate south to Judah; surviving northern traditions eventually inform a distinctive Samaritan form of Judaism.
701	Sennacherib, king of Assyria, invades Judah.

622	**Josiah's** reforms, including the centralization of worship in Jerusalem; the "book of the law" (2 Kgs 22:8) was probably the core of **Deuteronomy.** Traditions originally from prophetic circles in the Northern Kingdom are incorporated into an extensive history of Israel (an early version of the **Deuteronomistic History**, as found in Joshua—2 Kings).
612–539	Chaldean or Neo-Babylonian Empire, beginning with the defeat of the Assyrian Empire and the fall of its capital city, Nineveh, to a coalition of forces including the Medes and Chaldeans. In Jerusalem, prophets like **Jeremiah** and **Ezekiel** warn of coming judgment, then live through it with their people.
587–586	Judah falls to Babylon and its king, Nebuchadrezzar (or Nebuchadnezzar). The Babylonians, following the practice of the Assyrians before them toward conquered peoples, force members of the ruling class into exile in Babylon. There priestly circles produce the "Holiness Code" and an early **Priestly** version of the Torah.

600–300   IRON III (LATE IRON OR PERSIAN)

539–333	The Persian Empire, beginning with the defeat of the Neo-Babylonian Empire by Cyrus (hailed as the messiah of God by **Second Isaiah** in Isaiah 40–55).
520–515	The temple is rebuilt. The story of this reconstruction effort is depicted in **Nehemiah.** Beginning of the Second Temple Period.
c. 450	Restoration of Judah under Persian hegemony: **Nehemiah, Ezra,** and **Ruth.** Priestly circles create the final form of the Torah and the Prophets (incorporating the Deuteronomistic History, the Former Prophets, and the books of the Latter Prophets). Wisdom circles produce **Proverbs, Job,** and **Ecclesiastes.**

300–63 HELLENISTIC PERIOD

167–64: Judas Maccabeus leads a Jewish revolt against the Seleucid king Antiochus IV "Epiphanes." The revolt establishes an independent Jewish kingdom (the Hasmonean dynasty) and restores worship in the temple (Hanukkah). **Daniel** is written during this period.

63 BCE—323 CE ROMAN PERIOD

In 63 BCE, Pompey marches into Jerusalem and deposes the Hasmonean prince, establishing Roman lordship over Judea. The first century CE will see the rise of Christianity, the First Jewish Revolt (66–70), and the destruction of Jerusalem, including the temple in 70.

Chapter 12

The Torah (or Pentateuch)

Introduction to the

Pentateuch

Frank M. Yamada

The first five books of the Hebrew Bible or Old Testament (Genesis–Deuteronomy) are generally called the Pentateuch among Christians and some biblical scholars. In Jewish tradition the Five Books of Moses are known as the Torah. The Hebrew word *torah* literally means "teaching" or "instruction" and refers to what is the heart of the Hebrew Scriptures in both content and importance. The story lines within this collection stretch from the creation of the world and humanity to Moses's last speech on the plains of Moab as the Israelites prepare to enter into the land of promise. The Pentateuch, however, contains various forms of literature from many time periods. These five books have played a formative role in the religious beliefs and imagination of many Christian, Jewish, and Muslim traditions. The Pentateuch has also been one of the primary points of emphasis in modern biblical scholarship. In fact, one can trace the developments in the scholarly study of the Bible by surveying the history of Pentateuchal research. With such well-known stories as Adam and Eve in the Garden of Eden, Noah and the flood, the *Akedah* (or "Binding" of Isaac), the exodus, the Ten Commandments, and God's provision of manna in the wilderness, it is no wonder that these texts have inspired generations of people for millennia.

One must distinguish between the narrative arc found within the Pentateuch, beginning with creation and ending on the plains of Moab, and the historical contexts out of which the traditions in these books emerge. Historically, scholars agree that the Pentateuch is a compilation of sources, traditions, folktales, and legal material from different historical periods. Four primary sources have been identified within Genesis–Deuteronomy. The J and E sources, Yahwist and Elohist respectively, also known as the Epic Tradition, make up the main story line of the Pentateuch narrative. Both sources were written during the Israelite monarchy. Whereas the Yahwist source contains the perspective of the Southern Kingdom of Judah, the Elohist reflects ideas and themes associated with Israel, the Northern Kingdom. The J story line begins in the Garden of Eden (Gen 2:4b) and extends into Israel's journey through the Sinai wilderness. The D, for Deuteronomic, source is comprised of significant portions of the book of Deuteronomy and was written largely during the time of Josiah's reign (late-seventh century BCE). Finally, the P, for Priestly, document contains mostly cultic, genealogical, and narrative material written by a priestly school or group after the Babylonian exile (587 BCE). Genesis begins with the Priestly account of creation and its well-known phrase, "In the beginning…" (Gen 1:1). Hebrew scholars differ on exactly how that phrase should be translated.

Because of this complex textual process, the resulting five books are a richly diverse collection

that includes many different and even conflicting perspectives within it. For example, the Priestly account of creation depicts a well-ordered creation, with a sovereign God (*Elohim* in Hebrew) who structures the natural order through divine command. In this first creation story, plants and animals are created before humans, with humans made last as the climax of God's work. Immediately following the P version, the Yahwist's account of creation begins (Gen 2:4b) in a garden. The deity, represented by the divine name ("LORD" in most translations), forms humanity out of the ground. Animals are created *after* the human in response to Adam's need for companionship (Gen 2:18). Both accounts are self-contained creation stories. They provide different points of emphasis and depart from each other in significant ways—different names and images of the deity, different order of creation, and so on. Both accounts, however, are included in the biblical witness without significant editing to blur the variations. Thus the diverse and complex nature of the Pentateuch suggests that the final form of this collection was intended to reflect and keep in tension the various traditions that made up Israel's historical self-understanding. It is important to note, however, that textual versions such as the Samaritan Pentateuch, the Septuagint (a Greek translation), and fragments from the Dead Sea Scrolls represent different lines of tradition and thus point to other communities with textual traditions of their own.

The basic structure of the Pentateuch follows a narrative progression from creation to the journey of a particular ancestral family that becomes a nation. Here is an outline:

Genesis: Creation to the ancestors
    Genesis 1–11: Stories about creation
        and early humanity
    Genesis 12–50: Stories about the ancestors

Exodus: Liberation from Egypt to revelation
at Sinai
Exodus 1:1—15:21: Exodus from Egypt
Exodus 15:22—40:38: Journeys in the
wilderness and revelation at Sinai

Leviticus: Revelation at Sinai continued
Leviticus 1:1—27:34: Laws concerning
worship and holiness

Numbers: Wanderings in the wilderness
Numbers 1:1—25:18: The first
generation in the wilderness
Numbers 26:1—36:13: The second
generation in the wilderness

Deuteronomy: Re-proclamation of the
covenant
Deuteronomy 1:1—30:20: Moses re-
proclaims the covenant
Deuteronomy 31:1—34:12: Moses's
farewell and death

The plotline of the Pentateuch starts universally, beginning with the creation of the world and humanity. Genesis 1–11 contains universal stories about the beginning of human civilization and addresses common themes such as mortality and death (Gen 3, Garden of Eden), violence between human beings (Gen 4, Cain and Abel), God's comprehensive judgment through flood (6–9), and the creation of different languages and cultures (Gen 11, Tower of Babel). In 12–50, the narrative focuses on the particular family line of Abraham and Sarah, from whom God promises to make a great nation (Gen 12:2). This couple's progeny eventually become the tribes of Israel. A persistent theme throughout the ancestral stories is how the divine promise reaches fulfillment in spite of the circumstances and human decisions that threaten it. The theme of barrenness is frequent and appears in the

stories of Sarah, Rebekah, and Rachel. In each case, God eventually opens the woman's womb. The most significant story that involves an endangerment of the promise is in Genesis 22, where God tests Abraham by asking him to sacrifice his son, Isaac, as a burnt offering.

At the end of Genesis, Jacob and his family migrate south to Egypt, where Joseph had found favor in the household of Pharaoh. The book of Exodus begins with how the Israelites fell out of favor with a later pharaoh and were subjugated to slavery. Exodus 1–15 describes how the LORD delivers Israel from their bondage in Egypt. After a series of plagues, the Israelites are released. The climax of Israel's liberation occurs with the event at the sea, where the LORD delivers them miraculously. In the wilderness of Sinai, Moses receives the revelation of God, which will become the basis of Israelite community (Exod 19:1—34:35). The book of Leviticus, an extensive collection of laws with a primary focus on worship, is placed in the middle of the Torah and is set in the context of God's revelation at Sinai. The largest section of the book, 17:1—26:46, known as the Holiness Code, stresses this theme repeatedly. God's people are to be holy just as the LORD their God is holy (Lev 19:2).

The book of Numbers moves the narrative plot forward from the Mount Sinai event and tells of the people's wanderings in the wilderness. Themes of sin and rebellion recur in these stories, resulting in judgment and death. An entire generation of Israelites perishes in the wilderness journeys. Standing in tension with the theme of human rebellion is the equally persistent idea of God's provision in the wilderness. The LORD provides both water and manna to sustain the people on their journey. Numbers ends with a new generation poised to enter into God's promises and ready to go into the land.

In Deuteronomy, the Pentateuch concludes with Moses's final speech to Israel prior to their entrance into Canaan. The book contains a re-proclamation of the covenant that the LORD made with Israel on Mount Horeb, Deuteronomy's term for Sinai. The themes of Deuteronomy, however, are more than a simple rearticulation of earlier ideas. The book emphasizes the distinct character of Israel and its God. One of the primary motifs in the book is found in Deut 6:4-5, known as the Shema (*shema* in Hebrew is the first word in this passage and means "hear" or "listen"). The passage reads: "Hear, O Israel: The LORD is our God, the LORD alone. You shall love the LORD your God with all your heart, and with all your soul, and with all your might." The LORD is one, and therefore the people of Israel should be one and should worship the LORD exclusively. In practice this means that the people of Israel are to distinguish themselves from other nations in their community and worship. Similarly, they should worship in a central place of the LORD's choosing. As the last of the five books of Moses, Deuteronomy serves as a transition. It ends with the death of Moses, the pivotal figure who led the young nation out of Egypt. Moses is the central character in the Pentateuch, the Israelite prophet par excellence (compare Deut 34:10-12). His death marks the end of an era and hence is an appropriate conclusion to the Pentateuch. But the trajectories in Deuteronomy are central in the Former Prophets that follow. Many of Deuteronomy's themes can be found in Joshua, Judges, 1 and 2 Samuel, and 1 and 2 Kings. It is useful to think of Deuteronomy as a fulcrum point between the Pentateuch and the Former Prophets: it concludes the Torah and anticipates the continuing story of Israel.

The Pentateuch includes many possible points of entry for Asian American readers and communities of color in general. I am a *Sansei*, a third-generation Japanese American. The individual stories within these first five books have been a rich resource for the Asian American communities of which I have been a part. The theme of *ancestors* reminds us that our beliefs, religious practice,

and culture are not accidents but were preserved and maintained through the actions of those who came before us. As an Asian American reader, I am struck by the fact that the Torah chooses to tell its history not only through the lens of national events but through the particular struggles and triumphs of ancestors. Early missionaries to Asia discouraged the practice of ancestor worship, a community and family ritual that is common in many cultures of the world, including Asia. The biblical witness, however, while stopping short of the worship of ancestors, emphasizes the important role of ancestral faith and belief. In fact, the Torah tells its story primarily through the vehicle of ancestral lineage. When the LORD remembers Israel, who is suffering from the bondage of slavery in Egypt, the reason for God's remembrance is located in the promises made to the ancestors. In fact, the LORD is identified as "the God of Abraham, the God of Isaac, and the God of Jacob" (Exod 3:6).

Another important theme for this Asian American reader is found in the exodus. Following in the footsteps of African American interpreters and Latin American liberation theologians, many Asian Americans have continued to find meaning in the story of God's liberation of Israel from Egypt. The image of a God who liberates oppressed peoples continues to inspire communities that have experienced hostility within American society. The Asian American experience is one of exclusion. Legislation such as the Chinese Exclusion Act of 1882, which sought to restrict immigration to the United States, and government-sanctioned racism, as seen in the internment of Japanese Americans during World War II, points to a history of prejudice and fear toward people of Asian descent. In the first decade of the twenty-first century, South Asians who live in the United States have become targets of violence and hate crimes. The biblical idea of a God who liberates and sides with the oppressed provides a strong theological image from which the Asian American community can continue to build its self-understanding. Just as God loves justice and sides with those who are oppressed, so too Asian American community can be built on themes of liberation, siding with those in any community who suffer from injustice or prejudice at the hands of others. ❖

GENESIS

Randall C. Bailey

As the first book in the Hebrew Bible, Genesis speaks to beginnings. It opens with two differing stories on the creation of the universe (1:1—2:4a) and of the earth (2:4b-25). It contains narratives of the first family (chs. 3–4), first city (11:1-9), and the beginnings of the Hebrew people (chs. 12–50). Scholars have long noted how the creation story in Genesis 1 and the flood stories in chapters 6–9 are patterned on similar stories found in ancient Mesopotamia and how the creation story in Genesis 2 is patterned on creation stories in ancient Egypt. This borrowing from other cultures was common. As 2:10-14 claims, the Garden of Eden extended from Africa (ancient Cush/Ethiopia) to Mesopotamia (Euphrates River). All ancient cultures presented creation as controlled by their god(s) and set in their own backyards. Similarly, the idea of the seas being gathered into "one place" (1:9) is explained by people's knowledge of the Mediterranean. While the story line of Genesis goes from a *universal* story of the beginning (chs. 1–5) and rebeginning (chs. 6–11) of humanity to a story of a *particular* people, the descendants of Abram/Abraham (12–50), many different nations, cultures, and ethnicities are mentioned and engaged. The Table of Nations (Genesis 10) is an attempt to describe the interrelatedness of nations in the "known world" by depicting them as the descendants of Noah's three sons, Japheth, Ham, and Shem. Within the stories of Abraham's descendants are stories of the beginnings of Israel's neighbors, the Moabites and Ammonites (19:37-8), Ishmaelites (21:17-18), and the Edomites (36:1). In this way there is a claim that these nations were tribally related to Israel just as Lot, Ishmael, and Esau were related to Abraham and Jacob, though they were not from Israel, the line that God favored.

These stories were composed in a society that valued men more than women. The lists of generations in Genesis 4–5 and 29:31—30:24 are lists primarily of men. The promises made by God for a great nation stemming from Abraham are given to men (12:1-3; 15:7-21; 28:13-15). Divine promises to women are about giving birth to sons (16:11-12; 25:23). The women who are important characters in the story—for example, Sarah in 21:9-11 and Rebekah in 27:6-9, 46—are all depicted as trying to ensure a social place for their sons. Polygamy was the basic form of family assumed in the stories about the ancestors. God is depicted as male and is referred to as the God of Abraham (24:42), the God of Abraham and Isaac (28:13), or the God of your father (43:23; 46:3) and never as the God of your mother(s). Finally, the sign of the covenant for Israel, circumcision, is only given to the men (17:10-12a).

In the society in which these stories were written, it was normal for people to own slaves. Sarai/Sarah has an Egyptian slave, Hagar (16:1). Abraham has a slave, Eliezer (15:2). Laban gives his daughters female slaves as marriage presents (29:24, 29). Potiphar buys Joseph as a slave (39:1). All these slaves are exploited sexually. The women are forced to have sex with the slave master to produce children (16:2, 4; 30:3-12), and the male slaves have to be circumcised and service their slave masters (17:12; 24:2). As an African American, whose people were enslaved in the United States, I am always concerned about such passages in the Bible that present slave society as acceptable to the people and God of the Book. Bible translators often soften this abuse of slaves by calling these characters "servants" or maids. But such distinctions reflect the translators' embarrassment about the text, not the true social and cultural distinctions of those ancient societies.

Finally, some of the stories found in Genesis have played a major role in supporting political positions. Environmentalists adopt the biblical idea of God calling the creation "good" in Genesis 1. The divine curses on Adam and Eve (3:16-19) have been used to support concepts of men controlling women and their bodies. The so-called "Curse of Ham" (9:26-27)—really a set of curses on Canaan— was used to sanction the enslavement of Africans in Europe and the Americas. The destruction of Sodom and Gomorrah has been interpreted as a story of homosexuality rather than one of the sexual exploitation of daughters (19:8, 26, 33, 36) and has been used to sanction the oppression of gays and lesbians. The Lord's killing of Onan because he ended sex with Tamar before climax (38:9-10) is used as an argument against masturbation and contraceptives.

The good news about Genesis is that as we read the book, we have much to discuss, especially as it relates to our own lives, views of God, humanity, and the world in which we live. As we continue to interpret this richly diverse collection of texts, we engage interpreters past and present and participate in an ongoing dialogue with ancients and contemporaries who seek to locate their place in the world from "the beginning." ❖

EXODUS

Jorge Pixley

The book of Exodus is the centerpiece of the Torah (or Pentateuch)—the five books of Moses that begin the Hebrew Scriptures, for Christians the Old Testament. Exodus tells the story of how YHWH, the God of Israel, freed a group of slaves in Egypt and brought them to YHWH's chosen mountain in the desert to give them laws by which they should live. It is the foundational story of the people of Israel, celebrated to this day by the Jews on Passover. These liberated people will become, says YHWH, a special property (*segullah*) among all the peoples of the earth (19:5). Much of the Torah is devoted to the laws revealed at Sinai so that this special people might share the holiness of YHWH. That Exodus is so foundational for Jewish identity makes this a difficult book for many Christians to identify with—unless they are poor or oppressed Christians in Latin America and other places around the world.

The content of Exodus can be characterized in three great sections. In chapters 1–15, YHWH hears the cries of the oppressed slaves in Egypt and calls a prophet, Moses, to lead them to freedom. God had promised Moses that he would give the people land in Canaan (3:8), but when they escape from Egypt they find themselves in a desert. Chapters 15–18 describe the formative experience of the people's wanderings in the desert that lead them to the "wilderness of Sinai" (19:1). Next, in chapters 19–40, comes the third and longest section, the revelation of laws to guide the life of the people in their new social situation—to assure that they act justly toward one another *and* maintain the holiness of YHWH.

READING EXODUS IN LATIN AMERICA

I am the son of a medical doctor and a nurse who worked in a Baptist Hospital in Managua, Nicaragua. Though I am a U.S. citizen, my schooling through high school was done in Managua in Spanish. Later, my work with peasant native communities in Mexico, at the Seminario Bautista de México and the Instituto Teológico de Estudios Superiores, opened my eyes to the reality of most rural peoples of the world. I became convinced that if the Christian gospel had nothing for *them*, it had nothing at all. In his *Notebooks of 1858* and in *Capital*, Karl Marx gave a theoretical framework, and liberation theology gave the theological basis for a word to these poor.

Many Christian readers of the Bible in Latin America—and almost all of the Native (Indian) communities here—are peasants. Peasants are people who feel wedded to the land, of which they feel they are a part. They produce much of their own food and clothing, selling some surplus production in grains and animals to meet needs they cannot supply for themselves, such as salt and shoes. But with the penetration of capitalist agribusiness in the last one hundred years, they have seen their way of life threatened—and in many cases destroyed—by imported grains, which sell for less than their costs

of production, and by the sale and use of fertilizers and pesticides that were unnecessary in their traditional way of producing food. Many believe that Monsanto, Cargill, Dole, and other multinational corporations have driven them off land that God gave them, forcing them into urban slums.

These peasants, whether living on the land or displaced into slums, are a majority of the Bible readers in Latin America; it was among them that liberation theology emerged. With little economic sophistication, they nevertheless readily identify their oppressor as Neoliberalism or globalization. Those are *today's* names for Pharaoh as the peasants read Exodus in the context of their cultural situation. As the enslaved peasants of Egypt cried for liberation from Pharaoh, Latin America's peasants cry for liberation from Neoliberalism and the effects of economic globalization.

Others, including many of Latin America's more urbanized Christians, believe the root cause of their problems is control of their economies and political life by the world's leading imperial power, the United States. That empire, by determining what they should produce, destroys their *internal* national markets. It often determines what their democracy should look like, thus uprooting their political life from national realities. When things do not satisfy the U.S. empire, its troops or proxies intervene by destroying their coca fields or making certain that Latin American debts are directed to the "right" creditors. So, at the beginning of the twenty-first century, Pharaoh for them is the United States, and liberation means freedom from bondage to the United States; figures like Fidel Castro and Hugo Chávez become to them like Moses and Aaron.

THE COMPOSITION OF EXODUS

The original story of the exodus from Egypt— as opposed to the story narrated in the book—

must have arisen, and been told and retold, among the peasant people who rose up against the kings of the Canaanite plains and emigrated to the underpopulated hills of Canaan. That is the influential interpretation that Norman Gottwald proposed in his book *The Tribes of Yahweh* (1979). The laws of the so-called Covenant Code (20:22—23:19), though probably put together later in the monarchical period,

still reflect aspects of peasant life, the life of the original tellers of the exodus story.

The book of Exodus owes its present form to the scribes of Yehud (Judah), which was a Persian province from 538 to 322 BCE. Under priestly dominance, laws that make up the bulk of Exodus 24:15—40:38, what scholars call the Priestly Code, became prominent as the people strove to maintain their holiness under foreign hegemony. ❖

◼ LEVITICUS ◼

Madeline McClenney-Sadler

Leviticus, the third book of the Pentateuch, positioned between Exodus and Numbers, is one of the least studied books in contemporary churches. However, it is one of the most important books if we desire to understand the ethical system and religious practices of the Hebrew people, delivered by God from Egyptian bondage. In Hebrew, its title is the first word of the book, *wayyiqrā'*—"and he called." In the Greek translation of this book, its title is *Levitikon*, which probably refers generally to priestly ideals and issues. Leviticus, the English title, is the Latin rendering of the Greek.

We know that Leviticus was carefully copied over the centuries, because fragments found at Qumran do not reveal any meaningful variations from the much later manuscripts of the Masoretic tradition. The book's contents reveal stratification; that is, there are multiple layers reflecting multiple life settings. Thus, we do not need to assign the entire book of Leviticus to any one period or provide a single date for its composition, though much of the terminology of Leviticus points toward a preexilic date, during the First Temple period. Scholars

divide the book's chapters in different ways to study its content:

1–7	Sacrificial System
8–10	Ordination of Priests
11–16	System of Purity and Impurity
17–26	Holiness Code
27	Appendix

Or it may be divided into two sections:

1–16	Manual for Priests
17–27	Teachings Addressed to the Israelite People

The key to understanding Leviticus is to remember that the first half of the book provides instructions for priests, and the second half provides instructions about how the Israelites should live and treat one another. Its emphasis on holiness and holy behavior is a timeless admonition for believers all over the world. For the priests who recorded Leviticus 17–26, holiness must govern sexual relationships, relationships with strangers, relationships with enemies, and relationships with foreigners. Chapter 19 is where we first find a word from heaven that is timeless: "love your neighbor as yourself" (19:18). That is repeated in the New Testament, and Jesus introduced it as one of the two greatest commandments (Mark 12:31).

Holiness is an important touchstone in many churches and especially in many African American churches. To be holy is to love one's neighbor, even if the neighbor happens to be an enemy. The rationale for the pursuit of holiness is simple: we must be holy because God is holy (19:2). In this way, we may read Leviticus as constructing cultural identity through its religious and ethical ideals. Religious values are often a significant factor in the shaping of ethnic and racial identity. The book of Leviticus provides us with such an example, as holiness becomes a marker that defines the community of God's people and governs their interactions with one another.

My own reading of the Hebrew Scriptures has been shaped by many people and perspectives: a southern Baptist mother and an Episcopalian father, a conservative college campus ministry, liberation and womanist theology, feminism, and doctoral training in the Hebrew Scriptures. If I had to select the single most important theological influence on my understanding of Scripture, however, it would be the theological reflections of men and women I met at the homeless shelter on Second and D Street between 1986 and 1993. With particular regard to the themes of holiness in the book of Leviticus, I contend that all of us should grapple with what it might mean to be holy as we pass by a person in need on the street. Many of our homeless brothers and sisters are trying to return home from prison. The biblical precepts are clear: they require that we love homeless and formerly incarcerated persons—I might add: by any means necessary. I dedicate this introduction to homeless and formerly incarcerated friends everywhere. ❖

NUMBERS

Wilda C. Gafney

The stories in Numbers are a continuation of the exodus saga. Many of the most familiar stories from the wilderness sojourn of the Israelites occur in Numbers. Examples include the presence of the pillar of cloud and fire; provision of quails, the appearance of poisonous serpents, and a healing sculpted serpent; the sending of spies into Canaan; and murmuring and wandering on the part of the people. As the conclusion of the narrative that began in Exodus—and following a lengthy sermonic interlude formed by Leviticus—Numbers is significant

for anyone interested in the theme of liberation in the Hebrew Scriptures.

I approach the biblical narrative as an African American woman with feminist commitments. My identity, like all identities, is complex and constructed. As an African American Christian, I have been socialized to read the text from the dominant perspective and to identify with the Israelites—but that is an ironic posture for anyone in the African diaspora. While the Israelites are Afro-Asiatic, the Egyptians are continental Africans. The traditional and dominant interpretation of the exodus saga among U.S. and European Christians characterizes the Africans as enemies of God's people. The exodus story that is continued in Numbers is read as liberative for Jewish, African American, Feminist, Queer, and many other readers. But it is not liberative for indigenous readers. Native peoples in the Americas as well as colonized peoples in Asia and Africa encounter a text in which God dispossesses the inhabitants of the land. In the history of American expansion and European colonization, the broader Exodus narrative was used to justify invasion, slavery, colonization, segregation, and other violent intercultural practices.

Numbers gets its English title from its Greek version, *Arithmoi*. The book's Hebrew title, *BeMidbar*—"In the Wilderness"—comes from the fifth word (in Hebrew) in the first verse. The name *Numbers* in Greek, Latin, English, and other translations comes from the census that begins the book (1:1-4). This census, really a military muster (as are those in chapters 4 and 26), is a reminder that in spite of claims of a divine promise, entry into an inhabited land will not be seamless, or bloodless.

Among the more significant—but less familiar—narratives in Numbers are: a ritual for establishing the guilt of a suspected adulteress in 5:11-31; the establishment (and revision) of a community rule for female and male Nazirites in 6:1-8 and 30:1-5; Moses's questioning of God's parenting skills in chapter 11; conflict between Miriam, Moses, and Aaron in chapter 12; the fire-serpent and fire-serpent sculpture in 21:4-9 (described by Rabbi Arthur Waskow as a "copper copperhead"); the story of Balaam the gentile prophet in chapters 22–24; the stories of Mahlah, Noah, Hoglah, Milcah, and Tirzah—the women for whom traditional inheritance law was changed—in 27:1-11 and 36:1-12; and the initiation of rape-marriage, in which young girls are abducted and forced into marriage, in 31:1-20.

Numbers marks the end of the exodus journey and the beginning of Israelite self-determination. It also marks the passage into death—and not yet into the Promised Land—of the first generation to experience liberation. Numbers ends with the emergence of a new generation who will experience the fulfillment of the promise of liberation, eventually. However, the books of Joshua and Judges have very different portraits of how this liberation was experienced. ❖

DEUTERONOMY

Frank M. Yamada

Deuteronomy is the fifth book in the Pentateuch. The name of the book comes from Greek and means "second law." The Hebrew name is *'elleh haddebarim*, "these are the words." Both of these names point to two different aspects of the book. In Jewish tradition, there is only one Torah. However, this

last book of the Five Books of Moses represents a preached law, or a re-situating of Israel's covenant with its God for a new setting and a later generation. The Hebrew title comes from the first two words of the book and is descriptive of the contents. Deuteronomy is written as the final speech—or series of speeches—from Moses. Hence, it represents a last will and testament of this legendary leader of Israel.

The book is set on the plains of Moab prior to the children of Israel's entrance into the land of Canaan. In this way, Deuteronomy is a boundary document. It attempts to set forth Israel's identity, grounded firmly in God's revelation on the mountain, as the people seek to enter into God's promises made to the ancestors. As Israel is about to cross borders into a new land, Moses reminds the people of their distinctiveness, constructing boundaries for Israel's identity as a chosen community.

In 2 Kings 22–23, a "book of the law" is found in the temple during the reign of Josiah. The young king proceeds to reform the religious life of Israel according to the stipulation of this document, presumably with the assistance of his advisers, since he was only eight years old. Among the many named counselors are Jedidah, his queen mother (2 Kgs 22:1), and Huldah, the court prophet (2 Kgs 22:16-20), the latter providing the definitive word of the LORD in response to the royal inquiry about the "words of this book" (2 Kgs 22:13). Many scholars have associated this "book of the law" with large portions of Deuteronomy. Themes such as the LORD's intolerance of foreign shrines and altars, the oneness of God and of Israel, and the centralization of worship at a place of the LORD's choosing parallel the political and religious reforms of Josiah. Hence, scholars have dated significant portions of Deuteronomy to the last third of the seventh century BCE, during the reign of Josiah. After the fall of the Northern Kingdom in 722, the language of Israel's oneness and the LORD's oneness (compare Deut 6:4-5) represented an attempt to reestablish an ideal version of the former United Kingdom, one Israel. Scholars also have recognized that other portions of the book are written from a perspective after the Babylonian exile (587 BCE), long after the monarchy had collapsed. In this way, the specter of exile came to provide another recontextualization

of earlier ideas and themes. The idea of constructing an identity for the people of God in a promised land creates quite a different image when seen through the eyes of exile rather than through the lens of monarchy.

Deuteronomy is comprised of four sections, each beginning with an editorial comment that describes Moses's role as he re-situates the covenant for this new stage of Israel's journey and prepares the people for life beyond the Jordan (see 1:1-5; 4:44-49; 29:1; and 31:1-2). The first section (1:1—4:43) provides an introduction to the book as Moses summarizes Israel's wandering in the wilderness. The second and central section, 4:44—28:68, is a re-proclamation of the law that was revealed at Horeb (Sinai in other biblical traditions). In 29:1—30:20, the covenant is renewed on the plains of Moab. Moses exhorts the Israelites to choose life by being faithful to the "commandments, decrees, and ordinances" of the LORD their God (30:16). The book ends with the events surrounding Moses's death. This last section (31:1—34:12) includes Moses's commissioning of Joshua, a song of Moses, a final blessing, and the death and burial of this "prophet" (34:10) of Israel.

Deuteronomy 6:4-6 represents one of the central themes in the book. This passage, also known as the *Shema* (verse 4 begins with this Hebrew command, meaning "hear" or "listen"), calls Israel to locate their identity in a God who is one and who alone should be worshipped. The notion of exclusive worship of the LORD should be reflected in the Israelite community, which should be similarly unified as one people under the covenant of its God. This distinctiveness is reflected in Deuteronomy's laws through its emphasis on Israelite worship and social order over against Canaanite culture and practices. The theme of oneness can also be found in Deuteronomy's insistence that worship should be at one site, a place of the LORD's choosing. These themes in Deuteronomy can be understood as an exercise in constructing identity. To *be* Israel, the people must, on the one hand, be wholly dedicated to the LORD, and on the other they must distinguish themselves from the practices of other peoples. Group identity is created through the erection of cultural and religious boundaries. Both in its historical context and in its canonical/literary context, the authors and editors of this book sought to make clear what was distinctly Israelite for their day and age.

Establishing and maintaining cultural identity is a necessary and sometimes problematic business. There is a fine line between creating group boundaries to preserve a cultural heritage and erecting walls or fences to keep others out. I am a *Sansei*—a third-generation Japanese American. This double-edged sword of cultural identity bears itself out in my family's histories and in my own experience. Traditions, religion, and community have helped to preserve some aspects of Japanese culture for generations of Japanese Americans. Thus, culture can act as a force that binds together people of similar ethnic background, making them one. However, the Japanese in America have also been labeled as the cultural "other," or foreigner. During World War II, in a time of war hysteria, people of Japanese descent were perceived as threats by those who could not recognize the Japanese as belonging in America. This was made most clear when the U.S. Government unjustly imprisoned some 120,000 Japanese and Japanese Americans in camps throughout the West Coast without due process of law. In that case, cultural identity was the rationale that was used to exclude—setting "American" culture over against those of Japanese descent. Because of this double-edged nature of culture—the ability to both include and exclude—it is important to read the themes in Deuteronomy in context rather than assume them to be universal. The special nature of a place and people in relationship to their God can quickly turn into a rationale for the expulsion or extermination of a foreign "other." ❖

Chapter 13

The Historical Books

Introduction to the

Historical Books

Uriah Y. Kim

The Historical Books, a part of the Christian Bible (and many contemporary editions of the Bible), includes several books—Joshua, Judges, 1 and 2 Samuel, and 1 and 2 Kings—that appear in the Jewish tradition as the Former Prophets, part of the *Nevi'im* ("Prophets"), the second division of Scripture. Jewish tradition recognized that the material in Joshua–Kings was somehow similar to, yet different from, the prophetic writings—Isaiah, Jeremiah, Ezekiel, and the Book of the Twelve, Hosea through Malachi—that in that tradition are called the Latter Prophets (see the Introduction to the Prophets, beginning on p. 151). The emphasis in these writings on the role of prophets and the recurring theme of "prophecy and fulfillment," in which the word of God is given to a prophet and then fulfilled in events that happen "according to the word of God," give them a prophetic flavor.

THE DEUTERONOMISTIC HISTORY

In contemporary biblical scholarship these books are viewed as theologically and editorially connected in a self-contained work called the Deuteronomistic History. This work recounts a history of ancient Israel from its entrance into and settlement in Canaan (Joshua and Judges), to the establishment of the dynasty of David (1–2 Samuel), then to the division of the kingdom (1 Kings), and finally to the fall of Samaria and Jerusalem (2 Kings). This work is influenced by the ideals expounded in Deuteronomy, believed to be "the book of the law" mentioned in it (see 2 Kgs 22:8).

There are several overarching themes or messages in the Deuteronomistic History. From the perspective of the Babylonian exile, one theme shows that the Babylonian captivity was a result of centuries of Israel's unfaithfulness to its God, and therefore that God was justified in punishing the people. Some see a message of hope in the way the Deuteronomistic History ends with the report of the release of an exiled Davidic king from prison (2 Kgs 25:27-30), affirming a theme of God's special relation with the house of David that runs through the books of Samuel and Kings. Another theme is a call for repentance, prominent in the book of Judges, exhorting the people to turn back to God from their infidelity and to trust God to forgive and deliver them. Many scholars believe that a preexilic edition of the Deuteronomistic History was composed during King Josiah's reign (640–609 BCE). Two themes would have been especially powerful in the time of Josiah: the sinfulness of Jeroboam, founding king of the Northern Kingdom, who established illegitimate sanctuaries in Dan and Bethel and thus brought about the fall of that kingdom; and the faithfulness of David and God's promise of loyalty to David and his house.

In genre, the Deuteronomistic History is one of the first examples of historical narrative of a people, and it invites its readers to read it as history. Therefore, it is critical to have some knowledge of the historical background of events depicted in this work. Until the eighth century BCE, Judah, the Southern Kingdom, and Israel, the Northern Kingdom, were involved in regional conflicts with neighboring political entities but free from interference from the major powers outside the region, namely Egypt and the Mesopotamian powers, Assyria and Babylon. In the middle of the eighth century, however, the Neo-Assyrians invaded Syria-Palestine and eventually conquered the Northern Kingdom of Israel, sacking Samaria in 722 (2 Kings 17). Judah was spared the same fate when the Assyrian campaign against Jerusalem in 701 was thwarted miraculously, according to 2 Kings 18–19. However, even Josiah's faithful implementation of the "book of the law" (2 Kings 22–23) could not prevent what seemed like Judah's irrevocable march toward judgment. In 598, Jerusalem surrendered to Nebuchadnezzar, the king of the Neo-Babylonian Empire (2 Kings 24), which had replaced the Neo-Assyrian Empire toward the end of the seventh century. When Jerusalem rebelled against Nebuchadnezzar, he conquered Jerusalem, destroyed its temple, and took many of its residents back to Babylon in 586 (2 Kings 25). The books of the Deuteronomistic History are written against that background.

Joshua. The book of Joshua opens with God instructing Joshua to take possession of the land of Canaan, promising him sweeping successes if he obeys the book of the law (1:1-9). Obedience to God's instructions is a key theme in Joshua. The supposed quick campaign to conquer Canaan starts at a very slow pace. The procession across the Jordan (ch. 3), the setting of twelve stones as a memorial (ch. 4), the circumcision of the new generation, and the observance of the Passover (5:1-12) read more like priestly narratives than martial reports. Most of the subsequent conquest narrative centers around two cities in central Canaan, Jericho and Ai (chs. 6–9). The pace of the conquest narrative picks up with the description of the defeat of kings in the south (ch. 10) and the defeat of kings in the north (ch. 11), ending with the statement that Joshua "took the whole land" and "the land had rest from war" (11:23). It is critical to note that God's command to "utterly destroy" the indigenous people (8:26; 10:28- 43;11:1-23) is understood as a matter of faith, as a demonstration of obedience that propels the narrative forward; it should not be read as a moral precedent. Joshua then distributes the land according to the tribal allotments (chs. 12–22) and draws territorial boundaries. One has to wonder whether these artificial territorial boundaries followed or cut across cultural and ethnic boundaries that probably existed among the people of Canaan. The book of Joshua ends with Joshua's farewell speech to the people, exhorting them to be faithful to God (ch. 23), and with a renewal of the covenant with God at Shechem (24:1-28).

Judges. Despite claims in Joshua that Israel was able to conquer the entire land, the book of Judges describes the Israelites' ongoing conflict with local Canaanite tribes, emerging kingdoms, and the Philistines, who arrived about the same time as the Israelites. The Israelites were forewarned not to follow the gods of their neighbors and that they would be turned over to their enemies if they did not show loyalty to their God (2:11-15). This threat is carried out in chapters 2–16, where each crisis begins with the formulaic saying that the Israelites had done "evil in the sight of the Lord," followed by the Israelites being handed over to their foes (3:7-8; 3:12; 4:1-2; 6:1; 10:6-7; 13:1). But each time the people repent of their infidelity, God is moved by their cry and raises a judge to deliver them from their suffering. This pattern of apostasy, persecution at the hand of their enemies, repentance, and God's deliverance through the judges is repeated until the narrative reaches the last part of the book (chs. 17–21). This section describes a complete

disintegration of moral and religious integrity and a tragic civil war between Benjamin and the rest of Israel. Judges ends on an ominous note—"In those days there was no king in Israel; all the people did what was right in their own eyes" (17:6; 18:1; 19:1; 21:25)—driving home the point that these atrocities happened because there was no king.

First and Second Samuel. In the two books of Samuel—originally one book—there are voices for and against the establishment of a kingship. The story opens with Hannah's petition to the Lord for a son by Elkanah (ch. 1). After her son is born, she praises God in a prayer that predicts God's anointing of a king (1 Sam 2:1-10). Her son, Samuel, faithful as he is, is not the anointed one, however; neither are his sons (1 Samuel 8). Saul is anointed by God but is quickly rejected for another (1 Samuel 13, 15). God chooses a ruddy shepherd boy (1 Samuel 16). Once David appears, the narrative focuses on why he, and not Saul, is God's choice. The narrative ends with the ignominious death of Saul (1 Samuel 31). The story of David's rise to kingship continues until it culminates in 2 Samuel 5 when David becomes king of Judah and Israel. In 2 Samuel, David secures his kingdom through the founding of Jerusalem as his capital (2 Samuel 5) and military successes against the Philistines and other neighboring peoples (2 Samuel 8). Then the story takes an abrupt turn for the worse and begins what scholars call the Succession Narrative (2 Samuel 9–20), which recounts internal problems that threaten David's reign. Second Samuel ends with a collection of stories and poems associated with David (2 Samuel 21–24), which includes a song of David (2 Samuel 22) that parallels Hannah's song and expresses a full-blown theology of a divinely established monarchy.

First and Second Kings. First Kings continues the narrative that began with a young, daring, and charismatic David and now describes him as an old, impotent, and fragile man waiting for his death (1 Kings 1). David, however, is not finished yet. He has enough strength and sense to utter his last wishes and to put his son Solomon on the throne (1 Kgs 2:1-12). Solomon is famous for his wisdom, but his most important achievement is the building of the temple in Jerusalem (1 Kings 5–8). Upon his death, the kingdom is divided into the Northern Kingdom of Israel, led by Jeroboam, and the Southern Kingdom of Judah, ruled by Solomon's son Rehoboam (1 Kgs 12:1-32). Israel is condemned from the start, because Jeroboam commits the ultimate sin when he sets up royal shrines outside Jerusalem (1 Kgs 12:25-32). From this point on, each king is judged according to his loyalty to God as specified in "the book of the law," especially the law commanding all worship to be concentrated at one chosen site (compare Deuteronomy 12), which we should understand to mean the Jerusalem temple.

The narrative pays a great deal of attention to the house of Omri and is especially critical of Ahab (1 Kgs 17:1—2 Kgs 10:31). Then Samaria, the capital of Israel, falls to the Assyrians (2 Kings 17). Judah lasted another century and a half after the fall of Israel. It was miraculously delivered from the Assyrian aggression (2 Kings 18–20), perhaps due to Hezekiah's faithfulness. Only Hezekiah and Josiah receive unconditional praise from the narrator for their uncompromising loyalty to God and for abolishing the "high places," that is, local shrines for the common people outside Jerusalem (2 Kgs 18:1-8; 22:1-2; 23:24-25). However, even Josiah's unprecedented obedience to the instructions in the "book of the law" is unable to prevent God's long-delayed judgment on Judah. Nebuchadnezzar conquers Jerusalem, destroys the temple, and takes many of its inhabitants to Babylon (2 Kgs 24:8—25:21). Second Kings ends with an intriguing note that Jehoiachin, the Davidic king who was taken captive to Babylon, is released from prison in Babylon (25:27-30).

The centralization of worship and sacrifice implemented by Hezekiah and Josiah was an attempt to shut down the worship at the "high places." This policy forced the people to come to the Jerusalem temple, the royal shrine of the house of David, for sacrifice and worship. That made the people's access to God more difficult and costly. There also were other popular religious practices in which the common people participated but which were deemed illegitimate by the official religion of the kingdom.

It would have been easy for the people of Israel to resign themselves to the fact that political powers greater than they, namely the Mesopotamian empires, controlled their history. However, the Deuteronomistic History (and all of the Historical Books) clearly show that the Israelites believed that their history, aspirations, and destiny were guided by their God. They wrote a history of their own, without appropriating the ideologies and assumptions of the empires. The Historical Books are a testimony to Israel's faith that they were the subjects of their own history and that their God was its divine agent.

OTHER HISTORICAL BOOKS

The Christian Bible interrupts the Deuteronomistic History by inserting Ruth between Judges and 1 Samuel and adds 1 and 2 Chronicles, Ezra and Nehemiah (all of which come from the restored Judah of the fifth century BCE), and the book of Esther. The latter books are included in Jewish Scripture among the Kethuvim, or Writings (see the introductions to these books).

Ruth. This winsome story is not as forcefully didactic as the Deuteronomistic History but delivers a message nonetheless. It moves from lack (famine and the deaths of husbands, which leave Naomi and Ruth vulnerable) to fulfillment (as the two women make a new home for themselves in

Bethlehem). If, as many scholars hold, it was written in the period of return from exile (586-500 BCE), it may bear a more pointed message: that the concern expressed in Ezra and Nehemiah to separate Israelite men from foreign women (like the Moabite Ruth) is misguided. In Jewish Scripture Ruth is one of the five megilloth, scrolls read on special occasions (the Song of Solomon, during Passover; Ruth, at Shavuot or the Feast of Weeks; Lamentations, on the Ninth of Av; Ecclesiastes, at Sukkoth; and Esther, at Purim). The Christian Bible places Ruth between Joshua and Judges because it narrates a time before the rise of the monarchy.

1 and 2 Chronicles. These books, written in the period of Judah's restoration, "chronicle" some of the same history narrated in the books of Samuel and Kings (and indeed refer to them), but from a distinct theological perspective (see the introductions to those books). Their name in the Greek Septuagint, paraleipomena (literally "things left out"), suggests they are "supplemental" to the Deuteronomistic History, but they convey a vision all their own.

Ezra and Nehemiah. These two books in the Christian Bible are a single book in the Hebrew Bible; they pick up the narrative where 2 Chronicles leaves off. Because they describe the organization of a people in a restored Judah gathered around the Torah—which had been given its final form in exile—historians find these books of inestimable value for the history of early Judaism.

Esther. Also one of the megilloth, Esther is read at Purim, the feast that celebrates the deliverance that the book narrates. As the introduction to that book suggests, Esther may be more valuable as an inspiring story of courage and resourcefulness on the part of faithful Jews in a foreign environment than as a historical account. Though the plot revolves around the working of retributive justice, the God of Israel is never named (a perceived lack that was made up by additions to the Greek version of Daniel, which stand in the Apocrypha: see the introduction there).

I can appreciate Israel's determination to write its own history, despite the fact that it was not one of the region's great powers. In many ways I am no different from others in the United States in having multiple identities, for everyone is a mixture of cultures and ethnicities. I am ethnically Korean, culturally American, and "racially" Asian. However, due to identity politics in the United States, some people are more likely to be considered "foreign" than others. As a member of a minority community whose history is relegated to the margin of the historical narrative of the United States, I believe it is important to understand a history of Asian Americans or other groups without always referencing the national history of the United States. Creating or adopting a history of a people independent of a national history is an important step for a minority community. ❖

JOSHUA

Dora R. Mbuwayesango

The book of Joshua presents the fulfillment of the promise of land to the Israelites' ancestors. This fulfillment began with Moses leading the people from Egypt, through Sinai, to the verge of the Promised Land in the plains of Moab (Exodus–Deuteronomy). Joshua presents the movement of the Israelites from the plains of Moab into Canaan. Two major types of activities are reported in the book. The first half of the book (chs. 1–12) is concerned with the Israelites' dispossession of the Canaanites from the land. The second half (chs. 13–24) recounts the division of the land among the Israelites. Both the dispossession of the Canaanites and the settlement of the Israelites are presented as sanctioned, indeed as achieved, by Israel's God, YHWH.

The land-distribution narratives show how the land was divided among the Israelites according to YHWH's command. The focus of these narratives is on the people's internal unity. Despite tribal and geographical boundaries, Israel is united in the covenant with YHWH who had given them the land. However, this positive message is undermined significantly by the message of exclusivity in the first half of the book; God is portrayed as favoring one people, Israel, to the exclusion of all others. Chapters 1–12 are problematic because they are full of violence and destruction, which God sanctions. To me, an African person whose ancestors experienced dispossession and exploitation at the hands of European invaders, these narratives (6:1—12:24) are very disturbing, as they seem to be a blueprint for the barbaric acts that were carried out much later in southern Africa. The disturbing nature of these narratives is compounded by the historical alliance between the plunderers and European missionaries who brought the Bible and its God to that region.

In these narratives the conquest of the land is presented in an epic style, focused on the capture of a few key cities and the practice of *herem*. The Hebrew word *herem* has connotations ranging from "thing devoted to YHWH," to "ban," to "utter destruction." In Joshua, *herem* entails the utter destruction of the enemy. Thus Israel's occupation of the land involved systematic pillaging and the killing of the current inhabitants. The practice of the ban is demonstrated in the first battle at Jericho (6:1-24). The Israelites are guaranteed victory before they even set foot in the city. All they have to do is follow YHWH's instructions. When Jericho falls, they proceed to apply the *herem* requirement: all breathing things, "men and women, young and old, oxen, sheep, and donkeys," are killed (6:16-21). Only one Jericho family is spared, the family of Rahab, the Canaanite prostitute who had assisted the foreign spies earlier and kept their secret. While humans and other living things are killed, silver, gold, and vessels of bronze and iron are considered holy, that is, taken and set apart for YHWH. The city is burned down, along with everything in it except for Rahab's family, the silver, gold, and bronze and iron vessels (6:24).

The seriousness of the *herem* ban is demonstrated by Israel's initial failure to defeat Ai because the Israelite Achan secretly saved some of the treasures at Jericho for himself (7:1-5). Only after Achan and his family are destroyed (7:18-26) does the second attack on Ai result in victory (8:1-29). Ironically, in this episode the *herem* law is relaxed a little to allow the Israelites to keep spoil as "booty";

however, all humans are killed. Except for Rahab's family, the escape of other indigenous peoples from utter destruction is viewed as against YHWH's will. The fate of the Gibeonites, who tricked the Israelites into making a covenant with them, is to be "hewers of wood and drawers of water for the congregation and for the altar of the LORD" (9:27). Future divine dispossession is promised for other lands still undefeated when Joshua distributes the land (13:1-7).

The portrayal of God's exclusive favor in these narratives is troubling and difficult to reconcile with other biblical portrayals of God. The divine sanction of the extermination and dispossession of the indigenous peoples of Canaan is disturbing. Material goods such as gold, silver, bronze, and iron are deemed more precious than human life. The picture of God as a partisan deity, favoring one nation at the expense of others, is also disturbing.

These accounts of the conquest and settlement by the Israelites were written during the exilic or early postexilic period with the purpose of forging an identity among those who longed to return to Judah. These accounts define those who legitimately deserve to be in the land of Canaan. They seek to inspire the returnees to fulfill what they believe was God's original purpose for them. The exclusive ideology of Joshua is dangerous because history shows that it can be put into practice. A belief in exclusive divine favor for one people can lead to genocide and extermination of other entire peoples. ❖

JUDGES

Wilda C. Gafney

Judges 1:27-36 paints a portrait of the settlement of Canaan that is markedly different than the one sketched in Joshua. Judges indicates that the tribes did not drive out the inhabitants of the land, whereas Joshua recounts numerous unequivocal military victories. Judges 1:34-36 shows that Joseph's descendants continued in his ways; they forced the indigenous people into service—just as Joseph's adopted Egyptian people had earlier forced their own kindred into bondage (see Gen 47:19-26)—in spite of their own recent liberation from slavery.

There are several narratives of note in Judges: the story of Deborah, Barak, and Jael in chapters 4–5; Gideon in 6–8; Abimelech in 9; Jephthah and his daughter in 11; Samson and his women in 13–16; Micah, his mother, and their religion in 17;

the Levite, his wife, and her murderers in 19; and the rape of the Shilonite women in 20–21. Each of these stories involves folk who are in some way marginal: outsiders, members of undistinguished tribes, illegitimate children, thieves, makers and worshipers of images, abused and murdered women. Some of them describe horrible violence. As a woman from a marginalized, African American community and as a feminist biblical scholar, the book of Judges fascinates me.

Judges presents several narratives that turn on women's participation in warfare. The Deborah saga is introduced by a description of her predecessor, Shamgar ben Anat (whose name indicates either that he is the son of a woman named Anat, meaning his mother was named for the Canaanite warrior goddess, or that he is such a great warrior that he is perceived as semi-divine, as was Achilles). Deborah's saga includes the story of Jael, the woman who executes Sisera. Subsequent revisions of the biblical narrative erase Deborah and Jael: First Samuel 12:11 says that YHWH sent Barak to deliver Israel, without mentioning Deborah; and Hebrews 11:32 also lists Barak as the sole deliverer.

Jael is the first woman in the Scriptures to be called "most blessed of women" (5:24; Judith is the second, and Miryam, Mary of Nazareth, is the third). According to the Song of Deborah (ch. 5), Jael was so important that time was measured by her life; verse 6 speaks of events "in the days of Jael...." Jael can also be understood as an avenger of raped women, for Sisera's mother is represented (5:30) as boasting that her son is delayed because he is dividing up girls as spoil—literally, "dividing the woman-flesh" (she uses a Hebrew word for a woman's reproductive system).

Judges includes two particularly vicious stories of violence against women, the "sacrifice" of Jephthah's daughter (Judges 11) and the rape, murder, and dismemberment of an anonymous Levite's secondary wife in Judges 19. In Judges 20, the Benjaminites refuse to hand over the men of Gibeah who raped and murdered the Levite's *pilegesh* (the Hebrew word refers to a wife of secondary status). Israel goes to war against Benjamin, killing twenty-five thousand male warriors. The remaining Israelite tribes swear not to give their daughters in marriage to the six hundred survivors of Benjamin. Since the Gadite warriors of Jabesh-gilead did not join in the battle, these tribes also decide to annihilate their warriors, men and boys, and sexually active women, and to seize four hundred sexually uninitiated girls as wives for the Benjaminite warriors. But because these girls were insufficient in number, the tribes decide to abduct the innocent daughters of faithful Israelites from the house of God at Shiloh. The Benjaminites abduct young women performing a cultic service at the Shiloh shrine, in this case liturgical dance, as wives.

The abduction and rape of the Shilonite girls marks the end of Judges and is summed up with the refrain: "In those days there was no king in Israel; all the people did what was right in their own eyes" (21:25). Episodes of violence against women throughout the book thus serve an ideological purpose: to show that Israel's life without a king is wild, chaotic, and destructive.

To be sure, Judges also presents the intriguing story of the first king in Israel—a king before Saul ben Kish of the tribe of Benjamin, Gideon's son Abimelech ben Jerubbaal (see Judges 9). We read in 9:22 that Abimelech ruled three years, much longer than many later kings in the divided monarchy. He consolidated his reign by killing all of his brothers that he could find—sixty-nine; the youngest hid successfully. Abimelech also killed all of the people of Shechem in the fields outside of the city (9:42-45), then burned the nobles of Shechem in the temple of El-berith. Abimelech was dealt a deathblow by an unnamed woman; but he asked a young man to kill him before he died of his wounds, so that no one would say a woman killed him.

Unlike many other biblical texts, where such violence is narrated but not condemned, Judges provides an editorial conclusion: every sin, transgression, and atrocity recorded in its pages results from the lack of a king. The refrain "there was no king in Israel" is repeated four times: at 17:6, 18:1, 19:1, and 21:25. Judges thus prepares for the account of the rise of Israel's monarchy in 1–2 Samuel. In this respect it should be read as a document of pro-monarchical propaganda. ❖

RUTH

Wilda C. Gafney

The book of Ruth is the story of the mother of the Messiah. In the Hebrew Bible, David is the most significant character identified as God's *meshiach*, or anointed (*christos* in Greek). Jesus of Nazareth is the only character identified as God's anointed in the New Testament. Ruth is named in the genealogies of both David (Ruth 4:17-22) and Jesus (Matt 1:5-16).

As a member of both Jewish and Christian congregations, I am interested in Ruth's nearly identical role in both traditions. As a woman and a feminist biblical scholar, I am also interested in the women's relationships with one another and the sexual undertones in the story of Ruth. As an African American, I am interested in the cultural intersections in the text.

The story of Ruth begins with trauma—she and Orpah are abducted from their home in Moab and forced into marriage in an Israelite family struggling to survive a famine. The "taking" of the women in 1:4 is done with the same verb that describes the abduction and rape of the young girls in Shiloh in Judg 21:23, where it is translated as "abducted." The grooms die before producing children. The three women, Naomi and her daughters-in-law, Ruth and Orpah, are left to fend for themselves. Since the younger women are clearly not pregnant, they are of no use to Naomi, who tries to get rid of them. Ruth, however, decides to cast her lot with Naomi and Naomi's God, while Orpah goes to reclaim her lost life in her homeland.

The Moabite identity of Ruth and Orpah is interesting. Israel and Moab were perpetually embittered. In Israel's accounting, the people of Moab had come into being through an incestuous relationship between Lot and his daughters in Gen 19:37. Throughout the narrative, Ruth is identified as a Moabite woman; she seems never to lose her outsider status in spite of her beautiful poetic vow to Naomi in 1:16-17:

> Do not beg me to leave you anymore, woman,
> or to turn back from following you, woman.
> For where you go, woman, I will go;
> where you rest, woman, I will rest;
> your people, woman, will be my people;
> and your God, woman, will be my God.
> Where you die, woman, I will die
> and there I will be buried.
> May YHWH do this to me and more
> if anything but death separates me from you, woman.
>
> (author's translation)

While Naomi laments her circumstances, Ruth goes to work to support them. Naomi's land-owning kinsman notices Ruth following the reapers and gleaning grain in his fields and instructs his laborers to leave her extra grain. He also instructs them not to touch or injure Ruth—a verb now translated as "bother" in 2:9. Boaz's protection of Ruth underscores the vulnerability of poor, hungry women to physical and sexual abuse. It also prompts the question: Did Boaz protect *all* of the vulnerable women on his property?

The dramatic climax of the story is the after-hours tryst between Boaz and Ruth. Naomi advises Ruth to wait until it is dark and Boaz is well fed and intoxicated before lying down with him (3:3). She also tells Ruth to do whatever Boaz tells her, which, combined with the Hebrew expression "uncover his feet" (3:4), has a sexual connotation. (The word for feet in biblical Hebrew is regularly a euphemism for the genitalia.) Boaz accepts Ruth's offer of herself in marriage, and they discuss terms. After this, Boaz tells Ruth to lie back down with him until morning. Their activities are not elaborated upon.

The story of Ruth ends with the withdrawal of another potential suitor, Ruth's marriage to Boaz, and the birth of their son, Obed. At their union, all the people in the community bless Ruth and Boaz. Their prayer is that Ruth will be fertile. When Ruth gives birth, all the women bless Naomi, naming her as the baby's beneficiary; and the women name him Obed, from the verb that means both to serve and to worship.

The story of Ruth ends with the name of David, Ruth's most famous descendant at the point the text was composed, written, and received. The conclusion decenters Ruth in order to make a point about the messiah's lineage: even Israel's greatest king was descended from a poor, vulnerable woman from a despised foreign nation. ❖

1 SAMUEL

Uriah Y. Kim

First and Second Samuel, originally one book, are included in the Prophets, the second section of the three-part Jewish Scriptures (Torah, Prophets, and Writings) that Christians call the Old Testament. It made sense to view these books as prophetic because in them prophets such as Samuel, Nathan, and Gad play critical roles in advancing God's history, and the theme of prophecy and fulfillment is prominent throughout. In contemporary biblical scholarship the two books are viewed as part of the Deuteronomistic History (Joshua, Judges, 1–2 Samuel, and 1–2 Kings), which recounts a history of ancient Israel from its entrance into and settlement in Canaan (Joshua and Judges), to the establishment of the house of David (1–2 Samuel), to the division of the kingdom (1 Kings), and finally to the fall of Samaria and Jerusalem (2 Kings).

First Samuel responds to the problem noted at the end of Judges: "In those days there was no king in Israel; all the people did what was right in their own eyes" (Judg 21:25). There are voices for and against the establishment of kingship in 1 Samuel. The people of Israel were in transition, moving from one form of governance—tribal confederacy practiced during the period of Judges—to another—monarchy as practiced by their neighbors.

The story opens with a petition for a son by a barren woman named Hannah (1 Samuel 1). When God grants her appeal she praises God with a song, which predicts God's anointing of a king (1 Sam 2:1-11). The importance of having a male child in the biblical culture finds parallel in certain modern cultures, where male children are still preferred over a female child. This may not be the case in much of the West but is still the case in many parts of the world, perhaps more for cultural reasons than for economic reasons, as it was in the past. Hannah's son Samuel, faithful as he is, is not the one for whom the people are waiting; neither are his sons (1 Samuel 8). Saul, who appears physically superior to all others, is anointed by God but is quickly rejected (1 Samuel 13 and 15). Later in the story, God chooses a ruddy shepherd boy to be anointed (1 Samuel 16). Once David appears in the narrative, 1 Samuel focuses on why David is God's choice instead of Saul. The book ends with the ignominious death of Saul (1 Samuel 31). The story of David's rise to kingship continues in 2 Samuel.

First Samuel takes place during the time when Canaan was free from political powers outside the region; but there were conflicts within. Israel was one among several groups of people that wanted to establish or maintain their territories in Canaan. It was a time when there were more crossroads where these peoples interacted, often in conflict, than exact boundaries. The drawing of various kinds of boundaries—territorial, cultural, ethnic—was an ongoing process at the time. The Israelites saw themselves as different from their neighbors, especially from their archenemy the Philistines, whom they called the uncircumcised. They were, however, not very different ethnically or culturally from other peoples in Canaan, some who also practiced circumcision. Moreover, the relationship between David and the Philistines was ambivalent. David defeated Goliath of Gath to win the support of the people (1 Samuel 17) but served King Achish of Gath, a Philistine city, as the king's bodyguard (1 Sam 27:1—28:2). Later David's bodyguard was made up of the Cherethites and the Pelethites (2 Sam 8:18), who were closely associated with the Philistines. When David had to flee Jerusalem due to Absalom, Ittai the Gittite, who was in charge of six hundred Gittites (soldiers from Gath), escorted David (2 Sam 15:18-23).

My reading of 1 Samuel is colored by my experience as a member of a minority community in the United States. Together and separately, various groups construct the nation's cultural landscape. However, culture is often shaped through *collisions* between a dominant group and minority groups. When reading 1 Samuel, I pay attention to the interaction between various competing ethnic and religious groups. ❖

2 Samuel

Uriah Y. Kim

Second Samuel opens with David learning of Saul's death, thus picking up the story where 1 Samuel left off. The people of Judah immediately anoint David their king upon the news of Saul's death (2 Sam 2:1-4). Several years of war ensue between David's men and those who remain loyal to the house of Saul. When Ish-bosheth (or Ishbaal, in NRSV), son of Saul, is assassinated by his own servants (2 Samuel 4), the people of the northern tribes also embrace David as their king, making David king of Judah and Israel (2 Sam 5:1-5). It is important to note that the southern tribes and the northern tribes are distinguished throughout the narrative. In some ways, we might say the people of Judah under David's leadership *conquered* the people of Israel. It was to David's credit that the two distinct peoples came together as one nation. However, their union was tenuous; they always were only a crisis away from going their separate ways.

David secures his kingdom by establishing his capital in Jerusalem (2 Sam 5:6-16) and through military successes against the Philistines and other neighboring peoples (2 Samuel 8). However, the story takes an abrupt turn for the worse in 2 Samuel 11 when David has an affair with Bathsheba and has Uriah the Hittite killed. The subsequent chapters (2 Samuel 13–20) are filled with internal problems that threaten David's reign and put succession in jeopardy. Second Samuel ends with a collection of stories and poems associated with David (2 Samuel 21–24). These include a song of David (2 Samuel 22–23) that expresses a full-blown theology of a firmly established monarchy—a far cry from the earlier theology of a people gathered around the God of the exodus.

Jerusalem is a crossroads where different cultural and ethnic groups converge in peace but sometimes collide in violence. David conquers Jerusalem, a city belonging to the Jebusites, and builds his house there (2 Sam 5:6-12). The Jebusites were probably assimilated into Israel; at least, they were not exterminated. This is indicated by the fact that David buys land from a Jebusite that would become the site of the temple (2 Sam 24:18-25). Moreover, David, who is from the tribe of Judah, secures the loyalty of the northern tribes by bringing the ark of the covenant, which is associated with the northern religious tradition, into Jerusalem (2 Samuel 6). The Cherethites, the Pelethites, and the Gittites were David's inner circle of soldiers. Uriah the Hittite, an officer with a perfectly good Yahwistic name—indicating perhaps that Uriah was culturally and religiously an Israelite—has a house in Jerusalem and is married to Bathsheba (2 Samuel 11). She is an Israelite woman whose father, Eliam, shows up in the list of mighty warriors with her husband (2 Sam 23:34) and whose grandfather Ahithophel is a prominent member of David's court (2 Sam 15:12). But David has Uriah killed to cover up his affair with Bathsheba, triggering a series of violent acts that take place in the "city of peace."

I am ethnically Korean and culturally Northern American. There are predicaments and privileges that come with being a cultural hybrid in a society where the normative cultural identity is that of one particular racial group—white Americans of mostly European descent. If I let the normative identity politics define who I am, I will forever be marked a foreigner, just as Uriah the Hittite was labeled a foreigner in the text. I ask: What makes one an Israelite? What makes one an American? ❖

1 KINGS

Francisco García-Treto

The book of Kings—the division into "first" and "second" parts did not originally refer to two separate books—is a theological meditation on the religious and historical paths taken by the states of Judah and Israel. The theological point of view of 1 and 2 Kings is consistent with that of the other books of the Former Prophets (as distinguished from the Latter Prophets) of the Jewish canon—Joshua, Judges, Samuel, and Kings. Contemporary scholars call these books the Deuteronomistic History because, in their interpretation of the history of Israel from the conquest of the land of Canaan to the Babylonian overthrow of nation and temple, they build on Deuteronomy's distinctive views of the relationship the LORD established with a certain people. That relationship is marked by concepts such as covenant and election, recast by the framers of Deuteronomy in the ideological fires of religious reformation and nationalistic recovery that were kindled in the times of Kings Hezekiah and Josiah of Judah. Faithfulness to the LORD—which for the Deuteronomistic writers meant exclusive monotheistic worship and strict observance of Torah, especially on the part of the kings of David's line, who were for the authors the only rightful rulers of the LORD's people—is the key to enjoyment of the blessings of election, in particular possession of the land of Canaan. The opposite leads to calamity, national ruin, and the ultimate catastrophe of exile.

The story begins in 1 Kgs 1:1—11:43 with the death of David and the beginning of Solomon's reign in Jerusalem, under whom the growth and glory of the city culminates in the building of the temple. However, even Solomon, the builder of the temple, in the end succumbs to following other gods, a sin the writers of Kings identify as the cause for the split of the kingdoms (1 Kgs 11:1-13.)

The rest of 1 Kings (12:1—22:53) takes the story from the split of the northern tribes of Israel from Judah, resulting from the rebellion of Jeroboam son of Nebat against Rehoboam son of Solomon to the accession of Ahaziah son of Ahab to the throne in Samaria. The story alternates between the kings of Israel and Judah, driven by a categorical rejection of the possibility that anything good could ever be said about a northern king. So Omri, arguably one of the most successful and powerful of the kings of Israel, is given much less prominence in the story (1 Kgs 16:23-28) than his weak son Ahab, who is presented as the feckless husband of evil Queen Jezebel, and roundly condemned by Elijah (1 Kgs 16:29—22:40). The role of pointing out the failures of the rulers of Israel and Judah falls to prophetic figures, such as Elijah, who in 1 Kings appears on the scene not only to confront the cult of Baal (1 Kings 18) but to rebuke Ahab for his injustice and to speak prophecies of doom that, in a promise-then-fulfillment scheme, are basic elements of the plot of the work (1 Kings 21). ❖

2 KINGS

Francisco García-Treto

Second Kings 1:1—17:41 continues the story of the divided kingdoms of Judah and Israel begun in 1 Kings (see the Introduction to 1 Kings). This is a story increasingly marked by foreign intervention on the part of Aram and Assyria, a story in which the prophet Elijah plays a major part. It is at his instigation that Jehu carries out a military coup in which the House of Omri is overthrown. Chapter 17 briefly recounts the fall of Samaria to the Assyrians (vv. 1-6),

then follows with a Deuteronomistic justification of the doom of the kingdom (7-23) and a negative appraisal of the population settled by the Assyrians in the north, based on their mixed ethnicity (24-41).

Second Kings 18:1—25:30 moves quickly to the fall of Judah and Jerusalem to Babylonia. This is not a simple event, but a historical process in which the growing darkness is twice lit by the reigns of two reforming kings, Hezekiah (2 Kgs 18:1-8) and his grandson Josiah (2 Kgs 22:1—23:25). The other side of the Deuteronomistic claim—that a return to faithfulness to the LORD would reverse the results of breaking the covenant, voiced in Solomon's prayer at the dedication of the temple (1 Kgs 8:46-53)—echoes in the final notice (2 Kgs 25:27-30) that an heir of the house of David remained in Babylonia, leaving open the possibility of return and restoration.

My personal history as a Cuban exile has made me wary of the dangers of too-simple explanations of national catastrophes, particularly when they fan the fires of zealotry and flatten those who are blamed into the position of irredeemable *other*. I read Kings with care, understanding that its trust in God's covenant faithfulness and its offer of return and redemption are in truth for *all* God's people. ❖

1 CHRONICLES

Gregory Lee Cuéllar

The books of Chronicles are inspired by the events of Israel's exile in Babylon and the return from exile. In recounting these events, Chronicles reconstructs a distinct cultural memory of the people of Israel. For the Chronicler (as the anonymous author of these books is known), the exile and return represent far more than theological metaphors. From beginning to end, these traumatic events ordered all of Israel's past into a tension between two fundamental experiences: sojourning and settlement. Hence the readers of Chronicles are led to remember a people who were once "strangers in the land, wandering from nation to nation" (1 Chr 16:19-20), whom YHWH then "brought...out of the land of Egypt" (2 Chr 7:22; see 1 Chr 17:5, 21; 2 Chr 5:10; 20:10) to live in "the land that you [YHWH] gave to them and to their ancestors" (2 Chr 6:25; see 1 Chr 16:18; 22:18; 28:8; 2 Chr 33:8). The tension between sojourn and settlement, exile and return not only brings structure to the Chronicler's memory of ancient Israel; it also defines Israel's experience in terms of its relationship to the Neo-Babylonian

and Persian empires that shaped—and ultimately shattered—Israel's monarchical past.

It is apparent that in Judah's exile (587 BCE), key aspects of Israel's past were subsumed to the ideological requirements of the Neo-Babylonian Empire. As with any event in which peoples are displaced from their territories, the exile had the consequence of effacing some of the crucial particularities of Israelite identity and silencing the subjects who constituted it, such as the tribes of Judah, Levi, and Benjamin, the Davidic dynasty, the Levites, the Jerusalem temple, the priesthood, and the Judean cult. These subjects of ancient Israel's past re-emerge in the books of Chronicles in such a way as to allow the Jews returning from exile to recover a collective Israelite identity. As with any recovery of cultural identity, the Chronicler turns to the resources of the past: archives, including genealogical records, the writings of prophets, and royal court records, many of which are cited explicitly, and (in the view of many scholars) the books of Samuel and Kings as well. The Chronicler combines these resources to forge a text that will transmit a collective Israelite identity and mobilize support for Israel's cultic and political institutions. Throughout the text the Chronicler reveals that the archives on which he draws are a record of Israel's past at the same time that it points to the people's future.

The books of Chronicles can be divided into three major sections. First comes the genealogical section (1 Chr 1–9). This section merits readers' close attention and critical consideration, for in it the Chronicler legitimates Israel's divine claim to land ownership and governance in the region of Palestine. The genealogies do not merely summarize the prehistory of Israel and Judah before the monarchical period and the temple system; the lists are a strategically crafted composition that attempts to delineate the true Israel. Although imbued with theological meaning, the genealogical lists address the question of identity and inheritance in a very immediate way. The next sections are the accounts of David and Solomon (1 Chr 10—2 Chr 9); and the accounts of the kings of Judah (2 Chr 10–36). The whole comes to a conclusion on a note of hope (2 Chr 36:22-23) that in Jewish tradition is the final word in Scripture.

As a self-identified Mexican American from the Southwest, my reading of the exilic context of 1 Chronicles is informed profoundly by the Hispanic American reality and experience of exile in the United States. As an academic in biblical studies, I find that the Jewish experience of Diaspora in 587 BCE becomes an unavoidable frame of reference because of its pertinence to the development of the Hebrew Bible. ❖

2 Chronicles

Gregory Lee Cuéllar

This book continues the narrative begun in 1 Chronicles (see the introduction to that book). First comes a rather idealized account of the reign of Solomon (chs. 1–9), and then an account of the subsequent kings of Judah (chs. 10–36). Very little attention is given to the kings of the Northern Kingdom.

How readers respond to these two books depends, first, on how they view the historical record. In other words, what counts as history? What justifies a particular interpretation of history? If we remove these texts from their Diaspora context and treat them in isolation from the conditions of their emergence, it is easy for them to appear inconsistent and to lack historical value. Nevertheless, when the collective memory of displaced people is in fragments, members often resort to creative forms of re-creating their collective memory. As Martha Chew-Sánchez has argued in *Corridors in Migrant Memory*, these peoples may look elsewhere for new images to fill the gaps where the original collective memory was destroyed.

Our response also depends on where we stand. As someone who identifies himself as a Mexican American from the U.S. Southwest—a land where we find at the margins the lived experiences of those today who face internal colonialism—I am drawn to the marginalized stories of colonization and Diaspora in the Hebrew Bible. Even more tragic than this internal colonialism, however, is the dismissed experience of the displaced, an experience captured within marginal texts that are usually concealed from the fashioned histories of the ruling order. I read 2 Chronicles as an effort to affirm the text of the Other. Perhaps 1 and 2 Chronicles provide a helpful example of how such collective remembering may take place among contemporary peoples as well. ❖

EZRA

Alejandro F. Botta

The book of Ezra is part of a composition that also includes the book of Nehemiah. Origen and Jerome, two early Christian scholars, separated Ezra-Nehemiah into two books, but only after the fifteenth century did the books appear as separated compositions in Hebrew Bibles. The two books were unanimously accepted by Judaism and Western Christianity as belonging to the biblical canon, but they were rejected as such by the Syrian Church. In the Hebrew Bible, Ezra-Nehemiah are placed at the end of the Writings, after 1 and 2 Chronicles. The books were probably written in the land of Israel in the first quarter of the fourth century BCE.

The book of Ezra continues the story told in 1 and 2 Chronicles, beginning with Israel's return from exile in Babylon and the rebuilding of the temple in Jerusalem (chs. 1–6). It continues with an Aramaic section that includes the incidents with Rehum, Shimshai, Tattenai, and Shethar-bozenai (4:8—6:15) and the dedication of the second temple (Ezra 6:16-18). The narrative proceeds in Hebrew with the completion of the temple and the Passover celebration (6:19-22), and a narrative about the initial work of Ezra (chs. 7–10), which includes a letter written in Aramaic (Ezra 7:12-26). Ezra concludes with a third-person narrative about the resolution to send away foreign wives and children (ch. 10).

In 538 the Persian Cyrus, whom Second Isaiah calls God's shepherd and Messiah (Isa 44:28;

45:1), issued a decree liberating the exiles. The return from the Babylonian exile and the rebuilding of the Jerusalem Temple mark the beginning of the second temple period in the history of the Jewish people. This was a crucial time for the religious definition of Judaism, and Ezra played a pivotal role in its shaping. The destruction of Jerusalem and its temple by the Babylonians in 586 BCE and the subsequent captivity was one of the most devastating experiences for the people of God. Hope was proclaimed again in Babylon by prophets like Second Isaiah (Isaiah 40–55), who promised a new exodus from Babylon (Isa 43:14-21) and a glorious return to the promised land.

In contrast to that glorious vision, the harsh reality of life in Jerusalem after the exile represented a difficult challenge for the faith of the post-exile community. Long gone were the days of national independence and Davidic kings. The people of God, now constituted as a colony under Persian rule, had to redefine their identity around religious institutions and relegate to a future restoration their dreams of political independence. In this context, Ezra's mission is twofold: to appoint magistrates and judges (7:25) who should *apply* God's law; and to *teach* the law to those who don't know it (for example, in the reforms of King Jehoshaphat discussed in 2 Chr 19:4-11). Ezra will also strictly prohibit marriages to foreign women, a drastic decision but perhaps the only way he could imagine to preserve the integrity and hopes of the (again) liberated community. Thus, the book of Ezra reflects tensions and negotiations in the cultural identity of this early Jewish community upon their return from the exile.

I can resonate quite readily with the tensions in cultural identity raised by this book because they correspond in some ways to my own life experiences. I was born and grew up in Argentina, a few miles south of Buenos Aires. Three of my grandparents had emigrated from Italy and one from Spain, and that European connection set the tone of my childhood. During my high school and early college years, however, my country experienced a bloody right-wing dictatorship that murdered thirty thousand of my people. It was then that I made a conscious decision to side with those who were persecuted and oppressed by the military, most of whom still remain "missing." I understand society as being in constant struggle—more specifically a class struggle—and try my best to be an organic intellectual on behalf of my people. This class consciousness—both of myself as an interpreter, and of the class options made explicit in the texts—conditions my reading of the Bible in general, and the books of Ezra and Nehemiah in particular. ❖

NEHEMIAH

Alejandro F. Botta

The book of Nehemiah was originally part of a composition that also included the book of Ezra. Exactly how the chronology of Nehemiah's mission aligns with that of Ezra continues to be a matter of debate, but there is some agreement that "the twentieth year" of Neh 1:1 refers to the reign of Artaxerxes I (445 BCE). The name Nehemiah means "the Lord is compassionate." Appropriately, the book begins with a first-person narrative describing the return of Nehemiah from exile and the rebuilding of the walls of Jerusalem (1:1—7:73a), a clear manifestation of God's compassion for God's people. This section comprises roughly half of the book and tells how Nehemiah—after hearing that Jerusalem's wall had been breached in many places and its gates had been destroyed by fire—mourns, fasts, and offers a confessional prayer (1:4-11). In the prayer, Nehemiah reminds God of the promise that if the people would return to God and keep the commandments, "though your outcasts are under the farthest skies, I will gather them from there and bring them to the place at which I have chosen to establish my name" (1:9). The sequence of events shows that God has indeed heard the prayer, and shortly afterward Artaxerxes accepts Nehemiah's request to return to Jerusalem and rebuild its wall (2:1-10).

However, the task does not seem to be without opposition. In Neh 2:11—4:23, we see not only how the work is organized but also how Sanballat, Tobiah, and Geshem opposed Nehemiah. This conflict continues in Neh 6:1-14 until the completion of the wall (6:15-19). The tension within the community is evident in the class conflict described in Neh 5:1-13. The nobles and the officials have allowed an extreme situation of inequality to arise, forcing their fellow Jews into such poverty that to survive they had to force their sons and daughters into slavery. Their claim—"Now our flesh is the same as that of our kindred; our children are the same as their children" (5:5)—is a demand for a just society where all persons have their needs met. The struggle to bring reality into an approximation of the demand is all too familiar in colonial and postcolonial situations around the world today.

The second part of the book (7:73b—10:39) covers the central event of Ezra's mission in Jerusalem: the public reading of the Torah (7:73b—8:12) and the commitment of the community to observe God's commandments (9:38—10:39). The celebration of Tabernacles follows, a reenactment of the last stage of the exodus experience (see Deut 31:9-13). The book ends with the repopulation of Jerusalem (ch. 11), the dedication of the walls (12:27-47), and Nehemiah's religious reforms (ch. 13). These include the implementation of Sabbath observance and the condemnation of wives taken from Ashdod, Ammon, and Moab. ❖

ESTHER

Willa E. M. Johnson

The book of Esther is one of the most powerful and interesting texts in the Hebrew Bible. It is the only book in the Hebrew Bible that makes no overt reference to God. Neither does it mention other significant facets of daily Jewish ritual life. However, the events narrated in the book are the occasion for Purim, the holiday that celebrates the Jewish people's deliverance from government-sanctioned mass destruction. Therefore, despite those just-named omissions, Esther offers an important characterization of God's eternal commitment to and relationship with this people.

The book of Esther, set in a king's court during the Persian (Achaemenid) Era, is dated to c. 400–200 BCE. Many modern scholars have questioned the book's genre, though it was once simply considered historical. For those who continue to view Esther as a type of history, the book is termed a *historical novella*. One counterargument to that characterization relates to confusion about King Ahasuerus's identity. Even though some scholars settle this matter by conflating Ahasuerus with King Xerxes, for others that identification remains problematic. Some scholars propose that Ahasuerus represents an unspecified legendary figure. Assertions that the events narrated here cannot be verified historically in no way detract from the power of the work, nor do they limit the extent to which Esther can convey important general truths about the early Jewish Diaspora.

The rabbis included the ten-chapter book as a part of the Writings, or Kethuvim. The book involves an intricate cast of characters and its plot provides insights about the meanings of power, power relations, and liberation. The five principal characters are very different but interconnected. At the outset, the outspoken Queen Vashti is deposed; she has disobeyed her husband, Ahasuerus, and the king responds foolishly by issuing a decree that women must obey their husbands. Due to Vashti's unwillingness to appear before the king and his cronies wearing her crown—and *only* that, explained later rabbinic interpreters!—Vashti is banished. Her misbehavior in court paves the way for Queen Esther and her guardian, Mordecai. Haman, a Persian official, also surfaces early in the narrative, plotting genocide for the Jewish people. Ultimately, this architect of Jewish demise is led to his death by Esther and Mordecai, two purportedly weaker characters. Esther and Mordecai serve as a foil for Haman and the legislative acts of the puppet-king, Ahasuerus. The absurdity of the king's edict points to the unlikelihood that this aspect of the book of Esther, at least, is historical; but perhaps more important for the reader, it reinforces the king's ineptitude.

Based on what scholars know about the historical Achaemenid Empire, the notion that a member of an ethnic minority could become queen of Persia is as absurd as the edict against women (1:19-20). An extensive study of women in the empire makes clear that it is unlikely that anyone other than a Persian woman would have ascended to such a position of royalty. Nevertheless, both the edict against wives and the beauty pageant in which Esther was selected function in the plot to reveal who had *actual rather than perceived power*. The ultimate demonstration of this power emerges when Mordecai and Esther succeed in devising a plan to undermine the king's presumed authority.

One alternative to viewing the book of Esther as history is to understand it as illustrating Hellenistic comedy or farce. This interpretation is based in part on the ostensibly ludicrous actions of King Ahasuerus but also includes the way Esther is selected as queen. Contemporary humor is often used to broach society's thorniest issues. Indeed, some of the most biting commentary on political matters is delivered through comedic satire. For an ethnic minority to view its relationship to the empire in the fashion expressed in Esther provides for the Jewish Diaspora an opportunity to reckon with its reality. The experiences of being under the Achaemenid Empire—no matter how tolerant of diverse religious traditions the Persians might

have been—compounded with the aftermath of the Babylonian exile, which brought the loss of land and other traumas, placed the Jewish Diaspora in an unenviable and vulnerable position. That the genre of Esther may be comparable to Hellenistic comedy does not diminish the serious nature of the book.

The narrative pokes fun at the hapless king. This enhances even more the image of Mordecai, a towering figure of wisdom and strength who outthinks the king and his entourage of advisers at every turn. Esther, a member of the recently scolded gender, circumspectly presents her case to the king. As a representative of Yehud's ethnic minority, Esther is, in fact, doubly strong. She speaks to the king, who had earlier sought to quiet women. Esther thereby provides the means through which Mordecai is able to conduct his strategy to dismantle Haman's plan of genocide. By speaking to the king and *acting womanishly*—as a feminist—Esther obliterates Haman's devised doom for the Jewish people and grants to women of every ethnic background the wisdom to pursue worthy goals by practical means.

The book of Esther's harrowing drama of a people confronted with threats to the viability of its ethnic community, if not genocide, ought to inspire the survivor in all of us. I find inspiration here, not only as a biblical scholar, a spouse, and a mother, but also as a disabled African American survivor of breast cancer. Like Esther, I grew up without my mother, who died after she turned fifty and I nineteen. But although I missed my mother and best friend, I was far from motherless. The spirit of the woman who birthed me has guided me, and when I needed the gentle embrace of elders, women from the African American community loved and nurtured me. That experience leads me to take seriously a commitment to the welfare of a diminished and tattered African American community, a commitment not unlike Esther's own; my task is to help salvage from utter devastation the spirit that breathed life into me on bitter and difficult days. ❖

Chapter 14

WISDOM AND POETRY

Introduction to

WISDOM AND POETRY

Francisco García-Treto

Wisdom and Poetry, understood as terms of artistic form in the literary study of the Bible, can be found in many books of the Hebrew Scriptures, including the prophets—but six (or eight) books traditionally have been regarded as comprising the Wisdom and poetic writings. The Psalms, the Song of Solomon (also called the Song of Songs, or simply Songs), and Lamentations are labeled poetic, and Proverbs, Job, and Ecclesiastes (also called *Qoheleth*)

are considered wisdom books. All of these books belong in the third division of the Hebrew canon (the *Kethuvim*, or Writings), where they are joined by others (Ruth, Esther, Daniel, Ezra, Nehemiah, 1 and 2 Chronicles) that in Christian Bibles are placed among the historical or prophetic books. Because the Roman Catholic and Orthodox canons incorporate the books that others call Apocryphal or Deuterocanonical writings in the Old

Testament itself, rather than in a separate section, these churches thus add Ecclesiasticus (also known as Sirach) and the Wisdom of Solomon to the list of wisdom or sapiential books.

POETRY

A look at the way modern Bibles set the wisdom books in type is enough to show that they are entirely or in large part in poetic form. Only Ecclesiastes alternates poetry and prose throughout. Job surrounds a long series of poetic dialogues between Job, his friends, and finally YHWH with brief prose portions that serve as introduction and conclusion to the work. We customarily distinguish the books into the two groups mentioned above, wisdom and poetry, but there are nevertheless points of similarity between the two literary categories that go beyond the simple observation that they all have some kind of poetic form. But what *is* poetic form?

POETRY AND SONG

In the most general terms, poetry uses a variety of means to enhance language to communicate a wide range of emotion. Music is one of the most obvious enhancements available, and it is not surprising that song is among the earliest and most durable forms in which poetry appears in Hebrew literature, as in any other. David, the model king, is also the model singer and poet in 1 and 2 Samuel, from the time he joins Saul's court as a skilled musician (1 Sam 16:14-23), to the powerful scene beginning at 2 Sam 1:17, where the NRSV text says that he "intoned"—that is, sang—the "Song of the Bow," his moving funeral song for Saul and Jonathan. The Psalms are, for the most part, hymns from temple services, and many of them even have editors' notes addressed to the choirmaster, specifying the kinds of instruments

to use for accompaniment, or the name of a tune to which the psalm was to be sung. Psalm 150 even lists string, wind, and percussion instruments with which the psalmist entreats the congregation to "Praise the LORD!" Unfortunately, the ancient Hebrews did not develop a system of musical notation, so today we can only guess at how their music sounded; and for most of us, who depend on translations for reading the Bible, even the sound of the Hebrew words themselves is absent. Many characteristic features of Hebrew poetry—for example, the rhythm of accents in a line, the number of syllables in a verse, or the many forms of wordplay based on sound—are available only to the reader of the original language. That is not to say that all is lost; there is much that a good translation can convey.

THE CRAFT OF POETRY

Parallelism is the most distinctive and frequently seen feature of biblical Hebrew poetry. At its simplest—and the patterns and techniques of parallelism are a vast subject—it is a reinforcement of an idea or image by repeating it in the same verse using different words, or even by stating it in the opposite way. Psalm 1:5-6 can be used to illustrate both points:

> Therefore the wicked will not stand in
>   the judgment,
> nor sinners [stand] in the congregation
>   of the righteous;
> for the LORD watches over the way of the
>   righteous,
> but the way of the wicked will perish.

The ancient Hebrew poets also used devices such as similes and metaphors, universal tools of the poetic craft. Psalm 1, for example, pairs similes to say that those who delight in the law of the LORD are "like trees planted by streams of water, which yield their fruit in its season, and their leaves do not wither," while the wicked "are like chaff that the wind drives away" (Ps 1:3, 4). Perhaps the best-known and loved of the metaphors in the Psalms is the one that begins the Twenty-third Psalm: "The LORD is my shepherd, I shall not want."

GENRES

An important issue to take into account when reading any work of literature, poetry in particular, is its genre—that is, the kind of literature it is. A sonnet, for example, differs from a limerick not only in form and range of content but also in the audience's expectations of where and for what purpose it is fitting to use one or the other. That is not to say that creative poets may not displace genres to make powerful statements. The prophet Amos, for example, sings a funeral lament or *qinah* over the nation, as if he were lamenting an individual "maiden Israel" (Amos 5:1). David uses the same genre in his song in 2 Sam 1:17. Not all biblical poetry is of the same genre, nor was it intended for the same setting or purpose.

PSALMS, LAMENTATIONS, SONG OF SOLOMON

The book of Psalms reached its final form after the Babylonian exile, even though its collections of largely cultic poetry include some very ancient songs. By and large, the voices we hear in its 150 poems are those of Israel at worship, with the inclusion at times of the voice of the teachers of wisdom, promoting the study of Torah. Many Psalms can thus be classified as hymns in praise of God, while others are prayers of lament and petition, whether of individuals or of the entire community. Others are royal songs associated with ceremonies such

as the enthronement of a king, while yet others are songs for the pilgrimage festivals associated with Jerusalem, and so forth.

Lamentations (1:1) gives voice to the pain of the loss of Jerusalem, ravaged and desecrated by the Babylonians:

> How lonely sits the city
>   that once was full of people!
> How like a widow she has become,
>   she that was great among the nations!
> She that was a princess among the provinces
>   has become a vassal.

In Lam 5:15-16 the poet weeps for the suffering of the inhabitants in images whose power reaches across the gap of time and language and moves us:

> The joy of our hearts has ceased;
>   our dancing has been turned to mourning.
> The crown has fallen from our head;
>   woe to us, for we have sinned!

The Song of Solomon represents a totally different genre: it is a cycle of poems celebrating human love and physical beauty, universal and worthy themes of poetry. Placed in the canonical context of Scripture, however, these poems have been read as representing the reciprocal loves of God and Israel, or of Christ and the church, or have been used by Jewish and Christian mystics to convey the soul's desire for union with God.

WISDOM

An important trait shared by the poetic and wisdom books is their openness to international or intercultural influences. This shows in a variety of areas, ranging from form and style to content and scope of interest, where the Hebrew writers apparently knew, or even directly depended upon, the literary heritage of Israel's neighbors. Substantial parallels ranging from Sumerian laments to Babylonian hymns to Egyptian love songs, for example, inform our reading of Lamentations, Psalms, or the Song of Solomon, while the very words of the Instruction of Amenemopet, a well-known Egyptian wisdom text, stand behind the Hebrew text of Prov 22:17—24:22. On the other hand, the grandson of Jesus ben Sirach tells us, in his Greek translation of his grandfather's Hebrew text, that he has translated it "so that by becoming familiar also with his book those who love learning might make even greater progress in living according to the law" (prologue of Ecclesiasticus). In other words, he worked so that Greek-speaking Jews living in Egypt, some with a limited grasp of Hebrew, could read the book his grandfather had written in Jerusalem.

Royal and imperial courts, as well as major religious establishments such as the temple, needed literate, skilled personnel capable of keeping records and accounts, writing legal documents, and carrying out correspondence—in short, bureaucrats, administrators, and clerks—to conduct their varied affairs. As a class, these people are known as scribes (literally, "writers") because of the basic importance of literacy to what they did. Apparently there were schools and teachers in Israel, as there were in Egypt, Mesopotamia, and Syria, and they provided the likely context for the production of what we know as wisdom literature.

Proverbs is a large collection of texts that praise and recommend the acquisition of wisdom for very practical and this-worldly ends. Religious piety plays an important part in what Proverbs recommends, including that "the fear of the Lord is the beginning of knowledge" (1:7). But what will ultimately lead to success and to the reward of one's good name are human virtues such as prudence, understanding, diligence, honesty, temperance, and humility. An extraordinary poem in Proverbs 8 presents Wisdom in the figure of a merchant peddling and advertising her educational wares in the public square and, in verses 22-31, making the remarkable assertion of having been the first of God's creations, fashioned as a "master worker" (v. 30) to aid in the making of the world. The world, therefore, is comprehensible through wisdom. Much of the material in Proverbs is presented in the short genre that gives the book its name; in most cases it is a single verse in two parts, held together by parallelism:

A slack hand causes poverty,
    but the hand of the diligent makes rich. (10:4)

Pride goes before destruction,
    and a haughty spirit before a fall. (16:18)

Ecclesiastes and Job represent critiques *from within* of the central claim of the wisdom schools. In the view represented by Proverbs, the faithful practice of piety and virtue—of wisdom—leads to a good name, honor, and a long, prosperous, tranquil life, or at least it should. The writers of Ecclesiastes and Job are clearly among "the wise," but for them the results of wisdom are less rosy. The writer of Job questions the implied judgment on those who suffer—that it must be because of their own sin. Job is a wise and righteous man, at first rich, happy, and honored, who loses everything in a terrible series of events, through no fault of his own. Through the long poetic dialogues that compose the book, he defends his integrity against his wise friends, who encourage him to confess what in their opinion must be some terrible and secret sin. Job's refusal, and his appeal to YHWH—who finally appears, but in the end refuses to answer Job's query—pose the ever-unanswered questions that human suffering raises, and refute the too-easy answer that suffering is always the victim's fault. Ecclesiastes raises an even more universal question: does not the inevitability of death give the lie to any human idea of lasting achievement or accomplishment? A profound weariness sounds in the theme of the book, which goes on to speak of various areas of human effort as amounting to the same thing:

> Vanity of vanities, says the Teacher,
>> vanity of vanities! All is vanity.
> What do people gain from all the toil
>> at which they toil under the sun? (Eccl 1:2-3)

Two works of the later Hellenistic period, Sirach and Wisdom of Solomon, represent the development of the wisdom tradition in, respectively, Jerusalem and in the Diaspora (see the introductions to those books in the Apocrypha).

Being a member of the "Cuban Diaspora," having been a college professor in a department of religion for forty years, and, inevitably, getting old have given me an appreciation of the Wisdom writings and of the poetry of the Hebrew Bible. This appreciation has become deeper and richer than when I first encountered these texts as a child in church (Presbyterian), and in school (Methodist and Presbyterian), in the Cuba of my youth, or when I learned to read them with all of the historical-critical tools of a graduate education in the United States. I rediscovered these writings only when I became a new teacher, someone who had to come to grips with exile and with treading the thin line that exiles must always negotiate in order to survive, while simultaneously trying to succeed and serve others in a different country than the country of my birth and formation. In this process, I found the wisdom writers and the poets of the Hebrew Bible to be very different than what I had, early in my life, thought them to be. Now I think I understand them better, and because of my own experience, I feel more comfortable in their company. ❖

JOB

Cheryl A. Kirk-Duggan

Job, a poetic drama, asks how it is that evil and injustice seem to be allowed, permitted, or tolerated by God. Theologically, Job's dilemma is about *theodicy* or divine justice (from the Greek *theos*, "God," and *dikē*, "justice"): Why do evil things happen to innocent people? Is an all-powerful God good? Either a just God is not all-powerful, or a just God is not all-beneficent—or else the suffering person cannot really be innocent of wrongdoing and thus has earned retribution rather than beneficence.

The book's prologue (chs. 1–2) opens with God and "the Accuser" or "the adversary"—in Hebrew, *ha-satan*, an angelic figure who will only later develop into the New Testament's "Satan"—placing a wager on righteous Job to test his piety and faithfulness. The rich poetic dialogues that follow (chs. 3–27), filled with legal disputations and logical arguments between Job and his so-called friends, Eliphaz, Bildad, and Zophar, debate the question: Why *is* Job being punished? His friends insist that he must have sinned. They posit that God is and must always be good, right, and just. A poem (ch. 28) suggests that wisdom is only within God. In the monologues that follow (29:1—42:6), Job, Elihu, and God speak in turn. Job says God should not punish innocent people.

Job's friends fail to refute him. Elihu chastises Job for justifying himself and asserts that God can never pervert justice (32–37). Then YHWH appears in a storm theophany (a dramatic in-breaking of the divine) and questions Job, but avoids responding to Job's questions of suffering or divine justice through cosmological and mythological assertions (38:1—42:6). Job extols God's greatness and accepts God's decisions. Amid irony and dissonance, in the epilogue (42:7-17) God is angry with Job's friends, has them offer sacrifice, and has Job pray for them. Then God makes Job prosperous again, and Job dies an old man "full of days" (42:17).

SUBJECTS OF INTRIGUE

The rich, powerful themes within Job stand in tension. Job and his friends authorize their truth claims within different realities. The friends' traditional positions on suffering require authenticating Job's implicit wrongs. Job feels alienated from God, and amid relentless arguments, accuses God of injustice, while others accuse Job of wrongdoing. Job experiences agony, despair, and deep anguish.

Contradictions in the book mirror these tensions. Job's life descends into chaos, which is reflected in the dialogues as conflicting assertions regarding God are made by characters seeking to justify themselves. As the story develops, it presses us to question our own socio-religious and moral assumptions and values, our notions of personal faith and piety, of divine and human relationships, and of human suffering.

I relate to this book as a professor of theology and women's studies and an ordained elder in the Christian Methodist Episcopal Church, but also as the wife of a beloved husband, Mike, who was misdiagnosed with Alzheimer's disease and mistreated for four years. At last, by grace, his malady was found to be a side effect of a common statin drug.

We regard this as our own "Job experience"; indeed, Job is a representative figure for all who suffer in spite of all that seems to be right.

Carol Newsom has declared that the book of Job disorients and reorients the reader, offering a drastically different paradigm for God, creation, and human existence. In the story, Job's wife offers insight that shakes Job's presumptions. Regarding authority, his friends rely on common sense and various traditions about God (traditions very reminiscent of the language of Deuteronomy); Job, on the other hand, protests his own integrity. When Job was wealthy, he demonstrated empathy for women and the poor. Now Job expects God to treat him as he treats others in need: by being benevolent, paternal, and just. He and his friends seem to expect God to react to Job's benevolence: Doesn't God follow God's own justice (as later expressed in the Golden Rule) by treating Job as God wishes to be treated by him? But this question never receives a direct answer. Rather, the book implies, humans are made for God, not God for humankind. God seeks to reorient Job, apparently leaving the redress of injustice, oppression, and suffering as a human task.

SEAMS, COLLISIONS, AND CONVERGENCES

In the world represented by the book of Job, a chaotic God blesses the wicked and abuses the poor. This God is a tyrant and yet is declared just. René Girard posits that Job, like Jesus, is a popular hero who becomes a communal scapegoat, an innocent person who polarizes the community and attracts universal rejection. The Job of the prologue is a wealthy, popular potentate; but the Job of the dialogues is a victim of an awful reversal of fortunes. His friends' speeches reveal imitative hatred and envy, and truth is not their goal. Amid deception,

God's own delay to intervene appears cruel. Job's harshly accusatory language blurs his status as victim. The God described by his persecutors as a providential God stands in tension with the God who stands with the victims. The epilogue offers an incomplete, happily-ever-after scenario that masks the scapegoating dynamic of the story.

Holiness (*qōdesh* in Hebrew, *hagiosynē* in Greek) is an infrequent theme in the wisdom literature, and when it appears there it primarily concerns the fear of the Lord. Yet Job's holiness, and God's, are important. Calvin Samuel argues that Job's experience in the plot casts doubt on God's holiness and righteousness. Job fears God, is blameless and upright, and meets disaster with personal holiness; yet he suffers. Intriguingly, Job is from Uz: God must go outside the people, covenant, and cult of Israel to find this premier example of holiness. Here the sages who produced the wisdom literature have recast holiness to represent a holy, leprous Gentile who lives in an unholy land with unholy people, without cultic access to God's grace. In so doing the sages implicitly question God's holiness and portray God as a bullying, almost demonic caricature. God bestows holiness, yet it must be pursued by humans. The wisdom tradition holds in tension divine sovereignty and human responsibility. Job maintains personal integrity. Ultimately, however, the sages offer no conclusive explanations, and God's ways remain inscrutable. ❖

THE PSALMS

Stephen Breck Reid

The book of Psalms is a polyphony of song. It has voices from different times; its texts span five centuries. Moreover, the many historical contexts of different psalms reflect the needs of different locations and peoples, and help explain the diverse qualities of the poetry. Sometimes, if a piece of poetry is to retain its power, it requires alteration. This poetic reconstrual may involve a transformation from one culture to another. For example, a Canaanite storm image became part of a hymn to YHWH in Psalm 29, one of the oldest psalms. Most importantly, the social dislocation of exile and the postexilic context required new songs, such as Psalm 137.

The Psalms remind today's readers of the *plasticity* of great texts–that is, their ability to address different contexts simultaneously. These psalms originally came from a number of regions and historical periods; most were written from the perspective of the Southern Kingdom of Judah, but several psalms, including 80 and 81, came from the Northern Kingdom prior to its fall in 722 BCE. In the process of their being repeated, adapted, and inevitably reconstrued, the songs again and again became part of a new entity and developed new meaning for generations yet to come—in similar and, sometimes, in quite diverse settings and situations. The book of Psalms has several literary genres, but two dominate: laments and hymns. The Hebrew title of the book of Psalms, *tehillim* (praises), testifies to the importance of the hymn genre. This genre emphasizes God, while the laments focus more on the request of the speaker. The hymn has three sections: a call to praise; testimony about God; and a conclusion that expresses some prayer, wish, or blessing. The deity is typically depicted in these testimonies as creator (8, 19, 104) and redeemer (66, 98).

The laments comprise approximately one-third of the psalms. The structure of the lament is complex, often using seven elements: address to God; description of distress; plea for redemption; statement of confidence; confession of sin or affirmation of innocence; pledge or vow; and a conclusion. A lament is often part of a cultural response by which people seek to negotiate a changing social context. The lament psalms both reflect the specific culture from which they emerge and are able to be translated to serve in other historical contexts and situations.

In general, the book of Psalms addresses the complicated nuances of power and privilege as matters of *election*. The royal psalms (2, 18, 20, 21, 45, 72, 91, 101, 110, 144) and the songs of Zion (46, 48, 76, 87, 125) indicate the community's efforts to negotiate a responsible position in society through the images of God's choosing of king and city. The psalms of ascent (120–134) are probably a collection of pilgrim psalms sung as persons made their way to Jerusalem for worship. Overall, the prayers and songs create a poetry of particularity, but the breadth of the psalms nevertheless still evokes attention to the disenfranchisement evident at the margins.

The book of Psalms also includes a range of pieties. The debate on the social origins of the psalms reminds us that a religion lives not only in the priestly precincts but also in the so-called lay movements. The Psalter provides the best evidence for the coexistence of official religion (24, 95) and expressions of local lay piety (127, 131).

Finally, the book of Psalms is a collection of collections. The collections within the Psalter reflect different entities in the emerging religions of ancient Israel. The superscriptions—the historical notes that appear before many of the psalms—provide significant evidence of multiple groups or guilds, perhaps groups or families of Levitical priests: see, for example, the psalms ascribed to Asaph (50, 73–83) and the Korahites (42, 44–49, 84). Moreover, a preponderance of Yahwistic psalms, identifying the deity through the divine name YHWH, stands side by side with the Elohistic psalms, which name God as Elohim. The final form of the Psalter mediates these cultural differences within a fivefold structure (1–41, 42–72, 73–89, 90–106, 107–150), providing a parallel with the five books of Moses.

I read the psalms with music playing in the background, but this is more than an aesthetic preference. I grew up in an African American home, raised by parents who had suffered the loss of their own parents, in mid-twentieth-century Ohio, where de facto segregation gave to life a contingent, syncopated quality. The poetic rhythms and thematic countermelodies in the psalms evoke for me both the wonder and the precariousness of life. ❖

PROVERBS

Joseph F. Scrivner

A "proverb" is a short saying that summarizes some truth about life. Knowing and practicing such truths constitutes wisdom—the ability to navigate human relationships and realities. A literary collection of proverbs is thus intended to communicate wisdom. The biblical book of Proverbs is presented as such a collection: "The proverbs of Solomon son of David, king of Israel" (1:1). The book's title is, obviously, derived from this opening line. Similar phrases are found throughout Proverbs. These titles suggest two important points about this book: it is a collection of other, smaller collections, and it was collected by scribes.

Proverbs is comprised of six sections: 1:1—9:18; 10:1—22:16; 22:17—24:22; 24:23-34; 25:1—29:27; and 30:1—31:31. The first nine chapters introduce the book as a whole. The prologue (1:1-7) gives the book's purpose. It explains that these proverbs enable the learner to obtain wisdom and understanding (1:2). Learning to live wisely means practicing righteousness, justice, and equity (1:3). Such learning matures the naïve and deepens the wisdom of those already astute (1:4-6). This learning begins with "the fear of the LORD" (1:7). The prologue's paradigmatic introduction provides key concepts for the entire book.

Only the first section addresses its audience as "child" or "children," a common stylistic feature in ancient Near Eastern instruction, especially for young men preparing for service in royal courts (1:8; 2:1; 3:1, 21; 4:1, 10; 5:1; 6:1, 20; 7:1). Besides the use of "father" and "son" in the original Hebrew (but see the unusual "mother" in 1:8; 4:3), this orientation is evident in the warnings against the Strange Woman (2:16-19; 5:1-23; 6:20-35; 7:1-27).

In conjunction with counsel against the wicked (2:12-15; 3:31-32; 4:10-19), these denunciations present the Strange Woman as a *femme fatale*—a woman who seduces the innocent, unassuming male. This figure certainly promotes a caricature of women and displaces onto the woman the man's responsibility for the attraction he feels. Accordingly, any appropriation of this language today must creatively reimagine it in ways that do not perpetuate its potential for misogyny.

To counter the attraction of the Strange Woman, the author personifies the book's teachings as Woman Wisdom (1:20-33; 3:13-20; 8:1-36; 9:1-18). Wisdom, often capitalized (though not in the NRSV translation) because she speaks for herself, describes herself as the first creation, delighting the LORD and rejoicing in humanity (8:22-31). Because of her heavenly stature, she and her words are more valuable than precious stones. In a word, she is priceless (3:13-18; 8:17-21). Thus, those who seek to be wise must enter her house and dine with her, resisting the allure of the forbidden woman (9:1-6, 13-18).

Having chosen wisdom over foolishness, the learner passes from the parental guidance of chapters 1–9 to the various collections of 10–31. Here one must select the right counsel for the appropriate situation. Some situations require silence to avoid foolishness, while others require instruction about speech (26:4-5). Also, wealth may be viewed as a reward for righteousness (10:15, 22) or as the illegitimate possession of oppressors (15:27; 22:16, 22-29). Likewise, poverty can be spoken of as a consequence of laziness (10:4; 13:18; 14:23; 19:15) or as a condition created by the wickedness of others (14:31; 15:16-17; 16:8, 19:1; 20:10). Given the nature of any individual saying as well as the function of a collection of such sayings, this instructional variety seems appropriately balanced: such variety corresponds to life's genuine complexities.

The title of each section suggests that various scribes edited Proverbs over several centuries. Indeed, many of these proverbs are attributed to Solomon (1:1; 10:1; 25:1). Smaller sections are attributed to "the wise" (22:17; 24:23), and the final sections mention the otherwise unknown Agur and Lemuel (30:1; 31:1). Critical scholars have concluded that the attribution to Solomon is due more to the traditional practice of naming an important figure as author than to an actual literary history. As Moses is the lawgiver and source of the Pentateuch, and David the songwriter and composer of many psalms, Solomon is presented here as the paradigmatic wise man (described elsewhere as the author of three thousand proverbs: see 1 Kgs 3:16-28; 4:29-34).

Given the limits of ancient literacy, high-ranking government scribes probably composed and edited Proverbs, the book reaching its final form after the exile, in the fifth or fourth century BCE. The social status of these scribes is consistent with what we know from similar ancient Egyptian wisdom literature. It is likely that this literature was first used to instruct the apprentices of these scribes, and some may have been actual sons. In its original setting, the book was a means of transferring the privileges of the scribal position. It was the exclusive possession of the literate elite. Only with increased literacy in later Judaism and Christianity did the book become accessible to a wider audience.

Investigating the original context for this book creates interesting connections for me as an African American scholar. It reminds me of how education can be a means of exclusion or an instrument of liberation. African Americans have long viewed education as a primary means of freedom, the path by which one secures the ability to flourish. Yet education is perhaps the resource most often denied to those without socioeconomic status. Education is often cited as a key indicator of the distance between the privileged and the poor. The content and context of Proverbs reminds me that education can be a means of social mobility, on the one hand, or a tool for maintaining the status quo on the other. ❖

ECCLESIASTES

Madeline McClenney-Sadler

The author of Ecclesiastes is coping with a reality that most human beings either face directly or try to avoid: the reality and imminence of one's own death. As death approaches, the twelve chapters of Ecclesiastes are sprinkled with resignation. "All is vanity" (1:2).... "Look, the tears of the oppressed—with no one to comfort them!...I thought the dead...more fortunate than the living!" (4:1-2)...

"The fate of humans and the fate of animals is the same; as one dies, so dies the other" (3:19).... "The lover of money will not be satisfied with money; nor the lover of wealth, with gain" (5:10; 5:9 in Hebrew).... "The day of death [is better] than the day of birth" (7:1).... "It is better to go to the house of mourning than to go to the house of feasting; for this is the end of everyone" (7:2).

At some point during an encounter with death, as in the book of Ecclesiastes, most believers struggle with the meaning of life. At those times, Ecclesiastes may be a source of comfort. Well-wishers during rough times tend to sugarcoat the gravity of life, but the author of Ecclesiastes allows the reader to accept the bitter pill of life for what it is—bitter.

In Hebrew this book is known as Qoheleth, "The Teacher." The title Ecclesiastes is an anglicized form of the book's Greek title, which is a translation of Qoheleth. The book's content is most likely the product of an assembly of sages who instructed one another in wisdom schools. One might think it odd for a teacher who presumes the existence of God to be so thoroughly pessimistic, so decidedly negative, and so coolly logical; yet it is precisely the author's irreverence toward human effort that makes his fundamental claims holy, sacred, and wise. The subtext of his theological musing becomes the key to understanding: "when considering one's own mortality, be joyful in the day of prosperity, and in the day of adversity, consider God" (7:14, my translation). When all is said and done, the knowledge of God alone is sufficient. A wise person can eat, drink, enjoy life, and face death if she or he has wisdom and the knowledge of God (2:26; 3:14, 17; 5:7, 18; 8:12, 13; 12:1).

My reading of the Hebrew Scriptures is strongly shaped by my social location as an African American woman. For seven years, while pursuing degrees in business and divinity, I stood in solidarity with homeless people as they trained me for the ministry. The transformative power of instruction from the lives of the homeless has shaped my soul and revealed my strident classism and unexamined hypocrisy. The persistent threat of death that homeless people face forces them daily to grapple with end-of-life questions similar to those raised by the author of Ecclesiastes. ❖

The Song of Solomon

Alice Hunt

The Song of Solomon or Song of Songs—meaning, the most magnificent of all songs—demonstrates, perhaps more clearly than any other biblical material, the multivalent complexity and beauty of the Bible. On the face of it, the book—often called simply the Song—seems to have no religious connection, never mentioning God. Yet the book explores love—intimate, life-giving, provocative, mutual, erotic, dynamic, engaging, complex, longing, passionate love—and perhaps reveals that fully intimate relationships are a way of experiencing God, at once both immanent and transcendent.

Ancient writings were often attributed to people whose legendary name might lend the book credibility, and the Song is no exception: its authorship is traditionally ascribed to Solomon. The book's enigmatic form has led readers to make various suggestions about its genre, some seeing it as a series of love songs akin to Egyptian love poetry, others seeing it as including songs for recital at a religious ceremony such as a fertility festival or a marriage celebration. Earlier Christian interpreters read the book as allegory, revealing God's love for Israel or Christ's love for the Christian church.

The book continues to be used liturgically, read by some contemporary Jewish congregations at the end of the festival of Passover and by others prior to Sabbath.

Today's Western, Eurocentric philosophical way of reading often creates expectations for linear, documentary narratives that disclose characters involved in, and controlled by, a singular plot and clear imagery. The Song demands more from its readers, however. It portrays robust passion between clandestine lovers, often desperate to spend time together despite societal pressures. The book moves among a variety of speakers. The female lover speaks most often, answered by her male lover or by a chorus of females, daughters of Jerusalem, who encourage, cajole, voice concern, and celebrate with the female lover. Shifting in mood, intensity, theme, and setting, the Song craftily calls for examination of societal structures and still offers glimpses into the most intimate moments between the lovers. Innuendos—vineyards, clefts, gardens, locks, and hanging fruit, to name a few—permeate the Song. Many of the metaphors and allusions are inaccessible to today's readers, creating wonder over the apparent literary artistry of the writer.

The Song gives voice to females in a way unlike other portions of the Bible, which often reflect successful attempts to silence or control female expression. The speech and thoughts of women dominate the book. For example, while most biblical references to going to one's parents' home literally translate as "my father's house," the Song twice finds the woman speaking of going to "my mother's house."

The Song also seems to be countercultural in other ways. The Song addresses a wide variety of what we today consider justice issues. What are the implications of having dark skin? The woman proclaims, "I am black and beautiful" (1:5), and her lover agrees wholeheartedly. Who and what is considered beautiful? The woman defends the appearance of her small breasts against the teasing of her brothers, and her male lover continually extols her incomparable beauty. Does society have the right to decide who can love each other? The lovers often find themselves seeking each other but thwarted by interruptions. Even their supporters, the daughters of Jerusalem, sometime succumb to society's notions of appropriateness. The lovers must meet in private, even though the woman longs to have a public relationship. And the Song reveals possible undercurrents of class struggle. Perhaps a young man from among the elite has fallen in love with a poorer, less privileged young woman. In this way, the Song could be interpreted as a form of resistance literature. Other evidences of oppression appear throughout the book. The sentinels question, beat, and perhaps even rape the woman as she wanders the city streets at night searching for her lover. Concurrently, the Song magnificently displays the complexity of human life, both individual and communal, for even as the female's voice is freely heard, society seeks to control intimacy, social interaction, and notions of beauty.

Near the end of the Song, readers get a glimpse of the intended conclusion, if there is one, in 8:6-7, from which all can take courage in the face of oppression. Love is as strong as death; passion is as fierce as the grave. Love rages as flame. Water cannot quench it, floods cannot drown it, money cannot buy it. In the end, nothing matters but love.

I am a white, Protestant, upper-middle class, straight female who has been privileged with opportunities and choices. My social location with regard to race and ethnicity often goes unlabeled and, perhaps even more often, is considered normative. My racial context as privileged and unlabeled leave me, I believe, an extra responsibility to name contexts around me. Issues of gender remain omnipresent for me as I struggle to give voice to assumptions and values that often silence women. Recognizing my own context and the contexts around me feeds my interpretation of the Song of Songs. ❖

Chapter 15

THE PROPHETS

Introduction to the

PROPHETS

Lai Ling Elizabeth Ngan

The Christian Bible differs from the Hebrew Bible in its ordering of Scriptures. The second section of the Hebrew Bible is known as *Nevi'im*, "the Prophets." It consists of two subdivisions: the "Former Prophets," including Joshua, Judges, 1 and 2 Samuel, and 1 and 2 Kings (which in Christian Bibles and in *The Peoples' Bible* are numbered among a separate set of writings, the "Historical Books": see the introduction on p. 119), and the "Latter Prophets," including Isaiah, Jeremiah, Ezekiel, and the Book of the Twelve (Hosea–Malachi), which in Christian Bibles are simply labeled "The Prophets." These books are discussed here.

Prophecy and divination were common phenomena throughout the ancient Near East. While Israel shared in these experiences with its neighbors, the Hebrew Bible condemns diviners from outside Israel, but accepts prophets as divine messengers—even when they were associated with divination. (Divination—an umbrella category for a number of Hebrew words—is hard to define, but generally involves trying to determine the future by manipulating sacred things.) The Hebrew Bible further distinguishes "true" from "false" prophets in Israel, and tends to represent the former as a distinct minority (see, for example, 1 Kings 22)—even opposing the prevailing religion of the nation (as in the book of Jeremiah, for example, 1:18-19).

According to the Bible, the messages the (true) prophets delivered grew out of an intimate relationship with God. In *The Prophets*, Abraham J. Heschel wrote that a prophet was in "communion with the divine consciousness which comes through the prophet's reflection of, or participation in, the divine pathos." Prophets delivered words of indictment, judgment, comfort, and hope to their audiences; they also presented controversies to God and pleaded for the people.

A prominent theme in both the Former and Latter Prophets is the relationship between prophecy (or promise) and fulfillment. According to Deut 18:20-22, the words of a true prophet must come true. The stories and pronouncements of the prophets in the Hebrew Bible were likely preserved because what they said came true, and the people ultimately found their stories and sayings to be meaningful and formative for their understanding of YHWH and the LORD's activities in the history of Israel.

Another prominent theme is God's covenant faithfulness, which is often contrasted with Israel's infidelity and idolatry. The prophets preached the exclusive worship of YHWH, but the Israelites struggled throughout their history to determine who this YHWH they worshiped was. The prophetic books also present an ethical norm consistent with the teaching of the Torah: caring for the vulnerable of society, justice in every facet of life, and mutuality are expected of God's people.

THE FORMER PROPHETS

In Christian Bibles, the Former Prophets are considered part of the Historical Books because they purport to recount the history of ancient Israel, beginning where Deuteronomy left off. Because they present that history from the perspective of Deuteronomy, scholars have named them together the Deuteronomistic History. This history tells the stories of Israel from the time of Joshua to the end of Judah in early sixth century BCE. (See above, pp. 119–22.)

These so-called Historical Books are not historical as most twenty-first century readers understand that word. The stories in them are not the result of the objective, sequential reporting of events. They were selected and written to describe and emphasize God's activity in Israel's history, and they reflect the writers' social contexts, theology, and intentions. These stories and traditions went through a long history of transmission and editing. Most scholars agree that the Babylonian exile was the crisis that precipitated the formation of the Torah and much of the Prophets. As prophetic books, Joshua, Judges, 1 and 2 Samuel, and 1 and 2 Kings invite readers to reflect upon the messages they contain (Josh 1:8).

The stories and traditions were collected from many sources: tribes, clans, and families; royal archives and annuals; books of poetry; and songs such as the Book of Jashar (2 Sam 1:18), the Song of Deborah, and the Song of Hannah. The scholar Martin Noth was the first person to recognize that the editors of the Former Prophets were telling Israel's story within a Deuteronomic framework, and thereafter these four books have also been called the Deuteronomistic History. The Deuteronomistic History provided an explanation to readers in the exilic and postexilic periods for their predicament in the Diaspora and served as a resource for theological reflection.

LATTER PROPHETS

While the respective "Former Prophets" (the prophets who appear in the Deuteronomistic History) were portrayed through stories depicting their personal encounters and miracle-making, little is known about the stories of their counterparts among the Latter Prophets. The superscriptions introducing the following books provide some of the clues to the historical contexts in which these prophets served as YHWH's messengers.

The prophets' scrolls contain collections of oracles associated with the prophets for whom the books were named, but these are not stories about the respective prophets. The book of Jonah is the sole exception. It is a story about the prophet and includes only one oracle, of five Hebrew words (Jonah 3:4). To gain the most understanding of these texts, readers need to correlate the messages of the Latter Prophets with the stories and historical context provided in the Former Prophets. The Latter Prophets were addressing issues of their day, and their messages will be better understood when readers understand the historical contexts.

The Latter Prophets consist of four books: Isaiah, Jeremiah, Ezekiel, and the Book of the Twelve, also called the "Minor Prophets." The book of Daniel follows in Christian Bibles and *The Peoples' Bible*, but is not in this section of the Hebrew Bible, but rather in the third section, the "Writings." The books of the Latter Prophets are designated as major or minor, based on their length, not their relative importance. The oracles are primarily in poetic form; they were first spoken by the prophets, then later collected and arranged by their disciples and associates. The ministries of the Latter

Prophets ranged from the eighth century to the fourth century BCE, but the collection and editing of these books into their final form came even later.

The prophets used common life experiences and expressions to communicate the messages of God. The oracles often used a "messenger formula" that begins an oracle with "thus says the LORD" and ends with "utterance of YHWH," to show that the message had a divine origin. Some oracles are presented in the form of the *rib*, or covenant lawsuit, where God, through the prophet, takes Israel to court. These oracles may borrow their form from cultic pronouncements, blessings and curses, oaths, funerals, dirges and lamentations, and wisdom sayings. A feature common in many oracles is the use of "therefore" as a pivot on which words of indictment turn to words of judgment. The prophet's task was not only to announce condemnation; a major concern was to achieve the repentance of the people so that divine judgment could perhaps be diverted. The prophets often proffered the possibilities of hope and restoration.

The prophets whose oracles were collected into the books of the Latter Prophets were considered authentic messengers of YHWH, in some cases because what they said happened within a relatively short time. When Isaiah said to Ahaz that the threat posed by Rezin and Pekah would disappear in two or three years, it happened (Isa 7:1-9). When Micah and Jeremiah preached that Jerusalem itself would be destroyed, it happened. In other cases, the reader is given no reason why a prophet is recognized as authentic. It is clear, however, that the veracity of the prophets depended on the veracity of their words. The New Testament writers claim some of the prophets' sayings as messianic prophecies pertaining to Jesus of Nazareth. For example, Matthew appropriated the oracles in Isaiah 7–9 to refer to Jesus (Matt 1:23). Contemporary historians recognize that Isaiah's prophecies originally related to an immediate situation, the Syro-Ephraimitic crisis in 734–733; but this judgment has not prevented some readers from understanding that the words of the prophets may have had levels of meaning that the original prophets and their contemporaries may not have recognized. The prophets, both Former and Latter, were concerned about covenant faithfulness to God; they were equally concerned about justice and equity for all people. The relationship with God is reflected in the relationship with neighbors, especially the poor, the weak, and the vulnerable. *Orthodoxy* (right thinking or right belief) and *orthopraxis* (right practice) cannot be separated; they are two sides of the same coin. In a world filled with injustice and inequity, where the poor and hungry are ignored, where racial equality remains a still unfulfilled dream, where women are discriminated against and belittled, where all kinds of -isms are deeply entrenched, the words of the Hebrew prophets call us to judgment. How well would those who consider themselves righteous measure up to the indictments in these books?

As a Chinese American woman, I have experienced discrimination because of my race and gender. I am aware of the difficulty of fitting seamlessly into a predominately white society where Asian Americans are considered "perpetual foreigners." The ancient Israelites had similar experiences, as outsiders in Babylon and other locations of exile. I am aware of my privileged position as an academic who has had the luxury of studying the Bible and of my participation as a U.S. consumer in the exploitation of low-wage laborers to bring me cheap goods from around the world. The prophets preached against the rich who exploited the poor, and against the powerful elites who abused power and distorted justice. These indictments still ring true.

After 586 BCE, the Israelites came to live in diaspora, just as I and many other immigrants live in diaspora in the United States. Where, in the contemporary world, is compassion and understanding for those who are so far from home and struggling to survive? The prophets' words continue to be relevant for our time. ❖

ISAIAH

Hyun Chul Paul Kim

Isaiah is one of the longest books in the Hebrew Bible and one of the most quoted books in the New Testament. Its main content includes prophetic warnings against Israel and Judah (chs. 1–12), oracles against the nations (13–23), visions of apocalyptic victory (24–27), woe-oracles alongside the announcement of a righteous ruler (28–33), hope for restoration (34–35), and excerpts from 2 Kings 18–20 (36–39); and from a later time, an announcement of restoration and homecoming (40–55), and

a call for reform in a rebuilt community (56–66).

This lengthy collection of literature covers a wide range of historical events, including the end of King Uzziah's fifty-two-year reign (see 2 Kgs 15:1-7; 2 Chronicles 26), the Syro-Ephraimite war (735–732 BCE), the Assyrian King Sennacherib's siege of Jerusalem (701), the Babylonian destruction of Judah (587), the demise of Babylon culminating in the edict of the Persian king Cyrus (539), and the rebuilding of Jerusalem (450). For contemporary readers, the book is a crossroads of different but interconnected historical settings and texts, from the oracles of eighth-century Judean prophet Isaiah to anonymous prophetic messages from the post-exilic age (which scholars call Second Isaiah, chs. 40–55, and Third Isaiah, chs. 56–66).

One case of cultural clash between the prophetic vision and the prophet's people is the *call narrative* (ch. 6), which highlights the contrasts between the holiness of YHWH and the sinfulness of the people, between the corruption of the nobles and the cleansing power of YHWH. The historical setting refers back to the death of King Uzziah, the conclusion of whose long reign could signify an end of relative stability and a beginning of turmoil. In this sociopolitical situation—the anticipation of a new king—the prophet receives the divine call. The threefold chant of "holy" describing the divine presence emphasizes a cultural clash with the people of "unclean lips" (6:5). The moral corruption of the people, from the highest to the lowliest, is exposed (see 1:4, 6, 21). It is no wonder that they cannot truly "see" or "hear" the word of YHWH. A leading motif in Isaiah is humanity's inability to see or hear. Careful readers will find numerous occurrences of this motif throughout the book. Thus the nobles of Israel, in the north, are called mere drunkards whose vision is intoxicated and to whom YHWH's word sounds only as gibberish (28:7-13). The accusation is also applied to those who govern the southern nation, Judah, who are blinded in their own stupidity (29:9-10). Even the prophet himself had to be cleansed of his iniquity so as to hear the divine commissioning (6:7-8). Likewise, the qualifications of a new king include righteousness and the fear of YHWH rather than what is customary to his eyes and ears (11:3-4). In the end, it is YHWH alone who can open the eyes of the blind and the ears of the deaf (35:5; 42:18).

Near the middle of Isaiah is a narrative associated with King Hezekiah (chs. 36–39) that is almost identical to 2 Kgs 18:13—20:19. Scholars have identified the significant role these chapters play as a bridge between two seemingly disconnected portions of the book. Furthermore, the name Hezekiah in Hebrew means "YHWH has strengthened." This pun-name came to denote YHWH's strength united with the king's human faith as exemplified in Hezekiah's life and prayers. Hezekiah's firm faith contrasts sharply with that of King Ahaz, who opted instead for a political alliance with Assyria during the crisis of the Syro-Ephraimite war (7:9). Ahaz's decision demonstrated the influence of the prevailing culture, where military weaponry and the plans of superpowers were considered more powerful and appealing than any cry for prayer and for trust in God. This contrast in perspective continues in subsequent chapters, where the artisan's action of "strengthening" idols with nails is ridiculed by the prophet (41:6-7). In today's culture, the prophet's call to repent (6:10, 13; 66:2) collides with the pursuit of military supremacy, just as the poet's mockery resounds loudly against modern idolatries: economic pride, which comes at the cost of exploitation; progress at the expense of ecological decay; and social systems that disenfranchise many.

In reading Isaiah, I am often reminded of my social history and location. As a Korean Christian, I recall the hardship Koreans had to endure during colonization and occupation in the first half of the twentieth century. One of Isaiah's theologically most difficult themes surfaces in the call narrative, when the prophet is ordered to harden the hearts of the people (6:10). The notion that YHWH would whistle to the northern army, sending it to invade YHWH's own people, does show that giant empires are mere tools of YHWH. However, it also presents the challenging question of *theodicy*—the notion that God's goodness and justice will be vindicated (10:5-6, 12-14). Was Korea's hardship a divine chastisement? Was the imperial colonizer a divine instrument? If we turn to YHWH's divine pathos in rebuking the corrupt leaders and masses and listen to the message to the broken-hearted, "Comfort, O comfort" (40:1), the text offers a profound message: Isaiah's God is neither immobilized by nor indifferent to historical and sociopolitical wrongdoings. This God does interrupt and disturb wrongful affairs with divine indignation. But if we carelessly moralize instead, applying this notion to the misfortunes of others, we fall into interpretive misuse.

Such misuse parallels the way the powerful notion of the righteous servant's vicarious suffering (52:13—53:12) has been wrongfully abused in certain Christian interpretations of the passage, in which the servant is identified exclusively with Jesus, and his assailants identified narrowly with Jewish antagonists. Such interpretation leans toward anti-Semitism and fails to recognize potential continuity between the fate of Jesus and the prophet's vision of a righteous servant in the suffering people themselves.

The social settings of the final form of the book would be close to the settings of the so-called Third Isaiah (chs. 56–66), in the postexilic time of rebuilding during the Persian period. Unlike the hopes and dreams of the glorious return to Zion (43:3; 49:23), the rebuilding process became an ongoing experience of confusion, disappointment, and dissension (57:1-2; 59:5-8; 66:22-24). Many exiles lived as a diaspora of small ethnic groups, displaced to the margins yet essential parts of the dominating empires that oppressed them. To those who long to truly see and hear, Isaiah's cry resonates powerfully: "How long, O Lord?" (6:11). As an Asian American, my experiences of the English language barrier converge with the motif, throughout Isaiah, of the inability to see and hear. I wonder how often we see and hear but do not understand (43:8) the silences and voices of fellow aliens, sisters and brothers, in the marginalized locations of a multicultural world. Perhaps, in the prophet's cry "How long, O Lord?" and in a humble effort toward solidarity (1:16-17; 58:6-7), we too can hope to be like the ox and donkey who know their owners (1:3), acknowledging our Maker of weal and woe, darkness and light (40:27-31; 45:7). ❖

JEREMIAH

Angela Bauer-Levesque

The book of Jeremiah comes to us as a collection of laments, proclamations of judgment, and a few powerful eschatological promises, interspersed with stories about the life of the prophet during a time of trials and tribulations for the people of Israel. Located, in its initial layer of voices, in the seventh century BCE in the years leading up to the experiences of dislocation and exile in Babylon, the book warns of an impending disaster, then tells of the actual war and destruction and of the various ways the people and their leaders responded to the crisis. Two later editorial layers offer differing evaluations by the next generation of what had led to the calamities in which the hearers of exilic and postexilic times found themselves, having experienced deportation and disaster in and around Jerusalem.

The book of Jeremiah, like most prophetic literature in the Bible, testifies to the challenges and conflicts among the man Jeremiah, the people of Israel and Judah, and their God, YHWH, who is portrayed mostly as masculine yet sometimes also as feminine. Prophet and people search, together and separately, to make sense of their experiences of war and violence, chaos and attempts at resistance, defeat and daily life. A collection of poetry and prose, the book's fifty-two chapters lack a clear chronological order and offer several repetitions of some historical events. Complicating the interpreter's task is the fact that the Hebrew and Greek versions of Jeremiah differ significantly in length, order, and content.

ISSUES, COLLISIONS, AND CONVERGENCES

Biblical scholars have long debated the composition of the book and the identity—or identities—of the prophet Jeremiah. The leading theories on how the book was put together assume *three* sources and/or authors, posit *two* scrolls that eventually were combined, or propose various editors working at various times. Alternative interpretations have mostly dealt with the book in its final form. Feminist and womanist interpreters focus on the numerous layers of female imagery, on the gendered representations of power dynamics in the book, and on its descriptions of sexual violence. Postcolonial readers emphasize instances of resistance to the empires of the time: Assyria, Babylon, and Persia. Lesbian, gay, bisexual, transgender, and queer (LGBTQ) perspectives highlight the fluidity of gender dynamics in Jeremiah and the sexual connotations in interchanges between God and prophet.

In politics and ideology, Jeremiah portrays a prophet critical of the rulers of his time. He is also angry and dissatisfied with the people for not standing up against the injustices in their midst, and for worshipping in ways that make them feel good rather than honor their God, YHWH, in words and deeds. Resonances with current realities in the United States abound. Jeremiah constantly calls the people to turn back to faithful living laid out in the covenant made with their ancestors at Mount Sinai, meaning to act justly in community and to do God's work in the world. Such resonances with the contemporary world suggest the question, Who are prophets today?

As a point of caution, the rhetoric used to express the message of having strayed from God's way is full of powerful and problematic images. Addressed to a predominantly male audience, gendered and racialized metaphors invite the hearers to imagine being raped by divine power and shamed publicly (Jer 13:20-27). Contemporary readers may wonder about the effectiveness of rhetorical strategies that publicly shame their audiences into exhibiting changed behavior by means of misogynous, effeminizing, and racist accusations. Modern psychology has taught us that shaming evokes feelings of inadequacy and inferiority, rejection and powerlessness—the opposite of the strength needed for the challenging work of change. A first-generation immigrant from Germany who identifies as a white, anti-racist, lesbian feminist, I serve as a professor of Bible, culture, and interpretation at a divinity school, where in my teaching and writing I emphasize various aspects of social location (gender, race, sexual identity, to name a few.) and their interconnectedness in shaping our interpretations. Facing questions about the value of the prophet's rhetorical strategies is for me an inescapable part of our responsibility as interpreters today. ❖

LAMENTATIONS

Cheryl A. Kirk-Duggan

Laments—poetic liturgies of pain and anguish—evoke individual and communal agony over horrific loss. As passionate prayers of complaint, protest, rage, and grief over tragedy, they request divine deliverance. Some laments chronicle themes of funeral dirges, of weeping and wailing for the dead. In the company of God's faithful people, laments presume that God will intercede on their behalf. Whether concerning destruction of the city or the temple, the end of its rites, or the trauma of Babylonian exile, the book of Lamentations dramatizes visceral, catastrophic grief and tragedy and helps contemporary audiences as well to name and experience comparable realities, to grieve, and ultimately to heal.

The five laments of this book exude power and ambiguity, as they arise from difficult life dramas. Except for the third lament, each of the others contains twenty-two verses, forming an acrostic in which each line begins with a letter of the Hebrew alphabet sequentially. This use of acrostics unites diverse, often contradictory, voices, complex relationships, and tragic themes—from the slaughter of people to starving mothers reduced to cannibalism, to exile, and to the end of worship. Daughter Zion, represented as woman, princess, widow, lover, daughter, and/or mother, personifies Jerusalem, YHWH's punished spouse. Ancient societies viewed cities as the divine wives of the relevant god. Lamentations, a magnificent, artistic matrix, concretizes the community's suffering.

ISSUES THEN AND NOW

Throughout history, people have needed to express loss and to respond to death. Mozart, Verdi, Brahms, Fauré, and many others have written requiems, musical masses for the dead, featuring voices and orchestra. The blues—bad times captured in song form, originating from African American folk songs at the turn of the twentieth century—are responsorial, empathetic, and cosmological; they rely on a distinctive twelve-bar vocal melody form based upon a five-tone scale, with instrumental accompaniment. These songs are poignant, provocative laments reflecting the spectrum of daily life, from melancholy to complaint to celebration framed by thanks.

Emilie Townes, a womanist social ethicist, reminds us that lament precedes healing. Lament asks for deliverance, moving from crisis and tragedy to deliverance, and praising God. Lament, central to divine-human relations, is our cry for help. After exhausting human ingenuity and purpose, we become victims of our own arrogance. We begin actions we cannot contain and have to cry out to God, in anguish, for succor. Communal laments are forums for communal complaint, grief, and sorrow over physical or sociocultural devastation. Naming the pain makes it bearable. A lament helps us to be in covenant with God, to practice faith responsibly, to seek justice, and to anticipate God's salvific deliverance.

INTERSECTIONS OF COLLISIONS AND CONVERGENCES

The book of Lamentations includes imagery biased against women. Daughter Zion is the spokesperson for the community's grief and sorrow and later is an adversary against the divine to challenge mistreatment by God. Women and their suffering are valued as metaphors for communal pain. Yet Lamentations portrays the daughter as catalyst and collaborator in her own abuse; as inferior and subordinate to the divine male. As a menstruating woman, her body symbolizes humiliation and shame (1:8-11). Daughter Zion experiences bitter lament and reflects today's battered spouse: she experiences torture, abuse, and beatings (1:12-22).

Hebrew Bible scholar Linda Day reminds us that unwarranted and inexplicable suffering often triggers lament; victims are frequently blamed for the violence done to them. The suffering of the most vulnerable people problematizes the notion that suffering is necessary: Why, Lord? Jerusalem's ancient suffering and much suffering today cannot be redemptive. If we suggest that all suffering is redemptive, at what cost do we make that assertion? Amid great pain and agony, powerful questions arise: Where is God? Ancient times and the twenty-first century come together in the experiences of abandonment, violence, suffering, death, and helplessness. The book of Lamentations testifies to past pain, signals survival, and artistically renders suffering as classic poetry while questioning *theodicy*, God's justice. What happens when God, hope, or compassion seem absent? How do those who are privileged (rather than oppressed) know suffering?

Lament is not a resource for moments of grief alone. I am a professor of theology and women's studies at a divinity school and an ordained elder in the Christian Methodist Episcopal Church; I am also an athlete and a musician, on a quest for a healthy, holistic, spiritual life. The Lamentations remind us that we, with our limited anthropological categories, wrestle throughout our lives to address an inexplicable, mysterious God, and that as a community we must take time to grieve if we are to move toward healing. ❖

EZEKIEL

Gale A. Yee

Reading Ezekiel is a "trip" in more ways than one. The prophet was part of the first group forcibly exiled from Jerusalem and taken to Babylonia in 597 BCE. In his trance journeys, he is spirited back and forth, often violently, between the two places. Some scholars have wondered, in all seriousness, whether Ezekiel was having a hallucinogenic trip. He sees fantastic visions and performs bizarre symbolic acts. He speaks in strange parables and vivid allegories, some of which are pornographic. Others have thought he was mad or perhaps suffering from some type of paranoid schizophrenia. The extraordinary vision in Ezekiel 1 of God's chariot—with its exotic creatures, wheels within wheels and eyes in its rims—has even been interpreted as an encounter with a UFO!

Ezekiel's eccentricity can be explained, at least in part, by the traumatic context in which he lived. He was part of the priestly class that served in the great temple that Solomon built in Jerusalem. His was a turbulent period in Judah's history, a time of foreign colonization and conquest by the great superpower Babylonia under King Nebuchadrezzar (also spelled Nebuchadnezzar, as in NRSV). Babylonian foreign policy dictated the exile of the upper-class leaders of a conquered nation, cutting off its "head" so that the rest of the land could be more easily controlled. Ezekiel was thus one of the first to go into exile in 597, along with many from the ruling, military, and artisan classes (2 Kings 24). Several years later, Nebuchadrezzar conquered Jerusalem, sacked the temple of its enormous wealth, and burned it (2 Kings 25). A second elite group was deported in 587. Many of the exiles became unpaid laborers for Babylon's numerous building projects or were resettled as farmers in undeveloped parts of the empire. Ezekiel was probably among the latter, suffering not only deportation to a strange land but also a loss of status and prestige while forced to work like a peasant for his conquerors.

The book can be structured roughly into three parts:

1–24   Oracles against Judah and Jerusalem
        prior to 587 BCE
25–32   Oracles against the foreign nations
33–48   Oracles of hope and restoration for
        Judah

The first section details Ezekiel's prophetic words and visions of doom against the nation and city for their idolatry and faithlessness. The extraordinary vision of God's glorious chariot is a significant theological theme throughout. At the beginning of the book, the vision and his commission to prophesy leave Ezekiel literally speechless (chs. 1–3). He then performs a series of sign-acts that symbolize the state and the dismal future of the nation. (They are not unlike the street theater performed with a decidedly political edge in India today.) Because of the presence of foreign gods in the temple, God decides to quit the temple, leaving Jerusalem open to the invading Babylonians. Chapters 10–11 vividly describe God's glory as the fabulous chariot departs the temple and Jerusalem in three dramatic stages. God will not return in his chariot to the temple until chapter 43, after Ezekiel has a vision of the new temple in Jerusalem.

The second section begins with oracles against nations that are in close proximity to Israel: Ammon, Moab, and Edom (ch. 25). The oracles then shift to coastal nations and their monarchs (26–28). The section ends with diatribes against Egypt, Israel's historical and ancestral foe.

The third section of the book offers hope to a traumatized people. Chapter 34 foretells a new leader, a good shepherd, who will restore the exiles in Judah. Chapter 36 proclaims that the exiles' heart of stone will be replaced by a heart of flesh and a new spirit within them. Chapter 37 describes Ezekiel's famous vision of the dry bones, the inspiration for the Negro spiritual "Dem bones, dem bones, dem dry bones."

The book of Ezekiel will resonate with readers who have left their homelands, especially those forcibly wrenched from them. Their trauma is Ezekiel's. We recall only some of them here: Native Americans sequestered on reservations after the seizure of their sacred lands; Africans packed onto slave ships bound for cotton fields in the American South; Jews taken from their homes in Europe and sent to concentration camps; Japanese Americans put in internment camps; black Africans dumped into Bantustans in South Africa. Even more millions leave their mother countries because of famine, poverty, unemployment, war, or natural disasters. My own family members left the destitution of southern China to better their lives in Gold Mountain, the Chinese term for the United States.

The book of Ezekiel ends in hope: the hope of a people restored to their lands, of a rebuilt temple, and a new society of peace and prosperity. We must offer this same hope to the exiles and refugees of our time and work for justice in their name. ❖

Gallery

The Bible at the Crossroad of Cultures

*Much of the Bible can be read as a "grand narrative" of "the people of God" moving through history.
Many religious communities understand the Bible in just that way and identify with that people (see chapter
10). In recent decades, however, biblical scholars have drawn critical attention to thematic disagreements, breaks,
and dislocations in the biblical narratives. In the wake of the Shoah (or Holocaust), Jews and Christians alike
have challenged an earlier Christian presumption to have inherited what the Bible describes as ancient Israel's legacy.
Feminists, theologians of liberation in Black, Latin American, Asian, Native American, Palestinian,
and other communities, and postcolonial critics from previously colonized nations and missionized peoples
have all raised similar questions about the presumption of any culturally, politically, or economically
dominant group to identify themselves as the "people of God" more than others.*

*This gallery of images highlights questions about identity, diversity, and perspective that arise in the contemporary
reading of the Bible. Any of these images might be the subject of individual reflection or group discussion, or the
launching point for further research (how else do people visualize the people and events of the Bible?), or the inspiration for readers' own responses to biblical texts through visual, musical, or dramatic arts or other media.*

(detail)

Fig. 1

Ethnicity in the ancient world. Differences among peoples were recognized and
emphasized in the ancient near east. In these details from an Egyptian mural from the Middle
Kingdom (nineteenth century BCE), a variety of peoples request entry into Egypt for trade and food.
The artisans, hunters, and herders depicted in brightly colored robes are variously identified today
as "Semitic," "Asiatic," or "Hebrew" immigrants from Palestine, seeking Egyptian grain: compare the
biblical accounts of Abraham (Gen 12:10-11) and Joseph and his brothers (41:53–42:5).

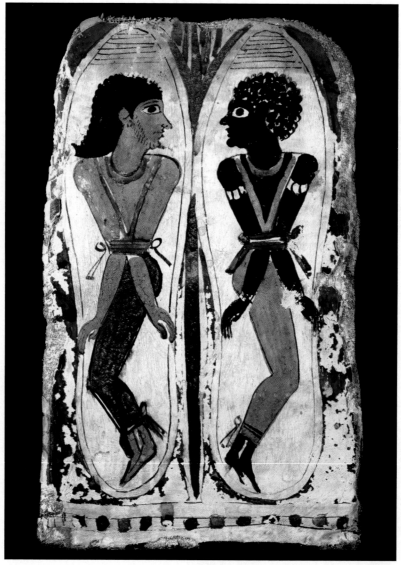

Fig. 2

Ethnic differences were emphasized by empires concerned
about cataloging the variety of peoples subservient to them or dependent
on them. Here a Nubian and an Asiatic prisoner are painted on the soles
of a pair of sandals crafted in the Egyptian New Kingdom.
The person who wore these sandals might have imagined the
figures looking at each other in consternation; others might
have seen a glance of recognition and solidarity.

Christian mission and evangelization often went hand in hand with European colonization of other lands and slavery in the Americas. This has meant that the Bible has often been introduced to a people—or imposed upon them—as if it were the possession of the colonizing or enslaving power. It is all the more remarkable, therefore, that characters, episodes, and themes in the Bible have been embraced by so many peoples as part of their own experience and heritage, as the following images show.

Fig. 3

Pictorial Bible Quilt, 1898. Born a slave in Georgia in 1837, Harriet Powers depicts scenes from the Bible in this piece. Powers's quilts are among the best known and best preserved examples of the quilting tradition in the U.S. South.

The Finding of Moses, 2004. Chinese artist He Qi renders the discovery of the future deliverer of Hebrew slaves as a moment of serenity and stately elegance in Pharaoh's court.

Fig. 4

Grapes of Canaan, 1983, by Sadao Watanabe (1913–1996), whose father converted to Christianity in the face of government persecution, mastered traditional Japanese printmaking in order to convey biblical narratives—here, the story of the Hebrew spies returning from Canaan (Joshua 2)—in indigenous Japanese style.

Fig. 5

Fig. 6

Sheba and Solomon. As the Book of Acts makes clear, Jesus' apostles traveled south, to Africa, as well as west, across the Mediterranean to Europe. But Ethiopia's biblical heritage is much more ancient. Here the meeting of Solomon and the Queen of Sheba is illustrated on pages from an illuminated nineteenth century manuscript of *The History of the Queen of Sheba* (Ge'ez and Amharic).

Song of Solomon, 2004. The amorous poetry of the Song of Solomon, addressed by an anonymous lover to his beloved, attracts contemporary interest as well. Interestingly, Chinese artist He Qi depicts the male lover as darker-skinned, though in the text it is the woman who declares "I am black and beautiful" (1:5).

Fig. 7

Nativity, 1993, by Chinese artist Lu Lan. As events in the life of Jesus have been portrayed through many eyes, Jesus and his family have been depicted as members of many cultures (see chap. 4). Of course, the "classical" Christian art of medieval Europe did nothing less.

Fig. 8

Feeding of the 5,000, 1999. Of Antiguan heritage, New York artist Laura James incorporates motifs and styles from Ethiopian art and iconography into her work.

Fig. 9

The Last Supper, 1973. Sadao Watanabe understood the social world of biblical cultures but used Japanese images—sushi at the last supper, for example—to indigenize biblical episodes. Here Jesus and his disciples eat while seated on the floor, in traditional Japanese style (and as Jesus and his disciples likely did as well).

Fig. 10

Peter Repentant. An African Peter feels remorse for his denial of Christ; an African Mary and John look on, in an illustration from a late-seventeenth-century manuscript of the Gospels and other scriptures from Gondar in Ethiopia.

Fig. 11

Mount Calvary, 1944. William H. Johnson (1901–1970) developed a "folk" style to represent the distinctive intensity of African American religious experience.

Fig. 12

Golgotha, 1945, by one of the leading artists of the Harlem Renaissance, Romare Bearden (1911–1988), bristles with weapons that echo the angular lines of cross and crucified.

Fig. 13

Mother and Son, 2001, by Jamaican-born Michael Escoffery, offers a realistic portrait of a black Christ and his mother. The style of some of Escoffery's other works is sometimes compared with that of Amedeo Modigliani—whose modernist style owed much in turn to the European and North American discovery of traditional African art.

Fig. 14

Fig. 15

Pieta, c. 1912, by German artist Käthe Kollwitz (1867–1945). Though the genre of the Pieta usually depicts a grieving Mary holding the body of her dead son, this Pieta is one of a number of Kollwitz's sculptures and paintings depicting parents holding their dead children—here, a daughter. A large replica of another of Kollwitz's sculptures, *Mother with Her Dead Son,* is featured in Berlin's Neue Wache, a monument "to Victims of War and Tyranny."

Fig. 16

An Ethnic Jesus. Perhaps the best known and most widely reproduced image of Jesus in the twentieth century, with over one billion reproductions mass-marketed around the world, Warner Sallman's *Head of Christ* (1940) depicts a serene Jesus with light skin, blue eyes, fair hair, and decidedly northern-European features. When Sallman painted more contemporary versions in the 1960s, he was concerned (as were his critics) that the portrait of Jesus not look too "feminine."[6] For a discussion of this and the following images see chapter 4.

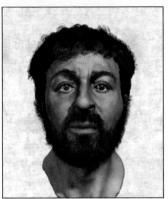

Fig. 17

A Scientific Reconstruction. The December 2002 issue of *Popular Mechanics* offered a portrait of Jesus created by forensic anthropologist Richard Neave, in its article "The Real Face of Jesus." Neave sought to base his image of Jesus on an objective, scientific basis rather than on the cultural predispositions of artists' imaginations. He relied on archaeological discoveries of Galilean skeletons from the first century CE, since according to the Gospels, Jesus' appearance was so similar to that of his disciples that he had to be singled out by Judas Iscariot (Matt. 26:48-50 and parallels).

Fig. 18

Jesus of the People, 1999. Artist Janet McKenzie sought in her portrait to depict a Jesus widely representative of the world's people, especially the poor. The image incorporates symbols from Asian and Native American cultures; the model was an African-American woman. "The essence of the work," McKenzie declared, "is that Jesus is all of us." The portrait won the National Catholic Reporter Jesus 2000 competition; the judge wrote, "this is a haunting image of a peasant Jesus—dark, thick-lipped, looking out on us with ineffable dignity, with sadness but with confidence."

The earliest pictures of Jesus were very different from the images to which we are accustomed today. In a typical portrait from a fresco in the Roman catacomb of St. Priscilla (first to third century CE), Jesus is portrayed as a beardless youth surrounded by sheep. The portrait depicts Jesus as the Good Shepherd of John 8:11, but similar frescos showing Jesus with a lyre may allude as well to the biblical image of David—or to Orpheus, a figure from Greek mythology associated with the afterlife.

Fig. 19

Still beardless, Jesus is depicted in this third-century mosaic in St. Peter's Basilica, Rome, driving his chariot across the sky, in the figure of the sun god Apollo.

Fig. 20

The style of portrait with which we are more familiar today—a bearded Jesus with long dark hair, parted in the center, seated on a heavenly throne and wielding a scepter as *Pantocrator* ("all-ruler")—first arose in the Christian Byzantine Empire, and reflects the fashion of the Byzantine court; Pantocrator was originally one of the titles of the Roman Emperor. This sixth-century mosaic is from the Church of St. Apollinare Nuovo, Ravenna.

Fig. 21

Fig. 22

Devon Cunningham's *Black Jesus* (1995) features a Black Christ as the heavenly Pantocrator ("All-Ruler") of Byzantine art. Mural at St. Cecilia Catholic Church, Detroit.

Although it is often easy for those who enjoy privilege and power to read the Bible as depicting a distant, ancient time, the peoples who make up the world's majority readily recognize biblical themes—such as crucifixion—as names for the historical realities they have themselves experienced. The following images depict such historical events. Can we understand the Bible differently by trying to see through the eyes of others?

Migration. Judaism, Christianity, and Islam find their shared ancestor in Abraham, described in the Bible as a "wandering Aramean" (Deut 26:5) who, in faith, left his family home in Ur and crossed national boundaries in search of a new home (Gen 12:1-4). Though historical migrations are often triggered by natural calamities (earthquake, famine) or political ones (war, economic deprivation, political oppression)—or, often, both—those who strike out, leaving homes and families behind, inevitably do so in hope that a better future lies ahead.

Here families who have lost their land to drought and bank foreclosure flee the Dust Bowl of the Midwest to travel westward (1939).

Fig. 23

During and after so-called counter-insurgency wars in Central America in the 1970s and 1980s and the economic hardship that followed, many Mexican and Central American men and women migrated to the United States, where they took work at low wages that many U.S. citizens disdained. Here Mexican migrant workers sort vegetables in California.

Fig. 24

Exile. The exile of much of the population of Judah following the Babylonian conquest of Jerusalem was one of the most traumatic events in Israel's history, and one of the most formative for its traditions. Contemporary peoples also remember, and have been shaped by, specific experiences of exile. How do these experiences shape their reading of the Bible?

Fig. 25

Cherokee Trail of Tears, 2001, by Cherokee artist John Guthrie. The Trail of Tears was a forced march in which the U.S. Army displaced the Cherokee from their native lands in the state of Georgia to the Oklahoma Territory in 1838. Some five thousand men, women, and children died on the Trail.

During World War II, Japanese-American families and individuals were compelled to board buses headed for forced internment camps in California and (here) Washington.

Fig. 26

Crucifixion. Images of those who have suffered abuse, torture, and death at the hands of military powers have for many people become contemporary icons of justice denied.

In 1917, Charlemagne Peralte, leader of the Haitian resistance to the U.S. invasion of Haiti, was killed by a Marine officer who came to his camp under guise of seeking to negotiate a truce; the Marines distributed photographs of his body tied to a door as a warning to others. The image of "Peralte crucified" instead became a rallying symbol of Haitian independence.

Fig. 27

On March 24, 1980, Salvadoran Archbishop Oscar Romero was assassinated while celebrating the Eucharist. Weeks earlier he had written an open letter to U.S. President Jimmy Carter asking that the flow of weapons to the Salvadoran military be cut off. Days before his death, he had called on the members of the armed forces to "stop the repression" of their brothers and sisters. Nine years later, Salvadoran theologian Ignacio Ellacuría and several of his Jesuit brothers were assassinated by a unit of the Salvadoran National Guard on November 16, 1989. Like Archbishop Oscar Romero before them, their deaths—but more importantly, their lives—came to symbolize the shared destiny of the Salvadoran people.

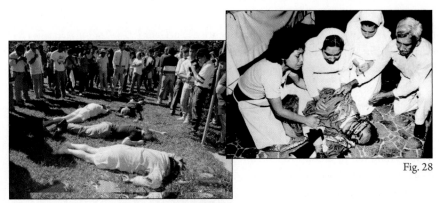

Fig. 28

Fig. 29

Shortly before his death, Ellacuría wrote:

If we are to understand what the people of God is, it is very important that we open our eyes to the reality around us. . . . This reality is simply the existence of a vast portion of humankind, which is literally and actually crucified by natural oppressions and especially by historical and personal oppressions. . . . The historically crucified people which remains constant although the historical forms of crucifixion are different . . . is the historical continuation of the servant of Yahweh, whose humanity is still being disfigured by the sin of the world, whom the powers of this world are still stripping of everything, taking away everything including his life, especially his life.[7]

Deliverance. Despite the energy with which slave owners in the southern U.S. sought to indoctrinate their slaves with the Christian duty to obey their masters, slaves heard another message in the Bible: that the God of the Exodus opposed slavery and willed the freedom of all people. Participants in the "underground railroad"—depicted here in a contemporary engraving—understood their efforts as a participation in a new Exodus.

The Underground Railroad often arranged for fugitives to travel in groups to the safety of the northern states and Canada.

Fig. 30

Fig. 31

Following World War II, the partition of Berlin into Western and Eastern sectors was for decades an occasion of misery. Even after the Wall was erected, East Germans attempted to flee to the West; refugees were often discovered, arrested, and even killed at the border. If they succeeded, their first stop was one of West Germany's refugee camps, as for this family of eight in 1962.

The wall's destruction in November 1989 was an event of public celebration around the world.

Fig. 32

Hope. One of the most enduring messages in the Bible is of hope for the human future.

Another episode of what Barbara Ehrenreich describes as the long history of "collective joy"[8] at moments of deliverance was the first election in South Africa in which blacks could vote, in 1994. The election ended decades of racial apartheid in that country.

Fig. 33

Within Christianity, Jesus' last supper with his disciples and the theme of his self-sacrificial action are central. The language of sacrifice has often been used harmfully, however, to elicit self-denial and renunciation from those from whom much has already been taken. Christian historians, theologians, and worship leaders point to a deeper wealth of symbolism surrounding the Lord's Supper or Eucharist: Israel's remembrance of liberation in the Passover meal; the miraculous provision of food—manna in the wilderness; bread and meal for a widow and her son in the days of Elijah; Isaiah's vision of the world's peoples gathered for a feast on a sacred mountain; and Jesus' own presence at wedding feasts and at the tables of those considered outcasts or notorious sinners.

Fig. 34

In *The First Supper*, 1989, Jane Evershed depicts a dinner gathering of diverse women—Native American, African, Asian, Chicana, Latina, Muslim and Jew—brought together by compassion, respect for the earth, and mutual empowerment. The painting accompanies a poem that reads, in part, "It is not too late for us to make a new world together."

Maps

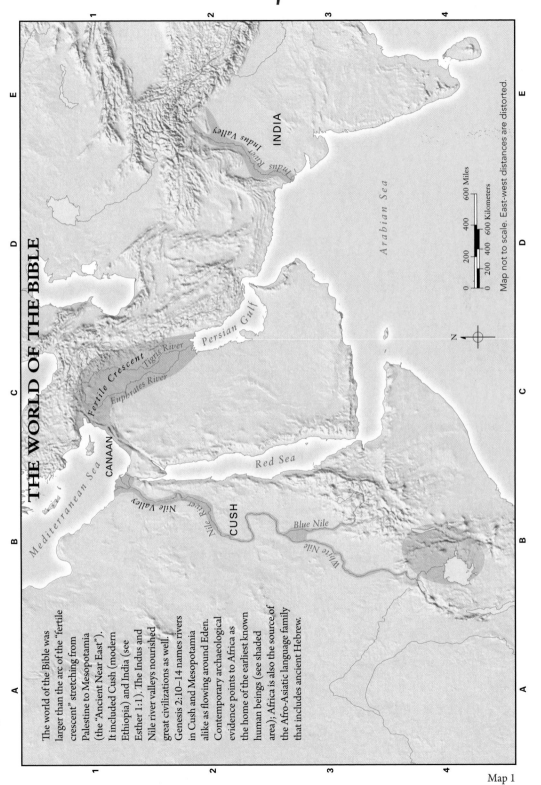

THE WORLD OF THE BIBLE

The world of the Bible was larger than the arc of the "fertile crescent" stretching from Palestine to Mesopotamia (the "Ancient Near East"). It included Cush (modern Ethiopia) and India (see Esther 1:1). The Indus and Nile river valleys nourished great civilizations as well Genesis 2:10–14 names rivers in Cush and Mesopotamia alike as flowing around Eden. Contemporary archaeological evidence points to Africa as the home of the earliest known human beings (see shaded area); Africa is also the source of the Afro-Asiatic language family that includes ancient Hebrew.

CANAAN

Mediterranean Sea

Fertile Crescent

Tigris River

Euphrates River

Persian Gulf

Nile Valley

Nile River

CUSH

Red Sea

Blue Nile

White Nile

Arabian Sea

Indus River

Indus Valley

INDIA

N

0	200	400	600 Miles
0	200	400	600 Kilometers

Map not to scale. East-west distances are distorted.

Map 1

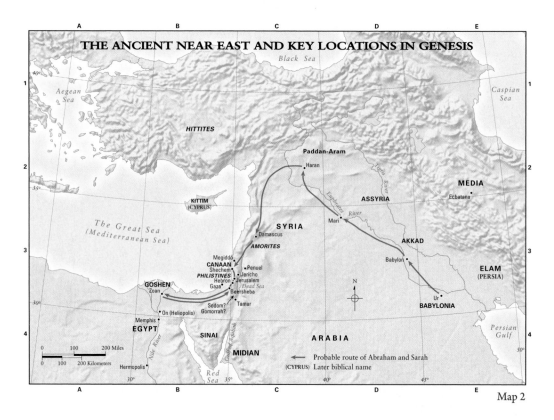

THE ANCIENT NEAR EAST AND KEY LOCATIONS IN GENESIS

Map 2

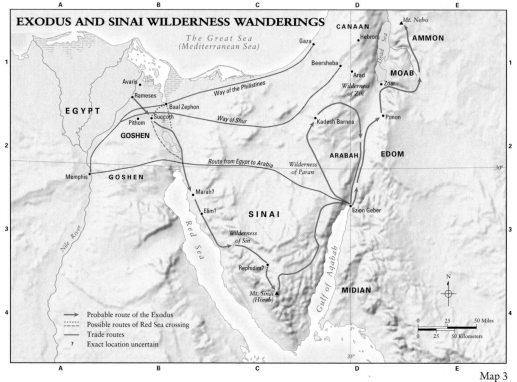

EXODUS AND SINAI WILDERNESS WANDERINGS

Map 3

CANAAN AND KEY LOCATIONS IN JOSHUA AND JUDGES

Map 4

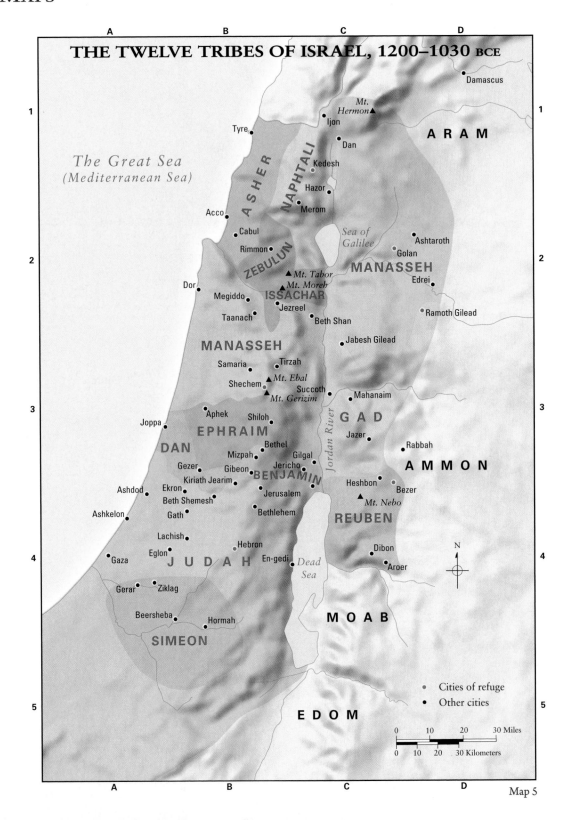

THE TWELVE TRIBES OF ISRAEL, 1200–1030 BCE

*The Great Sea
(Mediterranean Sea)*

Damascus

Mt. Hermon ▲

Ijon

Tyre

Dan

A R A M

Kedesh

ASHER

NAPHTALI

Hazor

Acco

Merom

Cabul

Sea of Galilee

Ashtaroth

Rimmon

Golan

ZEBULUN

MANASSEH

Dor

▲ *Mt. Tabor*

Edrei

▲ *Mt. Moreh*

Megiddo

ISSACHAR

Jezreel

Ramoth Gilead

Taanach

Beth Shan

Jabesh Gilead

MANASSEH

Samaria

Tirzah

Shechem ▲ *Mt. Ebal*

Mahanaim

▲ *Mt. Gerizim*

Succoth

Joppa

Aphek

Shiloh

G A D

EPHRAIM

Jazer

Bethel

Rabbah

DAN

Mizpah

Gezer

Gibeon

Gilgal

Jericho

Kiriath Jearim

BENJAMIN

A M M O N

Ashdod

Ekron

Heshbon

Bezer

Beth Shemesh

Jerusalem

Ashkelon

Gath

Bethlehem

▲ *Mt. Nebo*

REUBEN

Lachish

Hebron

Eglon

Dibon

Gaza

En-gedi

Dead Sea

Aroer

J U D A H

N

Gerar

Ziklag

Beersheba

Hormah

M O A B

SIMEON

● Cities of refuge
● Other cities

E D O M

0   10   20   30 Miles

0   10   20   30 Kilometers

Jordan River

Map 5

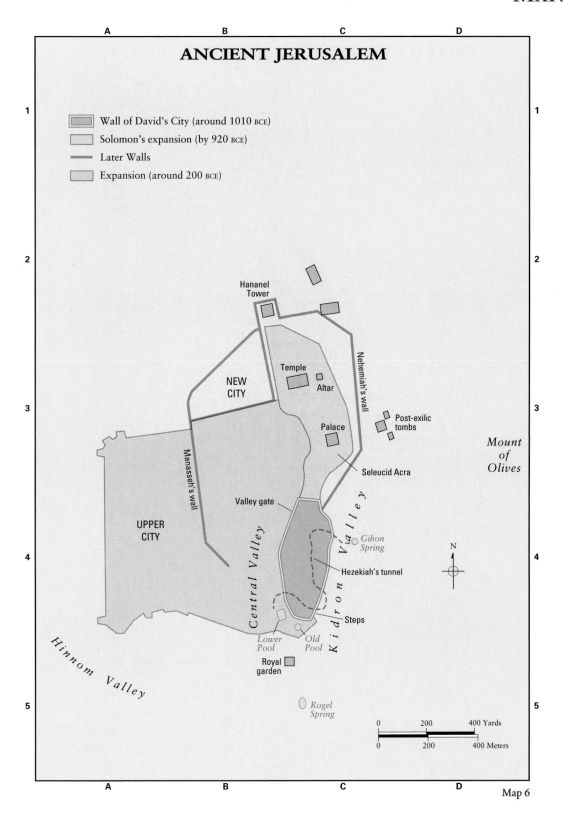

ANCIENT JERUSALEM

Wall of David's City (around 1010 BCE)

Solomon's expansion (by 920 BCE)

Later Walls

Expansion (around 200 BCE)

Hananel
Tower

NEW
CITY

Temple

Altar

Nehemiah's wall

Palace

Post-exilic
tombs

*Mount
of
Olives*

Seleucid Acra

Manasseh's wall

Valley gate

UPPER
CITY

Central Valley

*Gibon
Spring*

Hezekiah's tunnel

Kidron Valley

N

Steps

*Lower
Pool*

*Old
Pool*

Royal
garden

Hinnom Valley

*Rogel
Spring*

| 0 | 200 | 400 Yards |
| 0 | 200 | 400 Meters |

Map 6

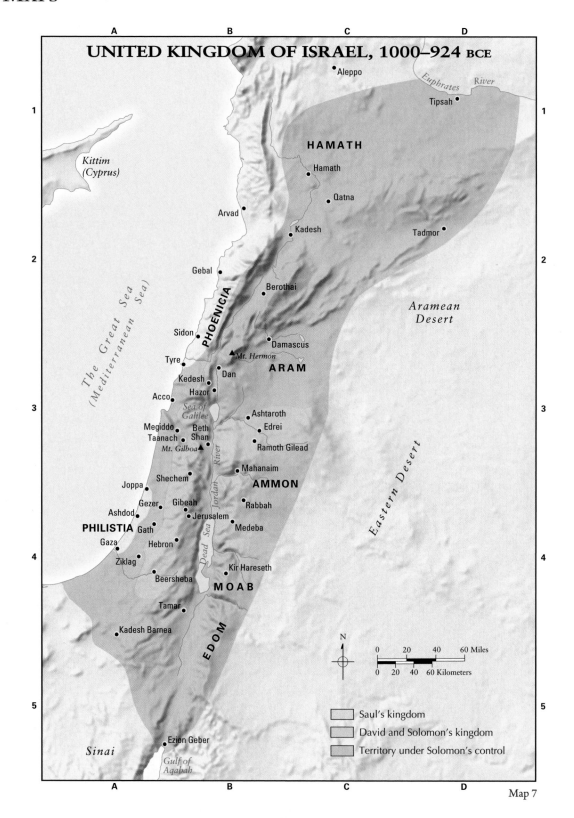

UNITED KINGDOM OF ISRAEL, 1000–924 BCE

Aleppo

Euphrates River

Tipsah

HAMATH

Hamath

Kittim (Cyprus)

Qatna

Arvad

Kadesh

Tadmor

Gebal

Berothai

Aramean Desert

PHOENICIA

Sidon

Damascus

Tyre

▲ *Mt. Hermon*

Kedesh

Dan

ARAM

Acco

Hazor

Sea of Galilee

The Great Sea (Mediterranean Sea)

Megiddo

Ashtaroth

Beth Shan

Edrei

Taanach

Mt. Gilboa ▲

Ramoth Gilead

Jordan River

Mahanaim

Shechem

AMMON

Joppa

Gezer

Gibeah

Rabbah

Ashdod

Jerusalem

PHILISTIA

Gath

Medeba

Gaza

Hebron

Eastern Desert

Ziklag

Dead Sea

Kir Hareseth

Beersheba

MOAB

Tamar

EDOM

Kadesh Barnea

N

0   20   40   60 Miles

0   20   40   60 Kilometers

Sinai

Ezion Geber

Gulf of Aqabah

Saul's kingdom

David and Solomon's kingdom

Territory under Solomon's control

Map 7

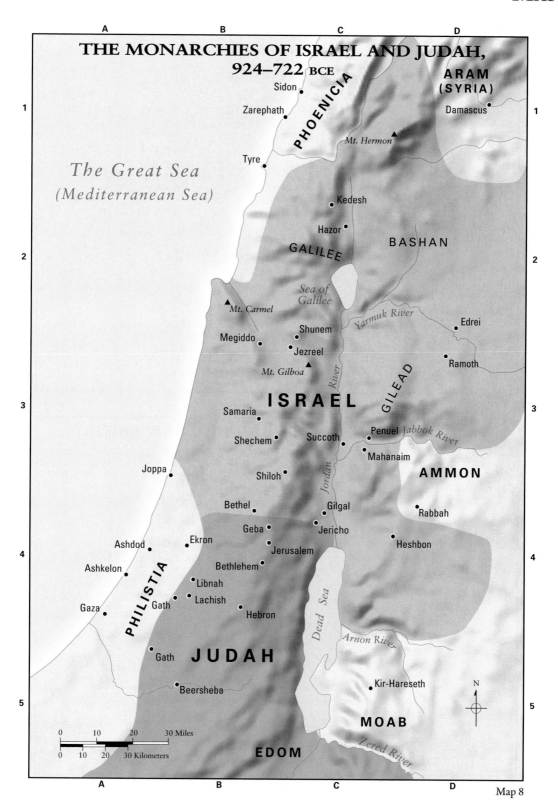

THE MONARCHIES OF ISRAEL AND JUDAH, 924–722 BCE

ARAM (SYRIA)

PHOENICIA

Sidon

Zarephath

Damascus

Mt. Hermon

The Great Sea
(Mediterranean Sea)

Tyre

Kedesh

Hazor

GALILEE

BASHAN

Sea of Galilee

Mt. Carmel

Yarmuk River

Edrei

Shunem

Megiddo

Jezreel

Ramoth

Mt. Gilboa

GILEAD

ISRAEL

River

Samaria

Jabbok River

Shechem

Succoth

Penuel

Mahanaim

AMMON

Joppa

Shiloh

Jordan

Bethel

Gilgal

Rabbah

Geba

Jericho

Ashdod

Ekron

Jerusalem

Heshbon

Ashkelon

Bethlehem

PHILISTIA

Libnah

Dead Sea

Gaza

Gath

Lachish

Hebron

Arnon River

Gath

JUDAH

Kir-Hareseth

N

Beersheba

0   10   20   30 Miles
0   10   20   30 Kilometers

MOAB

EDOM

Zered River

Map 8

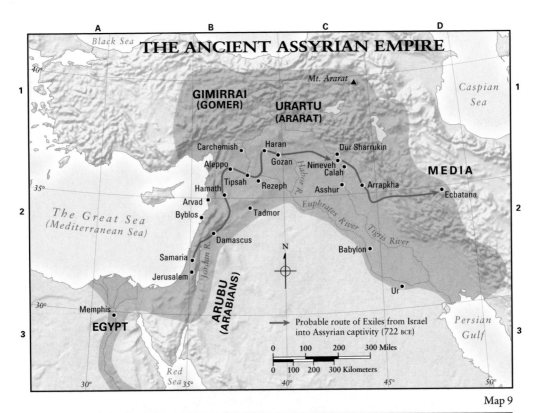

THE ANCIENT ASSYRIAN EMPIRE

Black Sea

40°

GIMIRRAI
(GOMER)

URARTU
(ARARAT)

Mt. Ararat ▲

Caspian
Sea

Carchemish • Haran

Dur Sharrukin •

Aleppo •
Tipsah •
Gozan •
Nineveh •
Calah •

MEDIA

35°

Hamath •
Rezeph •
Asshur •
Arrapkha •

Arvad •
Ecbatana •

Byblos •
Tadmor •

The Great Sea
(Mediterranean Sea)

Euphrates River

Tigris River

Damascus •

N

Babylon •

Samaria •

Jerusalem •

ARUBU
(ARABIANS)

Ur •

Persian
Gulf

30°

Memphis •

EGYPT

Probable route of Exiles from Israel
into Assyrian captivity (722 BCE)

0   100   200   300 Miles

0 100 200 300 Kilometers

30°   35°

40°   45°   50°

Map 9

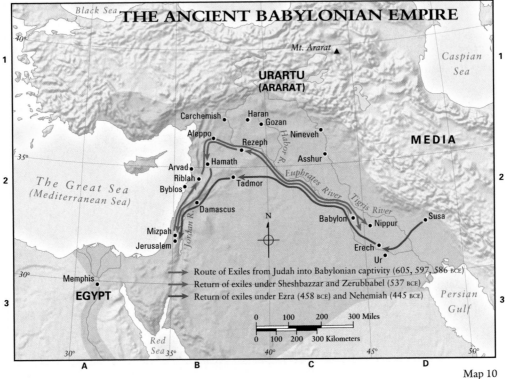

THE ANCIENT BABYLONIAN EMPIRE

Black Sea

40°

URARTU
(ARARAT)

Mt. Ararat ▲

Caspian
Sea

Carchemish • Haran

Gozan •

Aleppo •
Nineveh •

MEDIA

35°

Rezeph •
Asshur •

Arvad •
Hamath •

Riblah •
Byblos •
Tadmor •

The Great Sea
(Mediterranean Sea)

Euphrates River

Tigris River

Damascus •

N

Babylon •
Susa •

Nippur •

Mizpah •

Jerusalem •

Erech •
Ur •

Persian
Gulf

30°

Memphis •

EGYPT

Route of Exiles from Judah into Babylonian captivity (605, 597, 586 BCE)

Return of exiles under Sheshbazzar and Zerubbabel (537 BCE)

Return of exiles under Ezra (458 BCE) and Nehemiah (445 BCE)

0   100   200   300 Miles

0 100 200 300 Kilometers

30°   35°

40°   45°   50°

Map 10

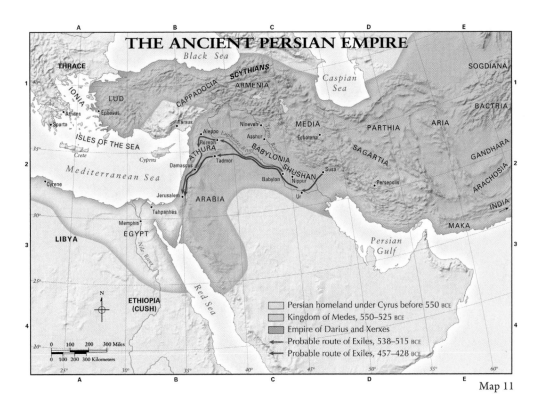

THE ANCIENT PERSIAN EMPIRE

THRACE

Black Sea

SCYTHIANS

Caspian Sea

SOGDIANA

IONIA

LUD

CAPPADOCIA

ARMENIA

Athens

Ephesus

Sparta

MEDIA

PARTHIA

ARIA

BACTRIA

Tarsus

ISLES OF THE SEA

Nineveh

Asshur

Ecbatana

SAGARTIA

GANDHARA

Crete

Cyprus

Aleppo

Ruzeph

ATHURA

BABYLONIA

Euphrates River

Tigris River

Mediterranean Sea

Damascus

Tadmor

SHUSHAN

Susa

Persepolis

ARACHOSIA

Babylon

Nippur

Ur

Jerusalem

ARABIA

INDIA

Cyrene

Tahpanhes

MAKA

Memphis

EGYPT

Nile River

Persian Gulf

LIBYA

N

ETHIOPIA
(CUSH)

Red Sea

Persian homeland under Cyrus before 550 BCE
Kingdom of Medes, 550–525 BCE
Empire of Darius and Xerxes
Probable route of Exiles, 538–515 BCE
Probable route of Exiles, 457–428 BCE

0 100 200 300 Miles
0 100 200 300 Kilometers

Map 11

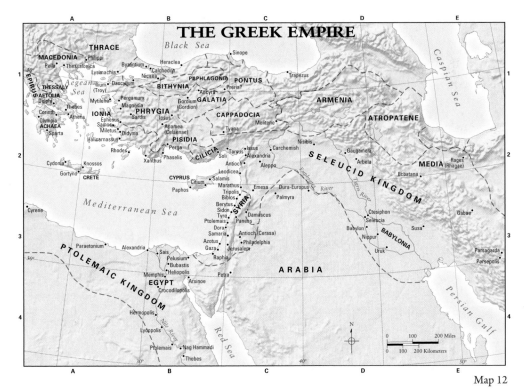

THE GREEK EMPIRE

MACEDONIA

THRACE

Black Sea

Sinope

Philippi

Pella

Thessalonica

Byzantium

Heraclea

EPIRUS

THESSALY

Lysimachia

Nicaea

PAPHLAGONIA

PONTUS

Trapezus

AETOLIA

Delphi

Thebes

Ilium (Troy)

Dascylium

BITHYNIA

Ancyra

Prusa

ARMENIA

Aegean Sea

Corinth

Olympia

Athens

IONIA

Mytilene

Pergamum

Magnesia

PHRYGIA

Sardis

Gordium (Gordion)

GALATIA

CAPPADOCIA

ATROPATENE

ACHAEA

Sparta

Ephesus

Samos

Miletus

Didyma

Apamea (Celaenae)

Ipsus

Tyana

Melitene

MEDIA

Rages (Rhagae)

Halicarnassus

PISIDIA

Perga

CILICIA

Tarsus

Issus

Carchemish

Nisibis

Gaugamela

Arbela

Ecbatana

Rhodes

Phaselis

Soli

Antioch

Alexandria

Aleppo

SELEUCID KINGDOM

Gabae

CYPRUS

Xanthus

Citium

Salamis

Laodicea

Emesa

Dura-Europus

Palmyra

Euphrates River

Tigris River

Paphos

Marathus

Tripolis

Biblos

SYRIA

Damascus

Ctesiphon

Seleucia

BABYLONIA

Susa

Cydonia

Knossos

Berytus

Sidon

Tyre

Paneas

Ptolemais

Dora

Antioch (Cerasa)

Babylon

Nippur

Uruk

Gortyna

CRETE

Samaria

Philadelphia

Mediterranean Sea

Azotus

Gaza

Jerusalem

Parsagarda

Cyrene

PTOLEMAIC KINGDOM

Paraetonium

Alexandria

Raphia

Petra

ARABIA

Persepolis

Sais

Pelusium

Bubastis

Heliopolis

Persian Gulf

Memphis

EGYPT

Arsinoe

Crocodilopolis

Hermopolis

Lycopolis

N

Red Sea

Nile River

0 100 200 Miles
0 100 200 Kilometers

Ptolemais

Nag Hammadi

Thebes

Map 12

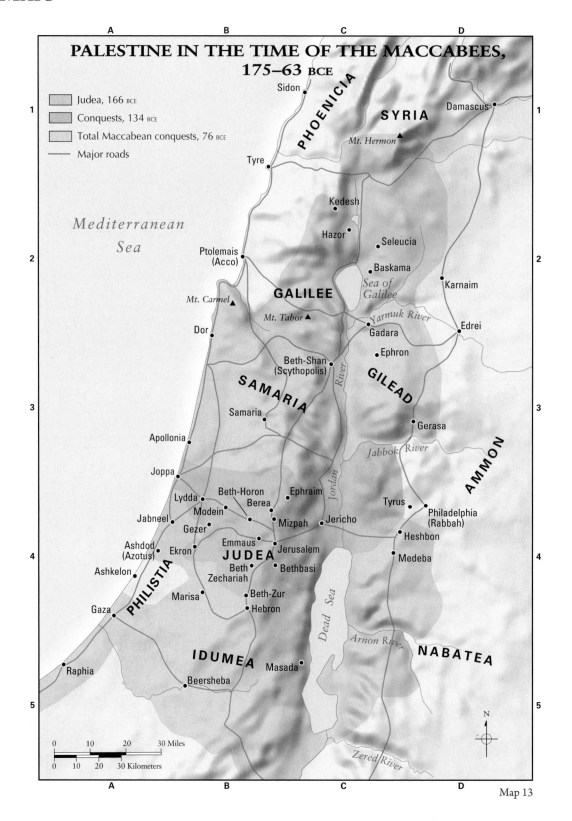

PALESTINE IN THE TIME OF THE MACCABEES, 175–63 BCE

Judea, 166 BCE
Conquests, 134 BCE
Total Maccabean conquests, 76 BCE
Major roads

Mediterranean Sea

Sidon

PHOENICIA

SYRIA

Damascus

Mt. Hermon

Tyre

Kedesh

Hazor

Seleucia

Ptolemais (Acco)

Baskama

Karnaim

GALILEE

Sea of Galilee

Mt. Carmel

Mt. Tabor

Yarmuk River

Dor

Gadara

Ephron

Edrei

Beth-Shan (Scythopolis)

GILEAD

River

SAMARIA

Samaria

Gerasa

Apollonia

Jabbok River

Joppa

Jordan

AMMON

Lydda

Beth-Horon

Ephraim

Berea

Tyrus

Philadelphia (Rabbah)

Modein

Jabneel

Mizpah

Jericho

Gezer

Heshbon

Ashdod (Azotus)

Emmaus

Jerusalem

Ekron

JUDEA

Bethbasi

Medeba

Ashkelon

Beth Zechariah

PHILISTIA

Marisa

Beth-Zur

Dead Sea

Arnon River

Gaza

Hebron

NABATEA

IDUMEA

Masada

Raphia

Beersheba

N

0   10   20   30 Miles

0   10   20   30 Kilometers

Zered River

Map 13

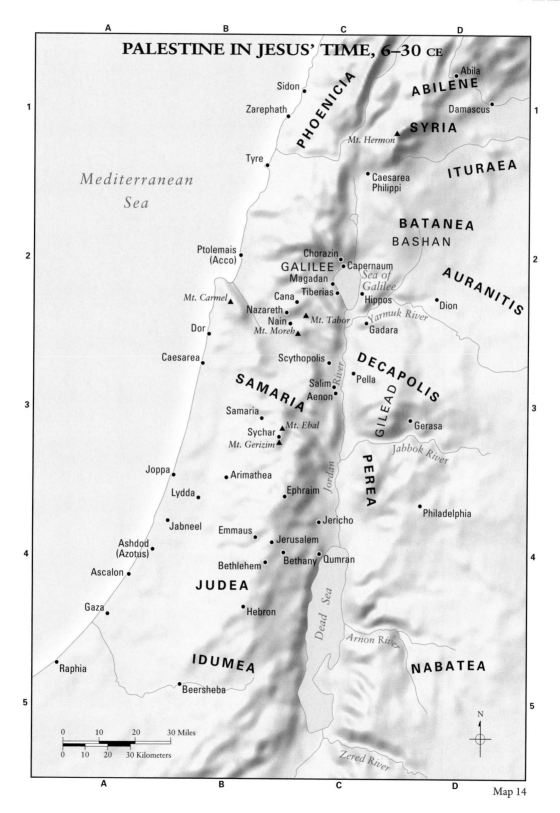

PALESTINE IN JESUS' TIME, 6–30 CE

Mediterranean
Sea

PHOENICIA

ABILENE

Abila

Sidon

Zarephath

Damascus

Mt. Hermon ▲

SYRIA

Tyre

ITURAEA

Caesarea
Philippi

BATANEA

BASHAN

Ptolemais
(Acco)

Chorazin

GALILEE

Capernaum

Magadan

*Sea of
Galilee*

AURANITIS

Mt. Carmel ▲

Cana

Tiberias

Hippos

Dion

Nazareth

▲ *Mt. Tabor*

Yarmuk River

Dor

Nain

Mt. Moreh ▲

Gadara

DECAPOLIS

Caesarea

Scythopolis

Salim

Pella

SAMARIA

Aenon

River

GILEAD

Samaria

▲ *Mt. Ebal*

Gerasa

Sychar

Mt. Gerizim ▲

Jabbok River

PEREA

Joppa

Arimathea

Jordan

Lydda

Ephraim

Philadelphia

Jabneel

Emmaus

Jericho

Ashdod
(Azotus)

Jerusalem

Bethany

Bethlehem

Qumran

Ascalon

Dead Sea

JUDEA

Gaza

Hebron

Arnon River

IDUMEA

NABATEA

Raphia

Beersheba

Zered River

0   10   20   30 Miles

0   10   20   30 Kilometers

N

Map 14

THE ROM

German
Sea

Atlantic
Ocean

BRITAIN

London

Cologna

GERMANY

Mainz

GAUL

Lyons

ILLYRICU

Solona

Adriatic Sea

Corsica

ITALY

Rome

SPAIN

Sardinia

Puteoli

Tyrrhenian
Sea

MAURETANIA

Carthage

AFRICA

Sicily

Syracuse

Mediterran

Roman Empire by the time of Julius Caesar, 44 BCE

Territory added by Augustus Caesar, 14 BCE

Territory added by Trajan, 117 BCE

Territory temporarily annexed by Rome

N

0°   10°

AN EMPIRE

0   200   400   600 Miles

0   200   400   600 Kilometers

50°

1

SARMATIA

Caspian Sea

DACIA

2

40°

Black Sea

MOESIA

THRACE   BITHYNIA   ARMENIA

CEDONIA   Byzantium   & PONTUS

ssalonica   • Philippi   PARTHIA

MYSIA   CAPPADOCIA   Edessa

Aegean   • Pergamum   MESOPOTAMIA

Sea   PHRYGIA   GALATIA   Tigris River   3

ACHAIA   • Athens   CILICIA   Euphrates River

Corinth   • Ephesus   Derbe •   • Tarsus

Antioch •   SYRIA   Dura-Europos •

an   Cyprus   Sidon •   • Damascus

Sea   Crete   Tyre •   • Pella

JUDEA

• Cyrene   Jerusalem •   NABATEA   30°

Alexandria •

4

CYRENE   Arabian

Memphis •   Desert

Nile River

• Antinoe

EGYPT   Red Sea

30°   55°   40°

C   D   E   Map 15

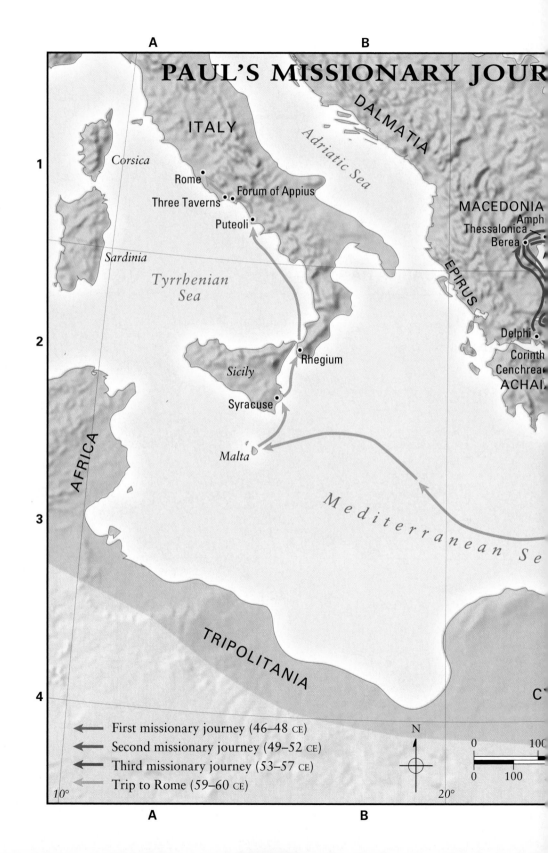

PAUL'S MISSIONARY JOUR

ITALY

DALMATIA

Adriatic Sea

Corsica

Rome

Three Taverns

Forum of Appius

Puteoli

Sardinia

Tyrrhenian Sea

MACEDONIA

Amph

Thessalonica

Berea

EPIRUS

Delphi

Rhegium

Corinth

Cenchrea

ACHAI

Sicily

Syracuse

Malta

AFRICA

Mediterranean Se

TRIPOLITANIA

N

First missionary journey (46–48 CE)
Second missionary journey (49–52 CE)
Third missionary journey (53–57 CE)
Trip to Rome (59–60 CE)

10°

20°

0   100

0   100

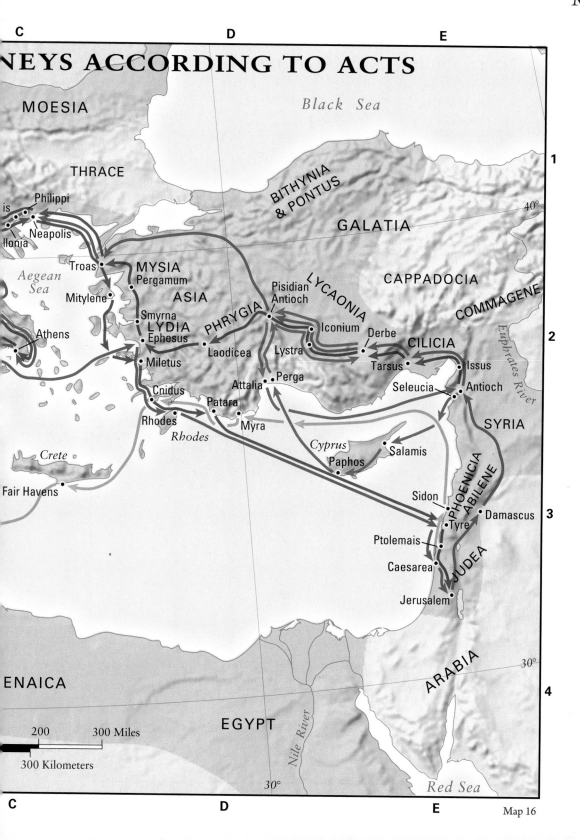

NEYS ACCORDING TO ACTS

MOESIA

THRACE

Black Sea

BITHYNIA & PONTUS

GALATIA

40°

is
Philippi

Neapolis

llonia

Troas

MYSIA
Pergamum

CAPPADOCIA

COMMAGENE

Aegean
Sea

ASIA

LYCAONIA

Pisidian
Antioch

Euphrates River

Smyrna

LYDIA

PHRYGIA

Iconium

Derbe

CILICIA

2

Athens

Ephesus

Laodicea

Lystra

Tarsus

Issus

Miletus

Attalia
Perga

Seleucia

Antioch

Cnidus

SYRIA

Rhodes

Patara

Myra

Cyprus

Salamis

PHOENICIA
ABILENE

Crete

Rhodes

Paphos

Fair Havens

Sidon

Damascus

3

Tyre

Ptolemais

Caesarea

JUDEA

Jerusalem

ARABIA

30°

ENAICA

4

EGYPT

Nile River

200   300 Miles

300 Kilometers

30°

Red Sea

Map 16

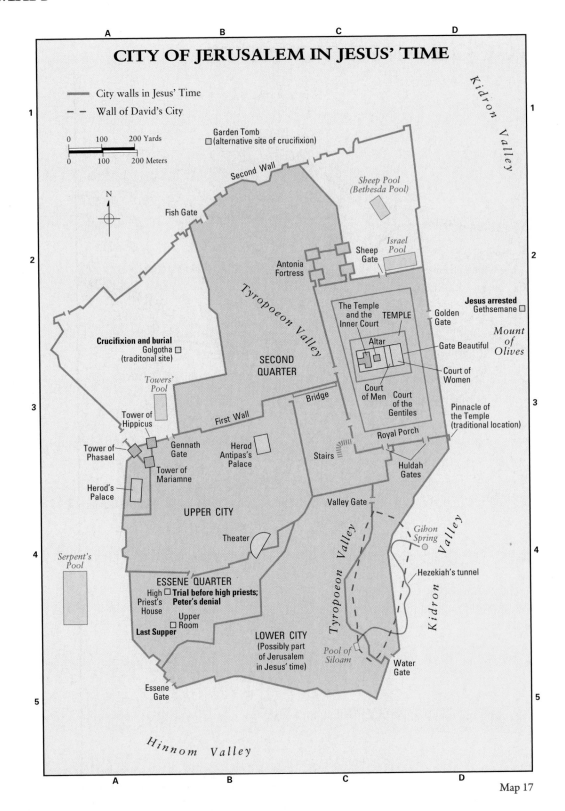

CITY OF JERUSALEM IN JESUS' TIME

City walls in Jesus' Time

--- Wall of David's City

0   100   200 Yards

0   100   200 Meters

N

Garden Tomb
(alternative site of crucifixion)

Second Wall

Sheep Pool
(Bethesda Pool)

Fish Gate

Antonia
Fortress

Sheep
Gate

Israel
Pool

Tyropoeon Valley

The Temple
and the
Inner Court

TEMPLE

Golden
Gate

Jesus arrested
Gethsemane

Crucifixion and burial
Golgotha
(traditonal site)

Altar

Gate Beautiful

*Mount
of
Olives*

SECOND
QUARTER

Court of
Women

*Towers'
Pool*

Bridge

Court
of Men

Court
of the
Gentiles

Pinnacle of
the Temple
(traditional location)

Tower of
Hippicus

First Wall

Royal Porch

Tower of
Phasael

Gennath
Gate

Herod
Antipas's
Palace

Stairs

Huldah
Gates

Tower of
Mariamne

Herod's
Palace

UPPER CITY

Valley Gate

*Gihon
Spring*

Theater

Tyropoeon Valley

*Serpent's
Pool*

Hezekiah's tunnel

Kidron Valley

ESSENE QUARTER

High
Priest's
House

Trial before high priests;
Peter's denial

Upper
Room

Last Supper

LOWER CITY
(Possibly part
of Jerusalem
in Jesus' time)

*Pool of
Siloam*

Water
Gate

Essene
Gate

Hinnom Valley

*Kidron
Valley*

Map 17

DANIEL

Barbara M. Leung Lai

Daniel is a book that includes six Diaspora stories (chs. 1–6) and four visions (7:1-28; 8:1-27; 9:20-27; 10:1—12:13), all set within a textual framework that extends over three empires: Babylonian, Median-Persian, and Greek. The book contains some of the best-known tales in the Bible, including the stories of Daniel's interpretation of Nebuchadnezzar's dreams (ch. 2) and "the writing on the wall" (ch. 5), Daniel's miraculous deliverance from a den of lions (ch. 6), and the courageous counter-Babylonian resistance of the three friends, Shadrach, Meshach, and Abednego (ch. 3). Within the Hebrew Bible, Daniel also contains the only full-fledged example of apocalyptic literature—a literary genre with a particular interest in revealing heavenly secrets to a visionary through dreams, visions, or angelic beings. The book was written in two languages (2:4b—7:28 in Aramaic, the rest in Hebrew) within a narrative framework based on the exilic experience and visions of a pious exile named Daniel.

I engage the text of Daniel as a first-generation Chinese Canadian and as a minority person in my profession. I see significant juxtapositions between Daniel's "captive" experience and my own experience. The Chinese individual "I" (small self) is situated within the collective "we" (big self). Within this perspective, reading and hearing the "I" voice of Daniel in chapters 7–12 allows for a sense of identification with him.

TEXT AND CULTURE

Daniel is a text surrounded by people of diverse cultures. Daniel's social world is unpleasant and difficult because of foreign rule. Perseverance and the ability to adapt are necessary tools for survival. If we read Daniel as a success story, the overall stance of the narratives in chapters 1–6 is one of loyalty, optimism, and accommodation toward the ruling power. Crossing borders between the home and the host culture, immigrant families today have to go through the same journey of alienation, adaptation, assimilation, and, for some, reorientation. As in Daniel, pleasure or pain and success or failure are among the possibilities of this border-crossing experience in the Diaspora. Likewise, remaining in a borderland existence or negotiating an ever-expanding "in-between space" are among the options in the life of an immigrant. Daniel exemplifies an individual's breaking away from a captive status to become an aspiring sage in an adopted culture. Failing to perceive this possibility in life, we would remain perpetual captives in a free land.

TEXT AND COMMUNITY

As a profoundly pastoral book, Daniel is a text for people of different faith communities. It was written at a time of great national peril to encourage faithful Jews that God is still in control, despite their current situations. Within my own interpretive communities, Daniel has been heavily employed, reflected upon, and critiqued among many postcolonial discourses. In my own culture-specific faith community, the book has been strategically appropriated in helping members come to terms with the new world realities after the tragedy of September 11, 2001. The world of Daniel is full of conflicts and turbulence, as well as the rise and fall of kings and kingdoms in the course of human history and beyond.

I am in the prime of my life, with a ministry among my privileged peers—well-educated, middle-class professionals, Chinese and non-Chinese baby boomers. Within this context, one reality persistently disturbs the community of baby boomers: our collective Canadian culture, our professional lives, and our social and economic status cannot adequately provide answers to our inquiry into the magnitude and intensity of human suffering. As in the case of Daniel, we look into the future with a high degree of uncertainty but glimpses of hope.

TEXT AND CONTEXTUALIZATION

Daniel is a text that often is appropriated by people who discover that it speaks to the contexts in which they find themselves. In 9:2, Daniel himself turns to a book—Jeremiah—as he seeks to understand his present situation. In doing so, he mirrors our own search for meaning and significance in our contexts. Daniel can be read as a manual for survival—and even success—under a hostile and dominating empire. Yet the means for resisting kings and empires as reflected in chapters 1–6 is the creative use of satire and humor, as David Valeta has argued. This may have profound implications for coping strategies on the part of minorities today, particularly in the academic religious or theological disciplines. The sharp contrast between the public Daniel as an aspiring sage (chs. 1–6) and the private Daniel as a dysfunctional seer (who speaks as "I" in chs. 7–12), suggests a degree of cognitive dissonance that contemporary minority students and scholars of the Bible may recognize. ❖

HOSEA

Lai Ling Elizabeth Ngan

Hosea was an eighth-century BCE prophet, a Northerner, who brought YHWH's words to his own people in Israel. He prophesied roughly from 740 to 724, from the death of Jereboam II to the fall of Samaria to the Assyrians. Therefore, Hosea saw the decline and social political upheaval of the last years of the Northern Kingdom. Hosea apparently experienced turmoil in his family life and, through it, realized God's deep love for Israel and deep pain for the people's infidelity to the covenant relationship.

A major theme in Hosea is *hesed*, "steadfast love" or "covenant loyalty," a concept that was meant to be reality in all relationships in life. God's desire for Israel was *hesed* and the knowledge of God—that is, to have an intimate relationship with YHWH (Hos 6:6). Hosea was the first to proclaim (2:16-17) that YHWH wanted to be called "husband" (or "man," Hebrew *ish*) and not *baal*—a word that means "master" or "lord," and was also the name of a rival Canaanite deity. (The English word LORD, when written in capital and small-capital letters in the NRSV, represents the Hebrew YHWH, the proper name of Israel's God.)

Hosea spoke of Israel's experience in the wilderness as a positive period in which the people were wholly devoted to YHWH. He used spousal and parent-child relationships as metaphors to describe the relationship between God and Israel. His view of covenant fidelity as marriage and the wilderness sojourn as honeymoon influenced later prophets, especially Jeremiah.

The book of Hosea consists of three sections. Hosea 1–3 tells of the prophet's marriage to Gomer, described as a "wife of whoredom," and the naming of the three children. "Whoredom" is a plural, abstract noun that refers to a personal quality or tendency, and not to the activities of prostitution. The Hebrew phrase might be better translated as "promiscuous woman."

The language of "whoredom" has led interpreters to debate whether Gomer was in fact a prostitute or whether she became one after she married Hosea. A prior question—and a more pressing issue—concerns prostitution in ancient Israel in general. While the prescribed roles for women were either as virgins in their fathers' houses or as son-bearing wives in their husbands' homes, prostitutes were accepted as a part of the social fabric. A woman who did not have male relatives to support her would have no recourse but to turn to prostitution to survive; she often had no other choice. Prostitution was thus a profession of last resort. Prostitutes were sexual playthings that men could use without fear of offending another male in the community. The association of females, more than males, with sexual promiscuity and evil continues to haunt us today. Ultimately, the point of Hosea's metaphor is that Gomer was like everyone else in Israel who did not remain faithful to covenant commitment with YHWH. Hosea's entire life and family thus became signs of God's judgment on Israel.

Hosea 4–12 consists of messages of indictment and judgment in the form of a *rib*, or covenant lawsuit. The leaders, especially the priests and kings, were called to account because they led the people into idolatry. Israel was pronounced guilty. This portion of Hosea offers glimpses of the frantic political activities in the last years of Israel, when wars and assassinations were frequent occurrences. Nevertheless, Hosea 14, the book's final chapter, provides words of hope. It urges the Israelites to turn back to YHWH, who would restore them like a beautiful, well-watered garden.

As a Chinese American and Christian woman, I am pained by the plight of women in Hosea's day. Their valuation as inferior to men and their powerlessness and lack of self-determination are issues that today's readers must address. Their experiences can be judged as inappropriate then and now. Today's readers need to consider carefully some of the expressions and ideas in Hosea. Gomer is described negatively as an unfaithful wife, but she is not given a voice to respond to the charges against her. The juxtaposition of male prophet, male God, and faithfulness over against promiscuous wife, female, and unfaithfulness gives the mistaken impression that male represents what is good and female represents what is evil. In a patriarchy such as ancient Israel, the female was frequently described in simplistic, clichéd ways to satisfy the expectations of a primarily male audience. The fact is that both males and females are equally capable of good and evil. A negative valuation of females continues to disadvantage women in today's society, not least in the church.

A third issue is the language of violent punishment that the husband (God) was going to mete out to the incorrigible wife (Israel, ch. 2). The correlations of husband and punisher, wife and punished can be misused as a justification for spousal abuse. Some men have claimed for themselves the right to "discipline" their wives through physical and sexual assaults, just as God punished wayward Israel. Even the wooing back of Hosea's wife (and Israel) in 2:14-23 sounds eerily similar to comforting words that many abusive husbands offer after severe attacks. The book of Hosea speaks clearly about the unwavering love of God for God's people, but like all other books in the Bible, it requires prayerful reflection and interpretation. ❖

JOEL

Claude F. Mariottini

The book of Joel is the second in the collection of prophetic books known as the Minor Prophets in the Christian Bible and the second book in the scroll of the Twelve Prophets in the Hebrew Bible. Although the name Joel is common in the Bible, the book does not provide any personal information about the prophet or the historical circumstances of his ministry. The introduction of the book identifies Joel as the son of Pethuel (1:1). His name means "The LORD is God." Unlike the other prophetic books of the Old Testament, no historical information establishes the date when the book was written.

Internal evidence provides an approximate date for the historical setting of Joel's ministry. The book seems to indicate that Joel lived in Judah during the Persian period. It mentions the restored temple (1:13-14) and the rebuilt walls of Jerusalem (2:9), the role of the priests in assembling the people (1:14; 2:15-16), the exile of Judah (3:2-3 [in Hebrew 4:2-3]), and the slave trade by the Ionians (Greeks) (3:6 [Heb 4:6]). The absence of the Assyrians, Babylonians, and Persians, the lack of reference to a king, and the apocalyptic imagery used by the prophet indicate that the book probably was written late in the postexilic period, roughly 500–400 BCE. Joel quotes from earlier prophets including Amos, Isaiah, Ezekiel, Zephaniah, and Obadiah.

In the Hebrew Bible, Joel has four chapters. The Septuagint and the Vulgate combined chapters 3 and 4 into one chapter; the Septuagint also includes as 2:28-32 what is 3:1-5 in Hebrew. English translations follow the Septuagint.

The prophet Joel used the devastation brought by a plague of locusts to announce the coming of the Day of the LORD as a day of judgment for the nations and of ultimate salvation for Jerusalem. The prophet used the plague and the drought that followed to call the people in Jerusalem to fast and to repent. Joel's graphic account of the locust invasion becomes a representation of the attack of the nations against Jerusalem and the final battle on the Day of YHWH.

The book begins with a vivid description of the plague of locusts and its consequences. Locust infestations have occurred in many parts of the world, including Africa, Syria, and Palestine. They can quickly leave fields, orchards, and vineyards stripped bare, bringing disaster to people who depend on the land and its produce for survival. As a Brazilian whose parents were born and grew up on a farm, I can sympathize with the plight of farmers confronted with plagues and drought. Many Brazilians live on small farms and have to work hard to earn a living. When plagues destroy their crops, they, like the people in the days of Joel, pray to God and seek divine assistance.

The locust plague was a national crisis and a test of Israel's faith, and the prophet used it to summon the people to repent of their sins and petition the Lord for assistance. The prophet demanded genuine brokenness of heart and issued a call to the people to fast, weep, and mourn.

The advance of the locust is compared to the advance of an army prepared for battle. Joel uses the plague to portray the events preceding the coming Day of the LORD. It will be a day of gloom and darkness and will be accompanied by the outpouring of God's Spirit, portents in the skies of the final battle, the judgment of the nations in the Valley of Jehoshaphat, and the manifestation of YHWH to restore the fortunes of Israel.

Joel is divided into two main sections, outlined below. The first deals with the locust plague and its aftermath. The second describes the events related to the Day of the LORD and the judgment of the nations.

The coming of the locust, 1:2—2:17
The locust plague, 1:2-12
A call to prayer, 1:13-20
The Day of the LORD, 2:1-11
Repentance and restoration, 2:12-27
The outpouring of God's Spirit, 2:28-32
The judgment of the nations, 3:1-21
A summons to judgment, 3:1-8
A call to war, 3:9-16
The restoration of Israel, 3:17-21 ❖

AMOS

Valerie Bridgeman

My grandfather, Kempis McKinney, was a well-respected gentleman farmer and a deacon in his Baptist congregation. People knew he was "a praying man." His business allowed him to interact with wealthy and poor people alike. He was a fair-skinned black man, which made it easier for him to interact with whites in the Jim Crow South. He fiercely defended those he perceived were vulnerable because they were uneducated, without means, or ill. I think often of my grandfather when reading about the persona and message recorded in Amos.

Amos came from Tekoa (1:1) in Judah, a city that we know had at least one famous wise woman (2 Sam 14:1-10). Amos may have been familiar with the banter and storytelling of the wisdom guilds, known for exposing the absurdity of life, the exploits of the wealthy, and the dishonest governmental behavior that affects people with little or no power. Amos, a person of means, got to see up close the self-centeredness of those with access to resources. He was a dresser of sycamore and fig trees and a "sheep breeder" (translated "herdsman" in 7:14-15 in the

NRSV; compare 2 Kgs 3:4), suggesting he owned flocks. According to his testimony, Amos was not a prophet (7:14-15), nor a member of a prophets' guild (not "a prophet's son"), a collection of people who kept alive the words of prophets or who surrounded prophets to practice discerning what ordinary, daily signs meant from a spiritual perspective (compare 1 Kgs 20:35; 2 Kgs 2:3).

Using a rhetoric of entrapment, the book of Amos draws listeners into position as the prophet elicits their agreement about the punishment of Israel's enemies. Slowly, however, the prophetic words turn on Israel and Judah, the presumed chosen people. Their status as chosen people (3:2) ultimately is repudiated as they learn that they are "like the Ethiopians" to the deity, who is God of all (9:7). Amos's poetic pronouncements against Israel were heightened by his day-to-day marketplace contacts. As a trader, he paid close attention to the ways merchants bargained or put extra weight on a scale in an effort to cheat. He noticed the plight of widows, children, and their vulnerability as he plied his own wares of wine, sheepskins, milk, and meat. He stood in city gates where officials meted out justice, listened to city elders give favor to the wealthy, abuse the poor, and take financial kickbacks. Amos was very conscious of the plight of poor people and decided to align himself, under God's influence, as a spokesman on their behalf.

Though attuned to the marketplace, Amos used primarily agrarian language that people would recognize: God's voice as lion's roar (1:1-2; 3:3-8); nature as testament to the name and character of Israel's God (4:13; 5:8; 9:5-6). His words are specific to his times; yet as he lifts up injustice done by powerful people against vulnerable ones, his words continue to speak today.

The book tackles corruption on three fronts: the courts, wealthy people's lifestyles, and sanctuary worship in Bethel and Gilgal. The terms "justice" and "righteousness" are Amos's linchpins for what constitutes a rightly ordered society; these two words are coupled at 5:7, 5:24, and 6:12 (see also 2:6-7; 5:12; 5:15). He favors a rightly ordered society over worship (compare Isa 1:10-17; Mic 6:6-8; Hos 6:6). He condemns the nations, and ancient Israel, for their unjust practices.

Amos aims at those entrenched in power and wealth. Like leaders during South Africa's days of apartheid, for example, they did not easily relinquish power, clothing it instead in religious language. The prophet provides a scathing indictment, noting that their worship is tainted by greed, sexual impropriety, and disregard for the poor (2:6-8). They rush through worship, or at least long for it to end, so they may return to their corrupt business practices (8:4-7). Amos mocks the call to worship and excoriates people for being pious without justice (4:4-5). His attacks on this manner of worship resemble those of his near contemporary, Hosea (8:11-14). As they have oppressed the poor, God will raise a nation to oppress them (6:14).

God's power is evident in the drama of the cosmos. God's identity as a warrior is revealed in nature, in the wind, the changing of night to day, the stars, the seas and rivers; indeed, God's palace may be in heaven, but its foundations are upon the earth (4:13; 5:8; and 9:5-6). In Amos, readers understand that Israel expected "the Day of the LORD" (5:18) to be an ultimate blessing for Israel. But Amos assures them that the day will be nothing like they imagine. It will be as if, trying to escape a lion, one runs into a bear, then, escaping the bear, is killed by a poisonous snake in the supposed safety of one's home (5:18-20). The answer for their plight is to "seek the LORD and live" (in various forms, 5:4, 6, 14). The repetition and doing of this phrase is the antidote for what ails them.

Like other prophets, Amos relies on attitudes toward women to make his point. He lays oppressive practices on the beds of women, "you cows of Bashan" (4:1). When the priest Amaziah challenges him, Amos declares that Amaziah's wife will become a prostitute or a spoil of war (7:17). Using women as scapegoats or in a pejorative way is a common biblical phenomenon (see Num 5:11-32; Ezekiel 16; Proverbs 5 and 7; Judges 16; 1 Kings 21).

Amos's visions for the Northern Kingdom were so powerful that Jeremiah later referred to them to make his own case toward Judah. ❖

OBADIAH

John J. Ahn

The name Obadiah means "servant of YHWH." Historically, the background to the book of Obadiah is the second forced migration, or exile, from Judah in 587 BCE. During this time, Nebuzaradan, the commander in charge of Nebuchadnezzar's Babylonian army, attacked, seized, and burned the palace, the temple, and all other major edifices in Jerusalem. Judah had been annexed ten years earlier, in 597, when Jehoiachin relinquished his throne and was taken to Babylon along with a first wave of Judean royal officials, elites, priests, and other noble and skilled workers for Babylonian economic gain. This second displacement of Judeans to Babylon was a further devastating blow to a vassal nation that was already broken. To add to this painful fracture, the Edomites—a geographical neighbor and related by blood as descendents of Esau—joined in on the pillage (v. 6) and slaughter (v. 10) and cut off the men, women, and children fleeing for their lives by handing them over to the Babylonians (v. 14). Obadiah, the shortest book in the Old Testament, speaks volumes about betrayal and the desire for revenge against a neighbor, one's own brother.

A neighbor's or relative's ill action becomes a source for a curse in Psalm 137:7-9. The motif of malediction against the Edomites has a unique role in the Hebrew Bible (Isa 34:5; Jer 49:7; Lam 4:21; Ezek 25:12; Joel 3:19; Amos 1:6; Mal 1:4). The atrocious action of one's enemy is understood; however, being trapped, deceived, and plundered by a neighbor or relative is a very different situation. The fact that one neighbor has turned away from another neighbor, relative has turned against relative, is seen as something that requires more than the standard reprimand. Throughout the twenty-one verses of

Obadiah, issues of betrayal and desire for vengeance cut across the text.

We know that families and religious communities *should* be among the last places that exhibit this betrayal-vengeance pattern. But ironically, where neighbors and sisters and brothers gather, we witness these traits. I am a second-generation Korean American and a third-generation Christian. My maternal grandmother was one of the first women to be educated by missionaries from the United States. For her generation, education was generally only for men and boys. She once noted that she was both grateful and embarrassed to be literate. She grew up in what we now call North Korea. After hearing and embracing the gospel, she was baptized, trained, and became an itinerant preacher. She went from village to village sharing the gospel. But for her in-laws and others in her immediate community, she was betraying the traditional religions of ancient Korea. She was ostracized by her own family. When her husband died, she was seen as the source of his death. She was left with nothing except her two young children. Her escape to South Korea is a modern-day tale like that of Harriet Tubman. She and her children escaped by hiding by day and traveling on foot at night.

North Koreans and South Koreans are brothers and sisters. However, betrayal and the persistent desire for revenge, or the threat of judgment and war, is constantly at bay. Both North and South Koreans see themselves as the victim and the other as aggressor—like Edom. With warriors (v. 9) on each side, and the North ready to pillage, "All your allies have deceived you, they have driven you to the border; your confederates have prevailed against you; those who ate your bread have set a trap for you—there is no understanding of it" (v. 7). Those *seem* not the ancient words of the sixth century BCE but words that describe some conflicts and hatreds of the twentieth and twenty-first centuries.

There is an important lesson to be learned, however. If one seeks judgment upon a brother or sister, be prepared to have it also fall upon oneself. In the oracles against the nations and Edom, Judah is also included (v. 18). In the end, however, those in forced migrations will be restored. "Those who have been saved shall go up to Mount Zion" to be one unified kingdom under the LORD. ❖

JONAH

Claude F. Mariottini

The book of Jonah is different from other prophetic books in the Old Testament. It is not a collection of prophetic oracles but a short story about an eighth-century prophet of the same name. It includes only one brief message proclaimed by Jonah.

The main character of the book is identified with the prophet Jonah, the son of Amittai (2 Kgs 14:25), who prophesied during the reign of Jeroboam II, king of Israel (786–746 BCE), that the borders of the Northern Kingdom would be expanded. The prophet Jonah was born in Gath-hepher, a village that belonged to the tribe of Zebulun (Josh 19:10, 13). His name means "Dove."

The traditional view assigns the composition of the book to Jonah himself, writing in the eighth century BCE. However, internal evidence suggests that the book was written not by Jonah but by an anonymous writer who lived in the later postexilic community, probably in the fifth century BCE. There are several reasons to date the book in the late postexilic period. Its language contains Aramaic expressions current in the Persian period. The implication that Nineveh was the capital of the Assyrian empire places it no earlier than late in the eighth century; and the title "king of Nineveh"

(3:6) is never used of the king of Assyria in biblical literature outside Jonah.

There is some debate about the literary characteristics of the book. Does it refer to a historical event, or is it a prophetic novel, a didactic story, an allegory, or a parable? The content of the book is loosely related to historical events, and the book includes a didactic story that seems designed to teach about God's concern for people who lived outside the covenant community.

The story begins as Jonah receives a divine commission to go to Nineveh and announce the coming of God's judgment against the city. But instead of going to Nineveh, Jonah flees to Tarshish, a city probably located in southern Spain, thus representing about the farthest place Jonah could flee from the Lord. En route, a storm threatens to destroy Jonah and the sailors who, to save their lives, threw Jonah into the sea. The Lord prepares a great fish to rescue Jonah. After Jonah is saved, the Lord commissions him a second time to go to Nineveh. Jonah goes, warns the citizens that the city will be destroyed in forty days, and the Ninevites repent and the judgment is averted. Jonah complains to God and sulks because the city's conversion moved God to suspend the judgment. God rebukes him and declares his concern for people and animals.

The story in Jonah may reflect a conflict of cultural values in postexilic Israel. The book's message is a criticism of the narrow nationalism of the people returning from exile. Some Jews believed that divine grace included the acceptance of Gentiles, while others, in the interest of self-preservation, held strong nationalistic views that excluded Gentiles from their community.

Some scholars believe Jonah was written as a protest against this exclusivist policy. Like Jonah, some Jews were not willing to share their faith with Gentiles, preferring that they be destroyed rather than saved. The author of the book wanted to show that the God of Israel is "a gracious God and merciful, slow to anger, and abounding in steadfast love, and ready to relent from punishing" (Jonah 4:2). The message of the book teaches about the Lord's desire to redeem people, forgive their sins, and honor their conversion. In presenting Jonah as a rebellious prophet, the writer was calling Israel back to its mission in the world.

Like Israel, the church has a mission to the world. God's desire to redeem people is manifested in the lives of thousands of immigrants who experience the grace of God in the fellowship of other believers. As a pastor of a church that includes people from South and Central America, I can testify that the gospel transcends culture and nationality. The message of hope that Jonah failed to proclaim is being proclaimed in multicultural churches all over our nation.

The book may be outlined as follows:

Jonah's flight from God, 1:1-17
Jonah's song of thanksgiving, 2:1-10
Jonah's mission to Nineveh, 3:1-10
Jonah's struggle with God, 4:1-11 ❖

MICAH

Daniel L. Smith-Christopher

The book of Micah is normally divided into three sections, chapters 1–3, 4–5, and 6–7, with only the first section definitively attributed to the sayings of the historical Micah. The first section can be dated at the end of the eighth century BCE, either anticipating or reflecting on the devastations of Assyrian campaigns in Samaria in 722 or attacks in Judah in 701 under Sennacherib. An apparent reference to Babylon and the exile (4:10) suggests that the second and third sections must be additions to the older chapters 1–3, made after 587 BCE. These additions may have been written or compiled by those who considered themselves students or followers of the prophet Micah, since the famous "swords into plowshares" passage of 4:1-5 has clear associations with Micah's rural imagery in chapters 1–3.

We know little about the prophet Micah other than the notable reference to his words in the later book of Jeremiah, quoted to defend Jeremiah from charges of treason, suggesting that Micah was well known (Jer 26:16-18).

Micah's village of Moresheth is located southwest of Jerusalem. It was among the smaller agricultural settlements that were under threat from invading armies that would have a far more difficult time making a successful assault on the walled city of Jerusalem, where the elite lived or sought refuge. And Jerusalem depended on the villages for both supplies and soldiers. Thus, in Micah we hear echoes of rural versus urban and workers versus elites.

As a Quaker reader of biblical texts, I am particularly attentive to the use and abuse of religious arguments as a defense of violence and privilege. Micah is a significant example of a prophet who resisted warfare as a crude means of exploiting the rural agricultural workers and village economies that formed the vast majority of Hebrew society. A Quaker-informed abolitionist reading of the Bible allows one to imagine a modern Micah complaining about the constant drain of local resources that militarism always creates, whether in developed or developing societies.

The angry judgments of Micah relate directly to the social and economic context of both Israelite and Judean policies as well as the pressures of Assyrian domination in the entire region. Micah, like many other prophets, angrily denounces the abuses suffered by the population of his agriculturally based village at the hands of elite city dwellers, including rulers, landowners, military leaders, and priests.

Micah's angry judgments are more understandable if we note that Israel's land-owning class was at the time consolidating its hold over both land and workers, with the cooperation of the nation's central institutions of religion and monarchy. This development was expressed in more detail by Micah's contemporary, Isaiah (see, for example, Isaiah 5).

Micah expresses the farmers' profound anger over the injustices they are suffering:

The punishment of the two capital cities, Jerusalem and Samaria, is that their lands would be returned to arable, useful land—"a place for planting vineyards" (1:6) and "plowed as a field" (3:12).

Warfare is resented for diverting usable farmers' tools into weapons; correspondingly, peace is represented as the people being free to pursue their farming, with the accompanying hope that nations would meet to settle their differences as rural households must do (4:3-4).

The abuses by the elite who "covet fields, and seize them; houses, and take them away" (2:2), and "eat the flesh of my people" (3:1-3) should be condemned.

True piety is described as living a just life rather than making many sacrifices of one's farm produce, which chiefly benefits the urban priests and other elites (6:6-8).

Next, Micah turns his attention to the larger empires that have designs on the smaller nations and communities. The Babylonian conquest of Jerusalem early in the sixth century BCE is alluded to in 4:10. Micah expresses the hope of God's judgment on the war machines of all the nations in 5:7-15, with the assurance that the Hebrew people will finally be left alone.

The book returns to judgment in the final section, chapters 6–7, with a warning not to follow "the statutes of Omri and all the works of the house of Ahab" (6:16)—two rulers whose legacy in the Northern Kingdom (1 Kings 17–19) resulted in the disenfranchisement of rural agricultural workers like Naboth. In the end, the Israelite peoples are condemned for their economic corruption (7:2-3), but the bigger nations are warned not to take advantage of this; they too will come to repent of their ravenous violence on the smaller nations: "The nations shall see and be ashamed of all their might" (7:16).

A careful reading of Micah raises questions about internal solidarity in the face of outside aggression—and about the fact that such aggression is often used to deflect attention from the seriousness of internal injustice. Too often internal corruption is tolerated in the name of loyalty to cultural or national liberation. But Micah condemns the corrupt exploitation of the peasant farmers (a majority of the population) by the Israelite elite who tax and conscript the workers to increase their own economic advantages *and* the threats posed by the larger imperial powers, Assyria and Babylon.

The book may be outlined as follows:

1:1-5	Introduction—Samaria and Judah on trial
1:6-7	Punishment for false ideology
1:8-16	Lamentation at the fate of Judah and Samaria
2:1-2	The injustice of the elite against the poor
2:3-5	The promise of punishment for oppression
2:6	Protest from the judged: "Don't talk like that!"
2:7-13	Affirmation of the judgment from Micah
3:1-12	Systematic accusations against leaders (3:1-4, against heads of households; 3:5-8, against false prophets; 3:9-12, against rulers and priests)
4:1-5	Judgment on militarism and its oppression of the poor
4:6-13	Reversal of fortune: the poor and "lame" will benefit
5:1-15	Promise of deliverance from the foreign oppressor
6:1-5	God resumes the trial
6:6-8	Justice is better than sacrifice
6:7-16	Words against Judean policies of oppression
7:1-7	Social instability after God's judgment
7:8-20	Hope for future restoration ❖

Nahum

Daniel L. Smith-Christopher

The book of Nahum has only forty-seven verses and a single theme: the punishment of the Assyrian Empire. It offers no internal critique of the behavior of either the Israelites or the Judeans, and its apparent nationalist sentiment creates unease in many contemporary readers and commentators. As a Quaker reader of the Bible, however, I am particularly interested in understanding the context of violent rhetoric, especially when expressed by those who have suffered military threat or domination. Can one be *informed* by the rhetoric of anger, acknowledging the useful attention it can bring to real injustices, and yet refuse to *endorse* the hastily advocated violence that often accompanies such rhetoric? Paying attention to contemporary debates among minority cultures or small nation-states, especially with regard to the role of nationalism or internationalism as a positive or negative step in self-determination, allows us to read Nahum with greater appreciation, especially when it is brought into dialogue with Jonah or others among the Twelve Prophets. If, on the one hand, Jonah holds out the possibilities of positive change among enemies, Nahum reflects vengeful anger on the other.

The book is often divided into smaller sections that separate oracles (for example 1:12-15 and 3:1-7) and taunt songs (3:8-13 and again in 3:14-17). But some scholars are correct in pointing out two main sections that divide at 1:15 and 2:1. The first part focuses on the appearance and description of God as divine Judge and avenger, often drawing on Canaanite cosmic battle imagery, as in 1:3-4. The second part focuses on—and almost relishes—the destruction of Assyria, to be lamented by none (3:7). That this destruction has not yet happened suggests that the writings we call Nahum were completed before the final destruction of Nineveh in 612 BCE at the hands of the Medes, in alliance with the Babylonians, who then rose in power themselves.

We know next to nothing about Nahum himself because all attention is focused on Nineveh, the major city of the late Neo-Assyrian Empire. (That empire was radically and efficiently reorganized under Tiglath-Pileser III in 744–727, called Pul in 2 Kings 15.) But Israel suffered its most significant attacks under Shalmaneser V (726–722) or Sargan II (721–705), and Judah was brutally attacked by Sennacherib (704–681) when Jerusalem only escaped when Hezekiah sued for terms (even though the Bible also says that God defended Jerusalem, 2 Kgs 19:32-34).

Assyrian inscriptions are notorious for bravado and brutality, and while historians are certain of their exaggeration of that nation's accomplishments, including booty taken and enemy killed, the sheer cruelty of Assyrian imperial design is striking. Nahum cannot be understood apart from some familiarity with these writings and the social and economic suffering they represent for Assyria's opponents (see "bloodshed" and "booty," 3:1). Not without reason was Assyria famous for its militarism and economic exploitation. Nahum's rhetoric expresses horrified familiarity with many of the details of Assyrian hegemony, including the armaments of invading armies (2:3-5; 3:3); enslavement (2:7); the numbers of dead (3:3b); and stolen wealth (2:9; 3:16).

Nahum and Jonah represent an interesting dialogue between Nahum—with its unrelenting and indiscriminate judgment on all things Assyrian as evil—and Jonah's sense that there may be Assyrians worth saving after all and his implied criticism of Judean resistance to God's intentions for foreigners other than destruction.

The book may be outlined as follows:

1:1-8	Announcement of God's coming in judgment
1:9-11	Accusations against Nineveh
1:12-14	The coming punishments of Nineveh
1:15/2:1 (Hebrew)–2:9	Announcement of attack on Nineveh
2:10-13	Nineveh compared to lion's prey
3:1-15	Like other oppressive empires, Nineveh will fall
3:16-19	Nobody will mourn Assyria's fall

A POSTCOLONIAL READING OF NAHUM'S ANGER

Nahum's rhetoric can be appreciated on a number of levels. While it may be disturbing in its unrelenting and indiscriminate judgment of national opponents, modern readers must reckon with the reality of angry rhetoric and actions that can result directly from real social and political exploitation. Thus, one way to read Nahum's anger is not so much with a sense of offended propriety (often a luxury of the privileged and powerful) as much as a discerning and compassionate understanding of the kinds of social, economic, and political subordination that inevitably—and often appropriately—provoke this kind of furious response. Who are the *modern* Assyrian Empires whose policies have nurtured such theologies of angry hatred among subordinated and exploited peoples?

Whether one takes modern offense at Nahum's angry celebration of Assyria's fall can depend entirely on one's point of view! Nahum's rhetoric can thus be helpfully compared to the angry rhetoric of movements such as the Black Panthers in the United States or the indigenous Maori (New Zealand/Aotearoa) *Hikoi* movements for social change and for justice long delayed. ❖

HABAKKUK

Valerie Bridgeman

I grew up forty miles southeast of Bull Connor's Birmingham, a place where dogs were loosed on children, where water hoses were turned on teenagers, and where some people were called "pickaninny." Faith played a pivotal role in the lives of those who willingly resisted oppressive and dangerous racism. It is from that history that I read Habakkuk. *How does one watch God watch evil?* That is the dilemma Habakkuk faced. It also is the question asked by enslaved people, by sexually abused people, and by those who ponder the reality of the mid-twentieth-century Holocaust and the plight of the dispossessed in the two-thirds world.

The book of Habakkuk addresses issues of violence, corruption, foreign occupation, and poverty. Habakkuk was probably written as Judah's existence as a nation-state came to an end, between 609 BCE, when it became a vassal state, and 586, when the inhabitants were forced into exile. Judeans were living under the brutal occupation of the Chaldeans and a corrupt government of puppet leaders. Using ancient lament and complaint forms, Habakkuk calls God to the witness stand, demanding to know how a just and holy God can allow destruction and violence to persist. Pairing the Hebrew words "destruction and violence" (1:3) connotes a legal phrase used to describe physical, political, and economic violence leveled against vulnerable

people (compare Prov 13:2; Jer 20:8; Amos 3:10; Ezek 45:9). In the presence of that violence, Habakkuk raised persistent questions of *theodicy*: Where is God when evil is rampant? Why is God silent? Habakkuk puts the question in distinctly theological language. Those reading or, perhaps, hearing the prophet's complaint no doubt experienced shock when Habakkuk accused God of complicity in violence. Habakkuk does not question God's power. For the prophet the problem is rather why God is willing to allow evil to continue, and even to participate with evil, since God is "pure" (1:13). God supported, even stirred up, Chaldean violence, using it to punish wickedness (1:5-11). Habakkuk rebuts the deity by saying that violence does not stem violence. The deity promises that violent culprits will get their comeuppance in the end.

The prophet takes a stand in order to be able to see how God will answer the controversy. He invokes priests who stood watch, suggesting that Habakkuk confronts God in a liturgical setting. He accuses God, who replies by instructing the prophet to "write the vision" that "will surely come" (2:1-3). YHWH tells Habakkuk to expect a messenger. The message will be so plain that runners will be able to read it. God's answer (2:4), that "the righteous live by their faith" (or faithfulness), is so compelling that it later becomes one of the cornerstones of

Paul's theology of justification (Rom 1:17; Gal 3:11; compare also Heb 10:38-39).

Habakkuk's concern is especially the way in which justice is perverted or "broken." For ancient Israelite and Judean prophets, justice was not an abstract concept. It was intimately tied to the lives of the defenseless. Injustices "cry out," even from the walls (2:11), indicating just how systemic broken justice was. Broken justice is supported by "the proud," whose appetite for wealth is treacherous and, like death, cannot be satiated (2:4-5; compare Prov 30:15-16). In the marketplace people become debt-slaves, booty for those with means (2:6). The prophet declares that all created order suffers. Animal cruelty and ecological mayhem (2:17) result from this violence and human bloodshed. Whole cities are established by violence, and streets are filled with blood (2:8, 12). This violent, dehumanizing life is sanctioned by the religious world, represented by the icons of their gods, plated with gold and silver (2:19-20). The only possible dam against the flood of blood will be the future flood of "knowledge of the glory of the LORD," which will be as significant as Noah's flood (2:14; 3:3).

The prophetic words shift from liturgical lament and prosecutorial complaint against the deity to taunts against the enemy (2:6-19). The doxology in 2:20, "But the LORD is in his holy temple; let all the earth keep silence before him!" serves as prelude to the hymn of faith in chapter 3, where the prophet prays (3:1-2), experiences a theophany (3:3-16), then declares unwavering and steadfast faith, even in the face of evil and violence (3:17-19). The prophet appropriates metaphors, typically used to describe the Canaanite storm-god, Baal, to describe a theophany of YHWH.

Habakkuk begs God to remember mercy, because God is so wrathful (3:2, 8). The prophet knows what happens when the deity gets angry. The theophany is overwhelming, destructive, awe-inspiring, and frightening. In response, the prophet's heart pounds, lips quiver, bones began to decay, and legs tremble (3:16) at the thought of this impending doom. The concluding verses of Habakkuk proclaim faith and trust in God in the midst of dire circumstances that suggested abandonment by God. Habakkuk rejoices and exults in a God who often seems inscrutable (compare Job 42:1-3). All that people need to survive—fig trees, grapevines, olive branches, crops, and livestock—is at jeopardy. Habakkuk's is a vision of stark nothingness. Yet, in the face of this dearth and desolation, the prophet declares he will rejoice in YHWH, who saves. He finds hope in God in withering times, much like the rabbis of Auschwitz, in spite of the evidence. ❖

ZEPHANIAH

John J. Ahn

The central message of the book of Zephaniah is God's impending judgment on Judah. The book begins with a superscription (1:1). Judgment on Judah and Jerusalem is found in 1:2—2:3.

A transitory section about oracles against the foreign nations is found in 2:4-15. Then, final judgment is transformed to salvation in 3:1-20. In its final, canonical shape, the book ends on a beautiful note of home, gathering, and praise for Judah (3:20).

Between the eighth-century BCE prophet Isaiah, son of Amoz, and the sixth-century prophet Jeremiah stands Zephaniah, son of Cushi, the most influential voice among the prophets of the intervening seventh century. For years, biblical scholars have suggested that Zephaniah may have been a disciple of Isaiah, heavily influenced by Isaiah's thought and preaching, and especially "Isaiah's Memoir" in Isa 6:1—9:6. Like Isaiah, Zephaniah too walked in the midst of the powerful inner circle (Zeph 1:1).

Isaiah of Jerusalem had two central means of transmitting judgment, using variations of the expression "the LORD's hand" (Isa 5:25; 9:12, 17, 21; 14:26-27; 23:11; 31:3; 40:2), and "on that day" (Isa 7:18, 20, 21, 23; also in Amos and Micah). In the book of Zephaniah, we hear both of these expressions. The theme "I will stretch out my hand against Judah" is found in the opening of the book at 1:4 and again at 2:13. Isaiah's fourfold "On that day" also is found in Zephaniah, beginning at 1:9-10 and continuing and concluding at 3:11, 16. But in the latter chapter Zephaniah gives the phrase a fascinating positive turn. Rather than the expected words of injunction, we hear a song of redemption and celebration. Here is a return to the original use of "On that day"—when it was employed as a celebration near the end of the grape harvest (Feast of Tabernacles or Succoth; compare the Song of the Vineyard, Isa 5:1-7). The image of crushed grapes became the impetus for words of judgment. Now a second-generation disciple preserves and employs his teacher's teaching, yet adapts it to promise hope and redemption for daughter Zion.

In Zephaniah we can also detect Deuteronomic or Jeremiah-like concerns that speak out against the worship of Baal and pronounce judgment against officials, judges, prophets, and priests for misconduct (Zeph 3:3-5). The only individual missing from the list is the king! Here is a prophet who indeed bridges the traditions of Isaiah and Jeremiah.

The name Zephaniah means "the Lord hides." As Zephaniah links the two great prophets, he also bridges the two great kings of Judah. Counting King Hezekiah as the first generation, and the first who attempted centralization and reform, Zephaniah is a direct fifth-generation descendent of this royal lineage. He prophesied during the reign of King Josiah (640–609 BCE). Josiah was only the second king of Judah who attempted and then actually advanced Judah's reformation. It is this "hidden one," Zephaniah—a prophet, not a king—who links these two great reformers of Judah.

Every generation has amazing stories to share and tell. The social philosopher Karl Mannheim, in his 1928 essay "On the Problem of Generations," was the first to systematically examine the impact of generational experiences on groups separated by geography, class, and other factors. Korean Americans and other immigrant groups in the United States (and, globally, Russian Israelis, Vietnamese Australians, and others) share some of the same generational divides. In "generation 1.5" are those who were pulled from their homelands and arrived in a new context as adolescents.

In the Korean-American church, we continue to live out generational issues, concerns, and tensions. Members of the first generation often seem quicker to criticize the second generation's lack of proficiency in Korean than to improve their own proficiency in English. In the first-generation context, one is expected to bow and speak in honorifics, showing deference; but the typical second-generation teen simply and directly asks, "Whassup, Elder Kim?" Attitudes and relationships among first- and second-generation Korean Americans can become complex.

My entry point into the book of Zephaniah is the role of bridge maker—between Isaiah and

Jeremiah, and Hezekiah and Josiah. The role of a transitional generation must be visionary. It must go beyond its own context and see the concerns of those who stand before and those who will come after. In the case of the Korean American church, the church must prepare for the third generation. However, without the second generation, there is no third generation. But all of this is entirely dependent on the first generation. Generation 1.5 has a special responsibility to help the first generation see things from a different perspective, because they are culturally closer to that generation. The second generation must respect and preserve cherished and functional traditions, but must adapt and amend them in ways that benefit ensuing generations. ❖

HAGGAI

Steed Vernyl Davidson

The book of Haggai provides some of the most reliable dating available in the Bible. Offering leadership during the reconstruction of the temple, the prophet Haggai dates his visions from August to December in 520 BCE, early in the reign of the Persian king Darius. The repeated formula (1:1; 2:1, 10) that consistently includes the name of Darius supplies both historical exactness and names the period in terms of imperial history.

Persian imperialism enabled deported Judeans to return to their homeland and provided resources to rebuild the temple. However, these measures alone did not result in economic prosperity or even communal cohesion. The book opens with a prophetic rebuke to a dispirited community accepting their fate (1:2) as imperial subjects in an economically ruined province. Details about Haggai's life are lacking, so it is not clear whether he returned to Jerusalem from Babylon. This uncertainty, though, eliminates arguments about his ethnic authenticity and helps focus greater attention on his message.

I read Haggai from the context of growing up in a recently independent country, Trinidad and Tobago, which achieved independence in 1962, but where several marks of colonialism remain in place. My formative years were developed against the background of a country trying to find its identity and unique place in the world.

Haggai communicates four visions from God (1:1-11; 2:1-9; 2:10-19; 2:20-23) that detail the value of a rebuilt temple. He begins by rebuking the residents of the city for their unwillingness to rebuild the temple (1:2). Their reluctance to work on the temple appears to be partly a result of poor economic conditions and partly the failure to establish a sense of community. A sense of scarcity had created among the residents a drive to take care of their individual needs to the neglect of the temple, the center of community life and identity. Haggai argues that as long as the temple is in ruins, the city's economic fortunes and the prosperity of the residents will remain bleak. He points out that drought conditions (1:9-11) and the futility of the efforts of the residents to eke out a living (1:6) result from the ruined temple. When eventually work had begun on the temple, he would ask the people to notice how their fortunes changed since the completion of its foundation (2:18-19).

Haggai's argument for the necessity of the temple lies not so much in its ritual and cultic functions as in its economic benefits to the people. Although he acknowledges that the completed temple would render the people ritually clean (2:10-18), Haggai argues that ritual cleanliness results in economic benefits, sharing the commonly held ancient worldview that the building of a temple guaranteed economic prosperity. Haggai helps the city see the temple as its central and focal point, but more importantly as the symbol of their identity as a people. The text constantly reminds the readers that Darius, the Persian, is king. The rebuilt temple serves to answer that reality with the statement of God's power and God's restoration of God's people to their land.

Haggai's fourth vision (2:20-23) pulls together the theme of restoration, but with a focus on a Davidic figure. This vision, exclusively delivered to Zerubbabel, the Persian provincial governor, contains promises in language reminiscent of early kings—"my servant," "signet ring," and "I have chosen you" (2:23). Throughout the book, the words of the prophet affirm the leadership of both Zerubbabel and Joshua, the high priest.

Although the prophecy's concern remains the temple, civic leadership receives in the last vision a focus that underlines a future role for Zerubbabel in partnership with God. Yet on that day Zerubbabel plays no role but merely stands by as a spectator of God's power. The centrality of the temple does not assume a central leader that accumulates power to himself. Both Joshua and Zerubbabel are subject to God's prophecy and are seen to obey the instructions of the prophet (1:12). This vision places God in opposition to other powers ("throne of kingdoms," "kingdoms of the nations," 2:22), without specifically naming any opponent. While the reader would expect this kind of judgment against the Babylonians or even the Persians, the vision offers a generic threat to all kingdoms. This vision offers a transhistorical perspective that shows a time when even the imperial powers will no longer exist. The prophet's message to the community in Jerusalem during the reign of Darius encouraged the rebuilding of the temple—the symbol of the presence of God and of the power of God in the face of empire, and a vision that outlasts temporal powers. ❖

ZECHARIAH

Steed Vernyl Davidson

I read Zechariah as an immigrant who was living in New York City during the attacks on the World Trade Center in 2001. I heard and felt the outrage of native New Yorkers toward such an insult to their national pride, and I also heard and felt the fear and pain of the rest of the world with regard to the responses to those attacks. In my reading of Zechariah, this context of double-vision that sees the whole emerges.

New Orleans will always remember Katrina not merely as the hurricane of 2005 but as a cataclysmic event that resulted in the displacement of vast numbers of the population. In its aftermath, many blamed the failure of government agencies to provide leadership necessary to prevent the scattering of people. Others blamed the disaster on the perceived permissive culture and lifestyle of the Big Easy.

Tensions over the deportation of Judeans to Babylon in the sixth century BCE are evident in the text of the book of Zechariah. The book can easily be divided into two sections: chapters 1–8 represent an optimistic prophecy of a time of restoration, guaranteed by the rebuilt temple and the consecrated leadership of Zerubbabel, the governor, and Joshua, the high priest. Chapters 9–14 angrily chastise other nations and various leaders of Judah for the population expulsion and call for faith in God to guarantee a secure future.

The prophet named Zechariah receives eight visions (chs. 1–7) that require angelic interpretation. In these visions, mostly relating to Jerusalem, he sees the restoration of the city (2:1-5), symbolic fixtures in the temple (4:1-7), the removal of idolatry from the city (5:5-11), and the affirmation of the leadership of Joshua (3:1-10; 6:9-15). All this sets the stage for the completion of the temple, built with the help of those from far away (6:15). As in Haggai, the reconstructed temple provides prosperity to the community (8:9-13).

Unlike Haggai, however, the primary leadership lies here with the priest Joshua, who receives purification and a mandate (3:3-10), a crown (6:11), and the messianic title Branch (6:12) to confirm the centrality of the temple and its priesthood in the restored community. The disaster that fell on the city as a result of the failure to heed Torah obligations (7:8-14) can be avoided by a commitment to keep these obligations (8:14-17). While Zerubbabel receives attention in Zechariah as the builder of the temple (4:8-10), this happens without him receiving the title "governor," and he is counseled on the superiority of the spirit of God over military might (4:6). The hoped-for future projected onto the restored temple envisages a community of people so attractive that they will compel the world to the temple by their presence (8:20-23).

This version of restoration in 1–8 contrasts markedly with the rest of the book, which takes on a heated tone in chapter 9. In these sections no prophet is named and some of the normal prophetic forms disappear. These chapters find little confidence in the institutions and leadership of Judah and blame them for the disaster. The priests, prophets, diviners, monarchs, and even the house of David receive strong criticism and find credibility only with divine forgiveness and cleansing. Perhaps reflecting the thoughts of someone outside the establishment, this section envisions that leadership of the people will rest firmly with God (11:7; 14:9). The center of the restored community lies in the city itself, not the temple (14:10-11). Foreign nations get blame and punishment for their part in the scattering of the people (9:1-8). The idyllic picture of universalism of the first part turns coercive as foreigners are compelled to participate in the festival of booths (14:16-19). All this comes with the renewed confidence that Jerusalem would never again be destroyed (14:12-14).

The reader may not find it necessary to arbitrate between these two different visions of renewal, as may be the case in real-life situations. Certainly, they continue, side by side, unresolved in the Bible. The main difference between the two sections of this book lies in their *anthropology* rather than in their theology. The first manifests a confidence in institutions and systems to work as they are designed. It sees the disaster as a result of the failure of the community to heed the law and believes that with another chance from God, a new start can be made for a repopulated and prosperous city. The second section lacks this optimistic view of institutions and pays attention to their flawed nature. While including strong mention of David (12:7-10), there is an acknowledgement that even this great dynasty remains defective and can only function from a strong theocentric focus. Such is the pessimism regarding institutions that the second section envisages its universalism not in human categories but in personified nations. Its reliance on God to effect the future restoration and prevention of more disasters distinguishes it from the first. Yet the first section presents a much starker picture of desolation in the passages relating to God's punishment (7:13-14), suggesting a recognition of the harshness of the experience of disaster and the abiding hope that someone—perhaps named Joshua—leading an institution like the temple can help the community work to prevent another disaster. The reader who comes to this book having experienced a disaster is unlikely to make any choice at all between these two perspectives. ❖

MALACHI

Osvaldo D. Vena

The book of Malachi is the last of the twelve Minor Prophets (Hosea–Malachi) in the Christian Bible, called simply the Book of the Twelve in the Hebrew Bible. It was most probably written after the reconstruction of the Temple in 516 BCE and before or during the time of the reforms of Ezra and Nehemiah around 450. One reason for this dating is that the word "governor" in 1:8 seems to indicate the postexilic Persian period and is also used in Hag 1:1, 14; 2:2, 21 and Neh 5:14, which were also written during this period. Another is the reference to the degeneration of temple worship, which seems to imply that the system must have been in place for a while. A third reason is that Malachi shares some common themes with Ezra-Nehemiah, namely, intermarriage with foreign women, tithing, and social injustices.

The name Malachi means "my [God's] messenger." And, more than a proper name, it may represent an anonymous prophet who speaks in the name of YHWH, the God of Israel. Therefore, the message is more important than the messenger.

The book begins: "An oracle. The word of the LORD to Israel by Malachi" (1:1). It ends with the announcement of the coming of the day of the LORD (4:1-3). That is followed by two postscripts (4:4, 5-6) that were perhaps added by the book's final editor. Most of the book consists of six oracles (1:1-5; 1:6—2:9; 2:10-16; 2:17—3:5; 3:6-12; and 3:13—4:3) in the form of disputations between God on the one hand and the priests and people on the other. Each disputation consists of a question that is misunderstood by the ones being addressed. This in turn leads to a divine answer to the original question. This answer includes a rebuke and a promise of judgment.

Malachi is written for a postexilic community experiencing deep divisions. Those in charge of the leadership—priests and powerful people—are forgetting their responsibilities and acting in ways that advance their own agendas. The priests are accepting sacrifices of lesser quality and perhaps using the good animals for their own benefit (1:7-8). The rich and affluent are divorcing their Jewish wives and entering into marital agreements with the leading families of the surrounding territories for economic self-aggrandizement (2:10-16). People are holding back their tithes, jeopardizing the temple's function as a center of redistribution of food for the poor (3:8-10). In the process, laborers are defrauded of their wages, widows and orphans are being oppressed, aliens are deprived of justice (3:5), and women are the objects of violence through unjust divorces (2:16). And the most astonishing thing is that the leaders of the people are surprised when God disputes with them and accuses them of all these things. They even wonder where the God of justice is (2:17). Therefore the prophet announces a day of retribution and judgment when God will come to the temple to purify the priesthood and make sure that the people will bring the appropriate offerings. On that day God will also secure a group of faithful ones who revere the LORD's name. The new age, which will dawn after God's coming, will be anticipated by the coming of the prophet Elijah. This text became important for the writers of the New Testament, who saw in John the Baptist the fulfillment of this prophecy.

The first readers of this text were imperial subjects of Persia. Judah was ruled by a governor, appointed by the Persian Empire, who extracted tribute from the people (1:8). At the same time the temple system required sacrifices and tithes. People were caught between two loyalties, the empire and the God of Israel. Some, the priests and the powerful, skirted their covenantal responsibilities by trying to shortchange God. The rest of the people, perhaps the majority, were the victims of this game of trying to please two masters. But God takes the side of these oppressed men and women and promises to come in judgment (3:5).

The book of Malachi presents a big challenge for today's readers: How can one fulfill one's responsibilities toward God and neighbor when one lives in the midst of an empire that demands total allegiance? Is it possible to live in the empire and at the same time be faithful to God? The Bible offers us positive examples of people who were able to do that, such as Daniel, Jesus, and Paul. The book of Malachi represents a negative example, for the people being indicted here were unable to remain faithful to God. It should serve the reader as a warning and a challenge.

I was born in Argentina and now live and teach in the United States. I live daily the tension between allegiance to God and to the society I have chosen. It is a difficult task, for I many times find myself doing the same things the priests and people of Malachi's community did. Like many of us, I tend to accommodate and to break faith with God and with those to whom I am accountable. The book of Malachi serves as a powerful reminder of what God expects of us. It announces with a clear voice that the consequence of being unfaithful to God is that innocent people suffer. My faithfulness, or lack of it, has social repercussions. ❖

Part III

THE APOCRYPHAL/DEUTEROCANONICAL BOOKS

16. THE APOCRYPHAL/
    DEUTEROCANONICAL BOOKS

Introduction to the Apocryphal/
Deuterocanonical Books   *Wilda C. Gafney*

Tobit   *Anathea E. Portier-Young*

Judith   *Wilda C. Gafney*

Esther (Greek)   *Nicole Wilkinson Duran*

The Wisdom of Solomon   *Scott Tunseth*

Sirach   *Scott Tunseth*

Baruch   *Frederick Houk Borsch*

The Letter of Jeremiah   *Frederick Houk Borsch*

The Prayer of Azariah   *Wilda C. Gafney*

Susanna   *Wilda C. Gafney*

Bel and the Dragon   *Wilda C. Gafney*

1 Maccabees   *Anathea E. Portier-Young*

2 Maccabees   *Anathea E. Portier-Young*

1 Esdras   *Stacy Davis*

The Prayer of Manasseh   *Stacy Davis*

Psalm 151   *Frederick Houk Borsch*

3 Maccabees   *Stacy Davis*

2 Esdras   *Stacy Davis*

4 Maccabees   *Stacy Davis*

THE APOCRYPHAL / DEUTEROCANONICAL BOOKS

Introduction to the

APOCRYPHAL / DEUTEROCANONICAL BOOKS

Wilda C. Gafney

More than any other division of Scripture, the Apocrypha (or Deuterocanonical writings) push readers to think about what they mean by Scripture. The very name we use for this literature stakes a claim. In my personal reading practices, I embrace a wide-open canon, recognizing, with respect, all Jewish and Christian canons as valid, from the five-book (Genesis–Deuteronomy) Samaritan Jewish canon to the not-quite-closed Ethiopian Orthodox canon that holds about eighty books, including *1* and *2 Enoch* and *1* and *2 Jubilees*. (I say "about" because the Ethiopian Orthodox have never published an official list or edition of the Bible.)

How do we categorize these books? Are they apocryphal (literally "hidden": compare 1 Macc 1:23) or deuterocanonical (a "secondary" or later canon)? *The Peoples' Bible* uses the NRSV translation of the Bible, which identifies these writings as *Apocrypha* and places them in a special section between the testaments. Use of the term *Apocrypha* is not meant to disparage the value of these writings (as the common use of the term "apocryphal" might imply) or that their meaning is somehow "hidden" (as a particular kind of Protestant interpretation presumes). The editors of *The Peoples' Bible,* come from largely Protestant contexts, and so we have chosen to present these texts as they are understood from a broadly Protestant perspective.

Of course, not all Christians are Protestant. A majority of Christians on the planet—Roman Catholic, Orthodox (in many configurations), and Anglican—read these texts as deuterocanonical, literally as a second canon that is interwoven with the texts that virtually all Christians regard as primary in the First Testament. As an Episcopalian, part of the worldwide Anglican communion, I understand myself to be both Catholic and Protestant. (Some Anglicans would go further and say that we are both Protestant and Catholic and neither Protestant nor Catholic!) We read this material as both deuterocanonical (as it is printed in Bibles such as the *New Jerusalem Bible*) and as Apocrypha (as printed in *The Peoples' Bible,* which uses the NRSV).

But neither are all readers of this book Christians, and so *The Peoples' Bible* is designed to be a resource for all people interested in the Bible.

At issue for readers is the question, What is Scripture? There is no single answer, as indicated by the number of different canons (or authorized lists of contents) for Jews and Christians around the world.

The ancient Israelites, exiled from their homeland by the Babylonians, produced two versions of the Scriptures, one including the texts now called apocryphal or deuterocanonical. The community deported to Babylon produced in Hebrew the books that are called the "Hebrew Bible" and that appear in Protestant Bibles, albeit in a different sequence, as the Old Testament. The community exiled in

Egypt produced in Greek a version called the Septuagint, which includes the books that are in Catholic, Orthodox, and Anglican Bibles. (Earlier biblical scholars taught that the Septuagint was a translation, expansion, and revision of a standard Hebrew Bible, but we now regard the two versions as somewhat independent of each other.) Some deuterocanonical or apocryphal material has been identified as a series of additions to the Hebrew Bible, particularly in the books of Esther and Daniel.

The discovery of the Dead Sea Scrolls changed the way many biblical scholars had thought about this material. Researchers discovered Hebrew scrolls that corresponded both to the previously known Hebrew versions of biblical books and to the Greek versions of biblical books, demonstrating that the Septuagint translators were faithful in translating the Scriptures they knew.

As a reader of African descent, I am reluctant to assign the Scriptures treasured by North African Jews to secondary status. As a Christian reader, I am interested in the use of the Septuagint and the Hebrew Bible in the Christian New Testament, where both are cited regularly. And as an Episcopalian teaching at a Lutheran seminary, I am interested in the manner in which Martin Luther understood these books and the ways that Lutherans have received them.

These texts generally date from 300 BCE to 70 CE. They are preserved in early Greek manuscripts (Codices Vaticanus, Sinaiticus, and Alexandrinus). Sirach, also called The Wisdom of Jesus Son of Sirach), chapter six of Baruch (also known as The Letter of Jeremiah), and Tobit were found in Hebrew among the Dead Sea Scrolls at Qumran. Most scholars believe that the majority of these works were composed in Hebrew or Aramaic and subsequently translated into Greek; Wisdom of Solomon and 2 Maccabees were most likely composed in Greek. These Jewish texts were initially understood as sacred, particularly in North Africa.

Eventually only those texts composed in Hebrew and collected by the earliest rabbinic authorities in the Babylonian diaspora became canonical, therefore authorized for all Jews in subsequent generations. How this happened is not clear. The story of a rabbinic council meeting at Jabneh and voting on the books of the Bible has been discredited. On the other hand, it is clear that early Greek-speaking Christians received the deuterocanonical books as Scripture. (Codices Sinaiticus, Alexandrinus, and Vaticanus all included the Greek New Testament as well as so-called New Testament apocryphal works: the *Epistle of Barnabas,* the *Shepherd of Hermas,* and the *Epistles of Clement*).

As already mentioned, the reception of these texts into the Christian canon has been uneven. In the fourth century, Jerome excluded them from the canon because he considered authoritative only the Hebrew manuscripts then available. In the sixteenth century, Martin Luther translated these texts and included them in his Bible, writing introductions to many of them, and designating them as apocryphal, along with the Epistle of James and the Apocalypse (or Revelation) of John. In response, the Council of Trent declared the Apocrypha to be deuterocanonical. This position is still held by the Roman Catholic Church.

The deuterocanonical or apocryphal literature can be divided into two categories. There are, first, distinct versions of books that also occur in Hebrew, such as Daniel and Esther:

Greek Esther. The differences between Greek and Hebrew Esther are centered in a few chapters that only exist in Greek. These unique portions of Esther include dreams and their fulfillment, prayers, plots and counterplots. One significant aspect of the Greek version is that the piety of the main characters is affirmed by mentioning God, who is not mentioned in the Hebrew version, some fifty times.

Greek Daniel. Several narratives in the Greek version of Daniel are not in the standard text of the Hebrew Bible, called the Masoretic Text. The Prayer of Azariah and the Song of the Three Jews are both psalms set in the midst of the fiery furnace. The stories of Susanna, which with Bel and the Dragon at one time served as the introduction to the book of Daniel, highlights Daniel's gifts as a wise and discerning judge.

Second, the vast majority of the apocryphal books are not included in the Hebrew canon. These texts, in the order of the Christian canon, are as follows:

Tobit is the story of a Jewish man, his wife, Anna, and their son Tobias, who are in exile after the first Assyrian deportation. The story also turns on a young woman named Sarah, whose seven husbands have been killed by a demon before any of their marriages were consummated. The angel Raphael heals Tobit, who has become blind, and enables Tobias to drive off the demon so he can marry Sarah.

Judith tells the story of a series of battles in the war between Israel and Assyria. The story's pious heroine saves the day by assassinating the enemy general, who has tried but failed to seduce her.

Wisdom is a collection of proverbial sayings attributed to Solomon. Similarities between Wisdom and Proverbs include the feminine personification of Wisdom and dependence on Egyptian and Greek philosophies.

Sirach is another collection of proverbial material, also called the Wisdom of Jesus Son of Sirach and, from its Latin name, Ecclesiasticus. Sirach venerates core Jewish values: the one God, the Torah, and the temple. It offers powerful critiques to Gentile culture and religion. Ben Sira, as the corpus is also known, employs strong language lamenting the birth of daughters and demeaning women in general.

Baruch offers reflections attributed to Jeremiah's scribe, Baruch ben Neriah. It includes practical advice for surviving Babylonian exile and a critique of idol worship. Its sixth and last chapter has circulated independently as the Epistle of Jeremiah.

First and Second Maccabees, books intended to look like the double books Samuel, Kings, and Chronicles, are in fact two separate works. First Maccabees tells the story of Judas Maccabeaus and his family as they lead their people, the Judeans under Syrian oppression, to revolt and then restore Jewish worship in Jerusalem. Antiochus (IV) Epiphanes was determined to forcibly Hellenize the Jews by slaughtering a number of men on Shabbat and by executing any who had been circumcised, had performed circumcisions, or possessed Torah scrolls. Antiochus also sacrificed a pig on the altar of the temple, desecrating it. Restoration and rededication of the temple is celebrated in the festival of Hanukkah (see John 10:22 for its observance in the New Testament).

Second Maccabees is a theological treatise that includes the only surviving excerpt of a historical text by the Jewish historian Jason of Cyrene. Second Maccabees advocates Jewish religious values, such as celebrating Hanukkah, and makes theological arguments for resurrection, divine revelation, miracles, and martyrdom.

First Esdras is a theological reflection on biblical history from the reforms of the prophet Huldah and King Josiah in 2 Kings 22–23 through the reforms of Ezra. The book of Ezra is known as 1 Esdras (and Nehemiah as 2 Esdras) in some Greek and Slavonic bibles, which designate our deuterocanonical/apocryphal 1 Esdras as 3 Esdras. This 1 Esdras/3 Esdras shares with Ezra, Nehemiah, Haggai, and Zechariah a preoccupation with the temple and the character Zerubbabel.

The Prayer of Manasseh presents a prayer of lament attributed to King Manasseh of Judah, who, though regarded as an apostate (2 Kgs 21:1-16; 2 Chr 33:1-9), was depicted as being repentant in the Chronicles account (33:12-13).

Third Maccabees doesn't mention the exploits of the Maccabees but recounts a somewhat parallel situation, with its own dangerous monarch, the Egyptian Ptolemy IV (Philopater), who profanes the temple with his presence. After being struck by God, he attempts to take his revenge on the Jews but is thwarted by God.

Second Esdras is a collection of seven apocalyptic visions concerning Jerusalem. The visionary is Ezra, the biblical scribe, who receives visions directly and is privy to an angelic apparition. He is ultimately assumed bodily into heaven, as were Enoch and Elijah.

Fourth Maccabees is set roughly in the Maccabean period but has little connection to the other Maccabean writings. Like the other literature that bears this name, the story turns on persecution and martyrdoms, in this case of the righteous Eleazar the sage, an elderly Jewish woman, and her seven sons. Here the antagonists are the Greeks.

While the full collection of these books varies significantly in reception and use by religious readers, all were at one time or another considered inspired and/or authoritative by some ancient Jewish and Christian communities. The preservation of these texts as Scripture, even in the most marginal sense, reminds us of Scripture's complexity and, ultimately, of its mystery. ❖

TOBIT

Anathea E. Portier-Young

In 722 BCE, the army of mighty Assyria destroyed the Northern Kingdom of Israel, as the prophet Amos had foretold. Survivors were taken captive and resettled throughout the Assyrian empire. Deportation ripped families apart, tearing the Israelite people from the land of their inheritance and from one another. So began the first Diaspora, or scattering, of the Israelites. For centuries and even millennia to come, Jews in the Diaspora continually negotiated their identity in relation to one another and to the people around them. How would they live as a minority people? Should they preserve their laws, stories, customs, religious practices and beliefs—and if so, how? Should they embrace the culture that now surrounded them? Even as they coped with the loss of homeland and kindred, they faced the dangers and difficulties of living in alien environments under foreign rule. They also built lives and formed families, prospered, and found joy.

This is the setting for the book of Tobit, a novella, or short romance, written around 200 BCE. The story is as fantastic as it is down to earth. An apocalypse enters the household: a demon haunts the bridal chamber while an angel plays matchmaker. The book's stunning revelation is that God answers prayer, is present with and within the family, and heals those who suffer. The book locates identity in the bonds of family, in religious praxis, in memory, and above all in acts of charity. By caring for members of the Israelite community in Diaspora—specifically by feeding the hungry, clothing the naked, burying the dead, and giving alms to the poor—the heroes of the book ensure the community's survival and welfare and free themselves from the bonds of death.

As a captive in Assyria, Tobit of Naphtali sets himself apart by abstaining from "the food of the Gentiles" (1:10), keeping the commands taught him by his grandmother Deborah, and marrying Anna, a woman from his own tribe (1:8-9). When his people suffer, he cares for them; he buries the Israelite dead at the risk of his own life (1:16-18). Tobit's fortunes rise and fall with the succession of kings: under one he conducts the king's business; under another he is a fugitive; under a third he is restored (1:13, 19-20; 2:1).

Yet sorrow lies ahead. Tobit suffers blindness (2:10). His nephew cares for him and his wife supports him, but he longs for death (2:10—3:6). Miles away in Ecbatana, Sarah, daughter of Edna and Raguel, also prays for death: the virgin bride has seen seven husbands strangled by the demon who loves her; she despairs of marriage and of life (3:7-15). God hears their prayers and sends the angel Raphael to heal them both (3:16-17). Disguised in human form, the angel leads Tobit's son Tobiah to Ecbatana (ch. 6). On the way, Tobiah conquers a fish (6:4). From its body he gains not only nourishment but also the means to banish Sarah's demon and heal his father's blindness (6:7-9).

Another happy ending is in store: the very day Tobiah arrives at Ecbatana, he marries his cousin Sarah (7:1—8:8). Raphael wrestles the demon (8:3); he also travels on to Rages, in Media, to retrieve a fortune Tobit had stored there in his days of prosperity (9:1-5). Finally, after much feasting, Tobiah, Sarah, and Raphael return to Nineveh, where Tobiah heals his father's blindness (11:1-13). Tobit sees his family and rejoices (11:13-15).

The book's recognition of suffering, message of comfort, and assurance of God's providence holds out a happy ending, not only for righteous individuals but for the people of Israel as a whole. In his testament before his death, Tobit warns his son of the destruction of Nineveh as well as Jerusalem (14:3-4). But he also foretells the ingathering of the scattered Israelites, the glorious restoration of the holy city and temple, and the conversion of all nations to true worship of the God of Israel (14:6). There is one exception to this vision of universal blessing: at the end of the book, Tobit's son, Tobiah, rejoices in the destruction of the people of Nineveh (14:15).

I read Tobit as a white woman in the United States who has received many privileges at the expense of others: I may more closely resemble the Assyrian than the Israelite. These verses, like the psalms of imprecation (for example, Psalm 137), challenge me to reckon with the anger of the oppressed, to acknowledge my part in oppression, and to promote healing for all God's people. ❖

JUDITH

Wilda C. Gafney

Judith has been celebrated in works of art as a Jewish and Christian example of piety, fidelity, courage, godliness, and celibacy, even though the book was not part of the Hebrew or Protestant canons. My interest in Judith stems from its canonical status in my church, my preference for feminist readings of the biblical text, and from my regular participation in Reconstructionist Jewish liturgy. Judith is one of the most active and vocal women in the canon, comparable to Rebekah (Gen 24:15-67). Like Deborah and Jael (Judges 4–5), she is (or becomes) a warrior and psalmist, and like Jael (Judg 5:28-30), she is a defender of raped women. In addition, Judith contains one of the few biblical references to rape from a woman's perspective.

The text is full of historical inaccuracies, leading many scholars to classify it as fiction. Nebuchadnezzar is depicted as ruling from Nineveh, even though it was destroyed before he ascended to the throne. Babylon is never mentioned, even though Nebuchadnezzar ruled Babylon, not Assyria. The temple is described as being rebuilt, although that would not happen until nearly fifty years after his death. In addition, Judith's hometown of Bethulia is unknown. It is depicted as being in Samaria, but this is problematic given the setting at a time when Samaritans were reviled and not recognized by Judeans as legitimate worshippers of YHWH. The conversion to Judaism of Achior the Ammonite at the end of the story is also a challenge to reading the text literally, because the Ammonites were perhaps more reviled than Samaritans. Holofernes, Nebuchadnezzar's general, is otherwise unknown, and the Persian form of his name makes it unlikely for an Assyrian (or Babylonian). While the exact date of Judith's composition is unknown, it must be dated no later than the first century CE because of Clement's discussion of the text. A likely period is 76–67 BCE, which would make Judith a celebration of the widowed and pious Queen Salome Alexandra.

Even though the book bears the name of its heroine, the first seven chapters do not mention her. The book opens with a long description, set in the time of Nebuchadnezzar, of the hostilities between Israel and Assyria. When Judith is introduced in chapter 8, she is presented with the longest genealogy of any character in the First Testament (Hebrew or Greek) and, with the exception of Jesus, any character in the Christian New Testament. It is hard for some scholars, myself among them, to accept the whole of Judith's lengthy genealogy as fictionalized, so perhaps the text should be understood as historical fiction. A number of Judith's most distant ancestors—Simeon, Shelumiel, and Zurishaddai—are mentioned in several other places (Num 1:6, 2:12, 7:36, 7:41, and 10:19).

In the story, Israel is besieged by the Assyrians and the people blame their leaders, particularly Uzziah the magistrate, for failing to capitulate to the Assyrians. He urges the people to wait five days for God to intervene, promising that if nothing happens he will surrender on their behalf. The people cry out to God in 7:29 in despair and defeat; Judith responds to the people's distress by summoning the leaders of the magistrates and exhorting them in 8:11-27. She will not demand that God perform on a human timetable, nor will she countenance surrender. Judith will become the vessel of God's deliverance; she is blessed by the leaders and people, even though they cannot know what she will do.

In chapter 9 Judith prays the longest prayer, thirteen verses, attributed to any woman in the Bible. Judith's prayer begins with the certainties that women will be raped in the coming war and that their rape is contrary to the will of God (v. 2). This aspect of the text leads some feminists to believe that Judith was composed in part by a woman. However, Judith also ascribes to God the practice of the abduction and rape of enemy women and girls, seeing that as God's justice (vv. 3-4).

In chapter 10, Judith rides off with her unnamed woman-servant on the adventure of her life. Judith dresses herself to display her beauty (10:3-4) and offers herself as an informant to Holofernes. Maintaining her piety by eating only her own kosher food (12:2), she dines with Holofernes as he gets drunk. Judith's virtue is suspect—and was condemned by Victorian readers—because she does not keep her servant with her (12:15). For his part, Holofernes intends to seduce her (12:12). But he passes out "dead drunk" before he can do the deed (13:2). With two blows, Judith decapitates Holofernes with his own sword (13:7-8). She puts his head in her now-empty food bag, and we must presume that no one notices a blood trail as she leaves the enemy camp to rejoin her people, as though she were just going for prayer (13:10-11).

When Judith arrives home, she proclaims (echoing Deborah) that Holofernes was struck down by the hand of a woman and (perhaps in opposition to Jael) that God had kept Holofernes from molesting her (13:16). Judith is then blessed in words given to Jael and Mary of Nazareth: "you are blessed by the Most High God above all other women on earth" (13:18). With the head of Holofernes on the wall (14:1, 11), Judith offers a psalm (16:1-17). She then returns to her widowhood, refusing all suitors, and lives to the age of 105, setting her servant free and giving away her substantial possessions before her death (16:21-24). Her epitaph is verse 25: "No one ever again spread terror among the Israelites during the lifetime of Judith, or for a long time after her death." ❖

ESTHER

(The Greek Version Containing the Additional Chapters)

Nicole Wilkinson Duran

The Greek account of Esther is significantly expanded, by more than 100 unique verses, beyond the Hebrew. It appeared with the Septuagint, the Greek version of the Hebrew Bible, at a time when Greek had become the most commonly spoken language of the Jewish Diaspora and of the Roman Empire, between 300 and 200 BCE. Within Judaism, the Greek account of Esther was recognized early on as a retelling and interpretation of the Hebrew text. Along with other books written in Greek and included in the Septuagint, the Greek version of Esther was accepted as Scripture in the formation of the Christian canon, only to be dismissed in favor of the Hebrew text by Protestant reformers when they defined the canon for themselves. It continues nevertheless to be accepted as the canonical version of Esther by the Roman Catholic and Orthodox Churches and by the Anglican Communion, including the Episcopal Church in the United States.

The two commonly cited texts of the Greek version of Esther are known as the *A* text, also known as the *Lucian* text, and the *B* text. Though they differ in some respects, both texts make two overall changes to the story as we have it in the Hebrew. First, references to God that are completely lacking in the Hebrew book have been added, and the hero's piety is enhanced. Second, Mordecai's role is extended in the Greek version, creating resonance between his character and endangered biblical wise men such as Joseph and Daniel. Both sets of changes point to a desire on the part of translators to bring the story into line with the readers' expectations of

Scripture, most likely because the canonical status of the Hebrew version was often questioned.

Significantly, the Greek version of the story begins not with Vashti's rebellion and the gender issue it raises but with Mordecai having an apocalyptic dream in which "the whole righteous nation" (11:9) narrowly avoids a vague but terrible destruction. Mordecai's discovery and report of an assassination plot against the king, an act that brings Mordecai to honor and power, occurs in detail before any woman enters the scene. In the *A* text the court's panicked response to Vashti's rebellion does not occur. Thus, the gender tension in the Hebrew account of that event is diffused, indeed all but erased in the Greek. Here the story is solely concerned with the conflict of Jew versus Persian (or Greek, as Haman becomes a Macedonian in translation), and God's preservation of the former. Other significant additions in the Greek include a lengthy prayer by Mordecai and one by Esther in which she makes a point of forswearing sex with Gentiles (this despite her marriage to the Persian king).

As an American Protestant, I first encountered the Greek version of Esther in a graduate-school classroom rather than in a faith context. As the only Bibles I knew growing up were the King James and Revised Standard Versions, I had not until seminary known that version of Esther's story. To me, a feminist and a Protestant, the Greek versions of Esther seem to obscure, rather than expand upon, the story of Esther herself. She was a girl born into an ethnic minority and torn between the survival strategies of assimilation on the one hand and advocacy for her people on the other. She was pushed by circumstance into exploiting her own sexuality to save her own life, Mordecai's, and those of the Jews. In place of that story, the Greek version tells the story of yet another "great man" (11:3), as the Greek refers to Mordecai, and the great man's interaction with God. The Greek version is valuable for me because it tells a story about the stories we tell. That is, it is a classic example and written record of one intriguing, maverick story—the Hebrew Esther—that through translation and retelling was pulled back within the limits of patriarchy and theological orthodoxy. ❖

THE WISDOM OF SOLOMON

Scott Tunseth

Although the Wisdom of Solomon mentions Israel's wise king in the title and is written as though Solomon were speaking, the book was probably written many centuries after Solomon lived. (It was not uncommon in the ancient world for writers to credit well-known and well-respected figures from the past. This type of writing is called pseudepigrapha; other examples include apocalypses and testaments of Israel's patriarchs and prophets such as the books of *Enoch*. Since Solomon was well known for being very wise, it is not surprising that the writer uses his name in a book that focuses on the meaning of true wisdom.

Some scholars have suggested that the book was written originally in Hebrew and translated into Greek, but no such Hebrew original has been discovered. This has led others to conclude that the language and style of the book point to a Jewish author who wrote in Greek and was very familiar with Greek thought. The Wisdom of Solomon was not included in the Jewish Scriptures but is placed between Job and Ecclesiastes in the Greek Septuagint.

The author probably wrote Wisdom to encourage the Jews living in Alexandria, Egypt, in the first or second century BCE to be faithful to God. Some had abandoned the Jewish religion and adopted Greek religions or turned to worshiping Egyptian gods. The author wanted to show fellow Jews that the wisdom of God was better than any Greek philosophy or Egyptian religion. To do this, the author also had to deal with a theme that appears in earlier books of Hebrew wisdom (Job, for example), namely, why evil people are sometimes successful while good people suffer. The author states that God will bring about justice when God judges all people after death. The wicked will be punished, but those who were faithful to God will live with God forever.

The author describes wisdom as "a breath of the power of God" (7:25), which is similar to the way earlier books describe wisdom as being present with God at creation (see Prov 8:22-31; Job 28:12-28). But a number of descriptions of wisdom in the book are similar to Greek understandings of wisdom. This likely reflects the author's Greek background in a city of Greek culture and language. For example, the author uses phrases such as "a pure emanation of the glory of the Almighty" (7:25) and as "a spotless mirror of the working of God" (7:26).

When the author quotes Scripture, he quotes from the Greek Septuagint, which tradition says seventy-two translators completed in Egypt shortly after 250 BCE. The author understands Jewish thought and knows Jewish history, but also is very familiar with Greek philosophy. Some scholars believe the book was written before the time of the Jewish philosopher Philo of Alexandria, who lived from 20 BCE to 54 CE. The author does not seem to quote from Philo's work, and Philo doesn't mention the Wisdom of Solomon in his writings. It has also been suggested, however, that the anti-Jewish riots that took place in Alexandria in 38 CE could be the background for the strong vision of judgment against the enemies of God's people found in 5:15-23 and for the strong anti-Egyptian tone of the book (see chs. 10–19).

These theories cannot be proved, but it is probably safe to say that Wisdom is one of the latest, if not the latest, book in the Greek Septuagint. In fact, in one early listing of books considered to be canonical, the Muratorian Canon, which dates from the late second century CE, the Wisdom of Solomon is listed as a book of the New Testament.

It is difficult for one who grew up in a Scandinavian Lutheran enclave to understand what it means to live in a hostile or unwelcoming environment—the kind of environment the Jews living in Egypt may have experienced and the sort of environment racial or religious minorities face on a daily basis. For me, the wisdom of God resided in the elders, including pastors and teachers, who attended the majority church in town, a place where most people seemed to look the same and most had names ending in -son. Prejudice and fear of others unlike us existed, but this was also an environment that taught me remarkable openness and tolerance. We imagined that God's light surely shined on us, as it had shined on the people of Israel. But we also learned that God's wisdom and God's grace were meant for all people. ❖

ECCLESIASTICUS, or the Wisdom of Jesus Son of

◼ SIRACH ◼

Scott Tunseth

The book of Sirach was written by one who described himself as a student of the law of the Most High (see 39:1-11) and as one who taught others (51:23). That writer was Jesus son of Eleazar son of Sirach (50:27). He is often also identified by the shortened Hebrew form of the name, Jesus Ben Sira (*Sirach* is the Greek for *Sira*). The author's grandson wrote the prologue and translated the book into Greek sometime after 132 BCE, "in the thirty-eighth year of the reign of Euergetes" (the latter a Greek-speaking Egyptian monarch from the Ptolemy dynasty: Ptolemy VIII Euergetes II Physcon, 145–116 BCE). Based on 50:1-24, Jesus son of Sirach likely wrote the book after the time Simon son of Onias was high priest in Jerusalem (219–196 BCE) and before the Maccabean-led revolts began, after 180 BCE.

The book of Sirach can be described as the class notes of a teacher of Hebrew wisdom who was seeking to help students learn the art of living well under the guidance of the Lord, the source of all wisdom (1:1). Sirach's notes contain many different kinds of literature, including prayers (23:1-6; 51:1-12), hymns (39:12-35), etiquette (32:1-13), numerical lists (25:1-2, 7-11), and poems honoring Israel's past heroes (chs. 44–50). But the book is primarily made up of typical wisdom sayings of the kind found in other wisdom books, such as Proverbs and the Wisdom of Solomon.

Themes in Sirach are also consistent with themes found in Hebrew wisdom. These include the importance of fearing (respecting) the Lord, proper use of wealth and the giving of alms to the poor, being honest and taking care not to use words to slander or lie, choosing friends wisely, practicing self-control, and raising children properly. Sirach also has specific advice for particular types of workers and for rulers (9:10—10:18; 38:1-15). Sirach does speak about facing suffering (2:1-6; 4:1-10), but the book holds to the belief common in earlier Hebrew wisdom that in this life good is rewarded and evil punished. The book does not raise the possibility of life after death.

I find that the attitude toward women depicted in Sirach is at times even more strident and unsympathetic than other biblical literature (see especially chs. 25–26), and this is troubling to me as a male reader. These words in particular are a reminder of the challenge we all face in hearing the text as *wisdom* for today. Again we recognize the difficulty of reading the Bible as God's Word when those words are presented through the lenses of a particular ancient cultural perspective. And yet compare those words to Sirach's more compassionate plea to avoid judging others by appearances (11:1-4). Reading the Bible is an exercise in wise discernment, in which we discern not only texts but also people, including ourselves.

No matter what vocational hat I wear—pastor, educator, editor, parent, spouse—Sirach challenges me not only to *seek* the Lord's wisdom but to be a channel for it as well. Yet, I do well to recognize that the channel does not flow in a single direction only, as if, being wise or powerful or privileged, one can simply own and dispense it. True wisdom, it seems, always runs in both directions. The Scriptures themselves invite us all into this sacred dialogue. ❖

BARUCH

Frederick Houk Borsch

In times of persecution and distress, people look for hope. They want to remember that other people have previously survived calamity. They need to know that even though their community and its leaders have sinned and broken covenant with God, God does not and will not abandon God's people.

The book of Baruch first recalls the year 597 BCE (1:1-14). Baruch, who had been the friend and scribe of the prophet Jeremiah, was, we are told, now with

the exiles in Babylon. Learning of the destruction of Jerusalem, Baruch sought to console and lead the people to confess their sins. After he read his book to King Jeconiah (called Coniah in Jer 22:24, 28 and by his royal name, Jehoiachin, in 2 Kgs 24:6) and to the rest of the exiles, the people wept, fasted, and prayed. Then they sent Baruch with his book, temple vessels, and other offerings to Jerusalem. The confession of sins of the exiles in Babylon (1:15—2:10) is similar to one found in Daniel 9; both are based in a Deuteronomic theology. Then comes a heartfelt prayer for deliverance (2:11-26), followed by a recollection of God's promise to restore and "make an everlasting covenant" with "my people" (2:27-35), and concluding with further prayer to the eternal God of mercy and might (3:1-8).

The second major section of the book (3:9—4:4) is a poetic praise of Wisdom and contemplation of her ways. While at first glance this may seem an interpolation into the book of Baruch, it was chosen to be an integral part of his message, again using language and themes found elsewhere in Scripture. The people are in the mess they are in because they have failed to follow the ways of Wisdom that are, indeed, God's ways and those of Torah (see Sirach 24). Although the fullness of Wisdom is mysterious, and God's ways can never be fully known (see Job 28), those who seek to follow Wisdom will find life and peace (see also Proverbs 1–7).

In its third and final section, the book of Baruch concludes (4:5—5:9) with words of encouragement and promise not unlike the prophetic hope offered in Isaiah 40–66. In four odes—each beginning "Take courage!"—and a psalm (much like Psalm 11 in the *Psalms of Solomon*), we hear that, yes, Israel has sinned, but a new day is coming. Through the prophet, and in the voice of mother Zion, God tells of deliverance and the end of exile. "Take courage.... Arise.... Look towards the east, O Jerusalem.... Take off the garment of your sorrow and affliction.... [E]very high mountain and the everlasting hills [will] be made low and the valleys filled up.... God will lead Israel with joy in the light of his glory" (4:30—5:9).

Now fast-forward to a time around the year 167 BCE, shortly after Antiochus IV came roaring out of Syria with his strong army, sacking Jerusalem, despoiling the temple, and forbidding the worship of the Lord and study of Torah. Once again God's ways and Wisdom may seem mysterious, but again there may be hope, and God's promises can be heard. Perhaps it was in this decade, or during some other time of difficulty and challenge, that the author of Baruch brought some disparate writings together into a message, similar in several ways to the overall message of the prophet Jeremiah, that speaks to oppressed people in every time and circumstance.

As a white, well-educated male who has been a university dean of chapel and professor, a divinity school professor and head, and a bishop, I have had to learn the ways that I am a person of considerable privilege. I have had to learn the "hermeneutics of suspicion" and how to try to listen to the voices of many others when interpreting Scripture. Baruch writes, "Take courage!" Those who confess their sins and trust again in God's ways and Wisdom will know a God of restoration, deliverance, and everlasting promise. ❖

THE LETTER OF JEREMIAH

Frederick Houk Borsch

The Letter of Jeremiah, a warning against idol worship, was perhaps first drafted in the fourth century BCE. It claims to be a letter from Jeremiah and bears resemblance to similar warnings found in Jer 10:2-16. The letter's first verses recall Jer 29:1-23, which advises that the exile in Babylon will last a long time (seventy years), but the letter now extends that time to "up to seven generations" (v. 3). A further historical link is made by reference (vv. 2-4) to the "gods made of silver and gold and wood" that the Jewish exiles will see being carried about in Babylon. The first nine warnings in the letter end in a refrain asking why anyone would think idols are gods, or declaring that "they are not gods; so do not fear them." Probably written originally in Hebrew or Aramaic, the letter likely received alteration and amendment during several centuries. A Greek version is found in the Dead Sea Scrolls.

In early Greek manuscripts the letter of Jeremiah was placed as a separate writing following the books of Baruch and Lamentations and in this manner was linked to the book of Jeremiah (there was a tradition that Jeremiah was also the author of Lamentations). Its scriptural placement, however, has never been secure, and in the Latin Vulgate and then in the King James Version of the Bible the "Letter of Jeremy" is attached to the book of Baruch as chapter 6.

While valued for its reinforcement of the dangers of idolatry, the argument is a rehearsal of the warnings found in other biblical passages (Ps 115:1-8; Isa 44:9-20; 46:1-12, 5-7). The popularity of such admonitions can also be seen in the Greek version of Daniel, the story of Bel and the Dragon, and is found in later legends, both Jewish and Muslim. Such parodies were in one sense easy to make. Lifeless idols are helpless; they cannot defend themselves. They cannot even wipe away the dust and soot that gets in their eyes and on their faces. They have to be carried about. More important, they cannot bring healing or wealth. However, one might at least sympathize with desperate people who pray to idols of one form or another. Foolish it may be, but humans often display a tendency to domesticate their deities and try to gain some power over their favors by paying obeisance, whether the idols be made of wood, stone, or precious metals or are other representations of the powers of this world.

Jesus warned that one cannot serve God and the god "Mammon" or wealth. We may want to laugh, but there are those today who demonstrate a near-religious reverence for obedience to, for example, the "invisible hand" of market forces that goes beyond mere economic theory, or call for obeisance to a flag or another symbol that goes beyond true patriotism. Seen in this light, the people of God perhaps always need something like the satire and ridicule of lifeless idols that we encounter here as reminders of their call to worship and serve the living God of justice and mercy.

As a white male who has enjoyed considerable privilege, I hear behind all such warnings the second of the commandments in the Decalogue: "You shall not make for yourself an idol, whether in the form of anything that is in heaven above, or that is on the earth beneath, or that is in the water under the earth. You shall not bow down to them or worship them" (Exod 20:3-5; Deut 5:7-9). ❖

THE PRAYER OF AZARIAH

and the Song of the Three Jews

Wilda C. Gafney

The Greek version of Daniel preserved in the Septuagint provides a fuller, richer account of the events found in the Hebrew version of Daniel. In many ways, the Greek version answers questions left unanswered by the Hebrew text, even when those questions are not apparent.

The character Daniel is a revered sage whose exploits were known to Greek and Hebrew writers long before the composition of either version of Scripture (see Ezek 28:3, "are you wiser than Daniel?"). The earliest stories of Daniel, known as *Dnil* and *Danel* in other Semitic literature, date from more than a thousand years before the setting of the stories about Daniel recounted in the Hebrew and Greek Scriptures. Because Daniel was a revered figure (in Ezek 14:14 he is listed as one of the righteous generation of Noah and Job), stories about Daniel abounded in the Ancient Near East. A number of those stories are preserved in the Greek version of Daniel.

Two units of Greek Scripture not present in the Hebrew book of Daniel are prayer hymns: The Prayer of Azariah and the Song of the Three Jews. These prayers are set in the scene in which Nebuchadnezzar throws the renamed Hananiah (Shadrach), Mishael (Meshach), and Azariah (Aved-Nego) into the fiery furnace for refusing to worship him.

In 3:23 the three Hebrew boys are thrown into the fiery furnace. The Greek account tells us what happens next. Azariah, whose name is usually listed last, indicating that he has the least status (perhaps he is the youngest, or the smallest), prays for twenty-one verses. His prayer is a prayer of confession on behalf of his nation: it is because of their corporate sin that they have been deported. In the Greek version (3:46), it is in response to Azariah's prayer that the furnace is heated seven times hotter than usual. It is also in response to Azariah's prayer that God's angel joins them in the fire and makes "the inside of the furnace as if a moist breeze were whistling through" (3:49-50). In response to their divine deliverance, the three of them sing praises to God together, calling on all creation to join them in verses 52-90.

After the young men finish their song, Nebuchadnezzar sees a divine presence in the fire and discovers that Hananiah, Mishael, and Azariah are untouched by the flames. The Hebrew and Greek texts merge after the hymn, with 3:24-30 in Hebrew corresponding to 3:91-97 in Greek. ❖

SUSANNA

(chapter 13 of the Greek Version of Daniel)

Wilda C. Gafney

The story of Susanna, now in chapter 13 of the Greek version of the book of Daniel (see the introduction to The Prayer of Azariah and the Song of the Three Jews), both circulated independently of biblical Daniel and as the prologue to the Greek version. In that narrative, a very young Daniel, whose name means either "God is my Judge" or "God's Judge," demonstrates his sagacity by saving the life of a virtuous woman falsely accused of adultery. This story demonstrates that Daniel is a sage from his youth; therefore it is no surprise that he is able to interpret dreams in the later story. Here Daniel separates the two rejected would-be lovers of Susanna and questions them separately. Their stories do not agree, they are proved to be liars, and Susanna is vindicated. ❖

BEL AND THE DRAGON

(Chapter 14 of the Greek Version of Daniel)

Wilda C. Gafney

The third section of Daniel unique to the Greek version (see the introduction to The Prayer of Azariah and the Song of the Three Jews) is also a double unit: the stories of *Bel*, a Babylonian god, and *the Dragon*, a live dragon, which Daniel kills. In the first story, the temple of Bel is unmasked as a fraud in which human attendants take away the food offerings so it appears as if the idol eats them. In a familiar display of sagacity, Daniel outwits the attendants by sprinkling ashes on the floor to record their surreptitious footprints (14:14-21). In the second narrative (14:23), people are worshipping a living dragon. In order to promote the worship of the one God, Daniel kills the dragon with a potion largely consisting of a magic hairball, "pitch and fat and hair" (14:27). Both of these stories are attributed to the biblical prophet Habakkuk (14:1).

I have an appreciation for dragon lore and am sorry that the dragons of Scripture, especially this one, fare so poorly. As an Episcopalian for whom Greek Daniel is canonical, I prefer the Greek text to the Hebrew one. I find it to be fuller and richer. It is for me most meaningful when read sequentially as an integrated text, as in the *New American* or *New Jerusalem* Bibles. ❖

1 MACCABEES

Anathea E. Portier-Young

Written in about 100 BCE, the national history of 1 Maccabees conveyed to its first readers a common identity and values in order to unite them as one people, liberated and led by the Hasmoneans. The book also solidified and defended the claims of the Hasmonean dynasty to the high priesthood and kingship of Judea.

Empire is the stage for the drama that unfolds in this book. The Hellenistic kings exploited their subject peoples through conquest, plunder, and slavery as well as systems of patronage and tribute. Under their rule, Judeans were compelled to serve two masters: God and empire.

Israel's covenant with God commanded circumcision, worship of YHWH alone, and adherence to the laws of Torah. It called Israel to be a people set apart from other nations. Their temple, their laws, and their practices symbolized their distinctive identity as God's own people. According to 1 Maccabees 1, around the year 175 BCE "certain renegades" (1:11) or "lawless" people in Israel (9:58) abandoned the covenant with God in order to "make a covenant with the Gentiles." This group of elite Judeans sought permission from the Seleucid king Antiochus IV Epiphanes, ruler of the Seleucid Empire and, by extension, of Judea, to "observe the ordinances of the Gentiles" (1:13). They built a gymnasium—the hallmark of Greek education and culture—and they "removed the marks of circumcision," masking the bodily sign of their covenant with God (1:15).

Before long, the same king who authorized the building of the gymnasium plundered the Jerusalem temple (1:21-24). Two years later his army plundered and set fire to the holy city, ripped down its houses and walls, and established a military garrison in its heart (1:29-40). In 167 he decreed a religious persecution of the Judeans under the pretense that "all should be one people" (1:41). Torah scrolls were burned (1:56). Judeans were commanded to eat pork, sacrifice to idols, defile their sacred space, and profane their sacred times (1:45-47). Antiochus erected a "desolating sacrilege" upon the altar of YHWH (1:54). Circumcised infants were killed and hung from their mothers' necks, and their families were killed (1:60-61). The king punished covenant obedience with death (1:50, 57, 63). Many acquiesced to save their lives (1:43-52) and many died as martyrs (1:63; 2:38). Others fled (1:53; 2:28-29). Some, spurred by the leadership of the Hasmonean priest Mattathias, chose to fight (ch. 2).

The story of revolt and liberation follows. It is also a story of the Hasmonean rise to power. As Mattathias was dying, he appointed his son Judas commander of the newly formed guerrilla army (2:66). The longest section of 1 Maccabees (3:1—9:22) tells of Judas's military victories as well as the purification and rededication of the defiled temple, an event commemorated today in the Jewish feast of Hanukkah. The next section (9:23—12:53) describes the savvy leadership of Jonathan, his brother, who became high priest and governor after Judas's death. Chapters 13–16 portray the idyllic rule of their brother Simon, who succeeded Jonathan and in 142 finally ended the occupation of Jerusalem and liberated the Judeans from Seleucid rule. At Simon's death his son John Hyrcanus assumed the high priesthood and Judean kingship, establishing a dynasty that would last until the rule of Herod the Great in 37 BCE.

The book begins with a collision: covenant identity clashes with the culture of "the Gentiles" (1:11). But by the book's end we see this as a deceptively simple—and indeed false—opposition. References to "the Gentiles" and "foreigners" were a rhetorical device designed to evoke feelings of national unity and even to justify policies of expansion (for example, 11:68 and 13:6). The Hasmoneans were brutal to their near neighbors in Azotus and Gaza and ruthlessly rooted out the "lawless" within the ranks of Israel (2:44; 5:68; 10:84; 11:61). But if they condemned those who "made a covenant with the Gentiles," the Hasmoneans themselves sought alliances with Rome and Sparta, whom they identified as "brethren" (8:1-32; 12:12-13; 14:20).

They resisted the persecutor Antiochus IV, but allied themselves with his successors (14:38). Like their "lawless" enemies, they secured power within a system of imperial patronage and adopted symbols of power from their "Gentile" patrons (10:20).

I read this book as a Catholic, a white woman, and a pacifist. For Catholics as for believers in the Orthodox traditions, including Anglicans, 1 Maccabees has the status of inspired Scripture. For me, this means that the Spirit uncovers through this sacred text the myth of false universalism, the injustice of religious intolerance, the rapacity of empires, the brutality of war, and the deceptive and destructive power of racial rhetoric. Such stories shape our understanding of ourselves and of one another. ❖

2 MACCABEES

Anathea E. Portier-Young

At the center of 2 Maccabees stands the Jerusalem temple. This sacred space provides a fundamental point of orientation for Jews in Judea and scattered in Diaspora. It is the place of worship, directing all attention to God. It is the chosen place through which God's presence is mediated to all God's people, ensuring their welfare. The temple links past and present, reaching back before the time of subjugation to foreign empires, before the exile and dispersion, to the days of Solomon and David, and even to the time of Moses when the tabernacle accompanied the people from their wilderness wanderings into the promised land.

Like 1 Maccabees, 2 Maccabees relates events leading up to the persecution of Jews by Antiochus IV Epiphanes in the year 167 BCE, the persecution itself, and the story of Jewish resistance. The story in

2 Maccabees is one of repeated threats to the Jerusalem temple—some of them realized. In this story, God and God's heavenly armies fought together with the faithful to protect and free it. Unlike 1 Maccabees, 2 Maccabees expresses belief in miracles and in resurrection (ch. 7). The book nuances its Deuteronomic theology of sin and punishment with the belief that suffering in this life can serve to discipline the faithful in preparation for life in the world to come (6:12-16; 7:18). Belief in bodily resurrection gave hope to those who suffered for their faith, enabling them to die for the law and for the temple in the hope of receiving the breath of life again (7:9-23).

The story of an unnamed mother of seven sons (later traditions will name her Hannah and Miryam) forms the heart and hinge of the book (ch. 7). As a mother and a Catholic raised in the traditions of the martyrs, I am drawn to her story. This mother and her sons were taken captive, tortured, and brought before the persecutor, Antiochus, who tried to make them eat pork (7:1). They refused. Six brothers suffered torture, spoke eloquently in defense of the law, proclaimed their faith in the resurrection and their belief in the justice of God, and so refused to defile themselves. Six brothers died (7:2-19).

Yet we are told that their mother excelled them all in courage, hope, and nobility (7:20). Speaking in their ancestral language, she encouraged each son (7:21). She related the mystery and miracle of gestation and childbirth to that of resurrection (7:22). The God who formed her children so mysteriously in her womb would by equal mystery give them the breath of life again (7:23). By their uncompromising faithfulness she and her sons would help to accomplish the work and plan of God for the redemption of Israel (7:37-38).

Antiochus asked her to intercede with her seventh son, to convince him to yield (7:25). He could not understand the words she had spoken in the ancestral language and did not know that she was exhorting her children to stand firm in their faith (7:24). She now instructed her youngest son to consider God's creation and so understand the providence in which they had their hope (7:27-29). Like the others, this seventh son made his choice freely (7:30-37). He prayed that the deaths of the martyrs would turn away God's anger from the Jewish people so that salvation might come (7:37-38). He died "in his integrity," placing all trust in God (7:39). The mother died last of all, having witnessed the sufferings of all her children (7:41). Immediately following the story of the mother and her sons, the narrator tells us that the faithful rallied together, asking God to hear the cry of the martyrs' blood (8:1-4). God's anger changed to mercy (8:5).

The sacrifice of the mother and her seven sons effected a turning point in Judas's revolt and in the fate of their people, atoning for the sins of a nation. She was confident that each one would receive back from God the life they gave so freely for the law. She did not try to stop them, but encouraged them, and watched and listened as each one made his choice, spoke, suffered, and died. Her story is one of incredible faith, a faith that she clearly instilled in her children as their first and most influential teacher. She did not speak for her children nor choose for them, but neither did she turn away in their time of greatest suffering. She offered them encouragement, perspective, presence, and hope. ❖

▨ 1 ESDRAS ▨

Stacy Davis

The titles of 1 and 2 Esdras suggest that they are connected, but that is not the case. First Esdras, found in Greek and Russian Orthodox Bibles, is a second-century BCE narrative that retells the story of life after the Babylonian exile (587/586–539 BCE) as also described in 2 Chronicles, Ezra, and Nehemiah. The book's only original section is 1 Esd 3:1—5:6, an account of a contest between three bodyguards about which is the strongest element on earth. The winner of the contest is Zerubbabel, the faithful Israelite, and his reward is authorization to rebuild the Jerusalem temple. Historically, this addition is unlikely, and it does not fit comfortably within the larger narrative.

I was raised as a Pentecostal Christian, so none of the apocryphal texts is canonical for me. However, graduate school, teaching, and personal devotion have introduced me to these books. Being an African American woman raised by a feminist makes it difficult for me to read 1 Esdras as anything other than problematic. My father was an Air Force sergeant for the first seventeen years of my life, so my mother was the one who kept the family together when he was away, which was frequently. As a result, I grew up seeing a woman who handled business not through charm or beauty but through brains and persistence.

As a feminist I am particularly interested in what 1 Esdras teaches about gender and in the construction of gender from a religious perspective both when the book was written and now. Zerubbabel, the governor of Yehud (the remnant of Judah), who figures prominently in Haggai, Zechariah, Ezra, and Nehemiah, claims that "women are strongest, but above all things truth is victor" (3:12). His argument adheres to the patriarchy common in the ancient world: women are powerful because they are mothers (4:15-16),

homemakers (4:17), and inciters of heterosexual lust, which may lead to marriage (4:18-31). Zerubbabel concludes that when a man, even a king, is smitten, he behaves as follows: "If she smiles at him, he laughs; if she loses her temper with him, he flatters her, so that she may be reconciled to him" (4:31). Contemporary with 1 Esdras, the biblical (Apocrypha) book of Sirach warns men against falling for women's sexual charms (9:1-9).

Feminists challenge the claim that women are powerful only insofar as they can manipulate men either through their seductive beauty or their chaste conduct. One of the first women to do so was Mary Wollstonecraft. In *A Vindication of the Rights of Woman* (1792), she insisted that the "power" Zerubbabel described was a false one that enslaved women by making them dependent upon their physical appearance and manners in order to gain male protection and thus survive. Freedom for women would come through equal educational opportunities for both sexes. Anyone reading 1 Esdras, regardless of religious belief or political philosophy, should wrestle with the sexism inherent in Zerubbabel's argument and what power meant then and means now. ❖

THE PRAYER OF MANASSEH

Stacy Davis

I encounter the Prayer of Manasseh regularly when I pray the midnight office. I use Phyllis Trickle's *The Night Offices*, based on the Book of Common Prayer (Episcopal Church, 1979), for evening prayers. Manasseh's plea to God is not part of the Protestant Bible that represents my canon as a Pentecostal Christian, nor is it included

in the Anglican-Episcopal canon; yet it forms part of that community's practice of prayer, and now my own. The Greek and Russian Orthodox communities do consider this short prayer to be Scripture.

This text purports to be a prayer of Manasseh, a seventh-century king of Judah, who in 2 Kgs

21:1-18 is described as the worst possible king. He is idolatrous, unrepentant, and partially responsible for Judah's fall to Babylon. In contrast, 2 Chr 33:10-17 describes the king as disobedient but later remorseful. The Prayer of Manasseh is a late first-century BCE expansion of the earlier view in 2 Chronicles.

The prayer's argument that God acknowledges and forgives the repentant was a common theme in Judaism, both before and after the exile in 587/586. This theme appears in the texts read today for Yom Kippur, the Jewish Day of Atonement, and for Roman Catholic and mainline Protestant Ash Wednesday services. ❖

PSALM 151

Frederick Houk Borsch

People loved to reminisce and romanticize about David. Dead Sea scroll 11QPsᵃ includes several extrabiblical psalms and also a notice that claims that King David composed 3,600 psalms and 450 songs. That is a great deal of composition and adds to the ascription to David of seventy-three of the 150 biblical psalms. For all his faults (his relationship with Bathsheba and betraying his loyal soldier, Uriah, to death), David remained a hero in Jewish lore. He was chosen and favored by God, and during his lifetime his kingdom and the people generally flourished. Michelangelo's statue of the handsome young David is a later expression of that love of heroes.

It makes sense, then, that there was a long tradition that added a 151st psalm to the Hebrew Psalter, recounting two important events in David's life. This short psalm served as a coda to the Psalter. Psalm 151 is preserved in most manuscripts of the Septuagint (LXX) and is found in other ancient biblical traditions; the Russian and Greek Orthodox churches include it in their authoritative Scriptures.

Psalm 151 is evidently a compressed version of two earlier psalms that are found—the second only in part—in Dead Sea scroll 11QPsᵃ. It appears that as early as the third century BCE an imaginative

editor hit upon the idea of concluding the Psalter with the voice of David himself recalling these great moments in his life. These are great moments because they are also significant events in the story of God coming to the aid of God's people. The first is the anointing of David ("I was small among my brothers, and the youngest in my father's house") to be king. Noted also are his musical skills that in the tradition made him such a fine composer of psalms and songs. The last two verses of the psalm recall his victory over the giant warrior Goliath, Israel's great enemy and oppressor.

As a white, well-educated male who has served in positions of great privilege (as a university dean of chapel and professor, a divinity school professor and head, and a bishop), I have had to learn to listen to the voices of many others when interpreting Scripture. In the saga of his people, David was the underdog. His victories showed that God was with him. His victories on behalf of his people showed that God is on the side of the lesser and the oppressed. Psalm 151 ends some versions of the Psalter with this encomium to David, the composer of many psalms and the underdog chosen by God, in order to bring further encouragement and courage to God's people. ❖

3 MACCABEES

Stacy Davis

The subject of 3 and 4 Maccabees is the same—religious persecution. Only their responses differ. Unlike 4 Maccabees, 3 Maccabees does not discuss the Maccabean Revolt, in which Israel's Jews successfully rebelled against Greek rule in the 160s BCE. Third Maccabees describes both faithfulness and unfaithfulness to Judaism, while 4 Maccabees emphasizes faithfulness to the point of martyrdom.

Classified as sacred Scripture in the Greek and Russian Orthodox communities, 3 Maccabees describes a third-century BCE conflict between Alexandrian Jews and their Egyptian rulers. For the Russian Orthodox who lived through waves of persecution and repression during the twentieth-century Communist era, 3 Maccabees would sound eerily like their own recent history. While the demise of Communism ended their struggle, the Jewish community in 3 Maccabees was rescued from extermination because God answered their prayers for deliverance. The book accurately describes the tension between the dominant Gentile culture and the minority Jewish one. Gentiles perceived Jews as haters of humankind because of their monotheism and dietary restrictions (2:27-30; 3:2-8). Writing in the first century CE, the Jewish historian Josephus repeated the critique. In *Against Apion*, he remarked that Jews are seen "as the very vilest of [humankind]" (2:236). In rebuttal, however, both the author of 3 Maccabees and Josephus insist that Jews should not be criticized or persecuted, because they are loyal citizens of the empire (3 Macc 6:26; *Against Apion* 2:225–35).

But 3 Maccabees' description of Jews who decide to obey the command of the emperor to worship foreign gods (2:31) is distinctive. Josephus later insisted upon the necessity of Jewish faithfulness to the Torah, which creates good citizens (*Against Apion* 2:144, 146, 291). The author of 3 Maccabees takes that a step further; once the threat of extermination has passed, those Jews who remained faithful receive state permission to kill the Jews who fell away (7:10-16).

The problem of what to do with apostates—those who abandon the faith—reappeared in early Christianity. In the mid-third century, Cyprian of Carthage responded to a time of persecution in which some Christians, under torture or fear, sacrificed to other deities. He concluded that those who had been tortured should without question be forgiven; all others must repent before being accepted back into communion with the church (*De Lapsis* 13, 16, 23, 29, 33, 35). There was no talk of killing the unfaithful, as in 3 Maccabees. This suggests that different communities can and do respond to apostasy in different ways, depending upon their context.

I have no personal or family experience of religious persecution. However, I am descended from African American slaves on both sides of my family. My family's history is shaped by slavery and its aftermath, including legal segregation in the South on my mother's side and the Great Migration to cities in the North on my father's. In both cases, my family's determination to build a better life for themselves against the odds enables me to respect the determination displayed by the communities described in both 3 and 4 Maccabees. As an African-American Christian, my religious and my ethnic context have suffering and persecution imbedded in them. These writings pose to me and to every reader this question: For what, if anything, are we prepared to die? ❖

2 ESDRAS

Stacy Davis

Second Esdras appears only in the Slavonic Bible and in Coptic Christian manuscripts, two traditions that give less attention to precise definitions of what is sacred Scripture than others do. The book was assembled from three parts that circulated in early Christian circles under other names:

CHAPTERS	ALSO CALLED	ORIGIN
1–2	5 Ezra	Written by Christians in second century
3–14	4 Ezra	A Jewish apocalypse from late first century CE
15–16	6 Ezra	Written by Christians in third century

The first part of the book (5 Ezra) argues that Christians have replaced Jews as God's chosen people. The last part (6 Ezra) warns Christians of impending judgment and encourages them to remain faithful. As a whole, 2 Esdras gives a Jewish and a Christian response to the fall of the Jerusalem temple in 70 CE.

The Jewish approach in the core of the writing (4 Ezra) is one of *theodicy*, a questioning of God's justice, of which the book of Job is a fine example. The author of 4 Ezra mourns both the loss of the temple and the mystery inherent in the world, but the grieving protagonist finds peace through an understanding that bad things sometimes just happen and that one day the Messiah will come (4:21-25; 11:5-24; 12:31-34).

The Christian approach in other parts of the book, however, blames Jewish unbelief in Jesus for the temple's destruction and rejoices in the devastation (1:24-35). This view was all too common in early Christian theology. Melito of Sardis, contemporary with 5 Ezra, blames Jews for the loss of their temple in the Roman-Jewish War (66–73 CE). Jews killed Jesus and deserve what happened to them (*Pevi Pascha* [*On the Passover*] 72–82, 86–90). "You smashed the Lord to the ground; you were razed to the ground" (*Pevi Pascha* 99).

Historically, both Jews and Christians suffered persecution at Roman imperial hands. Christians, however, did not see Jewish communities as their siblings enduring a common oppression but rather as their enemies. Writing about the educational challenges faced by oppressed peasants in South America, Paulo Freire observes in *Pedagogy of the Oppressed*: "But almost always, during the initial stage of the struggle, the oppressed, instead of striving for liberation, tend themselves to become oppressors, or 'sub-oppressors.'" Christian anti-Judaism was born in a context of imperial persecution but long outlived it, and became an often harmful force in its own right. Only after the mid-twentieth-century Holocaust did Christians seriously consider the theological consequences of their caricature of Judaism. Modern readers of 2 Esdras will confront those troubling images. As a feminist and a scholar and teacher of Judaism, 1 and 2 Esdras are distasteful to me; nevertheless, their ancient views on gender relations and interreligious dialogue exist in modern times and cannot be ignored. ❖

4 MACCABEES

Stacy Davis

Like 3 Maccabees, 4 Maccabees is concerned with religious persecution. Written probably in the first century CE, the bulk of the book (3:19—17:24) is a lengthy extension of 2 Maccabees 3–7, which describes the initial persecution and martyrdom that triggered the revolt. But the first chapters of 4 Maccabees outline the author's thesis that the Maccabean martyrs accept torture and death because they virtuously submit to reason and keep the Torah. This claim is summarized in 4 Macc 9:18: "Through all these tortures I will convince you that children of the Hebrews alone are invincible where virtue is concerned." The seven brothers choose death because they hope to "be with God, on whose account we suffer" (9:8). Once again, Josephus, who in this case is contemporary with 4 Maccabees, is useful. He insists that obedience to one's laws is the wisest course of action and that Jews are willing to obey their law to the point of death because of the hope of eternal life (*Against Apion* 2:144, 146).

Fourth Maccabees appears in an appendix to the Greek Bible but has never been explicitly declared Scripture by any church body. Nevertheless, any community that has ever suffered persecution can relate to the agony and courage described in the book. Oscar Romero, the martyred Roman Catholic bishop of El Salvador, speaks eighteen centuries after 4 Maccabees and Josephus in his book *The Violence of Love*. In spite of his different religious and cultural context, his words make the same argument:

> There is a hope. They are a people that march to encounter the Lord. Death is not the end. Death is the opening of eternity's portal. That is why I say: all the blood, all the dead, all the mysteries of iniquity and sin, all the tortures, all those dungeons of our security forces, where unfortunately many persons slowly die, do not mean they are lost forever. ❖

Part IV

THE NEW TESTAMENT

17. THE NEW TESTAMENT
    AS A TEXT OF CULTURES
    Neil Elliott (with Ann Holmes Redding)

❖ TIMELINE FOR THE NEW TESTAMENT

18. THE GOSPELS AND THE ACTS
    OF THE APOSTLES

    Introduction to the Gospels
    Cain Hope Felder
    Matthew   *Leticia A. Guardiola-Sáenz*
    Mark   *Emerson Byron Powery*
    Luke   *Stephanie Buckhanon Crowder*
    John   *Fernando F. Segovia*
    The Acts of the Apostles   *Rubén R. Dupertuis*

19. THE LETTERS OF PAUL

    Introduction to the Pauline Letters
    Elsa Tamez
    Romans   *Elsa Tamez*
    1 Corinthians   *Demetrius K. Williams*
    2 Corinthians   *Demetrius K. Williams*

Galatians   *Ediberto López-Rodríguez*
Ephesians   *Raj Nadella*
Philippians   *Aquiles Ernesto Martínez*
Colossians   *Gordon Zerbe*
1 Thessalonians   *Abraham Smith*
2 Thessalonians   *Abraham Smith*
1 Timothy   *Aída Besançon Spencer*
2 Timothy   *Aída Besançon Spencer*
Titus   *Aída Besançon Spencer*
Philemon   *Cain Hope Felder*

20. THE GENERAL LETTERS
    AND REVELATION

    Introduction to the General Letters
    and Revelation   *Henry W. Morisada Rietz*
    Hebrews   *James Earl Massey*
    James   *Margaret Aymer Oget*
    1 Peter   *David Cortés-Fuentes*
    2 Peter   *David Cortés-Fuentes*
    1 John   *Craig S. Keener*
    2 John   *Craig S. Keener*
    3 John   *Craig S. Keener*
    Jude   *David Cortés-Fuentes*
    Revelation   *Greg Carey*

The New Testament as a Text of Cultures

Neil Elliott

with Ann Holmes Redding

Give me that old time religion, Give me that old time religion,
Give me that old time religion, It's good enough for me.

It was good for Paul and Silas, It was good for Paul and Silas,
It was good for Paul and Silas, It's good enough for me.

A Point of View

I remember singing that gospel chorus in evening revival meetings as a young child, often gathered in the moonlight along the shore of a lake or on a wooded hillside in the Midwest. We prided ourselves on being a "New Testament church" and took apostles like Paul and Silas as role models. Making "converts" and founding new churches were

important to us. We took the modest buildings in which we met and the relatively low social standing of our members as proof that we were more like the early church than were the churches around us who could support large, ornate buildings and fine new cars for their pastors.

I came nevertheless to see as I grew older that for all the fervor with which we sang that chorus, *our* "old-time religion" was different in important ways from that of the apostles. Paul and Silas, we read, had preached a dramatically new message that took their hearers by surprise, "turning the world upside down" (Acts 17:6). We, on the other hand, invoked them with a sort of nostalgia, as hallowed ancestors in faith. Otherwise the sermons from our pulpits and the prayers our elders spoke over the communion table often carried themes of the same Cold-War conservativism that I could hear on the radio every day.

Paul and Silas spent a lot of their time in jail, but the sort of civil disobedience that landed the Rev. Dr. Martin Luther King Jr. behind bars was taken by our preachers as evidence that he was an "angry black man" who needed to learn Christian humility and patience. A quarterly church potluck was about as close as we came to the early practice of sharing "all things in common" (Acts 2:44-45): our preachers were more concerned to preach against the dangers of Soviet-style communism than to explore the apostolic variety. We read that there was "not a needy person" in the early church (Acts 4:34), but we looked on the charitable institutions to which Christians in other denominations devoted some of their wealth—offering food, shelter, and medical care to the needy—as indications of their "worldliness" and inclination to "socialism." I learned early on that whatever Paul and Silas's "old-time religion" was like, we could not afford to let ours resemble theirs too closely!

The desire to figure out such conundrums drew me eventually into the academic discipline of biblical studies. In contemporary historical study of the New Testament, the supreme value is to understand the origins of these early writings in the context of the first century CE—however different that context may be from our own context or from the beliefs of contemporary faith communities. Even though the New Testament is sacred Scripture for Christians (including many of the authors of this book) and even though many people read and study

these writings today with a sense of genuine connection with them, the academic discipline of New Testament studies requires that we take responsibility for distinguishing *our* interests in these writings from those of the ancient communities that produced them. Increasingly that has meant recognizing that the New Testament writings first appeared, not as the founding documents of a new religion, but as the varied expressions of popular hopes and aspirations for change among those communities.

THE DIVERSITY HIDDEN IN THE NEW TESTAMENT

The New Testament is a collection of twenty-seven writings composed by various authors at different times, from the mid-first to early second century CE. These writings were composed in a wide range of circumstances, in different provinces of the Roman Empire, and among diverse peoples. That diversity is obscured in our Bibles, however, by several factors.

1. The inclusion of the New Testament writings in the Bible. The way these writings are gathered together in our Bibles, alongside another collection of writings, the Old Testament, inevitably gives the false impression that they were originally intended to be part of a single book, "the Bible." That was not the case, however. The incidental character of the letters, for example, explains why so many of the topics they address remain obscure to us: their authors did not mean to address readers living decades, let alone centuries, after they wrote!

2. The composition of these writings in Greek. The original language in which the New Testament was written obscures the diversity of peoples behind it in several ways. First, we are reading the New Testament *in translation.* All these writings were composed in Koinē Greek, the "common"

Greek that developed after Alexander the Great and his successors spread Hellenistic empire and culture across the eastern Mediterranean and beyond. Their reliance on Koinē shows that the far-flung communities in which these writings emerged were already at a cultural and geographical distance from the soil of Jesus and his Galilean followers, whose native language was Aramaic.

> We know that Jesus and his followers spoke Aramaic because occasional word plays that still appear in the Gospels—like the play on Peter's name, *Kephas* (which means "rock" in Aramaic)—and from a few ecstatic expressions carried over into the worship of the Greek-speaking assemblies: *Maranatha*, for example— "Our Lord, come" (1 Cor 16:22)—or *Abba*—"father" (Mark 14:36; Rom 8:15; Gal 4:6). Scholars continue to debate whether Jesus would have spoken enough Koinē to understand the Lord's Prayer as it appears in Matthew 6!

Note that even the miracle of Pentecost narrated in Acts 2, in which people from "every nation [*ethnos*] under heaven" heard the apostles speaking in their various native languages, became evident, so the story goes, only as these people shared with one another their mutual amazement *by speaking Koinē*. Peter then addressed his multilingual audience, not in his native Aramaic, but in Koinē. And even though in the subsequent narrative "the word" spreads from east to west, reversing the direction of Alexander's conquests, we read that the apostles relied on Koinē, rather than any Spirit-endowed bilingualism, to preach the gospel. However spectacular it was, then, Pentecost was, on Luke's account, an isolated event. The actual diversity of the peoples who first spoke and heard about Jesus is obscured by the fact that they relied on the one language they all held in common—rather in the same way that very real ethnic and cultural differences in the United States are obscured by our reliance on English as a common language.

3. The way these writings are translated into English. Even though they used a common language, the New Testament authors display different degrees of linguistic ability, from the sophisticated prose of Luke to the rough Greek used in the Revelation to John, or from the terse staccato of parts of 1 Corinthians to the sonorous language of Ephesians (all of the second chapter of which appears in Greek as just two very long sentences!). Contemporary Bible translators work hard to smooth out those differences into a consistently stately English that sounds "biblical." But that practice obscures the diversity of cultures and rhetorical styles among the writers, which may indicate differences in education and, thus, wealth and social status as well.

4. The background all these writings share: Jewish Scriptures. The authors of these writings appeal, admittedly in very different ways, to the stories and symbols of the Jewish Scriptures in Greek translation (the "Septuagint" or LXX, named for the seventy scholars who created it, according to legend). Those Jewish writings are consistently referred to simply as "*the* Scriptures," *hai graphai*. That common practice reinforces the impression that we are reading the literature of a single people, a religious community continuous with ancient Israel. Careful reading shows, however, that often the people talking about "the Scriptures" were not themselves Judeans (or Jews). (The Greek word

Ioudaioi can be translated either way; in the first century it usually referred not just to religious belief but to national and ethnic identity as well.) In fact we see in various New Testament writings very different approaches to the question, Who are the people of God? Are they continuous with Israel, and if so, how?

Non-Jews were not first convinced of the "scriptural" character of Jewish writings and then drawn to the Jews as a "biblical" people. Rather they were impressed that these ancient writings had been handed down through many centuries by communities, now spread throughout the world in Diaspora ("dispersion"), who adhered to them with fierce and consistent devotion.

5. The mistranslation of the Greek word for "peoples." The diversity of peoples in the New Testament is significantly obscured when the very word for their plurality—*ethnē,* meaning "nations" or "peoples" (compare the English word "ethnic")—is translated, in the NRSV and elsewhere, as "Gentiles," and capitalized as if it referred to a single generic kind of people. In fact, no one in the ancient world would have thought of himself or herself as "a Gentile," any more than someone in the United States today would say, "I am an Ethnic!" Translating the word as "Gentile" tends to change one of the most vibrant themes in the New Testament—the remarkable gathering of individuals from many different ethnicities and nationalities, in fulfillment of ancient Jewish hopes (see Gen 17:4 and Isa 42:6 or 49:6, for example)—into a flat two-dimensional story in which the early church, including Jews and non-Jews ("Gentiles"), inevitably and necessarily outgrew the supposedly narrow confines of Jewish identity and culture.

This is not just a question of how we understand the ancient church. When nineteenth-century Christian missionaries from the colonial powers in Europe and the United States read the New Testament in these terms, they often saw themselves as carrying a divine gospel that transcended other, merely human cultures in Asia, Africa, South America, and Oceania, just as (they thought) the gospel had first transcended the merely nationalist prejudices of early Judaism. They could thus imagine that their own distinct ethnic experience and perceptions were in fact universal and therefore inherently superior to all others. Today biblical scholars recognize that stereotypes about narrow Jewish exclusivism have more to do with the racialized cultural politics of nineteenth- and twentieth-century Europe than with first-century social realities.

Similarly, postcolonial interpreters protest that the claim that the Christian gospel is "universal" has long been a pretext for European and North American colonialism and the imperial project of "civilizing" inferior peoples. It is still very common, unfortunately, for biblical scholars to describe the rise of Christianity in terms of transcending the limitations of Judaism. Identifying and "unlearning" these habits of thinking is as important a goal of contemporary scholarship as it is difficult.

HOW DID THESE WRITINGS BECOME THE NEW TESTAMENT?

Where Did They Come from?

Most or all of these writings were probably addressed to small assemblies of people who by the end of the first century were called *christianoi.* (Although Acts 11:26 indicates that it was in Antioch that the believers were first called "Christians," we have no evidence that this term was generally used by outsiders to refer to the movement until much later in the first century, or that it was widely adopted by insiders to indicate a single shared identity.) Those communities circulated and collected the writings and continued to read them after their initial purpose had been served. In Greek, the word for these assemblies is *ekklēsiai*, ordinarily translated "churches" in the NRSV, though the term did not have the same primarily religious connotation in the first century that "church" has today. These communities included people who felt different levels of comfort with the overwhelming presence and representation of Roman rule. Even among the letters of a single author, Paul, we see indications that various assemblies differed widely in wealth, privilege, and ethnic and cultural identity and expectations. (Indeed, if it weren't for that diversity Paul probably would not have written his letters!)

Who Wrote Them?

As subsequent chapters on specific books will show, the authors of some of the New Testament writings are anonymous. So, for example, even though subsequent tradition has named the four Gospels "according to Matthew," Mark, Luke, and John, none of the Gospel narrators identifies himself (or herself?) by name. (It fell to second-century church leaders like Irenaeus or Hegesippus to recite what they had heard from their predecessors about the authors of the Gospels; it is from their accounts—which do not always agree—that we receive the traditional identifications.) Other New Testament writings take the form of letters written by specific individuals, but there are reasons to question whether the letters from James (*Iakōbos*), Peter (*Petros*), or John (*Iōannēs*) were written by James the brother of Jesus and the apostles Peter and John, or by others, writing pseudonymously—that is, under a falsely assumed name. (Some scholars argue that writing in the name of another, more prestigious person was an accepted practice in the Hellenistic world, at least among the philosophical schools;

others point out, however, that forgery or fabrication, even for the most devout motives, were swiftly condemned when it was recognized as such.) It is unlikely that the John who wrote the letters (1, 2, and 3 John) was also the John who wrote the Apocalypse (or Revelation), which is written in inferior Greek. It is equally unlikely that Paul wrote all thirteen of the letters attributed to him: beyond differences of style and situation, we should note that 1 and 2 Timothy and Titus were not included in the earliest surviving manuscript of Paul's letters, from around 200 CE.

As chapters on the various New Testament writings will also show, scholars don't always agree in their judgments of these questions. The point here is not simply to cast doubt on traditional attributions of authorship but to show that we really do not know much at all about the *individuals* who wrote most of the New Testament. We are on much safer ground when we make inferences, from the texts themselves, about the *communities* in which they were developed and about the *issues,* including situations of both conflict and cooperation between cultures, that the texts were written to address. We are, then, inevitably confronted in the New Testament with the writings *of peoples* and texts *of cultures* (see the chapter "The Bible as a Text of Cultures").

How Did They Become "Scripture"?

We also know that it took time for the early assemblies to regard these writings as having sacred importance. We have a virtual snapshot of early Christians trying to make sense of the new writings of Paul in 2 Peter 3:15-16; clearly they were not embraced with unequivocal enthusiasm! An early Christian like Papias, at the end of the first century, still preferred the "living voice" of oral proclamation to anything written. Later, in the mid-second century, Justin Martyr wrote that Christian gatherings included readings from "the memoirs of the apostles or the writings of the prophets," implying that the former—the Gospels?—enjoyed an authority comparable to that of the latter. But when mid-second-century Christian apologists defended the faith by protesting the innocence of Christian practices, they did not argue first for the divine origin of their Scriptures; they relied instead on the analogy of Greek philosophical schools in asserting the reliability and unity *of Christian teaching* as it had been handed down through a succession of leaders. It was not until Irenaeus of Lyons, in about the year 180 CE, that a Christian apologist offered a defense *of the writings* that we call the New Testament. One of his evident concerns was to distinguish these writings from alternatives current in his day.

Sometime between 130 and 140 CE the Christian Papias wrote that he tried, whenever he met anyone who had followed "the elders," meaning Jesus' disciples, to ask them what they remembered of their teachings: "For I did not suppose that the things from the books would aid me so much as the things from the living and continuing voice."

How Were These Writings Selected?

The century and a half following Jesus' death produced a wide variety of writings concerned with the figure of Jesus and his apostles, many of which are *not* included in the New Testament and some of which are now lost to us. Most of the New Testament writings (and a few other writings like the *Shepherd of Hermas,* the *Letter of Barnabas,* and the *Apocalypse of Peter*) were used frequently enough in Christian gatherings that they came eventually to be considered sacred, alongside Israel's Scriptures,

as some fourth- to sixth-century Bible manuscripts demonstrate. Other writings, like the *Gospel of Thomas,* the *Gospel of Philip,* and the *Acts of Paul,* were also popular among at least some Christians, but came to be rejected by Christians like Irenaeus.

Obviously there were significant differences among various communities that claimed the legacy of Jesus. One weighty question in scholarship concerns just how early that diversity was evident, and how it should be interpreted. Irenaeus's claim to represent the faith believed by the true church "in the whole world"—in Greek, *kath' holos*—gave rise to the claim of a "catholic" (*katholikē*) faith and a "catholic" church, which originally meant "universal." For Irenaeus, all rival Christianities were spurious and wicked offshoots from the true root and stock.

In the early fourth century, Eusebius, Christian bishop of Caesarea, described the practices of different churches regarding the Scriptures they read. He found a general agreement regarding the four Gospels and the letters of Paul (variously numbered), but some disagreement about other letters, books of acts, and apocalypses (or "revelations"). It was not until 367 that the precise list of what we call the New Testament first appeared in a letter sent by Athanasius, archbishop of Alexandria, to churches in Egypt. After that authoritative statement, some of the writings still treasured among "catholic" Christians but not ultimately included in the New Testament continued to be read and are collectively known today as "the Apostolic Fathers." Other writings rejected by "catholic" Christians (in the sense just described) are available today in modern editions of the "New Testament apocrypha." Some ancient writings are lost to us; others have been discovered only relatively recently. Perhaps the most important discovery has been of the "Nag Hammadi library," a set of thirteen books, many of them representing gnostic Christianity, that were buried in the fourth century outside an Egyptian monastery (probably soon after Athanasius sent out his letter, which proscribed some of these writings!) and rediscovered only in 1947.

Early Christian Writings Not Included in the Modern New Testament

APOSTOLIC FATHERS

Barnabas

1 and 2 Clement

Didache

Diognetus

Shepherd of Hermas

Ignatius's letters

The Martyrdom of Polycarp

Polycarp's Letter to the Philippians

NEW TESTAMENT APOCRYPHA
AND PSEUDEPIGRAPHA

Acts of Andrew

Acts of Andrew and Matthias

Acts of Andrew and Paul

Acts of Barnabas

Acts of James the Great

Acts of John (two different texts)

Acts of Paul

Acts of Peter (two different texts)

Acts of Peter and Andrew

Acts of Peter and Paul

Acts of Philip (two different texts)

Acts of Pilate

Acts of Thaddaeus

Acts of Thomas

Apocalypse of Peter

Apocryphon of John

Apocalypse of Dositheus

Apocalypse of Messos

Apocalypse of Thomas

Apocalypse of the Virgin

Apocryphal Epistle of Titus

Apocryphal Gospel of John

Apostolic Constitutions and Canons

Apostolic History of Pseudo-Abdias

Arabic Gospel of the Infancy

Armenian Gospel of the Infancy

Ascents of James

Assumption of the Virgin

*Book of the Resurrection of the Christ
    by Barnabas the Apostle*

Book of Elchasai

Cerinthus

3 Corinthians

Epistle to the Alexandrians

Epistle to the Apostles

Epistle of Christ and Abgar

Epistle of Christ from Heaven

Epistle to the Laodiceans

Epistle of Lentulus

Epistles of Paul and Seneca

Gospel of Barnabas

Gospel of Bartholomew

Gospel of Basilides

Gospel of the Birth of Mary

Gospel of the Ebionites

Gospel of the Egyptians

Gospel of Eve

Gospel of Gamaliel

Gospel of the Hebrews

Gospel of Judas

Gospel of Marcion

Gospel of Mary

Gospel of the Naassenes

Gospel of the Nazarenes

Gospel of Nicodemus

Gospel of Peter
Gospel of Pseudo-Matthew
Gospel of Thomas
Gospel and Traditions of Matthias
History of Joseph the Carpenter
Hymn of the Dance
Hymn of the Pearl
Infancy Gospel of Thomas
Martyrdom of Bartholomew
Martyrdom of Matthew
Martyrdom of Paul
Martyrdom of Peter
Martyrdom of Peter and Paul
Martyrdom of Philip
Melkon
Memoria of Apostles
Preaching of Peter
Protevangelium of James
Pseudo-Clementines
Revelation of Stephen
Secret Gospel of Mark
Vision of Paul

NAG HAMMADI CODICES
Act of Peter
Acts of Peter and the Twelve Apostles
Allogenes
Apocalypse of Adam
Apocalypse of Paul
Apocalypse of Peter
Apocryphon of James
Apocryphon of John
Asclepius 21–29
Authoritative Teaching
Book of Thomas the Contender
Concept of Our Great Power

Discourse on the Eighth and Ninth
Eugnostos the Blessed
Exegesis of the Soul
First and Second Apocalypses of James
Fragments
Gospel of Mary
Gospel of Philip
Gospel of the Egyptians
Gospel of Thomas
Gospel of Truth
Hypostasis of the Archons
Hypsiphrone
Interpretation of Knowledge
Letter of Peter to Philip
Marsanes
Melchizedek
On Baptism A, B
On Eucharist A, B
On the Anointing
On the Origin of the World
Paraphrase of Shem
Plato, Republic 588b-589b
Prayer of Thanksgiving
Prayer of the Apostle Paul
Second Treatise of the Great Seth
Sentences of Sextus
Sophia of Jesus Christ
Teachings of Silvanus
Testimony of Truth
Thought of Norea
Three Steles of Seth
Thunder: Perfect Mind
Treatise on the Resurrection
Trimorphic Protennoia
Tripartite Tractate
Valentinian Exposition
Zostrianus

Although from the time of Irenaeus on, the New Testament writings were defended as having apostolic authority, it now appears to many scholars that some writings we might now consider pseudonymous (for example, 1 and 2 Timothy and Titus) were also accepted and that some of the included writings could be attributed to the apostles only at second hand. (Luke, for example, was identified as a companion of Paul, and Mark as an "interpreter" of Peter.) The early defense of these writings resembled the Hellenistic understanding that the truths of a particular philosopher were most reliably transmitted by the "school" of his followers, in unbroken transmission. (We see something similar in the early Jewish defense of rabbinic tradition, for example in the Mishnah tractate *Avot.*) The simple fact that the argument had to be made shows that early on, different Christians disagreed about which writings they valued.

What beliefs qualified these writings for inclusion? Other considerations clearly weighed heavily as well in the selection of our New Testament. The writings that came to be included speak of Jesus as "Christ" (the Greek *christos* translates the Hebrew *messiah,* "anointed one") and regard him as God's agent, calling him "lord" and "son of God." They declare that he died a physical death and was bodily raised from the dead; furthermore, his death had atoning significance as a sacrifice for the sins of others. His return from heaven in power is expected soon. While all these views are not uniformly expressed in every writing, none of the writings in the New Testament contradicts them; furthermore, the exclusion of many other writings can be directly explained by their expressing views at variance with these foundational beliefs. (For example, the recently published third-century *Gospel of Judas* mocks the other apostles for regarding Jesus' death as a sacrifice.) None of this is surprising when we reflect that those Christians, like Irenaeus, who were concerned with distinguishing holy from

spurious writings were also concerned to identify and safeguard correct thinking ("orthodoxy").

Which practices qualified these writings for inclusion? Specific practices ("orthopraxy") were also criteria for inclusion in or exclusion from the New Testament. Insistence that Christians accept circumcision and keep a kosher diet was a matter of heated controversy in the early churches; Acts 15 and Galatians reject that insistence, however, and no writing advocating these practices appears in the New Testament. Similarly, eating food, especially meat that had been associated with idol worship, was much disputed, as we learn from 1 Corinthians 8 and 10. Paul's own response there is nuanced and rather ambiguous, but no endorsement of eating idol meat appears in the New Testament and in some places the practice is roundly condemned (Rev 2:14, 20). Sexual immorality (Greek *porneia*) is uniformly condemned. While celibacy is accepted as appropriate (see Matt 19:12) and even preferred, it is discouraged as a general rule (1 Corinthians 7); and "Paul" (if it is Paul!) appears elsewhere to give a biblical endorsement of marriage (1 Tim 4:3-4).

Hospitality to strangers, at least within the community of believers, is encouraged, as is affection and unity within the assembly. But the boundary between members and outsiders is strongly felt and reinforced with language about purity and holiness that in Jewish Scriptures could serve to distinguish Israel from its neighbors. It is no accident, then, that people today who seek to draw sharp distinctions between "the saved" and "the lost" can appeal to the Bible. Another, more inclusive vision of all peoples eventually being drawn into the love of God, is also present in the New Testament, but it appears less frequently and is occasionally eclipsed by the concern to reinforce boundaries between "insiders" and "outsiders."

Impulses to transform social relationships in ways that might bring undesirable attention to the assemblies came increasingly to be discouraged and, especially in later writings, subordination within social roles—slaves to masters, wives to husbands—and to church leaders was urged (see Eph 5:21—6:9, Col 3:18—4:1, and 1 Timothy and Titus). Writings that show more emancipatory practices (like the *Acts of Paul,* in which Paul's companion Thekla draws women away from their obligations to pagan husbands) were eventually excluded. The expectation that adhering to the Christian faith would bring opposition, harassment, and even death as a witness (or "martyr") is clear and consistent; again, no writing in the New Testament denies this, though several writings excluded from the New Testament (like the *Testimony of Truth* found at Nag Hammadi) repudiate it explicitly. Hostility to the Roman imperial order is most forcefully expressed in the Revelation to John, though couched in symbolic imagery that outsiders might have found inscrutable. It was nevertheless clear enough to Christians that many churches rejected the writing, as Eusebius reported in the fourth century. Some Christians alluded to texts like Rom 13:1-7 when they faced hostile imperial officials and protested their innocence. But that passage came more usually to be read, like 1 Pet 2:13-17 and 1 Tim 2:1-2, as encouraging quiet subordination to the authorities.

THE HISTORY THAT SHAPED THE NEW TESTAMENT

A Puzzle: The Title "Christ"

The thematic center of the New Testament is the proclamation that Jesus of Nazareth is "the Christ." Many readers today—especially Christians—understand "Christ" as a divine title, equivalent to "son of God." It may come as a surprise, then, that literally, to call someone *Christ* was originally a Jewish way of saying that a person has been "anointed"

to be king of Israel. (Outside of Jewish literature, the Greek word *christos* would simply have meant "smeared" as with oil, without any special connotation.) The phrase itself no more implies Jesus' divinity than it meant that Saul or David or any other of Israel's early kings was divine. Even when the Hebrew Bible describes the king as God's "son," as in Ps 2:7-9, the title is honorific; it does not mean that the king was a heavenly being!

Obviously, then, the meaning of *christos* shifted over time in the Jesus movement, in specific ways and for specific reasons that scholars can investigate. Although the title originally would have meant that Jesus was being hailed as Israel's messiah, no writing in our New Testament uses the phrase "King of the Jews" to refer unambiguously to Jesus, nor is that a phrase used later in Christian worship. To the contrary, in all four Gospels that phrase appears as an accusation (which Jesus never accepts), a taunt thrown at Jesus by his enemies, and the title that the soldiers put over his head when they crucified him. As far as the Gospels are concerned, Jesus never declared himself to be "king." In all four Gospels, the crowds who hail Jesus as "king" or "son of David" as he enters into Jerusalem turn against him a few days later. (Matthew's Gospel repeatedly implies that although Jesus came to Israel as the people's king, the people fatefully rejected him. Luke is generally more careful to reserve the title "king" for what other people say about Jesus; his own followers use the phrase only when they address actual regents, as Paul addressees "King Agrippa" in Acts 25–26.)

The New Testament uses a wealth of *other* titles to refer to Jesus, notably "lord" and "son of God." Furthermore, the Gospels give the impression that Jesus himself had no royal ambitions at all (see John 6:15, where he flees from a crowd that wants to make him king). Subsequent centuries of Christian preaching have insisted that it is Jesus' divinity that matters and that it was nothing but a fateful misunderstanding on the part of his Jewish contemporaries to think of him in political, military, or "nationalistic" terms (that is, as an actual king)—even though that is what "christ" literally means! Early on, then, the term *christ* was somehow bleached of its original meaning. Scholars regard that shift in meaning as only one index—though an important one!—of the significant changes that occurred as talk about Jesus moved from one cultural and historical situation to another.

Just what happened between Jesus and the writing of the Gospels?

It is customary in contemporary scholarship to align different New Testament writings with specific stages in the history of the emerging Christian movement. Although it is hazardous to speak of a consensus regarding the date any writing was composed (see the various introductions in this book), there is at least wide agreement that we must distinguish Jesus' own context from that of the movement that spread after his death in about 30 CE and both of those periods from the time after the Roman war in Judea (66–70 CE) when all of the Gospels were written. The paragraphs that follow extend that scheme to include developments in the late first century.

A Word about Sources

Because the scholarly construction of this history differs significantly from the history given in the book of Acts, the former can seem to some readers both surprising and arbitrary. After all, Acts tells us that after Jesus' death, his disciples waited in Jerusalem, as he had instructed them, until persecution drove "all except the apostles" from the city (8:1). The rest of Luke's account unfolds geographically as "the word" spreads from city to city, region to region, around the northern arc of the Mediterranean. (Luke is remarkably uninterested about the south: the few references to Libyans, Egyptians,

and Ethiopians are the exceptions that prove the rule.) The story is very orderly, always under the miraculous direction of the Holy Spirit, and Luke ties it off neatly with Paul's successful preaching in the imperial capital.

But Luke's account doesn't tell us all that we need to know. If all we had were Luke and Acts, we wouldn't know, for example, that Jesus directed his disciples to meet him after his resurrection *in Galilee* (Matt 28:7; Mark 14:28; compare John 21:1-23). Where did such stories come from? We won't find out from Luke, who offers no mention of the existence of other Gospels, let alone explanations for them. Neither does he ever mention that his protagonist, Paul, wrote letters. On the other hand, if all we had were Matthew, Mark, and John, we wouldn't know anything of a person named Paul, nor could we explain how assemblies came into being in Asia Minor, Greece, Rome, or Egypt! Obviously, then, we must give a more complex account of history than Luke— or any of the New Testament writings themselves— alone provides if we want to understand the diversity of communities that these writings imply.

Furthermore, because the Gospel narrators don't tell us who they are, we are left to draw reasonable inferences about them—and more importantly, about what they were doing when they wrote the Gospels—from what we read in them. We need to explain the wide variations in phrasing and order that we see across the four Gospels, especially between John and the other three; but also the remarkable similarity, sometimes involving identical wording, in the way a story is told, especially among Matthew, Mark, and Luke (called the "Synoptics" because of this similarity). The frequent duplications of material (though often in altered form) and the lack of any cross-references (Luke mentions previous writers, 1:1-4, but does not identify them) suggests that each Gospel was written not to complement the others but to be self-sufficient in the community that received it.

Why Are the Gospels So Similar—and So Different? The most widely accepted explanation for similarities and differences among the Gospels relies on two assumptions.

(1) The stories that appear in the Gospels (especially in the Synoptics) were shaped by decades of *oral storytelling* in very specific settings in the lives of communities. *Form criticism* is a method that correlates those life-settings with specific story forms. For example, believers in Jesus told stories about him having power to heal when they gathered to pray in his name and to lay hands on the sick. Anyone who has been in such a setting today (as I have) knows that getting the details of a particular episode in Jesus' life "right" is much less important than getting to the punch line. As one woman asked me, as a group gathered to pray for her infant son who was undergoing chemotherapy for brain cancer, "Jesus can heal him, right?" This distraught mother could remember bits and pieces of different stories from the Gospels, but none of them exactly as it appears in any Gospel. Just so, ancient communities gathered for prayer were less interested in accurately passing historical reminiscences along to posterity than in affirming for one another that the same power Jesus had exercised to heal in the past was still available. That practice determined the shape of healing stories that now appear in the Gospels.

The same principle applies to other forms in the Gospels. Jesus engages in controversies over specific practices (what to eat, whether and how to wash, to fast, to pay tribute to Rome, to give money to the poor, and so on) when antagonists—usually stereotypical figures like "lawyers" or "scribes and Pharisees" or "elders"—confront him. Controversy stories all present a problem and provide Jesus' decisive answer. They do not provide us reliable information about lawyers as such, or Pharisees as such. But they *do* let us see the sorts of questions that communities had to face when

their own practices were challenged. That means that in an important sense, stories about Jesus *came from* the practices of those anonymous communities. (That is more obvious in stories where the challenges concern not Jesus but the actions of his disciples: see Mark 2:18; 2:23-24; 7:2, 5, and parallels.)

An important example of the role communities played in shaping the Jesus tradition is the words Jesus speaks over wine and bread at the last supper. The words over wine, then bread, then wine in Luke 22 are different from the words Jesus speaks over bread, then wine in Mark 14 or 1 Corinthians 11. To complicate the matter, the prayers for "eucharist" in the first-century writing *The Teaching of the Twelve Apostles or Didache*, first rediscovered in the nineteenth century, name Jesus but say nothing about his body or blood. It is reasonable to suppose that the form in Mark and 1 Corinthians—no less than the alternatives—has been shaped by the way some early communities practiced the Lord's Supper.

---

(2) The Gospel writers themselves are not recording their own memories. (Note that none of them even makes this claim: even John 21:24 makes clear that the authors—"we"—are different from the eyewitness disciple on whom they depend.) Rather the Gospel writers have creatively used the materials available to them to serve their own purposes and, presumably, the needs of their communities as they saw them. Pursuing such

questions involves *redaction criticism,* which asks how the Gospel writers have "redacted," or edited, their sources. For example, in Mark 7 Jesus answers a question about washing before eating by talking about what makes someone unclean: Is it what one eats, or what one says? The Gospel narrator declares (but the authors of Matthew and Luke do not) that with his answer Jesus "declared all foods clean" (7:19). No doubt that is what the Gospel's author—and perhaps the community of which he was a part—took as the meaning of the story as they made decisions about their own meal practices. But no such clarity was apparently available to Paul in the mid-first century as he wrestled with the question in Romans 14, or to Peter as he wondered what a vision about unclean foods might mean (according to Acts 10), or to the apostles as they met in Jerusalem (according to Acts 15). It is reasonable to conclude that Mark's interpretation of the story came not from a better memory of Jesus' words and intentions but from the practices of a particular community at some distance from the communities around Paul or Luke.

What Sources Did the Gospels Use? What did the Gospel writers "redact"? They would have relied, we can presume, on the oral traditions developed before them. One or more of them may also have depended on other written sources. There is continuing debate over whether the author of the Gospel of John had available the other three Gospels and freely adapted some of the stories he found in them. There is much stronger agreement that some literary dependence explains the similarities among order and wording in Matthew, Mark, and Luke (the Synoptic Gospels). On the leading hypothesis, Matthew and Luke both had available a copy of Mark and used it as the framework for their own writing, adding to it a number of sayings of Jesus that they both took from another source. That source, called "Q" (from the German word *quelle,* "source"), so far is only a scholarly hypothesis—no one has ever found an actual manuscript of Q—but that hypothesis is so strongly held that many scholars describe with conviction the (anonymous) community that produced it. (The leading alternative, a decided minority view, is that Matthew wrote first; that Luke borrowed heavily from Matthew; and that Mark used both Matthew and Luke, alternating from one to another and abbreviating both as he wrote his Gospel.)

Another example of communities shaping traditions about Jesus is the "Last Supper." Matthew, Mark, and Luke tell the story of Jesus' last supper with his disciples as a Passover meal, though they do not make any reference to the roasted lamb that is part of that meal. John, on the other hand, insists that Jesus was crucified on the day *before* Passover, when the lambs were being slaughtered (19:31), and even suggests that the way Jesus died fulfilled a scriptural prescription referring to the way the lambs should be roasted (19:36). So—on which day did Jesus die? Any answer we give will need to take into account the different theological motives of the different Gospel writers. Similarly, taking up a difference among the Gospels mentioned earlier, when we read in Matthew and Mark that Jesus instructed his disciples to meet him in Galilee, it is reasonable to suppose that one or both of those Gospels was written in Galilee or by a community that had grown up in Galilee. It's just as reasonable, of course, to suppose that Luke has a particular agenda in having the disciples stay in Jerusalem.

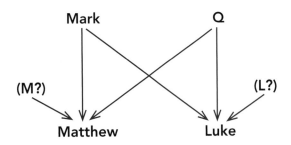

The Two-Source Hypothesis.

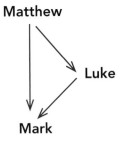

The Two-Gospel Hypothesis.

Different scholars will give different weight to either of these theories (or others). What they have in common is a matter of wide agreement that the New Testament traditions about Jesus cannot be explained as deriving either from a single authoritative tradition or from a disinterested desire simply to pass on firsthand testimony for its own sake. Rather, the traditions behind all four Gospels derive from the rich and complex practices of a number of diverse communities, in different lands, who shaped these traditions creatively to face specific challenges and to serve specific needs over a matter of a few decades.

We know enough today about the history of the first century to identify important events and developments that shaped the New Testament. At the risk of oversimplifying a complex period, that history can be sketched in four phases.

1. Jesus and His Contemporaries

Jesus first appeared as a public figure in Galilee shortly before the death of John the Baptist, whose disciple he was (for he accepted John's baptism). Although the Gospels seek to portray John as something of a herald for Jesus, they record more of Jesus' words about John's significance than the

reverse (Matt 11:11-19; Luke 7:24-35—both from Q?). Jesus accepted and, after John's death, himself took up John's proclamation that the reign of God, with its sudden reversal of injustice and judgment of the wicked, was near. But Jesus said more: in the person of John, that reign had appeared and suffered violence. The Gospels portray Jesus as a teacher, but much of what he said and did in Galilee should be seen as a very particular kind of teaching. He advocated a strict observance of the law and mobilized people to live out a different social reality for which the metaphor "reign of God" was a kind of shorthand. In his parables, furthermore, he described the exploitive dynamics that had placed many of his contemporaries in harsh circumstances.

Those circumstances were shaped by the aggressive and often brutal expansion of Roman rule. Rome had set Galilee and Judea under the client king Herod and, at his death in 4 BCE, had divided those territories among his sons. Together with a compliant Judean aristocracy, Rome opened Galilee up to economic exploitation, foreclosing on loans and consolidating fields so that on the estimation of some scholars, as much as 70 percent of arable land had been put in the hands of foreign investors. Jesus' parables are filled with figures occupying different roles in this new economy: powerful men who deal in extravagant sums of money, buying up new fields, planting export crops (installing new olive oil presses, for example), and building warehouses to store privately owned grain; poor people who struggle to obtain justice in the village courts; and farmers who have been thrown off their land and reduced to day labor or sharecropping. The rich are sometimes depicted as absentee landlords, leaving for distant countries and then periodically sending agents back to demand their profits. The Gospels later reshaped these stories into allegories about the way God deals with human beings, but contemporary scholars argue that Jesus was really trying to show how the newly "capitalized" agricultural economy actually worked in people's lives.

Jesus called twelve "disciples," or student-followers. But he probably meant neither simply to teach a small group of students a distinctive set of teachings (as teachers in the philosophical schools might have done) nor to establish what would later emerge as "the church." Rather his choice of twelve men was probably meant to symbolize a vision of a renewed Israel. The reports that he "sent them out" (that is, in Greek, he made them *apostoloi*, "apostles") into Galilee's villages and the occasional references to a larger, less distinct group as "disciples" suggest that Jesus meant to energize a

Gospel interests at work: All four Gospels tell what appears at first glance to be the same story about a woman approaching Jesus at dinner and "anointing" him. In Matt 26:6-13 and Mark 14:3-9, the scene is the house of Simon the leper; the woman pours expensive ointment on Jesus' head, and Jesus explains, when some (Matthew says his disciples) protest, that she has prepared his body for burial (Mark says *anointed* him.) In both, Jesus says the woman's action is so important it should be recited whenever "the gospel" is proclaimed. That has hardly been the case—we don't even know the woman's name—but apparently these Gospels understand her action in prophetic terms: she has "anointed" Jesus as a Messiah who must die.

In Luke 7:36-50, that theme has disappeared. The woman has become a prostitute (a "woman of the city") who approaches not Jesus' head, but his feet, and washes them with her tears and dries them with her hair before applying ointment. It is Pharisees who object, saying that Jesus should not tolerate the gesture by such a woman, and in Luke, Jesus' response takes the form of a parable about forgiveness. In John 12:1-8, the story more resembles that in Matthew and Mark, except that John identifies the woman as Mary of Bethany and places Jesus at her home; and here the woman "anoints" Jesus' feet. The objection comes now from Judas, who is motivated by greed.

These accounts cannot be harmonized. (When earlier generations of Christians tried to do so, they confused Mary of Bethany with Mary Magdalene and identified the latter as a prostitute—an egregious mistake with no basis in any New Testament writing!) They evidently result, not from the same scene being "remembered" (or misremembered!) differently, but from different authors taking liberty to modify elements of a story for their own purposes.

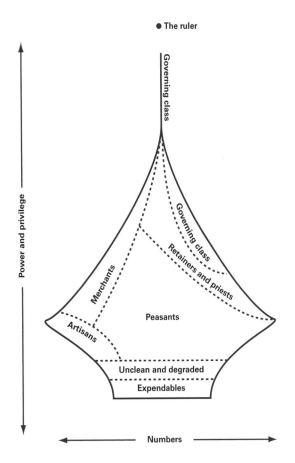

Classes in agrarian societies. From Gerhard E. Lenski, *Power and Privilege: A Theory of Social Stratification* [New York: McGraw-Hill, 1966], 284.

and exorcisms as a feature of Jesus' culture, even if not of their own. Comparative studies in circumstances of colonial violence suggest that demon possession may be a reflection on the personal, psychic level of the larger social dynamics of occupation—of being "taken over" by irresistible outside forces. (Note that in Mark 5 the demon identifies itself as "legion," using the term for the Roman military force in Syria-Palestine.) Note, too, that Jesus described his activity not as therapy for emotionally troubled individuals (as an earlier generation of Western interpreters suggested) but as his combat against the "house" or "kingdom" of Satan (Mark 3:23-27).

Though Jesus is often presented in Christian preaching as a teacher of peace, the Gospels also show him in confrontation with forces, whether human or superhuman, that oppressed common people. He spoke, in the tradition of Israel's prophets, about God taking the side of the poor and the oppressed; he also spoke of an imminent reversal that had already begun in his own words and actions. Some of the hardest sayings in the Gospels are Jesus' strong announcements of judgment against the indifferent rich (Mark 10:25 and parallels; Matt 25:31-46; Luke 12:16-21, 16:19-31).

Avoiding Stereotypes. Several cautionary notes should be sounded regarding the Gospel portrayals of Jesus in conflict. First, when the Gospels depict Jesus arguing against synagogue leaders or being accosted by Pharisees or "scribes" or "elders," we should ask whether these arguments were a feature of Jesus' own time or rather were projected back onto Jesus' day by later communities having their own arguments with local synagogues or seeking to counteract their appeal. The latter appears more likely once we recognize that the Gospels' harsh depictions of Jewish adversaries—ever-vigilant against healing and forgiveness, jealous of Jesus' success, eager to pounce upon any infraction of Torah observance, and constantly unaware that

movement in which communities would organize themselves along lines of mutual support as an alternative to the Roman economy. Scholars often prefer therefore to speak of "the Jesus movement." But the few tantalizing clues that the Gospels offer to such a movement make describing it more fully an elusive goal.

Jesus in Conflict. Jesus also performed healings and, according to the Synoptics, exorcisms (that is, he cast out demons). While earlier interpreters influenced by the European Enlightenment found all these stories incredible, more recently cross-cultural anthropology has allowed the scientifically minded to recognize demon-possession in their murderous rage they are ironically exposing themselves to self-condemnation—are historically improbable. They are better understood as literary caricature.

Second, although Christian preaching and interpretation has often set Jesus over against Jewish observance of Torah, in fact the Gospels never depict Jesus breaking a commandment of the law. Nor does he flout the laws regarding purity and holiness, for example by entering the temple after contracting uncleanness: to the contrary, he appears careful to observe the Torah's requirements, as when he tells a leper whom he has healed to show himself to the priests to confirm that his uncleanness has been removed (Mark 1:40-44). Further, although he is repeatedly criticized by Jewish adversaries for eating with sinners (Mark 2:15-17 and parallels; Luke 15:1-2), he breaks no law in doing so.

Finally, when some contemporary Christians praise Jesus for an open meal practice that welcomed all sorts of people, they often set that practice in explicit or implicit contrast to Judaism. We should note first, however, that so far as the Gospels indicate, Jesus was not the host, but the guest at such meals—so he was hardly responsible for who was invited and who was not. Second, however his associations might have scandalized some of his contemporaries, they did not constitute a violation of the Torah. Third, Jesus is also on record speaking prejudicially to women from other cultures (Mark 7:24-30 and parallel; John 4:21-22) and restricting his work to the "lost sheep of the house of Israel" (at least on Matthew's account: 10:6, 15:24). It would seem, then, that however much we may value intercultural tolerance today, it may be anachronistic to hail Jesus as its champion—especially if that means setting him over against a supposedly more ethnocentric or xenophobic Judaism.

The more we know about Jesus, the more we must understand him as a member of his own people and a participant in their culture. Further, we apparently should understand him as taking part in a larger social movement that seems to have attracted especially the poor. (The stories about *rich* people being attracted to Jesus show them either turning away when they realized what it would cost them, as in Mark 10:17-22 and parallels, or making restoration for all they had exploited from others, as in Luke 19:1-10.)

Jesus' Last Days. The Gospels agree in giving particularly close and sustained attention to the last days of Jesus' life, but they disagree in important ways regarding the sequence and meaning of different events. The Synoptics present Jesus turning decisively to Jerusalem; John makes this last journey one of his many visits to the city at festivals. He entered the city, the Gospels agree, seated on a donkey, as if to evoke the messianic prophecy of Zech 9:9, and was hailed by an enthusiastic crowd in messianic terms. According to the Synoptics, he then entered the temple and overturned the tables of money changers whose services enabled pilgrims to make the required sacrifices in the temple. The Gospels offer different reasons for this action (Matt 21:12-13; Mark 11:15-17; Luke 19:41-46; compare John 2:13-22), none of which may actually go back to Jesus himself. By comparison with other writings from the period, scholars have speculated that Jesus meant by his action to protest the widely perceived corruption of the temple leadership, their ill-gotten wealth, their cooperation with Rome, or the required use of silver coins, minted outside Jerusalem and bearing idolatrous images, to pay temple fees and tithes. Whatever his exact intention, his action could not have disrupted temple functions for long. Its symbolic force was enough, however, to mark him as a possible instigator of popular unrest and thus as a danger to the delicate rapprochement with Rome.

All the Gospels agree that Jesus was crucified—a form of execution widely used by Rome to intimidate subject populations, not least in Judea—and that his cross bore the mocking title "king of the Jews." Although the Gospels seek to interpret his death theologically in different ways, its fundamentally political character is also clear. Jesus' crucifixion was an instance of Roman imperial violence exerted to suppress whatever hopes he had stirred up (or others feared he might stir up) among a subject people.

2. Assemblies of the Risen Christ (30s–60s)

The Gospels all devote considerable attention to the last days of Jesus' life, with enough overlap to indicate that the sequence must have been one of the earliest components of the Jesus tradition to take shape after his death. An important theme running through each of the narratives is that Jesus died "according to the Scriptures," that is, in fulfillment of prophecies regarding the messiah in Jewish Scripture. However, the facts that *no* Scriptures explicitly predict the death of the messiah and that the Scriptures cited are often not predictions at all suggest that this theme arose out of a perceived necessity among Jesus' followers: they needed to explain why the one they had hailed as the messiah "had to" die.

That effort must have followed another, prior realization: namely, that Jesus' death was *not* the end of his story. All of the Gospels (and Paul in 1 Corinthians 15) describe encounters or visions that made clear to the disciples that Jesus was no longer dead but had been raised from the dead by God. Because this proclamation is so important throughout the New Testament, it is especially important to understand it in its original context.

Easter in Context. Although Paul makes clear that the sequence he knows was passed on to him as "of first importance," it does not agree with the sequence of any of the Gospel accounts, nor can comparison of these various accounts arrive at a single harmonization that explains their diversity. Furthermore, our sources narrate different types of events: discoveries of the empty tomb, terrestrial encounters with the risen Christ, and visions of the risen Christ in heaven "at the right hand" of God (see Acts 7:55-56; 2 Cor 12:1-4; Revelation 1). At the end of the first century or early in the second, Luke took great care to smooth out some of these scenes into a coherent narrative: first the empty tomb, *then* earthly encounters with disciples, *then* Jesus' ascension into heaven, followed by a few select appearances (or auditions) to Stephen and to Paul. But this careful organization appears secondary. More common and apparently earlier is the simple affirmation that Jesus was "raised" or "exalted to God's right hand," that is, raised *into heaven.*

That claim would have made sense within the thought-world of Jewish apocalypticism. It had to do primarily not with Jesus being revivified or levitated into the skies, but with his being vindicated in heaven as God's agent—that is, as the figure that different Jewish apocalypses identified under different names but always as standing "at the right hand" of God's heavenly throne. This figure would act soon to bring about the restoration of God's reign on earth and to vindicate the just.

The Church of Jews and Non-Jews. That expectation also explains why, when the movement that spread beyond Galilee and Judea in the years after Jesus' crucifixion began to attract non-Jews as well as Jews (first at Antioch in Syria, according to Acts 11:19-26), they were welcomed as signs that ancient prophecies were being fulfilled. Prophecies that the nations, long hostile to Israel, would submit to God's messiah and worship God along with Israel were at the heart of Paul's mission (see Rom 15:7-19). Indeed, Paul declares that the larger purpose of his mission among the nations was to make his fellow Jews "jealous" (Rom 11:11-14). Paul meant to convince them that the non-Jews that he gathered into assemblies in Asia Minor, Greece, and Achaia were the obedient nations of the last days about whom Isaiah had prophesied. To that end Paul exhorted his congregations to abandon the worship of all other gods, to live morally upright lives, and to share financial resources with one another and with the assembly in Jerusalem, headed by James. For their part, James and the other apostles in Jerusalem welcomed Paul's work in the Diaspora, not only for the relief it brought the poor among them but presumably because they shared Paul's vision of its end-time significance.

Because they have played such a central role in Christian misunderstandings and stereotypes about Judaism, the conflicts that swirled around Paul bear careful consideration. Heated and sometimes unclear things that Paul says about the law in Galatians and Romans have long fueled Christian generalizations about the inferiority or inadequacy of Judaism. Only since the 1970s has the center of gravity in scholarship on Paul shifted so that interpreters can no longer presume agreement regarding what, if anything, Paul found "wrong with Judaism."

Paul's vision of obedient men and women from "the nations" joining with Israel in worship of God (Romans 15) goes far to explain his concern in both Galatians and Romans. Facing pressures to "Romanize" or else appear to be enemies of civic order, non-Jews in the Galatian congregation apparently sought to appear less conspicuous and thus to avoid persecution and harassment from their neighbors by adopting certain signal practices of Judaism, notably circumcision. Paul warned them that accepting circumcision would obligate them to observe Torah as Jews—a warning that would have been ineffective if becoming Jews had been their actual motive! In Romans, Paul warned non-Jews against arrogance toward Jews, presumably both within and around the assembly. Though this arrogance is often attributed to Jewish rejection of the Christian message, it also resembles the contempt

toward Jews shown among the Roman elite at the time. In both letters, recent scholarship suggests, it is not Judaism but the perception of Judaism by outsiders that causes Paul's concern.

The precarious balance that Paul and the Jerusalem apostles struggled to maintain, hoping to see their work vindicated in a heavenly intervention—the appearance in power of the raised Christ—did not last. Paul's effort to bring a collection of money (and representatives) from his assemblies of "the nations" to Jerusalem (Rom 15:25-32) was premature. It ended in disaster. According to Luke's much later account, Paul's appearance in Jerusalem in the company of non-Jews stirred up hostility among Jewish antagonists, from whom he escaped only by appealing to the jurisdiction of Rome. For Luke, the ensuing series of hearings before Roman officials (Acts 21:17—26:32) allows Paul to fulfill Scripture: he gives testimony before "kings and governors" as Jesus predicted his followers would (Luke 21:12). Later tradition reveals that Paul was executed under the emperor Nero, along with Peter (presumably around 64). A year later James was put to death in Jerusalem and, according to one early tradition reported by Eusebius, the community of believers in Jesus that James had led abandoned Jerusalem in the face of impending war against the city. Luke recounts none of these deaths, however, nor does he give any indication about the fate of James's Jerusalem community. Rather his account shifts attention to the west, to Ephesus and to Rome—centers of an emerging non-Jewish form of Christianity.

3. The Gospels as Post-War Literature

The challenges facing churches in Asia Minor, Greece, Achaia, and Italy after the Roman war of 66–70 were considerable. The eschatological vision that Paul and the Jerusalem church had apparently shared had been dramatically disproved. As Roman armies (or hostile non-Jewish neighbors) attacked

Jewish populations in other cities, Judaism fell under a shadow of deep suspicion. Vespasian, with his son Titus, the conqueror of Jerusalem, consolidated power as the new emperor by portraying the destruction of Jerusalem as the necessary punishment of a spectacularly rebellious people who were incapable of civilization. The Jewish origin of the Jesus movement came to seem, to some, a distinct liability. Proclaiming as lord a Jew whom Rome had executed as a rebel could only seem provocative. Indeed, making a public claim that this Jew had been raised by the only true god, that he would return to subdue all powers and authorities, and that he would rule as that god's messiah seemed both politically reckless and profoundly unrealistic. Hadn't Rome destroyed the messiah's presumptive capital? Hadn't Rome vanquished his people without the messiah offering any sign of the promised intervention? In the face of imperial claims that the gods manifestly favored Rome, such silence on the part of the putative messiah must have made continued belief in him untenable for many.

The Gospels were written in the wake of this catastrophe, in part to provide feasible theological explanations for the destruction of Jerusalem and more generally to convince their readers that, the catastrophic disappointments of recent history notwithstanding, Jesus was in fact the long-predicted messiah and son of God.

For Matthew and Luke, the latter task required several things:

- They provided Jesus' descent from King David as his messianic credentials.

- They presented the coincidence of events in his early life with Scriptures regarding Bethlehem and (spuriously) Nazareth as prophecies fulfilled (Matthew), or narrated current "prophecies" from pious Jews and angelic announcements hailing the messiah's arrival (Luke).

- They offered an account of his recognition as messiah by a prophet, John, and the heavenly confirmation of his divine "sonship" at his baptism.

- Then, his identity established, they narrated a "temptation" in which Jesus resisted invitations to reveal his identity by performing classically messianic acts—feeding the hungry, proving himself invulnerable to harm, and seizing worldly power. In their own ways both Gospels would go on to show that Jesus in fact had these powers, but chose to exert them on his own terms. In Matthew, only as the risen Jesus leaves his disciples does he assert that he has "all authority in heaven and on earth"; for Luke, it is the heavenly Jesus who rules through his earthly agents, the apostles, in the book of Acts.

- They recast Jesus' teachings, which had already come to authorize specific practices in congregations of his followers, as the charter for distinctly Christian belief and practice. His parables became allegories concerning "the rule (or kingdom) of God," teaching particular themes of judgment (in Matthew) or reconciliation (in Luke). His sayings about the imminent rule of God were expanded and modified, in longer prophetic speeches (Matthew 24–25, Luke 21:5-36; compare Mark 13) and individual sayings alike, to urge the faithful to diligence for an indefinite but prolonged interim.

- They reworked stories and sayings to intensify the impression of implacable hostility from Jewish opponents, variously identified as "the scribes and the Pharisees," "teachers," or "lawyers," worked by Matthew into a crescendo of antagonism (chs. 21–25). Luke develops this theme more softly and, in the book of Acts, shows that hopes for Israel's restoration began to be realized by the church in Jerusalem after Easter.

- Matthew reworked the story of Jesus' last hours to fix the responsibility for his death on "the people" of Jerusalem "as a whole," who willingly accepted guilt on behalf of their children as well (27:15-26) in fulfillment of the doom that Jesus pronounced on the Pharisees and their "generation" (23:29-39). Matthew also depicted Pilate—against all that we know from historical sources outside the New Testament—as weak and indecisive (27:11-26). Thus Matthew effectively exonerates the governor and, by implication, Rome of any opposition to Jesus or his cause, but shows the people of the doomed city as implacably hostile to the way of peace. Luke softens some of these same notes and takes pains to depict Jesus as sympathetic to the innocent in Jerusalem, showing him offering public warnings of the city's doom (21:5-8, 37-38) and reporting that many of the people did not turn against him (23:27-31, 48). Again, Luke seeks to represent the early days of the apostolic community in Jerusalem as involving the repentance and reconciliation of a significant portion of Israel (see Acts 2).

Although the resulting narrative is intimately familiar to many Christians, especially because of its recital during Holy Week services, the net effect that Matthew created should astound us. Against historical probability, Matthew minimized or deflected those story elements that might have suggested that Rome had reason to hold Jesus (and, thus, his followers) in suspicion. At the same time, he relied on what must have been current stereotypes about Jewish rebelliousness to blame the people of Jerusalem for his death, thus confirming their own unfitness as Roman subjects and providing the counterintuitive demonstration that the city's destruction was proof of Jesus' true identity as messiah.

As already mentioned, Luke's narrative takes different turns because of the author's own theological agenda, which includes an appeal to at least some Jews to recognize the Jesus movement as an authentic continuation of Israel. For its part, the Gospel of Mark makes many of the same narrative moves, though it is missing some of the elements that in Matthew and Luke served to establish Jesus' identity specifically as Israel's messiah (his genealogy, fulfillments of messianic prophecies, and teachings concerning the law, for example). On the hypothesis that Mark was written first of the three, those elements in Matthew and Luke would have been developed later. On the minority view that Mark edited both Matthew and Luke, the purpose of such editing might well have been the removal of just such elements, in line with a certain stereotypic antagonism to Jews shown elsewhere in the Gospel. Note that Mark can sum all Jews up as people constantly preoccupied with washing their hands and "the washing of cups, pots, and bronze kettles" (7:2-4).

The Gospel of John goes even further to distance Jesus from the Jews (or Judeans, *Ioudaioi*), whose hostility to Jesus is aroused early, expressed constantly, and appears predestined. Jesus characterizes the Jews as children of darkness, born "from below" (8:23), and even as children of the devil (8:44); the narrator repeatedly calls attention to their hypocrisy throughout Jesus' last hours (18:28, 30; 19:15, 31). The dominant explanation at the end of the twentieth century for this negative portrait of "the Jews" was that the Gospel of John derived from a Jewish milieu: it was the product of a community of Jewish believers in Jesus whose faith had made them the targets of semi-official ostracism from local synagogues. That explanation has been challenged, however, by others who argue that postulating a non-Jewish author eager to counteract the continuing attraction of the synagogue could also account for this narrative antipathy toward the Jews.

No doubt scholars in the twenty-first century will continue to explore all of these aspects of these narratives, to raise and test new hypotheses against evidence within and outside of the Gospels, and to refine our understanding of the communities that produced them. The fact that different views may be proposed, or that one or another explanation may gain acceptance or be challenged at different times, should not lead readers to despair of scholarly exploration as such, in this any more than in any other field of academic investigation. Rather the continuing evolution of all these discussions points to the strength of a common and fundamental perspective that the particular differences among the Gospels are the result of particular interests and concerns held by specific communities in the years following the Roman destruction of Jerusalem. What contemporary readers make of those narratives will similarly reflect the interests and concerns of different communities today.

4. The Consolidation of Non-Jewish Christianity in the Early Second Century

In the wake of the Roman suppression of the Judean revolt (and of similarly brutal attacks on Jewish populations in other cities), the Christian churches came increasingly to be populated by non-Jews. Of earlier, distinctly Jewish hopes concerning Jesus as Israel's messiah, we have the evidence of Paul's letters and the glimpses they provide us of the Jerusalem community. However, the New Testament as we now have it is clearly the product of a later, fundamentally non-Jewish church.

Just as earlier Jesus traditions were increasingly cast in the years following the war in Judea into narratives that opposed Jesus to his own people and portrayed his Jewish contemporaries as incapable of truly recognizing or understanding him, so Paul's own letters were supplemented by additional letters, written by others, that proclaimed the end of the "law with its commandments and ordinances" that had previously distinguished Jews from "Gentiles"

(Ephesians 2). The unity of Jews and non-Jews was achieved through the marginalization of any distinctly Jewish identity. Other writings went further, explaining that the death of Jesus had not only served as a sacrifice for sins but had provided a *perfect* sacrifice, superseding and rendering irrelevant the sacrifices of the temple (the Letter to the Hebrews). *Barnabas*—included in early Bibles but now collected in the Apostolic Fathers—offered a tissue of allegorical interpretations of Israel's Scriptures showing that those Scriptures had always pointed forward to Christ: the Jews' acceptance of Torah as instruction for living had been their catastrophic mistake, willed by God.

Increasingly the efforts of Christian writers were aimed at countering the suspicions of outsiders and the misunderstandings of received truths on the part of insiders who came to the church through Greek culture and philosophy rather than Judaism. Against outside suspicion, the churches stressed the decorum and "keeping one's place" that were expected by Roman mores: thus the subordinationist ethic of the so-called "household codes" in Ephesians, Colossians, 1 Timothy, Titus, and 1 Peter. Impulses toward women's equality and independence and their leadership in congregation life were suppressed (1 Tim 2:11-15; 1 Cor 14:34-35, regarded by some scholars as a later interpolation into the letter) and dismissed as "old wives' tales" (1 Tim 4:7). The expectation—perhaps fueled by the earlier practice of Pauline assemblies, on one interpretation of Philemon—that the ownership of slaves should have no place in the church was quickly countermanded by warnings to slaves to obey their masters and not to affront them by addressing them as equals (1 Tim 6:1-2). Deference to rulers and prayers on their behalf became the rule (already in Rom 13:1-7; 1 Timothy).

The consolidation of what would come to be called "catholic" (that is, universal) Christianity also required the definition of correct belief over against error within the churches. So 1 John insisted that any who denied that Jesus came "in the flesh" had the "spirit of the antichrist" (4:1-3; similarly 1 Tim 3:16). In the Revelation (or Apocalypse), another John condemned the view that Christians could eat idol meat and thus participate in the wider civic life of their cities (2:14-15). And increasingly, the more spontaneous recognition of Spirit-inspired leadership evident in the earliest communities was replaced by the tighter definition of roles and offices and a heightened expectation of deference (1 Tim 3:1-13; Titus 1:5-9).

Other, more dramatic developments still lay ahead: waves of state persecution, at first sporadic and local, but in the third and early fourth centuries a matter of imperial policy. Struggles on the part of the "catholic" movement to disqualify alternatives, including Gnosticism and, later, the "New Prophecy" (or "Montanism"), as "heretical." And, at last, the astonishing sea change effected by the Emperor Constantine in the fourth century when he initiated an imperial policy of toleration and consolidated his power by presenting himself as the imperial patron of the Christian religion.

With Constantine, the cross became no longer the government's instrument of execution—Constantine proscribed its use—but, for the first time, the symbol of the religion, quite literally the emperor's gift to the church, for he (through the offices of his mother) recovered the relic of Jesus' cross and endowed the Church of the Holy Sepulchre in Jerusalem. With Constantine, catholic theology no longer remained the purview alone of bishops and theologians but was made a subject of imperial edict when he convened the Nicene Council and intervened decisively in its deliberations. With Constantine, the ancient hopes of the Christian movement were refocused around the policies of the emperor, who was hailed by the bishop of Caesarea as the representation of divine rule on earth, the fulfillment of messianic prophecy (Eusebius,

Life of Constantine). And after Constantine, one side or another of an ecclesiastical dispute could appeal to the channels of imperial power for enforcement. It was in the decades after Constantine that Jesus Christ first began to be represented in Christian art as a monarch, clothed in imperial purple and seated on a throne, hair and beard styled in the fashion of the Byzantine court (see Fig. 21 in the Gallery).

READING THE NEW TESTAMENT TODAY

Any of us who pick up the New Testament today inevitably read it knowing things that the New Testament writers did not—simply because we live so removed from them historically and culturally. That also means that to know what *they* knew requires tremendous effort on our part to investigate their world and to imagine our way into it. None of us should imagine that we can do that perfectly, without bringing our own presuppositions and questions, whether recognized or implicit, into the process.

That is not just a fact about the way individuals read. The Bible is used today in very many ways: as an instrument for supporting faith, awakening curiosity, inspiring hope. It is also *deployed* today in many ways to consolidate power, evoke fear, and coerce submission. This happens intimately, as the Bible is cited to foment suspicion and animosity toward homosexual men and women or to threaten women in domestic violence across the United States. It happens on a global scale as the Bible is cited to promote war, to reinforce systematic oppression of groups of people, and to justify indifference.

"The poor you will always have with you." As a child I heard that saying of Jesus (Mark 14:7 and parallels) regularly cited as if it revealed a deep and universal truth about the intractability of poverty. The point was clear enough: Why bother pouring time, attention—and *money!*—into efforts to ameliorate poverty when Jesus himself declared there would be no end to it? Wasn't it simply being realistic to give up on the poor? Of course, deeper currents of ideology are at work in U.S. society: the denial of class, the mythic assertion of equality of opportunity, the correlation of wealth and poverty with moral worth and the lack thereof, and the inevitable stigmatization of the poor as lazy and ungrateful beneficiaries of the exaggerated benevolence of the rich. But those beliefs have been protected, insulated from analysis, by being cloaked as a divinely inspired realism.

My point is that reading the Bible is never a neutral act: it cannot be in a society where the Bible is so intricately woven into the fabric of "the way things are." It follows that reading the Bible should not be just an academic exercise or the satisfaction of personal curiosity, but rather an opportunity to examine other deeply held beliefs and practices. But that requires a willingness to understand the Bible as the product of ancient communities that faced real historical challenges and responded to them, in part, by generating these writings.

Because I grew up in the United States as a white, middle-class, straight, Christian male and thus have enjoyed a variety of privileges and presumptions in this society that I haven't earned, it has been easy enough for me to assume that the Bible is somehow "mine" or "ours." I've usually been able to expect that the Bible will not be read against *me*, in ways that injure, insult, or demean me. A precious part of my learning the Bible has been *unlearning* the lessons of privilege. But listening and really taking in the experience of others who have not enjoyed that same privilege opens up another, deeper, broader way of experiencing the Bible, one that places me outside some parts of my past but alongside others as we work toward a common future.

Just that sense of a common cause drew me to take part in developing *The Peoples' Bible* and, now, *The Peoples' Companion to the Bible*. It helps me to recognize those parts of the Bible that point to similar impulses, similar struggles, in the ancient communities that produced it. After all, the words of Jesus that I cited above are only part of what he said, according to Mark; the rest of that saying is clear enough:

> "You always have the poor with you, *and you can show kindness to them whenever you wish.*" (Mark 14:7, NRSV)

I think it's likely that Jesus' words would have rung in the ears of those who heard them with echoes of the Torah, where God commands:

> Since there will never cease to be some in need on the earth, *I therefore command you, "Open your hand to the poor and needy neighbor in your land.*" (Deut 15:11)

But whether or not my surmise is correct, the responsibility for how I read the Bible—and for what I make of it as I respond to the needs and concerns around me—remains up to me. ❖

❖ Timeline for the New testament ❖

Before the Common Era (BCE)

387   Rome is sacked by Gauls (Celts), who temporarily occupy the city.

336–323   Conquests of Alexander the Great of Macedon extend Greek language and Hellenistic political forms throughout the East, to Egypt, Asia (modern Turkey), Syria, and Palestine. At his death, his successors (*Diadochi*) rule in Egypt (Ptolemies) and Syria (Seleucus and the Antiochi).

284–247   Ptolemy II Philadelphus of Egypt commissions the translation into Greek of Israel's Scriptures (commonly, the Septuagint).

279   Celtic peoples invade Macedonia, suffering losses at Thermopylae but threatening Apollo's sanctuary at Delphi.

264–241   The First Punic War establishes Rome as a naval power rival to Carthage; Rome makes Sicily, Sardinia, and Corsica provinces.

218–201   In the Second Punic War, Hannibal threatens Rome and its possessions until C. Scipio ("Africanus") reduces Carthage, gaining influence in Macedonia and Achaia as well.

195   Palestine comes under Syrian (Seleucid) rule.

189–188   Great Roman military force subdues Celtic peoples in Asia.

175–164   Antiochus IV Epiphanes rules in Syria, extending his empire to Egypt, renaming Jerusalem "Antiochia" and forbidding observance of Torah. 168–64: Judas Maccabeus and his brothers Simon and Jonathan lead a successful revolt and in 160 restore temple worship (Hannukah). Simon, then Jonathan—assume high priesthood—provoking pious Jews (Hasidim) to withdraw—the roots of the Pharisees and Sadducees? Expulsion of a "Righteous Teacher" precipitates formation of the sect responsible for some of the Dead Sea Scrolls.

171–168 Rome defeats Macedonia in the Third Macedonian War.

148–146 Third Punic War: Rome defeats Carthage and forms the province of Africa. Macedonia and Achaia are also reduced to provinces.

133–30 A century of Roman "civil war," sparked by attempted agrarian reforms by Tiberius Gracchus, pits Roman Senate and aristocracy against growing classes of dispossessed landholders and slaves from Rome's wars of conquest. A series of warlords arise, gaining popular support and seeking military supremacy in Rome; but none is successful until Pompey, Caesar, and Crassus form a political alliance and promise benevolence to the Roman masses and Eastern subjects alike.

66–64 Pompey conquers in the East, making Syria a Roman province, marching on Jerusalem, entering the temple and deposing the Hasmonean prince Aristobulus II.

58–50 Julius Caesar conquers Gallia and begins the conquest of Britannia. Caesar and Pompey become rivals until 48, when Pompey is killed in Egypt; in 44 Caesar is assassinated in Rome. Caesar's nephew Octavian and Marc Antony set out to avenge Caesar but quickly become rivals.

38–4 Herod the Great rules in Judea, secure after switching his allegiance from Marc Antony to Octavian. On Matthew's account Jesus could have been born no later than 4 BCE.

31 Octavian defeats Marc Antony at the Battle of Actium; Antony and Cleopatra subsequently commit suicide; Egypt becomes a Roman province. Octavian returns to Rome to be hailed as "Augustus."

27 BCE–14 CE Emperor Augustus. The ideology of the benevolent sovereign, "father" of the people, is celebrated by Virgil and Horace.

Common Era (CE)

14–37   Emperor Tiberius. 26–36: Pontius Pilate is Roman procurator of Judea, responsible for Jesus' crucifixion in 30. Soon afterward, the proclamation of a risen Christ takes hold: according to the Gospels, beginning with Mary Magdalene and other women; James, other followers of Jesus, and Paul have visions of the risen Christ. Tacitus later wrote that "under Tiberius nothing happened" in Judea.

37–41   Emperor Gaius (Caligula). Gaius threatens to set up his statue in the Jerusalem temple (the possible referent of the "desolating sacrilege" in the Gospels?); he is assassinated by his own officers. Philo of Alexandria leads a delegation to Gaius to protest city-wide violence against Jews. Paul begins his apostolic work in Syria and Cilicia.

41–54   Emperor Claudius. In 41 he puts down riots in Alexandria and issues warning to Jews; in 49, expels Jews and Druids from Rome. 41–44: Agrippa I is king in Judea. His suppression of the Jesus movement in Jerusalem (and execution of the apostle James, son of Zebedee) leads, according to Acts, to the spread of the movement beyond Judea and Galilee; James, brother of Jesus, takes leadership of the Jerusalem church. According to Acts, an "apostolic conference" takes place in Jerusalem circa 48–49 (if not earlier), determining that non-Jews will not be required to accept circumcision or keep a kosher diet in the Jesus movement. Paul writes 1 Thessalonians, works in Corinth, Ephesus.

54–68   Emperor Nero comes to power after his stepfather dies suddenly. Circa 54–58 Paul writes to Corinth and Rome and makes his fateful visit to Jerusalem. In 64 Nero accuses Christians of setting the great fire in Rome; Peter and Paul are among those executed, according to tradition. James is murdered in Jerusalem.

66–70   The Jewish War. Priests refuse the temple sacrifice in honor of the emperor, beginning revolt against Rome. Roman general Vespasian leads its suppression, conquering Jotapata (and its rebel leader Josephus) and besieging Jerusalem. A revolt in 68 by the governor of Gaul so threatens Nero that he commits suicide. 68–69: three emperors, Galba, Otho, and Vitellius, quickly succeed each other until Vespasian returns from Judea to seize command in Rome. According to one early Jewish tradition the Jerusalem church escapes the besieged city and settles to the east of the Jordan; in subsequent centuries Christian writers will refer to Jewish-Christian communities there.

69–79   Vespasian becomes emperor. His son Titus completes the sack of Jerusalem and returns to Rome in triumph. The defeat of "impious" Judea becomes a propaganda theme for the Flavian dynasty, not least in the history written by former rebel, now client "Flavius" Josephus. Gospel of Mark is generally held to have been written soon after the defeat of Jerusalem. Colossians and Ephesians may have been written in this time.

79–81   Titus is emperor.

81–96   Emperor Domitian. During these years many of the later writings of the New Testament may have been written. The Revelation to John envisioned the destruction of imperial Rome; likely the Gospels of Matthew and Luke were also composed (perhaps John as well), connecting the destruction of Jerusalem to the death of Jesus; the Jewish apocalypse *Fourth Ezra* also addressed the city's defeat in theological terms. Hebrews, 1 Peter, and the Pastoral Letters probably also derive from this period. On an alternative theory, some time later Mark may have used both Matthew and Luke to compose his Gospel.

96–98   Emperor Nerva. James and Jude written?

98–117   Emperor Trajan. Pliny, governor of Bithynia, asks Trajan regarding policy toward Christians informed against by their neighbors. Jews in Cyprus, Egypt, and Mesopotamia revolt while Rome is distracted by war against Parthia.

117–38   Emperor Hadrian. 132–35: Second Jewish Revolt, led by Bar Kochba. *Barnabas* and the *Shepherd* of Hermas are probably written around this time. Justin converts to Christianity c. 130; a gnostic school begins in Alexandria.

138–61   Emperor Antonius Pius; Marcion and Valentinus flourish. Polycarp is martyred c. 154-55; Justin writes his *Apologies.*

161–80   Emperor Marcus Aurelius; Justin is martyred (165), then Polycarp (166). "New Prophecy," revitalizing the message of John's Apocalypse, erupts in Phrygia c. 172. Irenaeus is made bishop of Lyons in 178.

Chapter 18

THE GOSPELS AND THE ACTS OF THE APOSTLES

Introduction to the

GOSPELS

Cain Hope Felder

If contemporary members of groups who historically have been the most marginalized and exploited
in the United States—African Americans, Hispan-
ics, Native Americans, and Asians—were suddenly
transported back to the first or second century of
the Common Era and brought face to face with
Jesus of Nazareth, the central person in the Gospels, they might well be surprised that he was not—
as he has so often been portrayed in this nation's

history—a mild-mannered spiritual teacher, a virtual priest to the status quo, whose guiding purpose
was to rush to Calvary to purge everybody of their
sins. Over the centuries, the Jesus of the Gospels
has been effectively spiritualized and depoliticized
beyond recognition. The stories of his courageous
speaking truth to power through his teaching, healing, preaching, and witnessing for righteousness
and justice have been greatly muted. The result

has been a Jesus with the accent on "Christ," rather than on "Nazareth." Fortunately, thanks to alternative traditions in subordinate communities that have kept alive a different memory of Jesus, the resilience of the original Gospels within the canon allows them still to speak for themselves despite the self-serving, morally skewed agendas that have too often been imposed on them over the centuries (see also pp. 43–50).

Scholars designate Matthew, Mark, and Luke the "Synoptic Gospels," because they present the career of Jesus in a similar manner, different from the Johannine Jesus of the Fourth Gospel. In the Synoptic Gospels, Jesus' public ministry essentially progresses from the cities of Galilee in the north to Judea in the south, culminating in the environs of Jerusalem. Jesus' movements are otherwise in the Gospel of John; there he travels back and forth from north to south. The Johannine portrayal of Jesus celebrating three Passovers in Jerusalem has also given rise to the common notion of a three-year framework for Jesus' ministry.

Scholars generally date the composition of the Gospels as follows: Mark, 68–70 CE (that is, during or immediately after the Roman war against Judea, 66–70 CE); Matthew, 80; Luke, 85; and John, 90. In general, the later the date in the first century, the higher the Christology one encounters in a writing. A "low Christology" emphasizes Jesus of Nazareth as prophet, wisdom teacher, preacher, and healer, and allows his human qualities to appear: weariness, self-doubt, and impatience in his journey toward his eventual dying and rising as the Messiah. The Synoptic Gospels generally represent a much lower Christology than that found in the Fourth Gospel, which depicts Jesus as the incarnate Word of God and his identity as virtually one with God's own person. In the course of Christian history, when imperial regimes have claimed the sanction of God and portrayed Christ as a heavenly emperor, this aspect of the Johannine portrayal

has seemed to offer little comfort to the men and women victimized by these regimes—and the Jesus portrayed in the Synoptic Gospels has seemed to them more a brother in struggle. But as we shall see, there is more to the Fourth Gospel than this.

Each of the canonical Gospels offers a distinctive version of the Jesus story, and each Gospel becomes more intriguing and even exciting as one discerns the particular community concerns that shaped the particular telling of the story. Although a number of scholars in recent years have sought to challenge the priority of the Gospel of Mark, the majority continue to regard it as the earliest of the four Gospels to reach its final form as a narrative about Jesus. Mark's Gospel presents Jesus of Nazareth as following closely upon the heels of John the Baptist's proclamations about the nearness of the reign of God and about the necessity for persons to repent and undergo public baptism in the Jordan River. Mark describes Jesus as the "Son of Man" who must suffer in order to fulfill his vocation as Messiah and Son of God. For Mark, Jesus is the preeminent miracle worker but one who intentionally hides the true significance of his miracles until he stands before the high priest of Israel. Mark casts Jesus' ministry as part of an urgent apocalyptic drama, because this Gospel evidently was written for a community that faced life and death decisions about either adhering to a boundary-breaking faith or abandoning it.

The Gospel of Matthew is a very appropriate version of the Jesus story to open the New Testament because this Gospel, far more than the others, has the strongest Jewish-Christian tone. Matthew emphasizes the continuity of Jesus' story with prophetic revelations of the Hebrew Bible, which, he claims through many proof-texts, were fulfilled in the ministry of Jesus. For Matthew, Jesus is the son of David who epitomizes a new understanding of the Messiah expected in Judaism. The organization of Jesus' teachings in this Gospel into five main discourses, and the characterization of Jesus as the teacher of a "higher righteousness" who routinely goes up and down mountains, indicate as well Matthew's effort to have his readers find in Jesus a new Moses. If Mark stresses a long list of miracles (Mark 1–11), Matthew has a penchant for Jesus' extraordinary, sustained teachings on themes of justice and mercy. It is clear, on the most widely accepted theory of Synoptic relationships, that Matthew composed his version of the Jesus story by making heavy use of Mark as a source.

The Gospel of Luke is less interested in a new Jewish Messiah than in a universal savior for all people. Luke's Jesus exudes compassion and mercy in his repeated emphasis on role reversals and in his bold ministry to the poor, to those unjustly imprisoned, downcast, or otherwise oppressed. Over the centuries, some scholars have shown a certain discomfort with the Lukan Jesus as he incarnates the Jubilee ideal (Luke 4:18-20; see Leviticus 25). Luke also has used Mark as a source but less than Matthew has. Instead, Luke introduces an extended, theologically distinctive narrative tradition, often called the Journey or Travel Narrative (Luke 9:51—19:27), in which one finds some of the most inspiring and challenging parables and episodes of all the Gospels.

The Gospel of John emerged out of the tense political and religious context of the closing decade of the first century. This unique Gospel raised the stakes for anyone claiming to be Christian. Many scholars believe members of the Johannine community had to cope with the double threats of heightened political and religious tensions with a besieged Judaism on the one hand, and on the other, increasing hostility from exasperated Roman officials which made little distinction between Christians and Jews. Pogroms against the Jews broke out throughout the empire, and the Johannine Christians were being summoned to take their last stand: accept or reject Jesus as the Word of God—the new center of a new religion coming of age—or imperil your very soul! For many interpreters, such threats and stresses make sense of the bold "I am" statements of the Johannine Christ—a new portrayal of Christ as mysteriously and ironically triumphant, even as he goes to the cross; a Christ who (in John 13 and 21) challenges the church to again set its sights on a suffering and oppressed humanity.

I read the Bible as an African American who sees clearly the centrality of the presence and voice of Africans in the Scriptures. As I peruse the Gospels, I cannot miss the fact that Jesus was born a Hebrew, a child of an Afro-Asiatic people. The Afro-Asiatic Jesus was rushed to safety on the continent of Africa shortly after his birth and his cross was carried by an African just before his death. We all need to bring "new eyes" to these first century Gospels and see not just the Greeks and Romans, but also Asians, Africans, and others. We have all been invited by Jesus to the banquet table. ❖

The Gospel According to

MATTHEW ▪

Leticia A. Guardiola-Sáenz

The Gospel According to Matthew has been the opening book of the New Testament since the end of the second century, when the formation of the Christian canon began. At that time it was regarded as the first Gospel ever written and as the testimony of the apostle Matthew. Now most scholars judge that it was probably not the first Gospel—that place belongs to Mark—and that it is an anonymous text, probably written around 85–90 ce. That dating is based in part on the perception in 18:15-20 of a more organized church, which most likely emerged after the year 70. Early church tradition held that Matthew was written in Hebrew, by a Jew writing for a Jewish audience. However, since the Gospel was evidently written in Greek, many scholars today point to a Gentile author who valued Jewish tradition and wrote for a Gentile audience familiar with it, or for an audience that included both Jews and Gentiles.

Matthew is considered the most Jewish of the canonical Gospels. He outlines Jesus' story as parallel to Israel and depicts him as constantly concerned with upholding the law (see 5:17-20). With more than 100 references to the Hebrew Bible, this Gospel presupposes an audience familiar with the Torah and the prophets, to whom Matthew seeks to prove that Jesus came as fulfillment of prophecy. He begins with a long genealogy, establishing Jesus' Jewish ancestry and his royal heritage as the Davidic Messiah. Then, following the literary patterns of ancient Greco-Roman biographies, Matthew offers a classic opening for a hero's life: a miraculous conception, then a sequence of events

under constant divine guidance through dreams and angels (the visit to Mary, Joseph, and the child Jesus by wise men from Persia in response to a cosmic invitation, then the flight of the holy family into Egypt to protect Jesus' life, then their return to Nazareth). Some details from this story, including Joseph's dreams and the trip to Egypt, are reminiscent of the dreams of the ancestor Joseph in Exodus as well as of Israel's journey.

Some scholars see in the structure of this gospel another indirect reference to the Torah. Just as the Torah has five books, Matthew has organized Jesus' message in five discourses. The most popular of them is the Sermon on the Mount (chs. 5–7); the others are 9:36—11:1; 13:1-53; 18:1—19:1; and 24:3—26:2. This structure seems to present Jesus as a "new Moses" and his teachings as a "new Torah." However, as Jewish as Matthew can be, it is also a very Christian Gospel. Besides its particular emphasis on discipleship, it is also the only Gospel that writes explicitly about the church (in Greek, *ekklēsia*; see 16:18; 18:17). This tension probably reflects the process by which a Christian group emerging from a larger Jewish community came to identify themselves over against that community. Thus Matthew's references to the synagogue as "their" synagogue uses us-them language that speaks of the strain experienced by the community. Perhaps that strain somehow explains the perceived need of a "new Torah."

In all fairness, however, it is impossible to speak of a clear separation of "Jewish" and "Christian" communities at this stage, or to use distinctive labels such as "Jewish Christians," "Jewish/Gentile Christians," or "Gentile Christians." The people in Matthew's community—including the Gentile converts—most likely considered themselves Jewish, but at the time the Gospel was written, things were changing, with new Gentiles coming onto the scene. What we see here is a process of cultural hybridization (mixture) taking place at ideological, religious, and ethnic levels. It is this hybridism, which seems to happen contrary to Matthew's plans, that fascinates me, because it resonates with my personal experience of growing up in a bicultural context. At the end of the Gospel, Jesus states that all nations will share in the faith of Israel (28:19-20); but by then non-Jews had already started sharing in the faith (8:5-13; 15:21-28). What was apparently expected to be a two-stage process—first the Jews, then the Gentiles (10:5-6)—never happens, because the Gentiles come to the table before they are invited. The Roman centurion and the Canaanite woman end up sharing the bread intended first for the house of Israel. They come seeking Jesus before they are approached, on their own terms and without being coerced—that is, without being "evangelized" in any imperialistic way.

Ultimately, what comes across as the central message in Matthew is the *inclusiveness* of faith. For me, the Gospel of Matthew—and the whole Bible—is about the encounter and dialogue of the divine and the human and how that interaction defined and continues to define both divine and human identities. Perhaps because I grew up in the borderlands between Mexico and the United States, I have seen such divine-human encounters—and all encounters between people and peoples—as constant negotiations of limits. Border-crossing is inevitable, but it needs to be done with respect, avoiding invasion, and acknowledging the inescapable hybridity that occurs in all contact zones, by which we are transformed. All border zones are vulnerable, and people living in them can survive only through interdependency. This and more we can learn from the way borders work in Matthew. ❖

The Gospel According to

MARK

Emerson Byron Powery

Of the written stories of Jesus' mission included in the New Testament, the Gospel of Mark is generally considered to be the earliest. Written outside Palestine, and possibly in Rome, this account is one of the initial writings responsible for carrying the message of the Jesus movement *westward*, toward Italy. The author makes the story of Jesus more suitable for a Latinized or European population. Mark includes a number of stories that highlight Jesus' contact with non-Jewish people. Especially significant among these encounters is one that results in the first *human* confession of Jesus—from the lips of a Roman centurion—as "God's Son" (15:39).

This story begins with Jesus' baptism by that radical countercultural figure John the Baptist. John's life ends when he questions the political activities of King Herod (6:14-29). Jesus' life comes to an abrupt end when he confronts leading Jewish religious figures (11:15-18). His death by crucifixion, a form of execution reserved for slaves or state criminals, suggests the complicity of the religious establishment in Jerusalem with political forces under the authority of Pilate, the Roman procurator.

Mark's message of Jesus' life and actions is bound up with the coming reign of God. This message should be read in light of the author's context, especially the Roman-Jewish War (66–70 CE). How should followers of Jesus live in a world in which Rome and its ruling elite stand in tension with the leaders of the Jews? Whose side should these Jesus followers take? Should they "give to the emperor" or to God? (12:13-17). Jesus' life-giving activity among the villages of Galilee had implications for the early Christian communities of first-century Rome, despite the potential for ethnic tensions between Jews and non-Jews (compare Rom 14:1—15:6).

Most of Mark's story concentrates on Jesus' activities among Jews within the borders of Judea. Yet the author does not avoid the ethnic collision of a Jewish Jesus—from "Nazareth of Galilee" (1:9)—with non-Jews. In fact, the author claims that Jesus also *attracted* non-Jews, from the "region around Tyre and Sidon" (3:8). This attraction leads to the direct confrontation with a Syro-Phoenician woman (7:24-30). Though the story ends well (the woman's request is granted), the author has Jesus reveal an ethnic bias as he implicitly calls the Gentile woman a "dog." Jesus' contacts with persons of other ethnic backgrounds are not uncommon elsewhere in the story: the tomb-bound Gerasene demoniac (5:1-20); the deaf man of the Decapolis (7:31-37); and a large crowd in that same region (8:1-9).

Although archeological evidence of a multiethnic population of Galilee is scarce, the fact that Mark's narrative highlights the encounters of Jesus with several Gentile characters suggests that the author's stories have a larger goal: he wishes to present what could be an ethnically exclusive story in a more inclusive time period and community.

This Gospel, unlike Matthew and Luke, omits a birth narrative with a genealogy or any other intentional Jewish identity markers. Neither does this story conclude with a global agenda comparable to Matt 28:16-20 or Luke 24:45-47. Rather, the story ends with an instruction to the disciples to return to Galilee, implying the development of an inclusive community of disciples (16:7) outside of Jerusalem.

I am part of the first generation of my family born in the United States. My two older siblings were born in the Cayman Islands in the Caribbean, and my two younger siblings were born in the United States. My parents moved to New York City in the early 1960s for economic *and* missionary purposes. Our West Indian American family comfortably receives other ethnic labels—Afro-Caribbean, African American. This mixed racial identity enhances my sensitivity to ethnic hybridity and to differences *and* tensions within the ancient biblical stories, including Mark's story of Jesus. ❖

The Gospel According to

▦ LUKE ▦

Stephanie Buckhanon Crowder

Composed around 80–90 CE, the Gospel of Luke bears the name of a person identified elsewhere in the New Testament as a physician and a companion of the apostle Paul (see Acts 16:10-17; 21:1-18; Col 4:11-14). The author employs a rhetoric of subversion, using a hidden or coded language that speaks against the control and domination of the Roman Empire, the ruling power in Palestine. While addressing the marginalization of the writer's audience, at the same time this secret speech reveals the source of such oppression and exclusion. For Luke's readers, *Pax Romana*, the Peace of Rome, might more accurately be called the pilfering power of Rome.

From the start the author recognizes the power dynamics typical of the imperial society of the time. In dedicating his Gospel to his patron, "you, most excellent Theophilus," Luke acknowledges the reality of Roman patron-client relationships and aligns himself with the client side of those relationships, perhaps even with the oppressed (1:1-4). The writer interweaves his narrative with personal experience rather than aesthetically removing himself from the imperialistic background of his "orderly account" (1:3). Nonetheless, the reader can detect a use of code even here, since the literal translation of the Greek *Theophilos* is "god-lover." Thus, this Gospel is for any who hear Luke's story who love God and believe in Jesus as God's son.

The Gospel of Luke presents Jesus as a savior accessible to all people. This Jesus transcends not only race and ethnicity but also wealth and poverty. Luke's Jesus confronts the rich so that rich and poor

have equal footing (6:24-26; 12:13-21; 16:1-13, 19-31). Women, the lame, the hungry, and those deemed "other" are also at the forefront (4:18-19; 8:1-3). The theology of Luke is grounded in a Jesus who comes not just to offer compassion to those who are wounded but also to speak to the evil of those who wound.

As an African American woman born and nurtured in the South, I have much affinity for this Gospel and for Luke's empathy with those on the outskirts. African Americans still occupy an inferior social standing when compared to other races. African American women are at the bottom of the social ladder. There have been some advances against race and gender discrimination, but the ceiling remains. As an ordained Baptist and Disciples of Christ minister, I am joined to other clergywomen who must constantly battle sexism against women in ordained ministry. Those who love God should equally show love for God's people. The portrayal of Jesus in this Gospel as one who releases, sets free, proclaims jubilee, and dialogues with an African (23:26) is quite appealing.

While in structure the Gospel of Luke is similar to Greco-Roman history and biography, its content makes it apparent (on the most widely accepted theory of Gospel relationships) that the writer had access to Mark's Gospel and to another source of "sayings" identified by scholars as "Q," for *Quelle*, the German word for source. Luke also seems to have used a source now called "L," because some aspects of Luke are found in neither Mark nor Q and are unique to Luke's work (chs. 22–24).

The Gospel of Luke can be outlined as follows: prologue (1:1-4); infancy narratives (1:5—2:52); preparation for ministry (3:1—4:13); ministry in Galilee (4:14—9:50); journey to Jerusalem (9:51—19:27); Jesus in Jerusalem (19:28—23:56); and leaving Jerusalem behind (ch. 24). ❖

The Gospel According to

JOHN

Fernando F. Segovia

why Peculiar

Traditionally, the Gospel of John has been attributed to John, the son of Zebedee, associated with the city of Ephesus in Asia Minor, and dated to the final decades of the first century CE. On these points of authorship, place of writing, and time of composition, there has been much debate but no consensus. Given the lack of evidence, the Gospel is best approached as a piece written by an anonymous author from an undisclosed location and at an unknown time. The Gospel of John has also been regarded, when compared to the other canonical Gospels, as a highly peculiar writing. Scholars have long debated its relationship to the other Gospels, arguing for a range of views, from this Gospel's creative dependence on the Synoptics, to its connection with the other Gospels at an earlier pre-Gospel stage, to its complete independence from the other Gospels. Despite shifting points of agreement and disagreement in this regard, the distinctive features of the Gospel are beyond dispute.

The Gospel presents Jesus as the incarnation of the Word of God, a divine figure existing with God before creation and responsible for all creation, and at last sent into the world to make the Father known. The Gospel presents two levels of reality that are engaged in conflict: a world "above," the world of "glory" where God rules—marked by life and light, grace and truth; and a world "below," the world of "flesh" where the evil one rules—marked by death and darkness, sin and falsehood. In this portrayal of Jesus' life he is a traveler, on a cosmic journey from the world above into the world below and on a series of geographical journeys up to and down from Jerusalem. Compared with the other Gospels, John's devotes much more attention to Jesus' words, the revelation entrusted to him by God, than to his works, the signs given to him by the Father. It depicts Jesus as bringing about a sharp division among all human beings between the "children of God" (1:12; 11:52), those who believe and who are reborn of the Spirit, and those who do not believe, who were "born...of the will of the flesh" (1:13). It reduces the expectations (evident in the other Gospels) of a coming convulsive end of the world and fulfillment of God's kingdom and instead highlights access to God's kingdom through belief in Jesus.

This Gospel raises keen questions about culture and society, both in the social-cultural context in which it was composed and in all subsequent contexts in which it is read, including our own. Fundamental are questions concerning the Gospel's depiction of reality in stark either-or terms: a world below, immersed in death and darkness, sin and falsehood; and a world above, in which all who believe are raised to dwell in the household of God, in life and light, grace and truth—but only through the agency of Jesus and his generations of followers. This view of reality has consequences, most important among which are the potential demonization of those individuals and groups who express no belief in Jesus and the divinization of those who do. Most specifically, the collective character of "the Jews" is singularly marked in negative terms in this Gospel, bringing to the fore the question of anti-Judaism, especially in the light of the history of the West toward these internal "Others." At the same time it is clear that where belief is lacking, no group fares any better in this Gospel—so we may as well ask about the legacy of this Gospel in the history of the Christian West's antagonism toward other non-Christians, what we might call its external Others.

I come to the Gospel of John and its either-or reality as a child of either-or realities in conflict. Born and raised in Cuba, I experienced life first under a right-wing dictatorship, then under a left-wing dictatorship. As someone who emigrated from Latin America to the United States, I experienced life first in the world of the colonized, as a citizen of a dependent country, and then in the world of the colonizer, as a member of what was in the United States a minority ethnic group. As someone who in effect crossed from "East" to "West" at the height of the Cold War, I experienced life first in a socialist state with a centralized economy and an autocratic regime, and then in a capitalist state, with a free-market economy and a liberal regime. All these situations involved variations of either-or contrasts. My whole life has been a reaction against polarization and "othering" and a search for freedom and justice, dignity and well-being. Before the Gospel of John, I stand in awe of its highly reassuring vision of enlightenment and love—and in fear of its deeply unsettling deployment of either-or rhetoric and ideology. The latter I can only resist; the former I can only admire. ❖

THE ACTS OF THE APOSTLES

Rubén R. Dupertuis

The Acts of the Apostles stands alone in the New Testament in telling the story of the spread of Christianity in the first years after Jesus' death and resurrection; it is the history of the apostolic period. But Acts is much more and, in some ways, less than that. In part because it follows the conventions of history writing at the time, Acts is selective in what it presents. Peter and particularly Paul—not all of the apostles—dominate the narrative. The picture of Paul that emerges in Acts differs from what can be gathered from Paul's own letters. Acts is far from being a dry reporting of facts and events—it is a narrative that articulates the author's theological perspectives and likely addresses the needs of the author's community at a particular point in time.

Later Christian tradition attributed Acts to a companion of Paul on the basis of sections of the narrative that speak in the first person plural (see 16:10-17; 20:5-15; 21:1-18; and 27:1—28:16). Unfortunately, we know little for certain about the author, his audience, or the circumstances of composition. It is clear that the same person is responsible for Acts and the Gospel of Luke in the forms in which we have them, making Acts part two of a two-volume work. In addition to prologues that address the books to a certain Theophilus, Luke and Acts share similar language, literary styles, and themes. Scholars typically date Acts anywhere from 80 to 125 CE.

The narrative carries out Jesus' charge to the disciples (1:8), describing the spread of the movement from Jerusalem into Gentile areas such as Samaria (chs. 1–9), Asia Minor, Greece, and finally Rome (chs. 10–28). The geographical movement coincides with a shift from a Jewish to a predominantly Gentile mission. In Acts we see a redefining of who and what Israel is and what the boundaries of membership are. The steps toward the inclusion of Gentiles are presented as the result of God's guidance (chs. 10–11) and the fulfillment of prophecy (ch. 15). The largely negative depiction of the Jewish reception of the gospel paves the way for Paul to characterize the Jews as failing to listen and to turn primarily to Gentiles (28:25-28).

Cultural differences and issues of identity surface often. This whirlwind tour of the Mediterranean world plays on contemporary conventions and stereotypes. When narrating scenes that take place in Jerusalem, the language of Acts strikingly echoes the Septuagint (the Greek translation of the Old Testament), while in Paul's visit to Athens he looks and sounds remarkably philosophical, even reminiscent of Socrates. The author of Acts can also use and allude to narratives that were probably familiar to his audience. Paul's shipwreck strikingly resembles the shipwrecks of the hero of Homer's Odyssey, except that where Odysseus's men drown, Paul's shipmates are all saved. But I see the author of Acts doing something more complex: carving out a space for his community in the cultural landscape of the early Roman Empire. Acts is a kind of apology. The identity the author creates is necessarily made from available materials, but it is nonetheless something new. The true people of God now includes Gentiles for whom the traditional markers of covenant membership do not apply. Gentile Christians are no longer regarded as Greeks, Romans, or anything else in the traditional ways these cultures are understood, in part because they now worship the one true God of Israel. Acts rearranges, bends, and even breaks old cultural and religious boundaries as it lays down new ones.

This cultural complexity and the ambiguity that goes along with it draw me to the study of Acts. I grew up straddling a number of different cultures, and that has always made clear and simple statements of national identity difficult for me. My family is from Argentina, although only my father was born there, and I never lived there. I split most of my childhood between Montemorelos, Mexico, and Michigan, in the United States. From an early age I developed a fairly good sense of the different sets of cultural rules in different places. I identify with several cultures but don't feel I fully belong to any one of them. This is why I am drawn to Acts. I like its complexity and messiness. Even if I can't fully identify with the particular space that Acts tries to carve out for Christians in its time, I can identify with the complex cultural world it presents and with the need to constantly negotiate one's place within it. ❖

Chapter 19

THE LETTERS OF PAUL

Introduction to the

PAULINE LETTERS

Elsa Tamez

Translated by Leticia A. Guardiola-Sáenz

Twenty-one of the twenty-seven New Testament writings are letters. We should be amazed by this fact, but we usually do not even notice it because we are accustomed to reading the Bible without thinking about its literary genres. We tend to hear and to study isolated verses, taking them out of their context. But in doing that we lose a great deal of the text's meaning. When reading Paul's writings in particular, we need to keep in mind that they are *letters* he sent to diverse Christian communities, to friends, or to coworkers. This teaches us that Paul's message comes in the midst of everyday life. His letters reflect his own day-to-day life, his thoughts about God from his particular context, and his joys and conflicts in his relationships with Christian communities. From a theological point of view, we who listen for the Word of God in the Bible—and I think especially of our communities in Central America today—may find it easier to understand the message of the biblical texts for us if we remember that God's message comes to us mediated through ancient letters that reflect people's experiences of God in the midst of daily life.

The letter was a common means of communication in antiquity. Archaeologists have found diverse types of ancient letters: personal, official, didactic, and so on. Letters provided a way of communication, mostly among literate people of means. Because the majority of the population were illiterate, those who wrote letters to them needed to ensure that someone would communicate the letter's content orally. That was clearly the case with Paul's letters. In 1 Thess 5:27, Paul asks the recipients of the letter to read it to the whole community.

Thirteen of the twenty-one New Testament letters bear Paul's name as the sender. These letters, often called the "Pauline corpus," were written or dictated either by Paul himself or by others—possibly his disciples—writing under the name of their teacher. (It was a common school practice in antiquity to compose a writing and sign it with the name of an important person, frequently a mentor, and some scholars have suggested that this practice accounts for the writings attributed to Paul that he did not himself write.) This is why there are important differences between the content of some of these letters, for example between Romans and 1 Timothy. Those two letters are dated by most scholars at two very different times: Romans in 57 or 58 CE; 1 Timothy in the 90s or perhaps even after 100. The letters reflect different contexts and the problems of two communities in different locations and different times. Scholars propose three different stages in the Pauline corpus:

Written or dictated by Paul, between 50 and 60: 1 Thessalonians, 1 and 2 Corinthians, Philippians, Philemon, Galatians, Romans

Written by others, circa 80s: Ephesians, Colossians, 2 Thessalonians

Written by others, circa turn of the second century, called Pastoral Epistles: 1–2 Timothy, Titus

Some scholars still debate whether there are more authentic Pauline letters than the seven just identified. But there is wide agreement that what is helpful for understanding any and all of these letters is to read them in their particular context.

The letters follow a structure that was common during Paul's time. Its elements are 1) an introduction that includes the sender's name, the name of the addressee, and a greeting; 2) often, a thanksgiving; 3) the body of the letter, its length and content varying according to the situation of the community or persons to whom Paul is writing; and 4) a closing word.

To the Galatians, who are Gentiles (that is, non-Jews; the Greek word *ethnē* means "nations"), Paul writes urging them to stay away from the false teachers who are demanding obedience to Moses's law through circumcision. He reminds them that God welcomes them by grace, not through circumcision. To the Corinthian community, Paul writes to advise them regarding specific practices that point to deeper theological and moral issues: how to deal with incest, for example, meat offered to idols, order during worship, and faith regarding resurrection. To the communities in Thessalonica and Philippi, he writes to strengthen their faith and to encourage them in their trials. To the Romans he writes, among other things, to clarify his position regarding the law and God's justice and regarding the inclusion of the Gentiles as children of God. He also hopes the Roman community will sponsor his visit to Spain. To his friend Philemon he extends a personal request—though it was read publicly in the church meeting in his house—to welcome his fugitive slave, Onesimus, and treat him with love as a brother. In all his letters Paul combines exhortation and theological teaching in order to edify the communities and help them conduct themselves within an often hostile Roman society. The theology we have from Paul comes out of these concrete realities.

At the end of the letters comes a closing or final word. It includes, variously, Paul's greetings to particular members of the communities, new exhortations, reference to his personal plans, and often a blessing. Sometimes he also includes a doxology, a word of praise to God, either in the closing or within the body of the letter.

The letter, as a literary genre, was a very useful missionary strategy. It acted as the presence of the apostle even when he was far away. Paul founded communities and then, through his letters, strengthened and exhorted them and clarified some doctrinal issues. We sometimes encounter him discussing unfinished topics or defending himself from those who were attacking him. Sometimes he talks about his personal situation, looking for solidarity and support from the community. We see this when Paul was in prison: he needed the prayers and solidarity of the community in Philippi. He also appealed for the solidarity of the Gentiles when he was collecting the offering for the needy in Jerusalem (Gal 2:10; 2 Cor 8–9). Later, when his relation with the church leaders in Jerusalem was tense, he appealed to the community in Rome for their prayers so that the leaders in Jerusalem would receive the collection (Rom 15:30-32). Paul was a good writer, and despite the clear evidence that he was often opposed, the fact that

his letters were collected and circulated among the churches shows that, at least some of the time, members of the churches found his messages persuasive and authoritative.

We know that some of Paul's letters were lost. In 1 Cor 5:9 the apostle speaks of a previous letter he wrote; and in 2 Cor 2:3-4 he speaks of a letter he wrote with "many tears." In Col 4:16 we read of a letter that Paul wrote to the church in Laodicea. Evidently, Paul wrote many more letters, but we have only a few in the New Testament. These survived because little by little they became known and shared among the Christian communities spread all over this part of the Roman Empire. They were copied and in time became a valuable heritage from the first apostle to the Gentiles, worthy of being handed on in the canon of the New Testament.

Many of the main theological concepts in our churches today—including sin, grace, salvation, and justification—come from Paul's theology, although we do not always understand them in exactly the way Paul did. Many of these concepts are expressed in rather abstract terms, which is why many have considered Paul more a theologian than a missionary. However, we should not underestimate his missionary work, since it was through his experience with God in everyday life, in his missionary work and his relationship with the people of the provinces of the Roman Empire, that his theology emerged. He traveled extensively, by boat and on foot, as we read in Acts. He founded a number of communities and worked with his hands day and night to take care of himself, since he did not want to be a burden on the communities he was evangelizing (1 Thess 2:9). He did not want to accept the support of important people either, because he did not want to lose his freedom. This seems to have been an urgent concern with some people from Corinth (2 Cor 12:13). Paul suffered persecution, imprisonment, whippings, beatings, hunger, cold, danger of death, and shipwrecks. He mentions all this in 2 Cor 6:4-7, in the course of a quarrel with some people he ironically calls the "super-apostles." For Paul, all this suffering was the true mark of his apostleship. Through his letters we see this man inspired by God, passionate about proclaiming Jesus as the Son of God, as *true* Savior and Lord, a Jewish man crucified by the Roman Empire but resurrected by God.

APOSTLE TO THE GENTILES

Paul directed his mission to the Gentiles, but—as he explains in Rom 11:13-16—even as "apostle to the Gentiles" he also had the welfare of his fellow Jews at heart. Although he was proud of being a Jew (Phil 3:4b-6), for him the God of Abraham and the Jews was also the God of the Gentiles. What Paul called "my gospel" (Rom 2:16; compare 2 Tim 2:8) had to do with an emphasis on God's grace that encompassed Jews and Gentiles alike, without Gentiles having to follow Moses's law. This is especially the theme of Galatians (Gal 2:7-9). Paul's concern for the Gentiles may be understood in part in light of his experience while growing up in a Gentile city. He was born and reared in Tarsus, a Greek city important for its schools and library. Paul was familiar with Roman culture and law. According to the books of Acts, Paul was a Roman citizen. Having a triple cultural heritage—Jewish, Greek, and Roman—he was interested in bringing all people to participate in God's promise to Abraham and to become part of God's people.

While Jewish, Greek, and Roman traditions imagined all the nations eventually becoming united, though in very different ways, for Paul this was a possibility to be pursued now, in obedience to the crucified and risen Jesus. The novelty of this message brought him trouble, misunderstandings, and conflicts with Roman officials and with the most conservative sector of the Jews, apparently including some from the church in Jerusalem. It was apparently not easy for some Jews to accept as an equal an uncir-cumcised Gentile who did not follow Moses's law. This cultural clash was not easy to overcome. Paul, on the other hand, urged the Gentile communities to affirm that those baptized in Christ had been made equals, regardless of ethnicity (Jew or Gentile), class (master or slave), or gender, as stated in Gal 3:28.

Through his letters we observe the passionate personality of Paul. He tells how, before becoming a follower of Jesus Christ, he had violently persecuted the churches out of his zeal for his ancestors' traditions (Gal 1:13-14). Later, after the resurrected Christ appeared to him, he changed radically and became just as passionate about the gospel, and particularly about preaching it to the Gentiles. The former persecutor now was persecuted, by Jews and Romans alike. Several times he was imprisoned and faced trials. He spent the last days of his life in prison, in chains. And, according to the church's tradition, he was sentenced to death by the Romans and died a martyr.

THE DEATH AND RESURRECTION OF JESUS IN PAUL'S THOUGHT

Paul's letters are the earliest documents that emerged from the Christian movement. The Gospels that speak of Jesus' life were written much later. In Paul's time, Christian communities remembered Jesus' life through oral tradition as they repeated stories about Jesus in their worship. They sang hymns proclaiming Jesus' death as a sacrifice offered for the forgiveness of sins through his blood. According to this interpretation of Jesus' death, neither Jews nor converted Gentiles needed to sacrifice animals in the Temple to be purified or to receive God's forgiveness; rather, Jesus' death was enough. In Paul's letters we observe him adopting these themes regarding Jesus' death. But he also *adapted* them, coming to emphasize more Jesus' crucifixion and resurrection. Our present emphasis on the importance of Jesus' crucifixion comes from

Paul. It was a key theme for him because it was a way of remembering the historic way Jesus died, and because from it emerged the question of who condemned him to die. Crucifixion was the death penalty imposed by the Roman Empire on slaves and subversives. Jesus was not a slave, but he probably died because he was seen as an insubordinate and dangerously charismatic person (compare John 11:48: "If we let him go on like this, everyone will believe in him…"). Paul declares that Jesus took "the form of a slave" (NRSV "servant"), language that may point to the shameful way Jesus died (Phil 2:7). To proclaim faith in a *crucified* man was crazy in the view of Greek wisdom and a scandal for Jewish culture (1 Cor 1:23). For Paul, however, it signaled God's solidarity with humanity. God was moved to compassion—even in the face of a perverse society that deserves to die for its injustice (Rom 1:18; 3:21-24)—moved enough to offer people a new way of life, modeled by Jesus.

Paul's theological emphasis on the resurrected Christ marks the faith in which this newness of life is possible. We may fairly summarize this aspect of Paul's thought by saying that God's justice was inevitably at odds with what the Roman Empire claimed was justice! (See Introduction to Romans for my thoughts on how my cultural background affects my biblical interpretation.) ❖

The Letter of Paul to the

ROMANS

Elsa Tamez

Translated by Leticia A. Guardiola-Sáenz

Paul addresses this letter to the Christian believers in Rome, most of whom were Gentiles. He writes from Corinth, as he travels to Jerusalem to deliver a collection for the needy (15:25-28). He dictates the letter to Tertius (16:22) while staying at Gaius's home (16:23), and sends it to Rome with Phoebe (16:1), a leader of the church in Cenchreae. Paul has never visited the church in Rome but now plans to visit them on his way to Spain, where he plans to travel with their help (15:24).

When Paul wrote this letter, around 57–58 CE, he was in a strained relationship with the church of Jerusalem. He had been evangelizing Gentiles without asking them to fulfill the law or get circumcised.

For Paul, faith in Jesus as the Messiah was enough. God's grace was equally enough for both Jews and Gentiles, but the tensions described in Galatians 1 suggest that some in the Jerusalem church did not seem to share this idea.

To better understand Paul, it is important to read this letter in its context of Roman rule and the customs of the Jewish culture. Otherwise his teachings can sound like dogmas that have nothing to do with real life.

In his letter Paul explains his position regarding the law and how it relates to both Jews and Gentiles (chs. 1–8). He illustrates how Gentiles and Jews have equally sinned, the Jews with their law and the Gentiles without the law, creating unjust and deceiving ways of social life (1:18). Paul calls this social reality, full of injustice, *sin* (3:9)—a major sin that leads everyone to destruction (3:9-20). This situation deserves God's punishment: death. But God's love is so immense that instead of punishing us, God shows us a *new justice* (3:21-26), different from the justice practiced by the Greco-Roman and Jewish societies. God's justice was present in Jesus' life, which moved him to give up his life in solidarity with many as he was crucified by the Roman Empire. The resurrection was then God's approval of Jesus' actions and life. By participating in the way Jesus lived and died, people are forgiven the sin produced through all the injustices committed by Jews and Gentiles. They are freed so that they can live out the justice they have received (6:1-23), like new people in a new creation, not according to selfish interests. This is only possible when people live according to the Spirit (8:1-4).

Paul also deals with the matter of *election*, since speaking of Gentiles as children of God raises the question of Israel as chosen people. He explains (chs. 9–11) that election has always been by grace, through God's mercy (9:16). God rejects exclusion, and out of mercy elects instead those whom society has rejected. God elected Israel, a small nation often oppressed by neighboring empires, in order to liberate it. But when those elected stop following God's paths of justice, the election is suspended and can only be resumed when people return to the paths of justice and make visible God's mercy (11:20-21). That is why Paul warns the Gentiles, using the parable of the olive tree, that they must "not become proud, but stand in awe. For if God did not spare the natural branches, perhaps God will not spare you" (11:20-21).

In the last chapters Paul writes about some issues of everyday life. One has to do with discrimination within the community due to certain dietary practices (14:1—15:7). Some Gentiles, who were the majority, were probably looking down on some people of Jewish background because they were refraining from certain foods and were observing certain days. Paul encourages them not to judge or despise one another because of these minor details, lest they lose sight of the fundamental reason for their gathering, "For the kingdom of God is not food and drink but righteousness and peace and joy in the Holy Spirit" (14:17).

At the end of the letter Paul sends greetings to a number of people, including women (who are eight of the twenty-five people named). Many women were leaders and coworkers with Paul. As he names the people to whom he is sending greetings, he praises them for their work. That is how we know that some women were ministers, teachers, and apostles—and that many of them, including Prisca (16:3-4), risked their lives or, like the apostle Junia (16:7), had been in jail.

Romans can be outlined as follows: greetings and plans (1:1-15); God's justice for all (1:16—4:25); practicing God's justice amid ever-present threats (chs. 5–8); God's election, exclusion, and grace (chs. 9–11); guidance for everyday life (12:1—15:13); and farewell: plans, greetings, and doxology (15:14—16:27).

My reading of Romans is conditioned by my personal and social contexts. I grew up in Monterrey, México—a city marked by dramatic social differences—in a large and poor family where eating meat once in a while and writing with a new pencil represented true happiness. My theological formation happened in Central America during the 1970s and 1980s. That was a context known for social injustice, oppression, and the dictatorships of El Salvador, Guatemala, and Nicaragua, where thousands were tortured, murdered, or disappeared and people cried out to God for justice. My awareness that 60 percent of Latin America's population—mostly women—live in poverty due to an economic system that mercilessly excludes the weakest has made me denounce the horrors of structural sin. Reading Romans from these realities helps me to see that the letter proclaims good news for all. ❖

The First Letter of Paul to the

CORINTHIANS ▨

Demetrius K. Williams

Paul's Corinthian correspondence is the most lively, lengthy, and informative of his letters because of its vivid portrayal of the actual life situations and challenges of this community of believers. First-century CE Corinth was socially and politically stratified under the empire of Rome. The empire had destroyed the city in 146 BCE, and Julius Caesar resettled it a century later (44 BCE), mostly with an ethnically diverse population of freed slaves conscripted from Italy, Greece, Syria, Egypt, and Judea. Corinth, the capital of the Roman province of Achaia, was governed by a proconsul sent annually from Rome, and its municipal government was modeled on that of republican Rome.

Located on Greece's Peloponnesian peninsula, Corinth prospered as a trade and communication center. Its rapid rise to prominence was inspired in part by intense competition for commercial success—Corinth sponsored athletic games second only to the Olympic games—and the opportunity its lack of a hereditary class offered for upward mobility. But Corinth's success did not come without criticism. It gained a reputation as a sin city where "anything goes." Such was its fame that an Athenian comic-poet coined the verb "Corinthianize" (*korinthiazesthai*), which meant to engage in sexually immoral behavior. This openness was also evident in Corinth's religious diversity, which included a thriving Jewish community, a cult to the emperor, and temples dedicated to Greek and Egyptian deities. Added to this were a host of ideas imported along with material goods to the city's two ports from various parts of the ancient Mediterranean world. The religious diversity and ethnic complexity

of Corinth destined it to evoke from Paul some impassioned and intense responses. The letters we call 1 and 2 Corinthians (another letter, lost to us, preceded 1 Corinthians; see 5:9) have long been viewed as primarily concerning theological or doctrinal issues, thus minimizing the cultural influences and social-political codes in them. Certainly Paul's responses were and are theological, because he brought to these matters his understanding of Scripture and the new reality brought about by Jesus Christ. Nevertheless, it is important to recognize that the Corinthians' beliefs and practices, and their challenges to Paul, were culturally informed and have their counterparts around the world today.

Paul wrote 1 Corinthians from Ephesus, most likely in 53 or 54 CE, to address various issues, which can be outlined in two parts: first, matters that "Chloe's people" reported to Paul (1:10—6:20), including factions in Corinth (1:10—4:21), incest and sexual transgressions (5:1-13), litigation before pagan courts (6:1-11), and sexual morality (6:12-20); and, second, the Corinthians' questions in their letter to Paul (7:1—15:58; see especially 7:1, 8:1, and 12:1), including marriage and celibacy, slavery and freedom (ch. 7), Christian liberty (especially Paul's refusal of the Corinthians' patronage, ch. 9) and the problems of idolatry (8:1—11:1), the dress and status of women in worship (11:2-16 and especially 14:33b-36), the practice of the Lord's Supper (11:17-34), the use of spiritual gifts in worship (chs. 12–14), and the future resurrection (ch. 15). In closing, Paul addresses some practical matters (ch. 16), including arrangements for the collection, travel plans, and final greetings.

The first readers or hearers of this letter would most likely have been familiar with these cultural practices: 1) rhetoric and rhetorical self-presentation, which was the basis of the Corinthians' allegiance to certain leaders, especially Apollos; 2) the practice of closely examining rhetoric—the basis of some Corinthians' negative evaluation of Paul's preaching (see chs. 4 and 9); 3) litigation in the courts, the foundation of Greco-Roman civil society; and 4) the buying of sacrificial meat in the marketplace, a practice common in Greco-Roman "pagan" society. What those first readers may have regarded as problematic innovations or violations of cultural boundaries were 1) Paul's teaching about sexual ethics—some Corinthians apparently believed those were matters of individual freedom, that "all things are lawful for me" (6:12; 10:23); 2) the (only slightly) elevated status Paul ascribed to women; 3) rituals such as baptism and the Lord's Supper; 4) Paul's

assessment of rhetoric (he insists he is a *herald*, not an orator or rhetorician); and 5) his teaching on the resurrection.

While many of these ideas and practices seem alien to our modern social and cultural experiences, contemporary readers will spot some convergences: 1) the role of women in church and society remains a problem for some faith communities; 2) especially for persons of African descent living in the West—including me—the legacy and continuing effects of slavery and racism remain a concern; 3) church schisms and disagreements remain painful realities, and, as a particular cause of these, 4) we see lively and often strained debate over the possibilities for a new sexual ethics that will include openness to and the affirming of loving same-gender and transgendered persons in church and society. Many of these issues, both in Paul's time and in ours, are not only theological but also relate in some degree to issues of culture and society. ❖

The Second Letter of Paul to the

CORINTHIANS

Demetrius K. Williams

Paul probably wrote 2 Corinthians in 55 CE, shortly after 1 Corinthians, in response to new developments within the community of believers involving even more acute issues related to the culture of Greco-Roman society. Competing missionaries and apostles had entered the Christian community at Corinth and their rhetorical eloquence and personal presence resonated with Corinth's cultural norms. In the closing of his previous letter to Corinth (1 Cor 16:1-9), Paul said he planned

to stay in Ephesus until Pentecost, then travel to Corinth and possibly remain there for the winter. He changed his plans, deciding to visit Corinth two more times (2 Cor 1:15). But his next visit to the city was a humiliating and painful one (2:5; 7:12) because one Corinthian member supported those other apostles and opposed Paul's leadership. Paul cancelled the second proposed visit and rushed back to Ephesus, where he composed an important letter, delivered by Titus and written "out of much distress and anguish of heart and with many tears" (2:4; some believe that chs. 10–13 represent that letter). Desiring to hear how the Corinthians had received his tearful letter, Paul traveled to Macedonia to find Titus (2:12). Upon finding him, Paul learned that the community was on his side (7:5-16). His letter had been successful in persuading the Corinthians of his leadership and ensuring their continued support of the collection for the Jerusalem saints.

Traditional commentaries have been preoccupied with two questions about 2 Corinthians. Was it written as a single letter, or was it originally several letters in which Paul addressed different situations, which a later editor compiled as the letter that has come down to us? And who were these opponents who attack Paul's gospel and apostolic self-understanding? While many interpreters today uphold the original unity of 2 Corinthians, those who view it as a composite writing cite its unevenness and digressive structure. Whichever way one reads the letter, it reflects religious and cultural influences that were part of Paul's heritage as a Diaspora Jew. Moreover, 2 Corinthians is written in the Greek used by educated people of his day, and displays features of Hellenistic rhetoric (lists of suffering and achievements, invective, and comparison) and epistolary form. All these features represent Hellenistic (Greek) cultural influence and also Paul's "hybridity," the Hebrew-Hellenist mix that can be seen in the contrast between Paul's interpretation of Moses's veil (3:12-18, drawing on Exod 34) and the "fool's speech" of chapters 11–12.

Paul's oratorical encounter with those other apostles can also be viewed against the background of Hellenistic cultural influences. The wealthier members of the Corinthian community welcomed the "super-apostles" as guests at their house meetings (11:4-5, 13-15) and served as their patrons. These traveling apostles came to Corinth—Paul's mission field, at least from his perspective (10:15-16)—with "letters of recommendation" (3:1; 11:4-5)

and were well received (11:4, 20). They, like Paul, are Hebrews, Israelites, seed of Abraham, and ministers of Christ (11:22-23a). Their hybridity, too, is evident: they are Greek-speaking, rhetorically competent Jewish-Christian missionaries. In the spirit of Hellenism, they viewed mission as competition and saw themselves as missionaries offering a competing model of rhetoric and apostleship (11:7-11; 12:13-15). For them success depended on the missionary's ability to express the divine in his or her performance—rhetorical eloquence, knowledge, and personal charisma.

These rivals and some in the Corinthian community felt that Paul did not measure up. He is unreliable. He changes his travel plans. He lacks letters of recommendation (3:1). He takes advantage of the Corinthians to enrich himself (7:2; 12:16). He is brave only from the safe distance from which he writes (10:1, 10). He is not a good orator (10:11; 11:6). He refuses financial support from the Corinthians, which must be evidence of his lack of love for them (11:7; 12:13). He is inferior to the super-apostles (11:5; 12:11). And he is not a "true apostle" (12:12).

If these charges are informed by Greek and Roman culture, Paul responds in kind, using well-known rhetorical techniques. But he also insists on the authority of Israel's Scripture and grounds his apostolic authority in his personal experience of humility, which he describes as strength in weakness ("for whenever I am weak, then I am strong," 12:10). His perspective is informed in light of the passion, death, and resurrection of Jesus Christ.

How should today's readers of 2 Corinthians view these issues? Some might recall contemporary televangelists who boast of charismatic powers—healings, words of knowledge, and ecstatic visions. Others might take notice of the rhetoric of some televangelists who proclaim a theology of personal success and material prosperity that can be had by all who have the proper faith practice. A focus on contemporary competitiveness in

Western capitalism and imperialistic politics in our contemporary world might gain the attention of other readers. Whatever perspective one takes, the issues in the time of Paul and the Corinthians and our time are not merely theological but also relate to issues of culture and society. ❖

The Letter of Paul to the

GALATIANS ▦

Ediberto López-Rodríguez

Galatians was written in the middle of the first century CE. If Paul was writing to the ethnic Galatians who lived in north-central Asia Minor, the *region* called Galatia before the Roman conquests, the letter was written in the years 53–57 and from Ephesus or Madeconia. If he was writing to the churches in the *Roman province* of Galatia—a region extended by the Romans to include the southern cities of Lystra, Derbe, Iconium, and Pisidian Antioch—the dates would more probably be 48–49 from Syrian Antioch, or 51–53 from Corinth. On either account, this letter emerges in the midst of a cultural debate between Jewish Christians and some converted Gentiles, the fruits of Paul's mission to the Gentiles.

To understand the letter to the Galatians, we need to read it in its cultural context. Early Christianity emerged out of the Jesus movement's mission to bring restoration to Israel. Originally this mission did not include Gentiles (see Matt 10:5, 6). However, Jesus' mission and compassion to the outcasts of Israel soon were extended to those Gentiles who feared God. Their attraction to what (for the sake of convenience) we may call early Jewish Christianity developed into the mission to the Gentiles. This mission provoked a controversy among the first Christians, who debated whether Gentiles needed to become Jews first in order to be part of the Christian community. Were Gentile Christians supposed to observe the Jewish Sabbath, the separation of meals as clean or unclean, and circumcision? Different answers were given to these questions.

The letter to the Galatians gives evidence of two positions regarding the cultural identity markers of the Christian community. Many Jewish Christians wanted to require Gentile converts to be circumcised and keep the Mosaic Law, in addition to believing in Jesus as the Messiah (perhaps in the spirit of Jesus' teaching as reflected in Matt 5:17-20). Another less restrictive group was willing to require only the minimum: monotheism and Jewish morals. The book of Acts presents some of the stories of these Hellenistic Jewish Christians (chs. 6–9, 12). In Antioch of Syria, Hellenistic Jewish Christians spread the faith among Gentiles, and Christianity made big inroads among them; Paul became one of the leaders of the Antioch church (see Acts 11:25-30; 12:25—13:3, and Gal 2:11-14).

The letters of Paul are evidence of his openness to the Gentiles. From the letter to the Galatians we know that Peter and Barnabas were ambivalent about socializing and worshipping with Gentiles (2:11-14). It seems that the people of James, Jesus' brother, were powerful enough to intimidate Peter and Barnabas into submitting to a major Jewish religious and cultural requirement for the Gentiles: circumcision. Some Jewish Christian missionaries came to Galatia and were preaching a message contrary to what Paul had preached (1:6-9). We don't know the content of their message because we have only one side of the controversy. But given Paul's reaction it is evident that they advised the Galatians to accept circumcision and to observe (at least aspects of) the Jewish law (4:10; compare 5:2-4). The Galatians probably started to observe the law in part because these teachers said that Paul himself was preaching circumcision (Gal 5:11; 1 Cor 9:20-22). To confuse them even more, the Judaizing teachers may have also added that Paul was not a real apostle (Gal 1:1, 11-12)—not like Peter, James, or the other early leaders in Jerusalem who were law-abiding Christians and also preached circumcision (Gal 2:4, 6-7, 12, 14).

Paul replies with a strong defense of his apostolic authority (chs. 1–2) and assures the Gentiles that adding observance of the Jewish law will not enhance the salvation they have in Christ: "We know that a person is justified not by the works of the law but through faith in Jesus Christ" (2:16). Paul said Gentiles were justified before God only through Jesus. Therefore, justification was a *gift*, received from Jesus, "who loved me and gave himself for me" (2:20). The Gentiles did not need circumcision or to observe the law to be saved.

What Paul thinks of the Gentiles accepting circumcision is clear enough. What is less clear—and more controversial, given the long tradition of Christian theological anti-Judaism—is the extent to which Paul's statements set him in opposition to his ancestral religion, Judaism, or to the other apostles, whom Paul represents as agreeing with him on theological principle (2:1-10, 14-16). These remain lively questions in contemporary scholarship.

As a Puerto Rican, growing up both in New York and San Juan within a fundamentalist family, I learned to live in two worlds and bear the violence of religious intolerance. Later on, through the process of finding my cultural identity, becoming aware of oppression, and encountering African American liberation theology and human rights theology for the homosexual community, I have learned to struggle and recognize the ambiguities of colonialism and the false certainties of religious intolerance. These experiences have given me a keen eye for equality, which I bring to my reading of Galatians. ❖

The Letter of Paul to the

EPHESIANS

Raj Nadella

Ephesians is one of thirteen New Testament letters attributed to Paul. Most contemporary scholars question its Pauline authorship because it is noticeably dissimilar to the undisputed Pauline letters in vocabulary, writing style, and theology. An emerging consensus among scholars holds that the letter was probably written by an interpreter (or perhaps a disciple) of Paul to congregations in western Asia Minor, sometime in the late first century CE. This was a time when the church was emerging as a force in the Greco-Roman world.

The letter, which appears to have been written from a prison (4:1), confronts divisions in the church. Although Ephesians contains few explicit references to conflict between Jews and Gentiles, a good part of it highlights the author's attempts to promote harmonious relations between the two communities. Issues of identity, concern about factors that engendered strife, and the need for unity figure prominently in this letter.

Ephesians comprises a brief introduction followed by two distinct sections and a short closing. The salutation (1:1-2) greets the readers and identifies the writer. The first section (1:3—3:21) is doctrinal in nature and emphasizes the Christ event and its ability to unite Christians. The second section (4:1—6:20) offers ethical instructions. The writer seeks to promote unity among believers and exhorts readers to challenge principalities and powers. The book's final verses (6:21-24) include a benediction.

The doctrinal section declares that the Gentiles, who were alienated both from God and from the Jews, have been reconciled with both through the Christ event. The ethnic identities of Jews and Gentiles have hitherto divided their respective communities, but now the dividing wall has been brought down by Jesus, who has united them in God.

The ethical or paraenetic section of the letter exhorts readers to live out the unity made possible through Christ and to manifest it in interpersonal relations in familial, ecclesial, and social settings. This part of the letter emphasizes unifying factors such as the Christ event and seeks to attenuate dividing factors such as rigid aspects of the law. It also encourages an ethic of subordination of wives to husbands, children to parents, and slaves to masters that goes beyond what we see in the seven unquestioned letters of Paul (5:22—6:9; compare Col 3:18—4:1). Although this ethic appears under the apparently mutual rule "be subject to one another" (5:22), the instructions are not completely reciprocal, leading some readers to conclude that the unity envisioned here is achieved at a greater cost to some than to others. Can equality between Jew and Gentile be purchased only at the cost of inequality in other relationships?

The letter's rhetoric calls our attention to the destructive potential that a particular identity—whether ethnic or grounded in some other difference—can play, and offers suggestions for achieving a common identity, based on the Christ event, that can transcend all dividing walls. Because the dividing walls have been brought down, the readers are to create an inclusive community around the Christ event, which offers a transformational and unifying identity for the new community.

Most identity markers unite members of similar communities while simultaneously separating them from those that do not share that identity. I am a member of the Naidu community, a caste group in Andhra Pradesh, a south Indian state with a multiethnic and multicultural population. My identity as a Naidu unites me to this group, but given the troubled history of caste relations in this state, it has the potential to alienate me from members of other caste groups. The same issue applies to members of other castes. It is possible for different caste groups to transcend barriers and arrive at a unifying identity by focusing on their common language—Telugu. Yet even as Telugu might provide a unifying identity for people in the state, it would separate them from other linguistic groups in India and thus can cause strife. It appears that divisions between diverse groups stem primarily from the absence of *unifying identities* that can transcend all barriers. But divisions arise also when individuals and groups choose to focus on the divisive, rather than the unifying, aspects of an identity. The message and the exhortations of Ephesians are relevant wherever two or more communities are more aware of the differences that separate them than of what can and should unite them as equals. ❖

The Letter of Paul to the

PHILIPPIANS

Aquiles Ernesto Martínez

Paul wrote this friendly missive to a community of Christians living in Philippi, the first church Paul founded in Europe (4:15; Acts 16:11-40). Philippi was an important Roman colony located in eastern Macedonia, now northeastern Greece, where many retired soldiers had received land. The city was located on the *Via Egnatia*, a main trade road of the region.

The letter to the Philippians expresses Paul's gratitude for the financial support they sent to him with Epaphroditus while Paul was in jail awaiting trial (1:2-26; 4:10-20). The letter also reassures the community that Paul is well and will soon be freed from prison (1:12-26). Paul responds to issues of selfishness and quarrels (1:27-28; 2:2, 14; 3:15; 4:2-3) and opposition to his gospel (1:15-17, 27-28; 3:1b-20). Paul writes that he intends to send Epaphroditus back to the Philippians and that he hopes to send Timothy to them as well (2:25-30).

The letter is organized as follows: after a salutation (1:1-2) and a thanksgiving (1:3-11), Paul reflects on his imprisonment (1:12-30), exhorts the Philippians to be humble in imitation of Jesus (2:1-18), and asks them to live in harmony even as Paul discredits the Judaizers and subordinates his own Jewish accomplishments to Christ (3:1b—4:9). Paul closes with a note of gratitude for the financial aid the congregation sent him (4:10-23).

Scholars have struggled to determine when and how this letter fits in the chronology of Paul's ministry in Acts. Depending on his imprisonment, Philippians could have been written from Ephesus around 56 CE (see Acts 20:31; 1 Cor 15:32; 2 Cor 1:8-10); from Rome, between 61 and 63 (see 1:13; 4:22; and Acts 28:11-31); or from Caesarea, between 58 and 60 (Acts 23–26). Some abrupt changes of subjects and emotions have led some scholars to argue that this letter is a composite, comprised of different letters (1:1—3:1a; 3:1b—4:1; 4:2-9; 4:10-20, 23). To others, however, Philippians reads as a single composition with natural and spontaneous thematic changes.

As a person born and raised in Venezuela, who moved to the United States and eventually became a U.S. citizen, I have learned to appreciate diverse ethnic experiences with their corresponding hopes and struggles. Therefore I tend to approach the Bible from angles and ideas that privilege the multi-colored and complex human experience. From this vantage point, a cross-cultural reading of Philippians brings to the fore some issues worth considering. Modeling Greco-Roman ways of expressing friendship, Paul writes this letter to strengthen his close relationship with the Philippians and evoke appropriate responses from them. The letter's fraternal imagery shows strong affectionate ties between the apostle and these Christians (1:7-8; 2:18; 4:1, 14). This invites reflection on how appropriate rhetoric can help to create a sense of community, especially in a diverse and fragmented society. Philippians offers glimpses of social reciprocity between Paul and this church on the matter of giving and receiving favors, particularly with respect to monetary support and the appropriate response to it (1:4, 7; 4:10, 14-15). And as we continue to create conditions for gender equality, the position and prominent roles played by women in Philippi is noteworthy. Although masculine language and ideology permeate this letter, Paul praises Euodia and Syntyche for the strong leadership they provided in this church's ministry (1:1; 4:2-7; see also Rom 16:3-5, 7, 12, 16).

Paul's attack on some unknown Jewish adversaries raises questions about religious and civil discourse in a multiethnic context (1:15-17, 27-28; 3:1b-20). He counteracts people who insist on having Gentile converts circumcised, denouncing such practice as "mutilation" and calling its advocates "dogs," "evil workers," and "enemies of the cross of Christ" (3:2; 3:18), and discounting several aspects of his Jewish pedigree as "rubbish" (3:8). We can understand Paul as shaming opponents in a situation of conflict and irreconcilable ideological differences, but in a contemporary context of boundary crossing, pluralism, and respect for others, do we think such rhetoric is appropriate for constructing religious (and especially Christian) identity? Paul also argues that Christian citizenship is heavenly (3:20), that Jesus is Lord and Savior (2:11; 3:8, 20), and that eventually all would be subjected to Jesus (1:28-30; 2:9-11, 15; 4:21). Such language would have challenged the views of people who were Roman citizens and believed that Caesar was the only lord and benefactor. Though not explicitly stated, the political and possibly counter-imperial implications of Paul's language seem clear.

As impoverished and persecuted communities experience hardships today, the joyful overtone of this letter encourages Christians to move forward with hope (1:4, 18-19, 25; 2:2, 17-19, 28; 3:1a; 4:1, 4, 10). The hymn recorded in Phil 2:5-11 reveals not only how early Christians perceived the nature of Jesus but also how they made such a perception a mediation of their faith and a point of encounter with the sacred. How do expressions of faith, including song writing and poetry, do something similar in contemporary worship? ❖

The Letter of Paul to the

COLOSSIANS

Gordon Zerbe

This letter to the "saints and faithful" at Colossae, a town east of Ephesus in Phrygia, Asia Minor, is a message of exhortation and encouragement. It commends the readers for their faith in Christ (1:4-7; 2:5-7), but also shows concern about the possible impact of an aberrant teaching (2:4, 8, 16, 18). Colossians highlights the sole supremacy of Christ throughout the cosmos and in the church (1:13-23). Christ is God's creative, reconciling, peacemaking, and saving power. Believers are to depend on Christ alone. All other claims to traditions, sources of wisdom, and forms of social ordering are dismissed as merely human (1:27-28; 2:2-15, 20; 3:1-4, 9-11, 15, 17). The letter emphasizes a communal life of moral and social virtue, especially a unifying love and a commitment to peace that embrace the cultural diversity of the peoples and nations (1:4, 27; 2:2; 3:5-16).

Seeking to extend Paul's apostolic authority and ministry (1:23—2:5; 4:3, 7-18), this letter—

addressed to a believing assembly not founded or visited by Paul himself (1:7; 2:1)—was also intended to be read by the neighboring congregation in Laodicea (4:16). Colossians is set during a period of Paul's imprisonment (4:3, 10, 18). The immediate occasion of the letter is the return of the slave Onesimus back to his home community (4:7-9; see Philemon).

The letter follows the pattern of most Pauline letters: salutation (1:1-2); thanksgiving (1:3-8); prayer for the readers and a review of Paul's apostolic ministry, interlaced with affirmations of God's work in Christ that set the foundation for the subsequent main appeal of the letter (1:9—2:5); the letter's main body of warning, teaching, and exhortation (2:6—4:6); and a closing with greetings, information, instructions, and a benediction (4:7-18).

The teaching opposed in the letter is marked by rigorous self-denial (2:18, 23); special regulations regarding food, drink, and contact with physical objects (2:16, 21); observance of a possible sacred calendar (2:16-17); and the worship of angelic beings and cosmic forces (2:8, 15). The letter asserts that these practices represent an accommodation to dogma and regulations (2:14, 20, 21) and elemental cosmic principles or forces (2:8, 20), and are based on a philosophy that is merely "human" or "earthly" (2:8, 20, 22-23; 3:2) and of no worth in truly checking human self-indulgence (2:23).

In opposition to such practices, Colossians offers the full knowledge of God, wisdom, and life (1:9-11, 13, 20, 26-28; 2:2-4, 23; 3:3). It stresses moral, mental, and social transformation made possible through Christ (3:1—4:6), and calls on believers to avoid destructive impulses (3:5-9). They are to make real the "new self" and new humanity (3:10), by pursuing virtues that make for communal unity while celebrating diversity (3:10-15), engendering a liturgical life of mutual teaching, song, prayer, and thankfulness (3:16; 4:2-4), assessing

all speech and conduct in the light of Christ (3:17; compare 1:10-12, 28), following the traditional codes of domestic life (2:5; 3:18—4:1), and promoting wise and timely speech and conduct before outsiders (4:5-6). These exhortations are grounded in the sole supremacy of Christ as God's agent in creation and redemption—and in the redemptive transformation of the readers through their baptismal status (1:12-14, 21-23; 2:10-15, 20; 3:1-4, 9-10). They are dead to the former world and humanity but raised and made alive again with Christ.

If this letter was written or endorsed by Paul himself when he was imprisoned by the Roman imperial authorities in Ephesus, Colossians may have been written as early as 55 CE; or it may have been written as late as the mid-60s if it was composed during Paul's imprisonment in Rome. If written by a disciple writing in Paul's name after his death, as many scholars hold (due to differences in style, language, Christology, and the inclusion of the household codes), then the letter can be dated between 65 and 90 CE.

Twenty-first-century Christian readers will be mindful of the ambivalent potential of Colossians, and especially how it has been used to suppress indigenous cultural and religious practices in colonizing situations. That happens, for example, when people cite 2:8-23 to emphasize the exclusive supremacy of Christ over all human traditions while neglecting 1:27 ("how great among the Gentiles") or 3:11 ("no longer Greek and Jew"). It happens when people use 1:16-20 and 2:10 to give legitimacy and encourage acquiescence to unjust rule and imperial domination, while ignoring 2:15 ("he disarmed the rulers"). It happens when people use 3:18—4:1 to promote oppressive social hierarchies or exclusions, while neglecting 3:9-11, Gal 3:26-28, and Philemon.

Growing up in Japan as the son of missionaries, my first memories are those of being a foreigner. That experience provided the trajectory toward my adult commitment to practice the Christian faith in an Anabaptist-Mennonite perspective, along with a concern for ecumenical and interfaith exchange. Consciously and unconsciously, my experience has affected my reading of Colossians through the lens of sociocultural dynamics, both in understanding the past and in engaging the present. Serving four years in the Philippines as a visiting professor sharpened my interest in local readings and the public performance of Scripture, leaving me more attentive to both the integrity of the cultures of others and to the positive potential of respectful cultural interactions. ❖

The First Letter of Paul to the

THESSALONIANS

Abraham Smith

From Paul's vantage point, the proclamation of the gospel in Thessalonica, the capital of the Roman province of Macedonia, brought multiple changes—some positive, some negative. Several Thessalonians warmly welcomed Paul (1:9), accepted his gospel (2:13), turned to God from idols (1:9), and began a new walk or way of life (2:12). Among the negative changes, Paul and his companions were separated from the Thessalonian assembly (the *ekklēsia*, usually translated "church" in English: 2:17), and the assembly itself—in kinship with assemblies in Judea—suffered from the relentless opposition of their own compatriots (2:14). Whether the Greek word (*thlipsis*) that describes the assembly's afflictions (1:6; 3:3, 4, 7)—here translated as "persecution"—refers to physical abuse or social alienation, Paul read his assembly's troubles as the typical and predictable afflictions of the tempting one and as apocalyptic end-time hindrances designed to steer the faithful off track (3:3-5).

In response, an anxious Paul first dispatched his trustworthy envoy, Timothy, to learn about his nascent followers and encourage them (3:2, 5). Hearing that the assembly had not been shaken apart by their travails (3:6), Paul then sent them what we know as 1 Thessalonians, an affectionate letter of exhortation written about 50 or 51 CE. This is Paul's first extant letter and indeed the earliest writing in the New Testament canon. The letter appears to have had two goals: to declare Paul's repeated thanks to God (1:2; 2:13; compare 3:9) for the assembly's reception of his gospel and their continuing maturation; and to offer a description or image of group distinctiveness (4:1—5:22) designed to build up their new cultural identity and solidarity in opposition to their former one.

Paul's repeated thanksgiving models the consistency of fidelity to God that he hopes the assembly will maintain and increase (compare 4:1, 10; 5:16-18). His message about group distinctiveness includes *sanctification* or being "set apart" (4:3-4; 5:23); the designation of the "Gentiles" as persons who do not know God (4:5), a Jewish cultural slur that in effect put distance between the assembly's present life and the ethnic profile by which Paul and other Jews would have earlier identified them (compare 1:10; 2:14); "we-they" markers that divided people into two groups: *those who really know eschatological realities* (for example, that the dead believers will arise [4:13] and that the day of the Lord, that is, the parousia or the return of Jesus will come like a thief in the night [5:2]) and *those who do not*; and a request for consistent love for each other and for all (3:12; compare 5:15). This consistent love is by contrast something that outsiders in Thessalonica cannot be said to have given their neighbors (2:14).

As an African American, I identify with Paul's assembly in Thessalonica for several reasons: their minority status in an imperial world; their attempts to remain faithful to their God despite affliction caused by many of their compatriots; and their quest to love all, thus modeling a new and better way of life. But I find Paul's own ideology in the letter troubling for three reasons. First, his we-they rhetoric, even if helpful for group-solidarity purposes, can be co-opted by majority cultures to serve the status quo. Second, Paul's casting of the assembly simply as "brothers and sisters" (used thirteen times) can also be co-opted by majority cultures to erase ethnic cultural identities and support notions of a false universalism. Third, I find patriarchal rhetoric (the view of God as father, 1:1, 3; 3:11) problematic, because it can so easily be co-opted to christen a male-dominated society. ❖

The Second Letter of Paul to the

THESSALONIANS

Abraham Smith

Written at an uncertain date, this short letter of friendly exhortation presupposes the continuation of the hostilities faced by Paul's assembly in Thessalonica (1 Thess 1:4). Likewise, it presupposes that there is, within and around this relatively new Christian community, an ongoing conflict, with one group being *the afflicted* and another being *the afflicters* (1:6). The letter bears striking formal similarities with 1 Thessalonians in its use of a simple letter opening (2 Thess 1:2; compare 1 Thess 1:1), repeated thanksgivings (2 Thess 1:3; 2:13; compare 1 Thess 1:2; 2:13), and an intercessory prayer (2 Thess 2:16-17; compare 1 Thess 3:11-13). But 2 Thessalonians depicts a deity who will exact an everlasting revenge upon the assembly's afflicters (1:6-9). Also different is the letter's presupposition of a *parousia*, a return of Jesus at an unspecified future time (2 Thess 2:1-12)—as opposed to 1 Thessalonians' support for an imminent parousia (1 Thess 4:13-18). Yet another difference is an emphasis on firm adherence to a set of Pauline traditions (2:15), as a basis for intragroup critique: against false teaching (the view that the day of the Lord, or parousia, has already come, 2:2) on the one hand; and against dissident or unruly behavior that contradicted the self-sufficiency ethos modeled earlier by the apostles (3:6-12), on the other.

The similarities lead some scholars to assume that Paul indeed wrote the letter shortly after writing 1 Thessalonians, with the differences then explained as a development in Paul's own teaching. Others, however, consider the similarities with 1 Thessalonians and other Pauline letters as a deliberate attempt by a later follower of Paul to imitate the apostle's words and style. They also find it difficult to believe that Paul would support an imminent parousia in 1 Thessalonians, shift to a delayed one in 2 Thessalonians, and then return to an imminent one in later letters (for example, 1 Cor 7:29; Rom 13:11; Phil 4:5). That the development of such a set of traditions, including an overall Pauline writing style (3:17), would not have been available until after the apostle's letters were collected, perhaps late in the first century CE, becomes yet another reason for relegating the work to the category of deutero-Pauline (that is, from a second generation of Pauline tradition).

As an African American, I resonate with the letter's emphasis on group distinctiveness, an often necessary move for struggle-laden communities. Intragroup critique is also necessary lest parts of such communities romanticize their affliction beyond any possible critique of their cultural values or behaviors. Troubling, though, are the letter's presuppositions about the nature of the assembly's God, the reach of its love, and the rigid defining of its boundaries. Can a group harbor for long an image of a God who seeks everlasting revenge (1:9)? In opposition to the intragroup and extra-group love presupposed in 1 Thessalonians (3:12; compare 5:15), the extent of the reach of the audience's love presupposed in 2 Thessalonians seems introverted (1:3). So too does the letter's clear and solid boundaries between the afflicted and the afflicters (1:6). The use of apocalyptic rhetoric can impede the efforts of struggling, culturally distinctive communities to form just the coalitions that might help them come together for the common good. ❖

The First Letter of Paul to

TIMOTHY

Aída Besançon Spencer

The first of the Pastoral Epistles is addressed to Timothy, Paul's coworker ("my loyal child in the faith," 1 Tim 1:2). In it, Paul describes his personal life as he ministers to other Christians. Some readers of 1 Timothy have criticized the letter because it appears to bow down to the surrounding culture. For example, it is urged that Christian women be silent and not teach (2:11-15), and that Christian slaves be subservient (6:1-2). These statements (which seem to refer to a later period of the church), differences in style and theological terms, and the lack of support in Acts (19:22) regarding Paul's request to Timothy "to remain in Ephesus" (1:3) have led some scholars to conclude that Paul could never have written this letter and to date it as late as the second century CE. Scholars who support Paul's authorship date it during his lifetime, usually between 62 and 64, assuming it was written after Paul was released from prison in Rome (see Acts 28:30-31) and before he was imprisoned a final time in Rome.

It is a letter of paradoxes, with positive exhortations to some and negative judgments to others (for example, 1:18-20). It advances love and mercy as well as orthodoxy.

The letter purports to be written by Paul to Timothy—that is, by one multicultural person to another multicultural person, for the sake of a multicultural church. Paul, a Jew and zealous enforcer of Jewish law, was reared in Tarsus, outside Judea, in the Diaspora. Tarsus, in Asia Minor, represented a harmonious balance of East and West; both Greek and Aramaic were spoken there. According to the Acts of the Apostles, Paul's parents were Roman citizens (Acts 22:28). Thus, Paul was reared in a multicultural setting, yet he traveled to Jerusalem to learn rabbinic law (Acts 22:3). Paul's coworker, Timothy, is a Jew on his mother's side, but his father is a Gentile (1 Tim 1:2; see Acts 16:1-3). He is also from Asia Minor (Lystra).

Ephesus (1:3) was itself a multicultural city. It was the greatest city of the province of Asia, set at a key intersection for trade. It had a synagogue (Acts 19:8) and Jews who were Roman citizens. Yet Ephesus also was well known for the study and practice of magic (Acts 19:18-19) and for the temple of the goddess Artemis, the largest temple of the ancient world. In the Roman period, the worship of Artemis represented a syncretistic (that is, a mixed or blended) belief system.

Although Paul and Timothy could be described as multicultural people living in multicultural settings, the doctrines to which Paul is represented here as urging Timothy to hold fast are not at all syncretistic (1:3-7; 6:3). In this letter of lessons in church guidance and opposition to false teachings, truth is an important theme, as is a "healthy" or "wholesome teaching" (phrases repeated throughout the letter). Elders or overseers are important for teaching truth (1:3; 3:2; 5:17). Some teachers at Ephesus were promoting myths, endless genealogies, speculations, fruitless discussions, godless chatter, and contradictions (1:3-6; 4:7; 6:3-4,

20). Timothy is urged to guard the message he has received and avoid false knowledge (6:20).

As a multicultural person myself (my mother is from Puerto Rico, my father is from the Netherlands, and I was born and reared in the Dominican Republic, but I have lived in the United States since sixth grade), I can affirm the multicultural aspect of the communication in 1 Timothy. Although the accommodation to the larger culture's codes of subordination poses a challenge for many today, we can regard the Paul who speaks here and the Timothy who is addressed as constructing a bridge to reach others in their different cultures. First, they affirm that despite differences among people, all can have the same Savior (God is "our Savior" and Jesus "our hope," 1:1). God bridges all cultures and desires everyone to be saved and to come to a knowledge of the truth (1:15; 2:3-6; 4:10). Second, prayer is for everyone, no matter their social, political, or economic class (2:1-2). The author even advocated that older widows be part of a praying order (5:5). Third, despite different cultures, all can share similar values. The descriptions for overseers (bishop) and ministers (deacons) are built on such widely accepted character attributes as godliness, not being quarrelsome, not loving money, not living for pleasure, and not being a gossip (2:2, 8-10; 3:2-8; 4:7-8; 5:6, 11, 13; 6:2-3, 5-10, 17-18). Being "above reproach" (3:2, 7; 5:7, 14, 25) would help believers lead a "quiet and peaceable life" (2:2) so that more of the Greek and Jewish people might indeed "come to the knowledge of the truth" (2:4). This letter holds firm the basic truths of the gospel yet encourages the sorts of virtues that would help advance the proclamation of the gospel in the larger culture. ❖

The Second Letter of Paul to

TIMOTHY

Aída Besançon Spencer

Traditionally, 2 Timothy is considered Paul's last letter before his death. In this view, Paul had been released from prison in Rome (Acts 28:30-31) but now has been imprisoned again in Rome after Nero has begun to persecute Christians (64–68 CE). Paul no longer expects to be released (2 Tim 4:6-8; compare Phlm v. 22; Phil 2:24). Some scholars note some good reasons to accept Paul's authorship, particularly the personal elements in the correspondence. Nevertheless, based on chronological discrepancies between the imprisonments recounted in Acts and this letter (1:16, 17; 2:9; 4:16-17), other scholars question Paul's authorship of this letter.

Second Timothy has some themes in common with 1 Timothy and Titus, including sound teaching and truth (1:5, 13; 2:2, 14-15, 18, 24-25; 3:6-8, 10, 14-17; 4:2-4) and God as Savior (1:8-10; 2:10; 3:15). The virtues recommended for elders in those letters (1 Tim 3:2-3; Titus 1:7-9; 2:3, 5) are also recommended to Timothy here—good works, not being quarrelsome, apt teaching, and patience (2:21-24); similar problems in the church are addressed here—wrangling over words, profane chatter, senseless controversies, and myths (2:14, 16-17, 23; 3:2-8; 4:3-4); and the importance of conscience, self-control, faith, love, peace, and godliness are affirmed here as well (1:3, 7; 2:22; 3:2-5, 12, 16-17). These observations suggest to many scholars that the three letters came from the same hand—whether Paul's or another's.

But 2 Timothy is primarily about the need for community in the midst of suffering. This letter purports to be a personal communication from the apostle Paul to the evangelist Timothy to help him succeed as a Christian and as a minister. Thus, the author begins by calling Timothy "my beloved child," a term of endearment Paul uses in the singular only for Timothy (1:2; see 1 Cor 4:14, 17; Eph 5:1). Paul appears here to have an emotionally expressive relationship with Timothy. As his spiritual father, he does not hesitate to exhort Timothy: "I remind you"…"Do not be ashamed"…"Hold to the standard"…"Guard" (1:6, 8, 13, 14). He also exhorts Timothy to remind and warn the church (2:14). These imperatives evidently flow from a warm relationship.

The author's main goal is to encourage Timothy to share in suffering with him (1:8; 2:3, 9; 4:5). We learn in Acts that Timothy was reared in Lystra as a devout Jew, though having a Gentile father (Acts 16:1), and that he was present at Antioch of Pisidia, Iconium, and Lystra when, after enthusiastic initial responses, unbelieving Jews stirred up persecution against Paul and Barnabas, eventually even stoning Paul almost to death (2 Tim 3:10-11; Acts 13:13—14:22). The letter reminds Timothy of those persecutions and how the Lord rescued him from all of them (2 Tim 3:11-12).

The author urges Timothy to recognize the importance of human community even when God strengthens the individual believer (2 Tim 4:17). Households were an important aspect of the early church. This letter provides some of the most intimate relational and familial language in the Pauline corpus. Here we read that Paul deeply appreciates the household of Onesiphorus, who, not being ashamed that Paul was imprisoned, searched for him in Rome and many times "refreshed" him (1:16-17); Paul uses the same language to describe how Stephanas's household had refreshed him in Corinth (1 Cor 16:18). In other households, the author notes, some in the women's quarters have still not learned the truth (2 Tim 3:6-7; compare 1 Tim 2:11), but Prisca and Aquila remain constant (2 Tim 4:19), and Eunice and Lois have passed on their faith to their son and grandson Timothy (1:5; 3:15). Paul asks that the Lord repay Onesiphorus's household with the same mercy they displayed (2 Tim 1:16, 18). After all, Paul is a dangerous person to visit; his visitor might be imprisoned too. Even Timothy, when he arrives with Paul's winter cloak and parchment writing materials (4:13, 21), might be imprisoned (as eventually he is, according to Heb 13:23). Paul even seeks the company of Mark (4:11), whom, according to Acts, he once had not been willing to accept as a coworker (Acts 13:13; 15:37-40). Now, it would appear, they are reconciled, even though all Paul's friends from Asia have "turned away" from him (1:15). Demas, who had (according to Col 4:14) been with Paul in the first imprisonment, has now deserted him (4:10). Even Titus has left (4:10).

The letter ends with pathos: "Only Luke is with me" (4:11). At the end, the zealous Jew has only a Gentile Christian with him. During Paul's first imprisonment he was under house arrest (see Acts 28:30; Phil 1:12-13), but according to tradition, Paul's final imprisonment and execution took place in a former dungeon, the Tullianum.

When you are a multicultural person such as I, sometimes you may feel anomie—without country or a standard of truth. Second Timothy reminds us of the importance of the community we experience with family and church, as well as the importance that Scripture holds for Christians in any culture— especially in the midst of suffering for faith in Jesus Christ. ❖

The Letter of Paul to

Titus

Aída Besançon Spencer

As with 1 and 2 Timothy, many scholars question whether the Apostle Paul himself wrote the letter to Titus. Because Crete is never mentioned in Paul's other letters—according to Acts, he was taken there only as a prisoner en route to Rome (Acts 27:7-13)—and because of differences in style and message from Paul's unquestioned writings similar to those evident in 1 and 2 Timothy, these scholars consider Titus a deutero-Pauline letter and date it as late as the second century CE, attributing it to the same hand that authored those letters. Scholars who hold to Pauline authorship date Titus to a time after Paul was released from prison in Rome (that is, between 62 and 64—or perhaps as late as 67).

Titus first appears in the narrative of Acts in Antioch in Syria, accompanying Paul on a relief visit to Jerusalem (Acts 11:29-30; see 15:2-4; Gal 2:1-3). As Paul's coworker and partner, he helped arrange the relief collection for the poor in Judea and was urged to go to Corinth as Paul's representative

(2 Cor 2:13; 7:6-7; 8:6, 16-17, 23; 12:18). At Corinth he functions as a peacemaker and as a representative of the Corinthians to Paul (2 Cor 7:6-7, 15).

As the letter now represents the situation, Paul left Titus behind in Crete to "put in order what remained to be done," which included appointing elders for every city (Titus 1:5). He commands Titus to act "with all authority" and allow no one to "look down on you" (2:15). And no wonder, because Titus is an uncircumcised Greek who has to silence "those of the circumcision" (Titus 1:10-11; see Gal 2:3)! Paul further encourages Titus by addressing him as "my loyal child in the faith we share" (1:4; 1 Tim 1:2).

The problems in the churches at Crete (Titus 1:5, 12) are similar to those in Ephesus (according to 1 Tim 1:3-7) but are more clearly tied here to apparently Jewish opponents (see 1:10, 14). They involve rebelliousness and idle and deceptive talk. Lack of wisdom, self-control, honesty, and courtesy also seem to be problems (Titus 1:8; 2:2, 5-6, 9, 12; 3:1-3), and thus the author pointedly names God as the God "who never lies" (1:2). There appears to be a play here on a common cultural stereotype concerning the people of Crete. The island was reputed to be the home of notorious pirates; perhaps it is because of their influence that "to Cretanize" meant to lie, as Epimenides may have said (Titus 1:12). But the letter also speaks antagonistically of "those of the circumcision," of the proliferation of "Jewish myths," of the commandments of people who "reject the truth," and of quarrels about the law (Titus 1:10, 14; 3:9). Some scholars question whether the letter has actual Jews in view (although Jews had been at Crete for many years: see 1 Macc 15:19-23, referring to Gortyna, which lies in Crete, and Acts 2:11, which names Jews from Crete as present at Pentecost) or instead attacks the Judaizing practices of Gentiles (a problem against which the second-century bishop Ignatius of Antioch also inveighed).

Titus, 1 Timothy, Galatians, and 2 Corinthians are the only four letters in which the wrong thinking of the recipients (or the false teaching of opponents) has reached such proportions that no thanksgiving for the church appear at the letter opening. As in 1 and 2 Timothy, wholesome or "sound" teaching is very important for the author (Titus 1:9, 13; 2:1, 2, 8, 10). Elders (also called bishops) must have a "firm grasp" of the truth in order to teach and preach (1:9). The women elders must "teach what is good," and Titus himself is to have "integrity" and "gravity" in his teaching (2:3, 7). The gospel is summarized in a lengthy self-description in the letter salutation (1:1-3), including themes the author will develop in the letter, such as "knowledge of the truth" and recognizing God and Jesus as "our Savior," important themes also mentioned in 1 Timothy.

But an equally important concern is that the "word of God may not be discredited" (2:5, 8, 10). It is crucial that orthodoxy (right thinking) be reflected in orthopraxy (right practice: 1:16; 2:3, 7, 14; 3:1, 8, 14). A major theme of the letter is that "those who have come to believe in God may be careful to devote themselves to good works" (3:5, 8). Idleness can lead to idle talking.

As a minister and an intercultural person myself (of Hispanic and Dutch heritage), I am impressed that the letter represents Paul sending a *Gentile* to silence *Jews* (so I read "those of the circumcision"). Whether Jews or Gentiles adopting Jewish practices were the problem imagined by the author of Titus, the letter offers us an opportunity to recognize our own responsibility to minister across cultures today. Such cross-cultural engagement in our postmodern world requires *modeling* the truths and behaviors we teach and proclaim. Does Titus also suggest that we may also need, from time to time, to show errors, offer warning, and even seek to silence the voices of those who upset communities "for sordid gain" (1:11)? What might that responsibility entail? ❖

The Letter of Paul to

PHILEMON ▨

Cain Hope Felder

The apostle Paul's letter to Philemon has been the cause for much debate about the complex matter of slavery in relation to the early church. The central person in this the third-shortest book in the New Testament (2 John has only 13 verses, and 3 John has 15), is apparently a runaway slave, Onesimus, who has fled from the household of his owner, Philemon (see vv. 11, 15). Biblical scholars have used the historical-critical method in their attempts to understand the original context and the theological significance for us of this letter. Unfortunately, interpreters have too often allowed the relatively modern aftermath of the transatlantic slave trade to serve as a definitive prism through which this epistle is to be understood. That has distorted the actual sociopolitical and economic issues of the first century CE. Although the protocols for Roman slavery are evident in this letter, many of the prevailing interpretations should be approached with caution.

This is one of the seven "prison epistles" among Paul's writings—that is, letters that purport to have been written from prison; the others in this category are Philippians, Colossians, Ephesians, 1 and 2 Timothy, and Titus. Of these, only Philemon and Philippians are universally regarded as unquestionably coming from Paul himself.

Several factors evidently moved Paul to write to Philemon regarding Onesimus. First, Paul had been responsible for converting Philemon, a wealthy slave owner in Asia Minor, while Paul was in Ephesus (so much is implied in the document itself—see v. 19—though there is no external evidence of this).

Second, Paul then enjoyed a close friendship with Philemon and hoped to visit him after his release from prison. Third, it is clear that Onesimus has also become a Christian through the direct influence of Paul while in prison. Other, later letters will purport to have been carried by Onesimus traveling with Tychicus, one of Paul's virtual secretaries, to Ephesus, Colossae, and Laodicea. Paul's authoritative tone in the epistle stems from the simple fact that he was responsible for both master and slave becoming Christians.

That Paul wrote this letter from prison is clear enough (vv. 9, 13, 23), but the date of the letter is not. Rome, Caesarea, and Ephesus were sites where Paul was imprisoned. If Paul wrote from Rome, the letter must have been written about 61 CE; if from Caesarea, it would have been written about 58; and if from Ephesus, Paul would have written it in 55. The argument for Rome has the most merit, because many runaway slaves came to Rome rather than remain too near the place from which they had run. Those arguing for Ephesus claim that Paul's needing lodging with Philemon is a hint that Paul was nearby. But a runaway slave would most likely attempt to flee as far as possible from their master in order to avoid possible recapture. So Paul was most probably in Rome when he authored this epistle, sometime in the period 61–63.

The occasion and purpose for the letter appear straightforward. Paul wrote to Philemon because he wanted him to receive Onesimus back—certainly without penalty but also with a new status. A few modern interpreters have offered creative alternative views. One contemporary scholar has argued that the letter should not be regarded as a personal letter; it was actually written to a *congregation*, of which the addressee was a member (see v. 2). That is, Onesimus was no runaway but was sent to Paul on behalf of the church in Colossae. Paul writes to request that Onesimus now be released from his obligations in Colossae so that he might remain with Paul and work in Christian ministry as a free man. More recently, another scholar has argued that Philemon and Onesimus were blood brothers and that the issue of slavery thus had no bearing at all on the document. In my view, both these perspectives seem to go too far to deny Onesimus's identity as a slave, which seems to me irrefutable; it is because of Onesimus's conversion that Paul implores Philemon to accept him back as both a Christian and a free man.

The ancient but peculiar institution of slavery was a common practice during the Greco-Roman period. It was an acceptable form of socioeconomic and sociopolitical life. The rich owned slaves, and the slave had few if any rights. Even Aristotle contended that there were "natural slaves and natural masters." For him the structure of the human soul demands that some people be ruled as slaves. The early church did not deal in any uniform or persistent way with slavery as an ethical and theological issue. The seven undisputed Pauline epistles tend not to endorse slavery. But today one wishes, especially an African American like myself, that Paul had been more explicit in developing a clear and distinctive Christian position about slavery, that institution where one person is another's property.

Today commentators are careful not to assign Onesimus a racial or ethnic identity. Most biblical scholars now realize that in ancient times there was no *racial* policy that determined one's eligibility for slavery. Onesimus was likely not an African, as has so often been assumed. He probably was of the ethnic and racial identity of persons living in the Lycus Valley in Asia Minor. The letter to Philemon in fact has much less to do with slavery than it does with the radical difference Christianity should make when one becomes a Christian—a difference that would seem to leave no place for slaves or slavery. Paul has far too long been conveniently presented as a defender of slavery. Readers can judge for themselves the extent to which Philemon provides evidence to the contrary. ❖

Chapter 20

THE GENERAL LETTERS AND REVELATION

Introduction to the

GENERAL LETTERS AND REVELATION

Henry W. Morisada Rietz

Rome. Caesarea. Ephesus. Reading the General Letters (or Epistles) and Revelation in the context of *The Peoples' Bible* draws our attention to the peoples of the Bible in those places. Who are the people of the Bible? Certainly they are the authors *and* their communities, the original readers whom we imaginatively reconstruct as best we can. But the people of the Bible are also its present-day readers (whatever that present is), who actively participate in the creation of the Bible's meanings *today* and whose identities and social locations affect the construction of those meanings.

As a commentator on these biblical books, I am one of those people. I was born in Hawaiʻi in the 1960s. My mother was born in Germany to parents who were Jewish, French, and Hungarian gypsy. My father's ancestors emigrated from Japan to work in Hawaiʻi's sugar plantations. I am what we in Hawaiʻi call *hapa*—half—although I consider myself to be whole. I have spent much of my life in secrecy. In Hawaii in the 1960s, it was a bold act for my father to marry a *haole*—literally "foreign," but now it has come to mean whites generally—woman and have a *hapa-haole* son. I now live and teach in a small, predominately white town in rural Iowa. I have experienced both alienation and the threat of assimilation, but as an educated, financially secure, healthy, heterosexual male who is a citizen of the United States, I also know the power of privilege.

My identities and misidentifications, my social locations and dislocations, lead me to value *particularity*—and similarity as well as difference. From my experience of privilege and discrimination, of being both insider and outsider, I have learned to espouse for myself a hermeneutic—that is, a method of interpretation—of self-critique; I try to discern the ways that I may be implicated in the very critiques I make of other interpretations. The contractions and tensions that I embody sensitize me to listen for the tensions *within* the biblical texts, the conversations and arguments among the people *behind* the texts, and to make room for the various voices of the people who stand *in front of* the texts, reading them. Rather than seeking to resolve these tensions and trying to adopt fixed interpretations— which might involve silencing or alienating some voices, and assimilating others—I invite the reader to a practice of living within the tensions of multiple voices. Perhaps in this way we can all find nourishment for living within the diversities and ambiguities of life.

The General Letters and the Revelation to John represent a mixed collection of documents produced by the early followers of Jesus. Except for their having been gathered together at the end of the Christian canon, there is no inherent reason to treat these documents and collections together.

Hebrews, James, 1 and 2 Peter, 1–3 John, and Jude are called the General Letters, or sometimes the Catholic Epistles (from the Greek word *katholou*, meaning "general" or "universal"), since most of them do not name a specific addressee (2 John is addressed to "the elect lady and her children" and 3 John is addressed to "Gaius"). The English word "epistle" comes from the Greek word *epistolē*, which means "letter." The conventional form of a Greco-Roman letter included four elements:

> an opening formula—*praescriptio*—that included the name of sender, the name of the addressee, and a greeting or salutation (often "greetings," or, in Jewish contexts, "peace"); an expression of thanksgiving; the body of the letter; and final greetings.

But not all of the General Letters are really epistles, that is, formal letters. While the ending of Hebrews resembles the final greetings of a letter (Heb 13:18-25), indicating that it was sent from one community to another, it lacks the opening formula and thanksgiving of a letter. Hebrews refers to itself as a "word of exhortation" (Heb 13:22), the phrase used in Acts 13:15 to refer to a sermon. First John also does not have the form of a letter; it is more of a theological treatise. The title "Revelation" translates the first word of the document, *apokalypsis*, but the author identifies what he has written as a "prophecy" (1:3; 22:18-19), and embedded within the work are letters to the seven churches (Rev 2–3). Nevertheless, modern interpreters have associated the book with a more specific genre called an apocalypse—a revelatory document mediated by an other-worldly agent.

Historically, these various documents come from diverse communities and contexts. Although there is some debate over their dating, most are generally assigned to the late first century CE or early in the second century (although some have argued for dating Jude in the 50s, which would make it one of the earliest Christian documents). They are thus mostly the products of second- or third-generation followers of Jesus (see, for example Heb 2:3, 1 Pet 1:8). The authorship of most of these books is disputed. Hebrews is anonymous, as are 1–3 John (although those documents are related to the community that composed the Gospel of John: see John 21:24). James, 1 Peter, and 2 Peter claim to have been written by the named apostles, but most scholars judge them to be written by followers of the disciples who wrote in their name; thus they are pseudonymous. It is possible that Jude was actually written by "Judas . . . brother of James" and thus also the brother of Jesus, but that is not certain. The author of Revelation was probably named John (1:1, 4, 9; 22:8), but which John we cannot be certain.

Literarily and historically, nothing demands that we treat these documents together. Nevertheless, perhaps it is in this diversity and even serendipity that our reflections may be sparked, since to some degree it reflects that of the Christian canon as a whole: Why *these* particular documents and not others? What happens when we place disparate and diverse voices side by side?

Many of these documents are struggling with issues of identity and reveal the complexity of ways that identity is negotiated and contested. While personal or group identities are often negotiated vis-à-vis an *other*, in reality there are *many* others and thus many identities. Since Jesus and his original followers were Jews, it is fair to say that Christianity emerges out of the Judaisms of the first century. The inclusion of Gentiles only happened after Jesus' death, and it was the source of much conflict. The Jewishness of the movement is evident in the language of James, which is addressed to "the twelve tribes in the Dispersion" (from the Greek word *diaspora*), and refers to the community's "assembly" or *sunagōgēn*, from which we get the English word "synagogue" (Jas 2:2). How do the followers of Jesus make sense of their experiences in light of the traditions they inherit—or steal?—from Judaism? First Peter is addressed

to "the exiles of the Dispersion" (*diaspora*), who are also called "a chosen race, a royal priesthood, a holy nation, God's own people" (2:9), and who are now distinct from Gentiles (see 2:12). This is language that identifies the addressees as Jews. But there are also clear indications in 1 Peter that the addressees were born Gentiles (1:18; 2:10). Thus we see the centrality of Judaism—that one is either a Jew or a non-Jew, that is a Gentile—*assumed* among these followers of Jesus. As another example, the author of Hebrews compares Jesus to various traditions from the Hebrew Bible (or more probably a Greek translation of it) and from early Judaism—for example, the prophets (1:1-3), the angels (1:4-11), Moses (3:1-6), Joshua (4:1-11), the priesthood (4:14—5:10; 7:1-29), the covenant (8:1-13), the tabernacle (ch. 9), and the sacrifices (10:1-18). From the point of view of that author, those Jewish traditions prophetically anticipate or foreshadow the fulfillment or reality that Jesus represents. In doing so, an identity is constructed that degrades—but also is imbedded in—the Jewish *other*.

Some of the identity conflicts also occur within the community. Jude, 2 Peter, James, and 1–3 John all represent contestations within the movement. Reflecting the milieu of the ancient Mediterranean world, where religion was not focused on belief but on practice, these were not primarily theological or doctrinal controversies but arguments about praxis, what people should *do*. The author of Jude takes issue with other leaders within the movement—"intruders"—who are promoting licentiousness (vv. 4, 8, 16, 17-18). Jude responds to this situation, in part, by quoting as an authority *1 Enoch*, a Jewish document that most modern-day Jews and Christians do not recognize as biblical (vv. 14-15, quoting *1 En* 1:9). The author of 2 Peter is also combating people he or she identifies as "false prophets" and "false teachers," who are likewise teaching freedom leading to licentiousness (2:1-2,18-22; 3:3-10). While the author of James doesn't explicitly address false teachers, that book's arguments nevertheless seem directed against particular ideas and notions, namely the privileging of faith over works (2:14-26). As is well known, Paul developed such a position in order to justify the inclusion of Gentiles among the early followers of Jesus, who were Jews (Gal 2:15-16). Interestingly, the argument in Jas 2:14-26 parallels Paul's argument in Rom 3:21—4:24, including the affirmation that "God is one" (Rom 3:30; Jas 2:19), an allusion to the *Shema* (Deut 6:4), and the example of Abraham, recalling Gen 15:6, "Abraham believed God, and it was reckoned to him as righteousness" (Rom 4:3 and Jas 2:21-23). A close reading of Paul shows that he himself was not a teacher of licentiousness, although it is easy to see how his opponents and even his own followers could interpret him that way (for example, 1 and 2 Corinthians).

One of the fiercest internal debates occurs within the community that produced the Gospel of John along with 1–3 John. Here the author's opponents are labeled as "antichrists" who "went out from us" (1 John 2:18-19), indicating that originally they were members of the community. These opponents deny that Jesus came "in the flesh" (1 John 4:2-3; 2 John v. 7), probably taking what would later be called a proto-docetic position, namely that Jesus was only a spirit being and not a physical human. This controversy is also reflected in the later editorial layers of the Gospel of John, such as the prologue, where it is asserted that "the Word became flesh and lived among us" (1:14), and resurrection scene with Thomas (20:24-29). In these controversies we see strong emphasis on materiality and praxis—Jesus cannot be just a theological affirmation and Christianity is more than a belief system. Flesh and blood matter; actions count. We cannot, of course, forget that we are only hearing certain sides of the arguments. The opponents also considered themselves to be faithful followers of Jesus and were trying to figure what that means and how to act accordingly.

These documents also reveal how imbedded they are within the cultural contexts of their times. Many of the documents were written to communities facing persecution (1 Pet 1:6, 17; Heb 10:32-34; Rev 13:5-10). These documents provide a variety of responses to persecutions, reflecting tensions between the need for civil order and perhaps enabling survival, and calls for resisting imperial forces and civil disobedience. First Peter encourages acceptance of suffering as punishment (1 Pet 4:1-2, 12-19). The persecutions experienced by the community may have been in response to the early Christian movement being considered a threat to Roman "family values" (Gal 3:28; 1 Cor 12:13; Col 3:11). The author of 1 Peter diminishes that threat by commanding submission to authority, whether authority of the emperor and other governmental rulers (2:13-17), slave masters (2:18-25), or husbands (3:1-6; 3:7). Thus, 1 Peter advocates for the traditional Roman patriarchal family structure that on the micro-level has the father at the head of the household, with wives, children, and slaves below him, and at the macro-level has the emperor over all the members of the Empire (see similar "household codes" in Col 3:18—4:1 and Eph 5:21—6:9). The assumption that individual families mirror the nation on the whole underlie much of the modern debate over family values and explains why, for some people, individual families are thought to threaten national security. Nevertheless, the endorsement of master-slave relationships in these biblical texts should counter any easy application of these texts as a model for godly modern family relationships.

While 1 Pet 2:17 explicitly endorses the empire with even a slogan ("Honor everyone. Love the family of believers. Fear God. Honor the emperor."), Revelation is a testimony against imperial forces. When reading Revelation, it must be remembered that it was written for a specific place and time. It is addressed "to the seven churches that are in Asia" (1:4), namely Ephesus, Smyrna, Pergamum,

Thyatira, Sardis, Philadelphia, and Laodicea, all within 150 miles of one another. Most scholars date Revelation to the time of the Roman emperor Domitian, who reigned 81–96 CE. From the point of view of the author, the events described are about to happen, "for the time is near" (1:3; compare 22:20). Thus, Revelation was written for a specific place at a specific time, the Roman province of Asia Minor at the end of the first century. Revelation is not a blueprint or script for now in the twenty-first century or for future events. That does not mean, however, that it cannot have meaning for today. The hope of Revelation is a specific one. Steeped in Jewish tradition, Revelation anticipates the reconstitution of Israel. The 144,000 that are sealed include 12,000 from each of the twelve tribes of Israel (7:1-8). Alongside these representatives from Israel "was a great multitude ... from every nation, from all tribes and peoples and languages" (7:9). But Israel is still at the center, a specificity that Gentile Christians must struggle with as we seek to appropriate this book.

Revelation is also a powerful witness to the reality of evil. Through its fantastic imagery and dependence upon mythical traditions, it testifies that evil is real and cosmic and has specific, concrete manifestations on earth. Steeped in the traditions of Israel, evil has manifested itself in the past through the imperial conquests of Babylon, and for the author now is manifested in the Roman Empire, which claims to bring *pax* (peace), but does so at the price of conquest, oppression, exploitation, and death. This is not peace. The "beast rising out of the sea" (13:1) is Rome, and its ten horns are its vassal rulers, client regimes it has set up to exploit the colonies. In this book, as one would expect in the first century, there is no dichotomy between religion and politics, or economics. Without the "mark of the beast" (16:2; 19:20)—whatever that was—"no one can buy or sell" (13:16-17). Evil permeates the imperial machine. At the beginning of the twenty-first century, imperial forces are alive and well,

except that many of us find ourselves inextricably implicated in its machinery. For many, the empire now is the United States, or perhaps better, the complex system of global capitalism that is centered in the United States, propagated through electronic media, and enforced by its diplomatic and military forces and those of its clients.

Revelation's vision of the future reign of God is inspiring. It is not, ultimately, of an other-worldly, disembodied spiritual existence; rather it is an earthly vision of the transformation of the social, political, and ecological realities of this world. Offering an alternative to imperial Rome, Revelation envisions a new heaven and a new earth, centered in the new Jerusalem, where God and the Lamb will reign. This earthly hope of the Israelites restored to their land, restored to a sovereignty free from imperialism, parallels the hopes of many present-day indigenous peoples, from Palestinians, to Native American tribes, to the Kanaka Maoli (so-called native Hawaiians). Revelation affirms such particular dreams with a universalist pitch, where the nations will live together in peace—true peace free from oppression, exploitation, and death. The challenge to us is *how* to realize this vision; "Let ... the righteous still do right" (22:11).

While coming from different perspectives and often taking different positions, hearing the voices of the people of the General Letters and Revelation can challenge and inspire us, today's people of the Bible. Let us not abdicate our responsibility as interpreters who seek to find meanings in these texts, but let us own our voices and the ethical choices we make based on those meanings. Let us also listen to the voices of other readers, who are also constructing their own meanings from these texts. Rather than too quickly relaxing the tensions and resolving the contradictions—moves that often do violence to the text as well as against others—let us dwell within them, for those are the tensions of living with other beings. ❖

The Letter to the

HEBREWS

James Earl Massey

Of the twenty-seven writings that comprise the New Testament, the Letter to the Hebrews is arguably the most culturally specific. The social and religious experiences and beliefs of the Jewish people are so explicitly discussed in this writing that its title, "To Hebrews," found in the most ancient manuscripts of the work, seems well justified. At the same time, however, the message of the letter extends beyond Judaism because of what it teaches about Jesus. That message is that Jesus, the Son of God, became fully identified with all human experience so that his life, death, and resurrection could make access to God readily available to all who look to him as their Savior and exalted advocate. Here the Jewish Scriptures, the religious cultus of the tabernacle in the wilderness and, later, the temple, and historical Hebrew persons are all presented as provisional and prophetic in character, all pointing beyond themselves to what God has now made available to all people in the person and ministry of Jesus the Christ (the God-anointed One).

Among the many details specific to Jewish Scripture and tradition in the letter are references to the prophets (1:1); to the Hebrew people as descendants of Abraham (2:16; 6:13); to Moses and Joshua as exemplary leaders (chs. 3–4); to the nation's sojourn in the wilderness (ch. 4); to covenant concerns, the priestly system, and the necessity of sacrifices and offerings (chs. 5–10); and to a panoply of biblical heroes and heroines such as Abel, Enoch, and Noah (ch. 11). The Jewish flavor of the New Testament is nowhere more evident than in the Letter to the Hebrews, a writing whose understanding requires an awareness of the history, sacrificial system, Scriptures, beliefs, and covenantal obligations of the Hebrew people.

This close attention to aspects of Jewish belief and practice has convinced many readers that the letter must have been directed to Jews to attract them to faith in Jesus. For example, a nineteenth-century Christian commentator on the letter wrote that a Jew, reading Hebrews for the first time, "would be favourably impressed with the evident love and sympathy which the writer displays towards the Tabernacle, its ministers, and its ritual," and "would thus be led, insensibly and without offense, into a consideration of the argument that these symbols found in Christ their predestined and final fulfillment."[10]

Other scholars, however, have argued that the author's insistence that Christ has superseded aspects of the Jewish covenant must have come from, and been directed to, Gentile Christians. The first recipients of the Letter to the Hebrews cannot be stated with unquestioned certainty. But because 1 Clement, written in Rome about 96 CE, quotes copiously from it, it may be that Jewish (or possibly, Gentile) members of the church in Rome were its intended audience.

In addition to Paul, many others have been suggested across the centuries as responsible for writing Hebrews. Most were members of the Pauline circle. They include Luke, Clement, Barnabas, Apollos, Priscilla (with her husband, Aquila), Epaphras, Timothy, and Silas. Although no final word can yet be given on its author, features of the letter suggest that its author was a Hellenistic (Greek-speaking) Jew who was skilled in rhetoric, seems acquainted with Paul's teaching but was an independent thinker, and was a second-generation Christian (2:3). The writer knew the group to which the letter was addressed (5:11-12; 6:9-10; 10:32; 13:7, 19). The writer also knew Timothy (13:23). As an African American preacher, the sermonic feel, especially the cadences of the biographical miniatures (11:1-39), causes me to resonate with the thought that perhaps the author was that first-century African preacher Apollos.

Hebrews should be dated about 64 CE, and certainly prior to 70 and the destruction of Jerusalem, because mentioning that devastating event would have strengthened the writer's argument in chapters 7–10. Rome seems to match best what seems indicated in the letter as the locale of its intended recipients: 10:32 refers to the group's "hard struggle with sufferings," which could suggest the time when Emperor Claudius exiled Jews from Rome (chs. 49–50) or a severe period for Christians in the mid-to-late 60s under Nero's rule. Since further suffering was anticipated (12:3-4, 7, 12-13), the writer wanted to strengthen readers for a sustained faith in the mission and meaning of Jesus (10:15-19; 13:6, 20-21).

Concerned to encourage Christians as they faced persecution and slights, the writer reminds them anew that the Hebrew cultic forms actually pointed to the "new and living way" (10:20) opened by the expiatory death of Jesus, a death that grants believers an "eternal redemption" (9:12). The old covenant offered to Jews has been superseded by a new covenant offered to all people (10:16-18, citing invokes Jer 31:33-34). Backed by the Jewish Scriptures and the apostolic message, the writer explains that the animal sacrifices demanded under the old covenant really represented and foreshadowed the offering Jesus made of himself to God, and that because of this those sacrifices are no longer necessary, nor is the priesthood that administered them.

A warning is voiced to trust fully the gospel they had received because it had been attested "by those who heard" the Lord Jesus (2:1-4). The readers are encouraged to "exhort one another" (3:13), remain confident in faith (3:14), hold fast to the Christian "confession" (4:14; 10:23), show "diligence" (6:11), and keep living by faith (10:36-39). They are to look steadily to Jesus (12:2) and not look back or return to an obsolete ritualistic order, since to do so would be to commit apostasy (6:4-6; 10:26-31). Under persecution, some persons have abandoned the fellowship (10:25), so the writer cautions all others against neglecting to gather together.

Hebrews is a dynamic restatement of the Christian faith. The conditions its first readers faced demanded such a treatment, and the writer prepared and sent it as an encouraging word flavored with the evident caring of a pastoral heart. Christians today continue to value the writing as a doctrinal manifesto about the meaning of Jesus and a strategic word of encouragement for believers beset by life and fretful or confused about what they see and experience in the world. Hebrews offers a needed word for believers facing difficulties because they are Christians.

Briefly outlined, the structured argument of Hebrews is as follows:

God's Son as God's supreme agent (1:1—4:13)
Jesus the great High Priest (4:14—10:39)
The meaning and necessity of faith
    (11:1—12:29)
Concluding remarks (13:1-25)

Hebrews appears in the oldest version of the New Testament canon. It won acceptance into the canon on the strength of the Eastern church's tradition that Paul wrote it or was otherwise somehow behind its creation. The churches in the West did not view the writing as Pauline, but they accepted Hebrews as authoritative, and it appears in our

English versions immediately after Paul's writings rather than among them—an order influenced by that in the Latin Vulgate, the version on which the first English Bible was based. ❖

The Letter of

JAMES

Margaret Aymer Oget

Almost hidden among the many letters written by or attributed to Paul is James's brief letter to his churches. We who read this letter today are left with some unanswered—and possibly unanswerable—questions. We don't know who really wrote the letter or when it was written. Some biblical scholars think it was written by an anonymous author in the second century CE; others, that it was written by James, the brother of Jesus, which would put it in the 50s and make it contemporary with the letters of Paul of Tarsus. But this we can say with relative certainty: James is an *advice letter* to those James calls his "brothers and sisters" (1:2) and " my beloved" (1:16).

James gives his community two striking identities. First he calls them the birth-children of God! This is a startling image, because Christians are used to identifying Jesus as God's begotten son and understanding themselves as God's adopted children. But James says God gave birth to the faithful by means of the "word of truth" so that they, like Christ, might be the "first fruits of his creatures" (1:18). Equally startling to me as a woman is the *femaleness* of James's God. James testifies that God, the source of wisdom (1:5), the giver of the royal law (2:8) and the law of freedom (1:25), is also the one who "gave us birth" (1:18); the metaphor depicts God as the community's

birth-mother, laboring over the birthing stool to give them life!

James's people have another identity. He calls them "the twelve tribes in the Dispersion" (1:1). James probably does not mean that they are literally the people—or even the descendants of the people—who were exiled in 587 BCE. Rather, James is reminding his community that they are not "from here." Remembering that one is not from here is a constant theme in immigrant families such as my own. Even thirty years into my U.S. sojourn, I am reminded that my origins are with black and brown peoples outside the continental United States: from Africa, yes, but also of the Carib peoples and from the Indian subcontinent, all forcibly dispersed—exiled—in what the Rastafarians call Babylon, the islands of the British Caribbean.

To my immigrant ears, two of James's themes resonate. First, I am reminded that sojourners should be careful about whom they befriend. For as James remarks angrily, "friendship with the world is enmity with God" (4:4). Second, I am exhorted to endure when times are difficult, for although God "tempts no one" (1:13-14), this world in which we live can at times be a trial.

In light of the trials of life in exile, James in effect tells his community that "you must have that true religion." For James, true religion is marked by the person who prays, "Bridle my tongue; let my words edify," for James despises bragging, slander, grumbling, and other misuses of the tongue (3:2-5, 9; 4:1; 5:9). True religion requires an active faith that can be demonstrated in what one does (2:17). Importantly, true or "pure" religion means meeting the needs of the poor, the orphaned, and the widow (1:27). James excoriates the wealthy who oppress his people (5:1-6). In short, true religion, or what James calls "the wisdom from above" (3:17), is a life lived in worship of God, justice to others, and self-control. It is to this life that James's community, and all of us who understand life in exile, are called. ❖

The First Letter of

PETER

David Cortés-Fuentes

The First Letter of Peter is an exhortation written with the dual purpose of *encouraging* Christians going through difficult times due to the distinctiveness of their way of life and *witnessing* to them the "true grace of God" (5:12). The letter exhorts readers to rejoice even in time of unjust trials and suffering (1:6-7) and to maintain good behavior in the world (2:11-12; 4:7-11). It is directed to Christians in a broad region of Asia Minor whose social and religious identity made them "exiles" (1:2) and "aliens" (2:11) within the much larger non-Christian population. These terms had earlier been used to refer to Jews living outside Palestine, but now they refer to the dispersion of Christians. This experience of alienation is the result of their being called by the grace of God to be "a chosen race, a royal priesthood, a holy nation, God's own people, in order that you may proclaim the mighty acts of him who called you out of darkness into his marvelous light" (2:9; see Exod 19:5-6). God made these exiles and aliens into God's people (2:10; see Hos 1:6-9 and 2:23).

First Peter is usually dated sometime during the last quarter of the first century. It was probably written from Rome (5:13—"your sister church in Babylon") by someone who was ministered to and influenced by Peter. One reason for doubting Peter's own authorship has to do with the refined Greek used in the letter, unlikely the style of a Galilean fisherman. The letter follows the regular pattern of other letters in the New Testament: a greeting or opening formula (1:1-2); a blessing (1:3-12); the body of the letter (1:13—5:11), consisting of a call to holy living (1:13—2:10) and the adoption of appropriate behavior for Christians in a strange world (2:11—4:11), followed by an exhortation (4:12—5:11) and a closing formula (5:12-14).

First Peter calls Christians to recognize their distance and difference from the dominant culture and to resist cultural assimilation, even in times of repression and persecution (4:12-19). As a first-generation Latino from Puerto Rico, the identification of the letter's addressees as exiles gets my attention. Although the language may be used figuratively for the audience of the letter, for those whose experience of exile (voluntary or not) is a daily experience, this expression has a personal meaning. When the dominant culture discriminates and alienates people because of the color of their skin, their gender, their accent, or other cultural differences, the experience of exile becomes real and painful. As it happened to many Christians during the time of the Roman Empire, many immigrants now are discriminated against not because they are criminals but simply because they are different.

To the Christians suffering alienation in a strange land, 1 Peter declares that they have been chosen and destined by God and sanctified by the Spirit to be obedient to Jesus Christ (1:1). This community of believers are called to live not according to their former lives but as holy people, different from the common expected behavior of the time (1:13-16). These aliens are "God's own

people," a "chosen race," a "royal priesthood," and a "holy nation," called to witness to God's grace (2:9-10).

Written for a people struggling in the midst of affliction, suffering in spite of their innocence, the letter encourages the believers to persevere and remain faithful. God is the hope, strength, and support of the discriminated and persecuted (5:10-11). Even the people of the letter writer's "sister church in Babylon" (5:13) identify themselves as faithful partners with these aliens and strangers in struggle and in pilgrimage.

In our multicultural global context, we may read 1 Peter as a challenge to defy discrimination based on social-cultural markers and to find creative ways to celebrate our human diversity. ❖

The Second Letter of

PETER

David Cortés-Fuentes

Second Peter follows the form of a testament or farewell letter. The author uses it to remind readers of the teachings they have received and urges them to recall all of these things after his—the author's—death (1:12-15). He also warns them about false teachers (2:1-3) and encourages them to remain faithful and hopeful in a context of moral decay (2:10b-22).

The letter begins with a salutation (1:1-2), from Simeon Peter to fellow Christians, greeting them with grace and peace. The body of the letter (1:3—3:16) includes an exhortation to Christian character (1:3-15), the writer's claim of witnessing Christ's glory (1:16-21), a condemnation of false prophets and teachers (ch. 2), and a reminder of the coming

of the Lord (3:1-16). The book concludes with an exhortation and blessing (3:17-18).

Although the author identifies himself as "Simeon Peter, a servant and apostle of Jesus Christ" (1:1), the letter reflects the language and concerns of a church of a much later period. The fact that the writer acknowledges Paul's letters (3:15-16) makes it clear that this letter was not written by Peter, since it is unlikely that Paul's letters had the status of Scripture during Peter's lifetime. Furthermore, the effort the author makes to show readers that his letter represents an authentic witness to the apostolic tradition (1:19-21; 3:2), the view of an eyewitness to the transfiguration of

Jesus (1:16-18), and a sequel to an earlier letter they received from the same writer (3:1) all point to the pseudonymity of this letter—someone else writing in Peter's name. That was a common practice in antiquity, used by some to vest their writings with the authority of another author. The close similarity between this letter and the letter of Jude lends additional support to the argument that someone other than Peter was the author of 2 Peter.

The letter includes a denunciation and condemnation of false teachers and false prophets. It is directed against their greed, exploitation, and corrupt lifestyles as well as against their teachings (2:1-22; 3:1-13). The false teachers are similar to fallen angels, the people in the time of Noah, and the inhabitants of Sodom and Gomorrah (2:4-10). They deny the promise of the coming of the Lord, falsely contending that ever since the death of the earlier church leaders ("our ancestors") nothing has changed (3:1-7). The letter offers a more positive explanation of the delayed coming of the Lord: it is an extension of time, offering opportunity for repentance (2:8-9).

Second Peter is similar to the letter of Jude in its apocalyptic language and allusions to the stories of the Hebrew Bible as paradigms of the experience and struggles of the church. Especially distinctive is a statement that envisions a future similar to the one in the book of Revelation. Just before concluding the letter, the author urges the community to wait and hope "in accordance with his promise,... for new heavens and a new earth, where righteousness is at home" (3:13).

For many people who witness the lack of justice and live as victims of injustice, this declaration summarizes the hope of the letter and their own hope. The current system that perpetuates injustice by destroying natural resources, exploiting people, and putting too many resources in the hands of the few while too many people live in poverty and need cannot represent the final word of Scripture. This letter's call to faithfulness and hope is grounded in the certainty that believers will live "where righteousness is at home."

The hope expressed here for new heavens and a new earth finds its echo in the hope of many immigrants who come to the United States searching for a better life. My own experience as a first-generation Puerto Rican helps me understand this hope with a double perspective. First, I am keenly aware that not everyone experiences justice or enjoys the same opportunities to succeed. Second, I hear the message of the gospel as an invitation to continue the struggle for justice, and as an assurance that although there is still much to be done, God's promise is secure and firm. This hope sustains our struggles and strengthens our solidarity as people of God, waiting and working for a better future. ❖

The First Letter of

JOHN   ■

Craig S. Keener

Traditionally, readers attributed 1, 2, and 3 John to the anonymous author of the Fourth Gospel, who has conventionally been identified as the apostle John. But many scholars now debate that attribution. Because members of a theological "school" are more likely to share common ideas than a common style, I favor attributing the common style among these three epistles *and* the Fourth Gospel to a single author. In any case, all scholars use John's Gospel as background for understanding these epistles and, although it is impossible to date them precisely, most scholars place them around the end of the first century, 90–110 CE.

Scholars also debate the background of these epistles beyond their apparent connection with the Fourth Gospel. Many think the author opposes an early form of what later became known as Gnosticism, because the opponents deny that Jesus truly "has come in the flesh" (1 John 4:2)—perhaps meaning that, in the eyes of the opponents, he only *seemed* to be human. Other scholars point out that we lack explicit evidence of Gnostics this early, although not of other theological opponents.

Some scholars suggest instead a situation in which local synagogues have expelled Jewish believers in Jesus, as John's Gospel presupposes (John 9:22; 12:42; 16:2). In this case, those who "went out" and "denie[d] that Jesus is the Christ" (1 John 2:19, 22-23) might now be returning to the synagogues. But just as the seven churches of Asia Minor (Revelation 2–3) faced a variety of situations, including conflicts with synagogues and compromises with immoral practices, we need not assume that these epistles address precisely the same situation as the Fourth Gospel.

Clearer indications of the background may be inferred from the Johannine epistles themselves.

Some people have withdrawn from the fellowship of the community and no longer believe what the author considers the truth about Jesus. First John encourages believers not to let this departure by others shake their own faith. The Spirit within them assures them that they belong to Christ (1 John 3:24; 4:13; 5:7-8). The writer also offers a theological test by which believers can discern the true Spirit and Christ's true followers: they must believe in Jesus the incarnate Christ (1 John 2:22-23; 4:1-6; compare 2 John v. 7).

First John further offers a moral test: although the author knows that even believers sin sometimes, he graphically emphasizes that they must avoid sin, behaving righteously (1 John 2:3-4, 29; 3:4-10; 5:3, 18; 2 John v. 6). This righteous obedience to God's will especially involves loving their fellow believers (1 John 2:9-11; 3:10-17; see 2 John vv. 5-6). If faith and love are signs that one has eternal life (1 John 3:14-16, 23), the "mortal sin" (1 John 5:16) would be apostasy from faith and love.

Some issues that Christians debate today are more important than others. For John, recognizing that Jesus is Christ and Lord and that he fully shared our humanity are central and nonnegotiable tenets of Christian faith. But John also cares about ethics. By the time John wrote, the Christian movement was spreading among Gentiles (3 John v. 7). What does his teaching about love and remaining in fellowship say about Christians today who refuse to fellowship across racial or cultural lines? In addition to truly confessing Christ, a true Christian must love others who are Christ's. One who does not love one's brother or sister, God's children, cannot truly love God (1 John 4:20). If we are loyal to Christ, we share a deeper bond with fellow believers of different cultures, nations, or ethnicities than we do with others of our own culture who serve different lords. We must reject ethnocentrism (including all versions of apartheid) and chauvinistic nationalism.

A white convert from atheism to Christianity, I find John's message of cross-cultural love vital. In the time of my deepest brokenness, an African-American grandmother and her grandchildren welcomed me into their family. I found a spirit of strength in the black church, which knew how to deal with pain and nursed me back to wholeness. I was ordained in an African-American (National Baptist) church in North Carolina. Later I taught at an African Methodist Episcopal seminary. I continue to be nurtured spiritually by the black church. My wife was a refugee for eighteen months during war in the Congo. When ethnic strife between regions led to war, her family lost their home and nearly their lives. Painfully, such stories are not rare. Ethnic conflict, which is human selfishness on a corporate level, is widespread in the world. The ethnic reconciliation in Christ for which we work, on both my continent and hers, is for us a necessary expression of the love-in-action to which the Johannine epistles call us. ❖

The Second Letter of

JOHN

Craig S. Keener

Shorter than 1 John, 2 John shares its message and probably its author (see the introduction to 1 John). The writer offers a theological test by which Christ's true followers may be discerned: they must believe in Jesus the incarnate Christ (v. 7). They must also avoid sin, behaving righteously (v. 6). This righteous obedience to God's will especially involves loving their fellow believers (vv. 5-6). ❖

The Third Letter of

JOHN

Craig S. Keener

The Third Epistle of John is the last and shortest of these epistles (see the introduction to 1 John). Though it shares with 1 and 2 John a common author, a common milieu, and a similar message, 3 John appears to address a different, nontheological division in the community. The principle at the heart of the author's message is nevertheless the same: loving one's fellow believers is central to the meaning of being a Christian (vv. 5-12). ❖

The Letter of

JUDE

David Cortés-Fuentes

Jude is one of the briefest letters of the New Testament. Its twenty-five verses are an apology—a defense—of the faith in response to threats from false teachings and the dangers posed to the church by teachers whose morality and ethical behavior do not conform to "the faith that was once for all entrusted to the saints" (v. 3b). In spite of its brevity, its passionate defense is an example of early Christian apologetic literature, written to encourage the church to remain faithful in times of uncertainty and moral decay.

Jude is often considered a circular letter, addressed not to a specific community but to all believers "who are called, who are beloved in God the Father and kept safe for Jesus Christ" (v. 1b). But the claim that the letter was intended for a particular community is also plausible, based on the reference in verse 4 to some strangers who had disrupted the community. It seems that the author's original purpose, to write about the common salvation he shared with the community of faith (v. 3), changed due to the crisis of the false teachers. He calls the people propagating the false doctrine "intruders" and "ungodly" (v. 4), "dreamers" (v. 8), "blemishes" (v. 12), and "waterless clouds carried along by the winds; autumn trees without fruit, twice dead, uprooted; wild waves of the sea, casting up the foam of their own shame; wandering stars, for whom the deepest darkness has been reserved forever" (v. 13).

The structure of the letter follows the pattern typical of early Christian letters, which in turn used a pattern common to letters of the Greco-Roman time. The opening formula (v. 1a) identifies the sender as "Jude, a servant of Jesus Christ, and brother of James." Later tradition identifies this Jude as a brother of the Lord mentioned in Mark 6:3 (Judas) and a plausible author of this letter—which if true could make Jude one of the earliest letters in the New Testament. The letter is addressed to "those who are called, who are beloved in God the Father and kept safe for Jesus Christ" (v. 1b). Immediately after this opening, the letter includes a salutation wishing the audience mercy, peace, and love (v. 2). As an introduction to the main body, the letter incorporates a statement of purpose: to appeal to the Christians to contend for their faith because of the false teachers infiltrating the church (vv. 3b-4).

The main body of the letter consists of an alternate description of the character of the false teachers and appeals to the faithful to avoid their mistakes. The letter uses examples from the Hebrew Scriptures and other early Jewish traditions (vv. 5-23). First the writer reminds readers of the exodus, the story of Sodom and Gomorrah, and of the fight for the body of Moses by the archangel Michael (vv. 5-10). Next he invokes the stories of Cain, Balaam, and Korah (vv. 11-13). Then the writer alludes to the mysterious character of Enoch and some prophecies preserved in an early Jewish apocalyptic text not included in the Bible (vv. 14-16). Also in this last section, the letter appeals to prophecies of the apostles that announced the moral character of the people of the last days (vv. 17-19). The main body of the letter concludes with an exhortation to keep the faith and engage in works of kindness and compassion for the people (vv. 20-23). The letter closes with a doxology, praising God for caring for and strengthening the faithful in times of trial.

Although the letter begins with an apologetic tone, its main purpose is to urge the community to watch themselves, to avoid the mistakes of others, and above all to continue the fight for the faith. The last verses of the body of the letter (vv. 20-23) give readers some specifics on how they should conduct their fight for the faith: mutual support, common prayer, and mercy for those who waver.

I believe I am one of the few who finds the letter of Jude exciting. As a member of a so-called minority (a first-generation Puerto Rican), I find the exhortations of Jude fascinating. It seems easier to imitate and accommodate to the way of life of the dominant society, to assume their values, and be dragged into accusing and condemning the poor, the immigrants, and all those who are different for everything that goes wrong in our society. Jude reminds me that we are not alone in the struggle for justice, peace, and freedom. On the contrary, his witness, as that of many other Christians, sustains our faith and energizes our hope. ❖

The

REVELATION

to John

Greg Carey

The book of Revelation describes an "apocalypse" (1:1). As such, it narrates the revelation experience of one of Jesus' followers, John, to other followers in the Roman province of "Asia," today's western Turkey. In his vision John encounters the risen Jesus (1:9-20). Jesus dictates letters to seven churches scattered across Asia. Praising the churches for their faithfulness and admonishing them for their failures, Jesus promises eternal blessings for those who "conquer" in the face of the pressure to compromise their witness to Jesus. In his mystical state John enters the realm of heaven, where he visits the heavenly throne room, watches as the judgments of God unfold upon a violent world, observes Jesus' victory over the forces of imperialism and idolatry, and wonders as the New Jerusalem, the heavenly city, descends to earth. Revelation begins and ends by blessing those who see and hear the vision and do what it teaches (1:3; 22:18-19).

Many contemporary readers find Revelation hopelessly mysterious—or irrelevant. Their aversion is partly due to the bizarre ways in which self-made prophets today have distorted Revelation into a road map for the last days—always *these* days. Revelation's strange symbols also baffle modern audiences. Some people object to Revelation on ethical grounds as well, finding it too bloodthirsty, too vengeful, too world-denying, and misogynistic. Others simply cede Revelation to the "prophecy teachers," focusing their own attention instead on the more familiar stories of Jesus in the Gospels. Many of the self-styled prophecy teachers condemn ecumenical collaboration, environmental activism, global peacemaking, and a host of other causes as signs of satanic deception in the last days. Tragically, their influence continues to expand beyond North America to the rapidly growing churches of the global South.

But Revelation embodies perhaps the Bible's most forceful critique of imperial ideology, militarism, and commerce. Like many ancient Jewish and Christian literary apocalypses, Revelation speaks to the circumstances of its time and place, interpreting the ways of God for the crises of its own day. Not only does Jesus address seven actual churches made up of real people; Revelation insists that it reveals what "must soon take place" (1:1, 3, 19; 22:6, 10, 12). Even its most remarkable symbols—the dragon, the beast, and the whore—are familiar to readers of ancient Jewish and Christian literature. Revelation identifies the dragon as Satan (12:9), and it uses the beast and the whore to convey the wicked, idolatrous, and exploitative nature of Roman imperialism. The beast (prominent in ch. 13) and the whore (chs. 17–18) make war against "the saints." The beast is worshipped due to its surpassing power: "Who is like the beast, and who can fight against it?" (13:4). The whore generates unfathomable wealth for the few who benefit most from her commerce (18:11-13).

Revelation's most striking symbol applies to Jesus. In the heavenly throne room, John awaits the arrival of the "lion of the tribe of Judah," who has authority over the world's destiny. Yet the lion never appears. In its place stands the Lamb (5:5-6), who remains standing although it has been slaughtered. The Lamb conquers the forces of imperialism and evil through the word of its testimony—that is, by

faithfully witnessing to the ways of God, even to the point of death. Revelation calls its audience to demonstrate their loyalty to the Lamb by following its example. They bear witness ("the word of their testimony") to the ways of justice and peace (12:11), and they resist the economic, political, and religious trappings of Roman imperialism (3:4; 18:4). Thus they endure in their faithful testimony to Jesus, the Lamb.

We know only a little about the churches John addresses. They must have been small, relatively powerless groups of believers. Some were wealthy (3:17), but far more would have been poor (2:9). Perhaps the churches included some merchants who benefited from imperial commerce. Revelation describes these little churches as under intense pressure, even persecution (1:9; 2:13; 6:9-11), from their neighbors. While we lack hard evidence for such persecution of Christians in Revelation's specific cultural context, Asia was well known for popular devotion to the cult of the emperor. Revelation's call for faithful witness and abstention from the imperial cults placed the churches at odds with their neighbors. The churches' emulation of Jesus cost them good will, economic and social benefits, and occasionally their lives.

I interpret Revelation as a citizen of the United States, the world's greatest military and economic empire today. As a young convert to Christianity, I adopted the virulent nationalism and militarism promoted by prophecy teachers. I believed that serving God and serving the nation went in lockstep. Then, in college and seminary, I encountered interpretations from Latin America and South Africa that emphasize how Revelation speaks out against imperial oppression. They challenged me to ask what is beastly in my nation and to bear faithful testimony to the ways of peace and truth. ❖

Notes

■   ■   ■   ■

A Self-Inventory for Bible Readers

1 This self-inventory is inspired and adapted from a "Student Self-Inventory on Biblical Hermeneutics" used at New York Theological Seminary. See Norman K. Gottwald, "Framing Biblical Interpretation at New York Theological Seminary: A Student Self-Inventory on Biblical Hermeneutics," in *Reading from This Place*, 251–61. Special thanks also to Curtiss Paul DeYoung for his Assessment Tool on Developing and Sustaining Authentic Multiracial Congregations and to Ann Holmes Redding for consultation regarding the use of their Self-Assessment.

The God of the Bible and the Peoples of the Earth

2 Dag Hammarskjöld, *Markings*, trans. Leif Sjoberg and W. H. Auden (New York: Alfred Knopf, 1965), 205.

3 Huston Smith, *The Religions of Man* (New York: Harper and Row, 1965), 62.

4 Martin Buber, *The Eclipse of God: Studies in the Relation between Religion and Philosophy* (New York: Harper, 1957), 28.

5 Eduard Schweizer, *Luke, a Challenge to Present Theology*, trans. David Green (Atlanta: John Knox, 1982), 58.

Gallery

6 See Colleen McDannell, *Material Christianity: Religion and Popular Culture in America* (New Haven: Yale University Press, 1998), 190.

7 Ignacio Ellacuría, "The Crucified People," 580–604 in *Mysterium Liberationis: Fundamental Concepts of Liberation Theology*, ed. Ignacio Ellacuría and Jon Sobrino (Maryknoll: Orbis, 1993).

8 Barbara Ehrenreich, *Dancing in the Streets: A History of Collective Joy* (New York: Metropolitan Books, 2007).

The Hebrew Bible as a Text of Cultures

9 David Mura, *Where the Body Meets Memory: An Odyssey of Race, Sexuality and Identity* (New York: Anchor Books/Doubleday, 1996), 19–20.

The Letter to the Hebrews

10 F. W. Farrar, *The Epistle of Paul the Apostle to the Hebrews* (Cambridge: Cambridge University Press, 1891), 19.

SELECT BIBLIOGRAPHY

on Culturally Aware Interpretation of the Bible

◼   ◼   ◼   ◼

Bellis, Alice Ogden, and Joel S. Kaminsky, eds. *Jews, Christians, and the Theology of the Hebrew Scriptures*. Atlanta: Society of Biblical Literature, 2000.

Bible and Culture Collective. *The Postmodern Bible*. New Haven: Yale University Press, 1997.

Blount, Brian K. *Cultural Interpretation: Reorienting New Testament Criticism*. Minneapolis: Fortress Press, 1995.

Blount, Brian K., Cain Hope Felder, Clarice J. Martin, and Emerson B. Powery, eds. *True to Our Native Land: An African American New Testament Commentary*. Minneapolis: Fortress Press, 2007.

Brooks, Roger, and John J. Collins, eds. *Hebrew Bible or Old Testament: Studying the Bible in Judaism and Christianity*. Notre Dame: Notre Dame University Press, 1990.

Choi Hee An, and Katheryn Pfisterer Darr, eds. *Engaging the Bible: Critical Readings from Contemporary Women*. Minneapolis: Fortress Press, 2006.

Coote, Robert B., and Mary P. Coote. *Power, Politics, and the Making of the Bible: An Introduction*. Minneapolis: Fortress Press, 1990.

De La Torre, Miguel. *Reading the Bible from the Margins*. Maryknoll, N.Y.: Orbis, 2002.

Deloria, Vine, Jr. *God Is Red: A Native View of Religion*. Rev. ed. Golden, Colo.: Fulcrum, 2003.

Dube, Musa W. *Postcolonial Feminist Interpretation of the Bible*. St. Louis: Chalice, 2000.

Felder, Cain Hope, ed. *Stony the Road We Trod: African American Biblical Interpretation*. Minneapolis: Fortress Press, 1991.

Foskett, Mary F. and Jeffrey Kah-jin Kuan, eds. *Ways of Being, Ways of Reading: Asian American Biblical Interpretation*. St. Louis: Chalice, 2006.

Fredriksen, Paula, and Adele Reinhartz, eds. *Jesus, Judaism, and Christian Anti-Judaism*. Louisville: Westminster John Knox, 2002.

Fredriksen, Paula. *From Jesus to Christ: The Origins of the New Testament Images of Christ*. 2nd ed. New Haven: Yale University Press, 2000.

Freire, Paolo. *The Pedagogy of the Oppressed*. Translated by Myra Bergman Ramos. New York: Seabury, 1968.

Gottwald, Norman K. *The Hebrew Bible: A Socio-Literary Introduction*. Philadelphia: Fortress Press, 1985.

Gottwald, Norman K., and Richard A. Horsley, eds. *The Bible and Liberation: Political and Social Hermeneutics*. Rev. ed. Maryknoll, N.Y.: Orbis, 1993.

Horsley, Richard A., ed. *In the Shadow of Empire: Reclaiming the Bible as a History of Resistance*. Louisville: Westminster John Knox, 2008.

Jobling, David, Peggy L. Day, and Gerald T. Sheppard, eds. *The Bible and the Politics of Exegesis.* Cleveland: Pilgrim, 1991.

Kelley, Shawn. *Racializing Jesus: Race, Ideology, and the Formation of Modern Biblical Scholarship.* London: Routledge, 2002.

Knowles, Melody, Esther Menn, John Pawlikowski, and David Sandoval, eds. *Contesting Texts: Jews and Christians in Conversation about the Bible.* Minneapolis: Fortress Press, 2007.

Koester, Helmut. *Introduction to the New Testament,* vol. 1: *History, Culture, and Religion of the Hellenistic Age,* 2nd ed.; vol. 2, *History and Literature of Early Christianity,* 2nd ed. Berlin: Walter de Gruyter, 1995, 2000.

Kwok Pui-lan. *Discovering the Bible in the Non-biblical World.* Bible and Liberation Series. Maryknoll, N.Y.: Orbis, 1995.

Malina, Bruce. *The New Testament World: Insights from Cultural Anthropology.* 3rd ed. Louisville: Westminster John Knox, 2001.

Nasrallah, Laura, and Elisabeth Schüssler Fiorenza, eds. *Prejudice and Christian Beginnings: Investigating Race, Gender, and Ethnicity in Early Christianity.* Minneapolis: Fortress Press, 2009.

Page, Hugh R., Jr., Randall C. Bailey, Valerie Bridgeman, Stacy Davis, Cheryl Kirk-Duggan, Madipoane Masenya, Samuel Murrell, and Rodney Sadler, eds. *The Africana Bible: Reading Israel's Scriptures from Africa and the African Diaspora.* Minneapolis: Fortress Press, 2009.

Patte, Daniel, J. Severino Croatto, Nicole Wilkinson Duran, Teresa Okure, and Archie Chi Chung Lee, eds. *Global Bible Commentary.* Nashville: Abingdon, 2004.

Prior, Michael. *The Bible and Colonialism: A Moral Critique.* Biblical Seminar 48. Sheffield, England: Sheffield Academic, 1997.

Schüssler Fiorenza, Elisabeth. *The Power of the Word: Scripture and the Rhetoric of Empire.* Minneapolis: Fortress Press, 2007.

————. *Rhetoric and Ethic: The Politics of Biblical Studies.* Minneapolis: Fortress Press, 1999.

Segovia, Fernando F. *Decolonizing Biblical Studies: A View from the Margins.* Maryknoll, N.Y.: Orbis, 2000.

Segovia, Fernando F. and Mary Ann Tolbert, eds. *Reading from This Place: Social Location and Biblical Interpretation in Global Perspective.* 2 vols. Minneapolis: Fortress Press, 1995, 2000.

————. *Teaching the Bible: The Discourses and Politics of Biblical Pedagogy.* Maryknoll, N.Y.: Orbis, 1998.

Segovia, Fernando F., and R. S. Sugirtharajah, eds. *A Postcolonial Commentary on the New Testament Writings.* London: T. & T. Clark, 2007.

Sugirtharajah, R. S. *Asian Biblical Hermeneutics and Postcolonialism: Contesting the Interpretations.* Maryknoll, N.Y.: Orbis, 1998.

————. *The Bible and the Third World: Precolonial, Colonial, and Postcolonial Encounters.* Cambridge: Cambridge University Press, 2001.

Sweeney, Marvin A. *Reading the Hebrew Bible after the Shoah: Engaging Holocaust Theology.* Minneapolis: Fortress Press, 2008.

Tinker, George E. "Indian Cultures and Interpreting the Christian Bible." Pages 88–99 in *Spirit and Resistance: Political Theology and American Indian Liberation.* Minneapolis: Fortress Press, 2004.

van Wijk-Bos, Johanna W. H. *Making Wise the Simple: The Torah in Christian Faith and Practice.* Grand Rapids, Mich.: Eerdmans, 2005.

Vander Stichele, Caroline, and Todd Penner, eds. *Her Master's Tools? Feminist and Postcolonial Engagements of Historical-Critical Discourse.* Global Perspectives on Biblical Scholarship, Series 9. Atlanta: Society of Biblical Literature, 2005.

Von Kellenbach, Katharina. *Anti-Judaism in Feminist Religious Writings.* Atlanta: Scholars, 1994.

Acknowledgments

■　　■　　■　　▦

GALLERY

Fig. 1: Mural from tomb in Beni-Hassan, Egypt (nineteenth century BCE); Kunsthistorisches Museum, Vienna, Austria; photo © Erich Lessing/Art Resource, N.Y.

Fig. 2: Sandals from the Egyptian New Kingdom, Museo Egizio, Turin; photo Erich Lessing/Art Resource, N.Y.

Fig. 3: "Pictorial Quilt" (1895–1898) by Harriet Powers; photo © 2007 Museum of Fine Art, Boston.

Fig. 4: *Finding of Moses* by He Qi (China). For more information and art by He Qi, please visit www.heqigallery.com.

Fig. 5: *Grapes of Canaan* (Kappazuri dyed stencil print on paper, 6/100, 23 x 26 inches, 1983) by Sadao Watanabe (1913-1996). University Fund Purchase. Brauer Museum of Art 85.02.005. Valparaiso University. Photo © Brauer Museum of Art.

Fig. 6: Meeting of Solomon and the Queen of Sheba from *The History of the Queen of Sheba* (Ge'ez and Amharic); photo © Bildarchiv Preussischer Kulturbesitz/Art Resource, N.Y.

Fig. 7: *The Song of Solomon* by He Qi (China). For more information and art by He Qi, please visit www.heqigallery.com.

Fig. 8: *Nativity* by Lu Lan; © Lu Lan.

Fig. 9: *Feeding of the 5,000* by Laura James; © Laura James. Used by permission.

Fig. 10: *The Last Supper* (Japanese stencil, 1973) by Sadao Watanabe (1913-1996) from *Biblical Prints of Sadao Watanabe*. Reprinted with permission of Shinko Publishing Company.

Fig. 11: *Peter Repentant* from Ethiopian Octateuch (late seventeenth century); photo © British Library. All rights reserved. OR 481, folio 104v.

Fig. 12: *Mount Calvary* by William H. Johnson (oil on paperboard, c. 1944); photo © Smithsonian American Art Museum/Art Resource, N.Y.

Fig. 13: *Golgotha* by Romare Bearden from the Metropolitan Museum of Art, Bequest of Margaret Seligman Lewisohn, in memory of her husband, Sam A. Lewisohn, 1954 (54.143.9); image © The Metropolitan Museum of Art.

Fig. 14: *Mother and Son* by Michael Escoffery (oil on canvas, 2001); © Artist Rights Society (ARS), New York. Photo © Art Resource, N.Y.

Fig. 15: *Pieta* by Käthe Kollwitz (1867-1945); lithograph © Artist Rights Society (ARS), New York. Photo © Bildarchiv Preussischer Kulturbesitz/Art Resource, N.Y.

Fig. 16: *Head of Christ* by Warner Sallman (1892-1968); © 1941 Warner Press, Inc., Anderson, Ind. Used by permission.

Fig. 17: Portrait of Jesus from BBC One's documentary *Son of God*, based on forensic anthropologists' research; illustration © BBC Photo Library. Used by permission.

Fig. 18: *Jesus of the People* by Janet McKenzie. "Through my inclusive painting *Jesus of the People* I hoped to remind that we are all created equally and beautifully in God's image." Copyright © 1999 Janet McKenzie, www. janetmckenzie.com.

Fig. 19: Romanized Christ as Shepherd from the catacombs of St. Priscilla, Rome, Italy (fresco); photo © Erich Lessing/Art Resource, N.Y.

Fig. 20: Christ as sun god Apollo from St. Peter's Basilica, Vatican State (mosaic); photo © Scala/Art Resource, N.Y.

Fig. 21: Christ as Judge enthroned with two angels from St. Apollinare Nuovo, Ravenna, Italy (mosaic); photo © Erich Lessing/Art Resource, N.Y.

Fig. 22: Mural of Black Jesus by Devon Cunninham, St. Cecilia Catholic Church, Detroit, Mich.: photo © Jim West/The Image Works.

Fig. 23: Dust Bowl refugees; photo © Bettmann/CORBIS.

Fig. 24: Migrant workers pick tomatoes in a field in Camarillo, Calif., Tuesday, Oct. 26, 2004; photo © Damian Dovarganes/Associated Press.

Fig. 25: *Cherokee Trail of Tears* by John Guthrie; © John Guthrie.

Fig. 26: Japanese-American evacuees in Washington State; photo by Wartime Civil Control Administration, 1942.

Fig. 27: 1919 photo of execution of Charlemagne Peralte in Haiti by U.S. Marines Corps. http://static.wikipedia.org/new/wikipedia/en/articles/p/e/r/Image~Peraltebody.jpg_b176.html

Fig. 28: Assassinated Oscar Romero; photo © Perez Garcia/Bettmann/Corbis.

Fig. 29: Bodies of the assassinated Jesuits; photo © Patrick Chauvel/Sygma/Corbis.

Fig. 30: Underground Railroad; photo © Art Resource, N.Y.

Fig. 31: Family of eight flees East Germany, 1962; photo Will McBride; Bildarchiv Preussischer Kulturbesitz/Art Resource, N.Y.

Fig. 32: Berlin Wall in front of the Brandenburg Gate, Nov. 10, 1989; photo Klaus Lehnartz; Bildarchiv Preussischer Kulturbesitz/Art Resource, N.Y.

Fig. 33: South Africans waiting to vote, c. 1994; photo © David Turnley/CORBIS.

Fig. 34: *The First Supper* by Jane Evershed; © 1989 Jane Evershed.

OTHER IMAGES

Page xxiv: Rabbinic Bible: *Mikroat Gedolot* (Vilna: Ram, 1912).

Page 224: Classes in agrarian societies. Reprinted by permission of McGraw-Hill Publishers.

INTERPRETING THE BIBLE IN ITS CULTURAL CONTEXT
Path-Breaking Books from Fortress Press

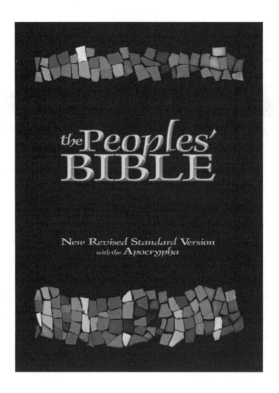

The Peoples' Bible
New Revised Standard Version with Apocrypha

Curtiss Paul DeYoung, Wilda C. Gafney, Leticia A. Guardiola-Sáenz, George Tinker, and Frank M. Yamada, Editors
ISBN: 978-0-8066-5625-0 / 1786 pages
$35.00, Hardcover

"The publication of *The Peoples' Bible* calls for celebration! This new and different study Bible is a rich resource for students as well as faculty. Written in accessible language and using the NRSV as text, it offers a wide array of interpretations from different cultures and ethnicities. *The Peoples' Bible* envisions the Bible and biblical interpretation as a crossroads where people from different social and cultural locations can meet. I am looking forward to using it in my classes and highly recommend it to anybody interested in serious Bible study."

— **Elisabeth Schüssler Fiorenza,** Krister Stendahl Professor, Harvard Divinity School

Available from most booksellers or from Fortress Press
www.fortresspress.com
1-800-328-4648

INTERPRETING THE BIBLE IN ITS CULTURAL CONTEXT

Path-Breaking Books from Fortress Press

Reading from This Place

**Volume 1: Social Location and Biblical
Interpretation in the United States**
Fernando F. Segovia and Mary Ann Tolbert, Editors
ISBN: 978-0-8006-2812-3
336 pages
$29.00, Paper

Reading from This Place

**Volume 2: Social Location and Biblical
Interpretation in Global Perspective**
Fernando F. Segovia and Mary Ann Tolbert, Editors
ISBN: 978-0-8006-2949-6
336 pages,
$29.00, Paper

These two volumes signal the critical legitimation of reading strategies that supplement or modify or even, in some ways, dethrone the historical-critical paradigm that has dominated academic biblical studies for two hundred years. They provide immediate and enduring guidance to scholars and students sorting through the complex epistemological, social, historical, and religious questions that issue from this momentous change.

Available from most booksellers or from Fortress Press
www.fortresspress.com
1-800-328-4648

Interpreting the Bible in Its Cultural Context

Path-Breaking Books from Fortress Press

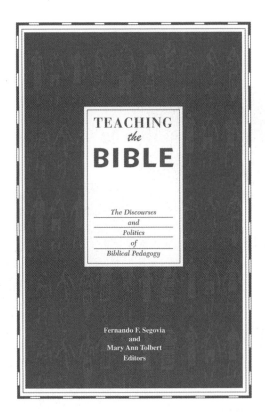

Teaching the Bible

The Discourses and Politics of Biblical Pedagogy
Fernando F. Segovia and Mary Ann Tolbert, Editors
ISBN: 978-0-8006-9698-6
384 pages
$29.00, Paper

"An absolutely indispensable compendium of resources for charting the changes in the discipline of biblical studies, for exposing the operations of power in past and present interpretations and uses of the Bible, and for discovering a variety of postmodernist and postcolonial pedagogies in the reading and teaching of the Bible in a radically pluralistic age."

—**Abraham Smith**, Perkins School of Theology, Southern Methodist University

Available from most booksellers or from Fortress Press
www.fortresspress.com
1-800-328-4648

INTERPRETING THE BIBLE IN ITS CULTURAL CONTEXT

Path-Breaking Books from Fortress Press

Mark

Texts @ Contexts series
Nicole Wilkinson Duran, Teresa Okure, and Daniel M. Patte, Editors
ISBN: 978-0-8006-5998-1
320 pages
$40.00, Hardcover

Genesis

Texts @ Contexts series
Althalya Brenner, Archie Chi Chung Lee, and Gale A. Yee, Editors
ISBN: 978-0-8006-5999-8
368 pages
$40.00, Hardcover

The Texts @ Contexts series presents cutting-edge scholarship on select books of the Bible from authors writing from a rich array of social, cultural, and ethnic locations. The result is a series of dazzlingly new and thought-provoking readings that foreground the perspectives and commitments of the interpreters as well as issues of identity, ethnicity, gender, class, location, and power.

Available from most booksellers or from Fortress Press
www.fortresspress.com
1-800-328-4648

INTERPRETING THE BIBLE IN ITS CULTURAL CONTEXT

Path-Breaking Books from Fortress Press

From Every People and Nation

The Book of Revelation in Intercultural Perspective
David Rhoads, Editor
ISBN: 978-0-8006-3721-7
288 pages
$23.00, Paper

Discusses the interpretation of Revelation from Hispanic/Cuban American and African American perspectives and in terms of ecological issues, postcolonial themes, and liberation theology. Provides a set of guidelines for intercultural Bible study. Contributors include Brian K. Blount, Justo Gonzáles, Pablo Richard, Barbara R. Rossing, Khiok-Khng Yeo, and more.

Available from most booksellers or from Fortress Press
www.fortresspress.com
1-800-328-4648